Aviation Psychology and Human Factors

Second Edition

Aviation Psychology and Human Factors

Second Edition

Monica Martinussen and David R. Hunter

CRC Press
Taylor & Francis Group
Boca Raton London New York

CRC Press is an imprint of the
Taylor & Francis Group, an **informa** business

CRC Press
Taylor & Francis Group
6000 Broken Sound Parkway NW, Suite 300
Boca Raton, FL 33487-2742

First issued in paperback 2023

© 2018 by Taylor & Francis Group, LLC
CRC Press is an imprint of Taylor & Francis Group, an Informa business

No claim to original U.S. Government works

ISBN 13: 978-1-03-256983-3 (pbk)
ISBN 13: 978-1-4987-5752-2 (hbk)
ISBN 13: 978-1-3151-5297-4 (ebk)

DOI: 10.1201/9781315152974

Library of Congress Cataloging-in-Publication Data

Names: Martinussen, Monica, author. | Hunter, David R. (David Robert), 1945-author.
Title: Aviation psychology and human factors / Monica Martinussen, David R. Hunter.
Description: Second edition. | Boca Raton : Taylor & Francis, CRC Press, [2017] | Includes bibliographical references.
Identifiers: LCCN 2017005035| ISBN 9781498757522 (hardback : alk. paper) | ISBN 9781315152974 (ebook)
Subjects: LCSH: Aviation psychology. | Flight--Physiological aspects.
Classification: LCC TL555 .M365 2017 | DDC 155.9/65--dc23
LC record available at https://lccn.loc.gov/2017005035

Visit the Taylor & Francis Web site at
http://www.taylorandfrancis.com

and the CRC Press Web site at
http://www.crcpress.com

Contents

Preface

In a lecture at the University of Lille on December 7, 1854, Louis Pasteur noted that in the field of observational science, "...*le hasard ne favorise que les esprits préparés*"—fortune favors the prepared mind.

We would suggest that statement is equally true in the field of aviation. However, reversing the statement might make it even more cogent, since for aviators, *misfortune punishes the unprepared mind*. To survive in the demanding domain of aviation, one needs to approach the task fully prepared. This means having a comprehensive knowledge of not only weather, aerodynamics, propulsion, navigation, and all the other technical disciplines, but also a comprehensive knowledge of what is simultaneously the most fragile and most resilient, the most unreliable and the most adaptable component—the human being. The study of aviation psychology can give you some of that knowledge and better prepare you for the demands that a lifetime or an hour in aviation will make.

This book is about applied psychology. Specifically, it is concerned with the application of psychological principles and techniques to the specific situations and problems of aviation. The book is principally meant to inform the student of aviation how psychology and human factors issues affect their performance in the cockpit. A secondary aim is to inform the student of psychology how their discipline is applied to aviation. We attempt to maintain this balance of perspectives and needs throughout the book, but when we slip we do so in favor of the student of aviation. There are many books written by psychologists for psychologists. There are few books written by psychologists for pilots. It is to this neglected segment that we offer the main thrust of this work.

The overall goal of the book is to make pilots aware of the benefits psychology and its application can offer to improve aviation operations, and to provide specific information that pilots can use in their daily operations. Besides making pilots aware of the benefits of psychology, the book should also make pilots informed consumers of psychological research and studies, so that they may better evaluate and implement future products in the field of aviation psychology. Further, although most of the studies and examples we cite are focused on pilots, the principles apply equally to other aviation professionals, such as air traffic controllers and aviation maintenance technicians.

In this second edition, we have kept the overall structure of the first edition, while revising and updating the material. Specifically, this edition contains two entirely new chapters: Aviation Physiology, and Abilities and Personality Traits. The Aviation Physiology chapter was added at the suggestion of reviewers who noted that this topic was often discussed in the context of human factors training for aircrew. Since, as the chapter will demonstrate, behavior is often influenced by physiological issues, it seemed appropriate to begin the new edition with a discussion of that topic. The chapter on Abilities and Personality Traits was added to provide a basic understanding of those topics, since they are important in many of the succeeding chapters—for example, Selection, and Aeronautical Decision-Making. Also at the suggestion of reviewers, we have moved the material on Aeronautical Decision-Making into a separate chapter and expanded considerably on that topic. In addition, the other chapters have been extensively revised to include recent research results and emerging topics, such as the selection of operator/pilots for unmanned aerial vehicles (UAVs), and mental health in aviation.

An early version of this book was originally published in Norwegian with the title *Luftfartspsykologi* in 2008 by the publisher Fagbokforlaget.

Authors

Dr. Monica Martinussen is a licensed psychologist and currently professor of psychology in the Regional Center for Child and Adolescent Mental Health at the UiT Arctic University of Norway and professor II at the Norwegian Defence University College. Dr. Martinussen conducted her doctoral research in the area of pilot selection, and has been engaged in research on that topic for many years, both for the Norwegian Air Force and at the University of Tromsø. Her research interests include research methods and psychometrics, aviation psychology, mental health, and work and organizational psychology. Dr. Martinussen has been a member of the Board of Directors of the European Association of Aviation Psychology for 8 years, and is currently associate editor of the journal *Aviation Psychology and Applied Human Factors.*

Dr. David R. Hunter has over 30 years of experience as an aviation psychologist. He is a former military helicopter pilot with combat experience in Southeast Asia, and holds a commercial pilot's license for both fixed-wing aircraft and helicopters. Dr. Hunter has conducted research on the use of computer-based tests for the selection of pilots for both the U.S. Air Force and the U.K. Royal Air Force, and has served as an advisor for the human factors design of new aviation systems for the U.S. Army. He also served as the principal scientist for human performance with the Federal Aviation Administration, where he conducted research and managed programs to improve safety among general aviation pilots. He is currently an independent consultant with a practice in Phoenix, Arizona.

1 Introduction

1.1 WHAT IS AVIATION PSYCHOLOGY?

Since the primary target of this book is the student of aviation, not the student of psychology, it seems prudent to begin with a few definitions. This will set some bounds for our discussions and for the reader's expectations. The title of the book includes two key terms: "aviation psychology" and "human factors." We included both those terms because they are often used interchangeably, although that is a disservice to both disciplines. While we will touch on some of the traditional areas of human factors in Chapter 7 on the design of aviation systems, our primary focus is on aviation psychology. Therefore, we will dwell at some length on what we mean by that particular term.

Psychology[*] is commonly defined as the science of behavior and mental processes of humans, although the behavior of animals is also frequently studied—usually as a means to better understand human behavior. Within this broad area, there are numerous specialties. The American Psychological Association (APA), the largest professional organization of psychologists, lists over 50 divisions, each representing a separate aspect of psychology. These include several divisions concerned with various aspects of clinical psychology along with divisions concerned with such diverse issues as consumer behavior, school psychology, rehabilitation, the military, and addiction. All of these are concerned with understanding how human behavior and mental processes influence or are influenced by the issues of their particular domain.

Clearly, psychology covers a very broad area—literally, any behavior or thought is potential grist for the psychologist's mill. To understand exactly what this book will cover, let us consider what we mean by aviation psychology. Undoubtedly, students of aviation will know what the first part of the term means, but what is included under psychology, and why do we feel justified, even compelled, to distinguish between aviation psychology and the rest of the psychological world?

First, let us immediately dismiss the popular image of psychology. We do not include in our considerations of aviation psychology reclining on a couch recounting our childhood and the vicissitudes of our emotional development. That popular image of psychology belongs more to the area of clinical psychology, or perhaps even psychoanalysis. Although clinical psychology is a major component of the larger field of psychology, it has little relevance to aviation psychology. That is not to say that pilots and others involved in aviation are not subject to the same mental foibles and afflictions that beset the rest of humanity. Neither would we suggest that aspects of the human psyche usually addressed in a clinical setting could have no influence on human performance in an aviation setting. Quite the opposite, we assert that all

---

[*] The term "psychology" is derived from the Greek word psyche, meaning both butterfly and soul. Psychology was first used as part of a course title for lectures given in the sixteenth century by Philip Melanchthon.

1

aspects of the mental functioning of pilots, maintainers, air traffic controllers, and the supporting cadre inescapably influence behavior for better or worse. Rather, we wish to dissociate aviation psychology from the psychotherapeutic focus of traditional clinical psychology. Aviation psychology may concern itself with the degree of maladaptive behavior evidenced by excessive drinking or with the confused ideation associated with personality disorders, but it does so for the purpose of understanding and predicting the effects of those disorders and behaviors on aviation-related activities, not for the purpose of affecting a cure.

Ours is a much more basic approach. We are concerned not just with the behavior (what people do) and ideation (what people think) of those with various mental disturbances. Rather, we are concerned with how people in general behave. Psychology at its most inclusive level is the study of the behavior of all people. Psychology asks why under certain conditions people behave in a certain way and under different conditions they behave in a different way. How do prior events, internal cognitive structures, skills, knowledge, abilities, preferences, attitudes, perceptions, and a host of other psychological constructs (see Section 1.4) influence behavior? Psychology asks those questions, and psychological science provides the mechanism for finding answers. This allows us to understand and to predict human behavior.

We may define aviation psychology as the study of individuals engaged in aviation-related activities. The goal of aviation psychology then is to understand and to predict the behavior of individuals in an aviation environment. Being able, even imperfectly, to predict behavior has substantial benefits. Predicting accurately how a pilot will react (behave) to an instrument reading will allow us to reduce pilot error by designing instruments that are more readily interpretable and that do not lead to incorrect reactions. Predicting how a maintenance technician will behave when given a new set of instructions can lead to increased productivity through reduction of the time required to perform a maintenance action. Predicting how the length of rest breaks will affect an air traffic controller when faced with a traffic conflict can lead to improved safety. Finally, predicting the result of a corporate restructuring on the safety culture of an organization can identify areas in which conflict is likely to occur and areas in which safety is likely to suffer.

From this general goal of understanding and predicting the behavior of individuals in aviation environment, we can identify three more specific goals. They are, first, to reduce error by humans in aviation settings; second, to increase the productivity; and third, to increase the comfort of both the workers and their passengers. To achieve these goals requires the coordinated activities of many groups of people. These include pilots, maintainers, air traffic control operators, the managers of aviation organizations, baggage handlers, fuel truck drivers, caterers, meteorologists, dispatchers, and cabin attendants. All of these groups, plus many more, have a role in achieving those three goals of safety, efficiency, and comfort. However, since covering all those groups is clearly beyond the scope of a single book, we have chosen to focus on the pilot, with only a few diversions into the activities of these other groups. Another reason for choosing pilots is that the majority of research has been conducted on pilots. This is slowly changing, and more research is being conducted using air traffic controllers, crew members, and other occupational groups involved in aviation.

In this, we enlist contributions from several subdisciplines within the overall field of psychology. These include physiological psychology, engineering psychology, and its closely related discipline of human factors, personnel psychology, cognitive psychology, and organizational psychology. This listing also matches, to a fair degree, the order in which we develop our picture of aviation psychology—starting from fairly basic considerations of human physiology and culminating in an examination of human decision-making and accident involvement.

Although aviation psychology draws heavily upon the other disciplines of psychology, those other disciplines are also heavily indebted to aviation psychology for many of their advances, particularly in the area of applied psychology. This is due primarily to the historic ties of aviation psychology to military aviation. For a number of reasons aviation, and pilots in particular, have always been a matter of very high concern to the military. Training of military pilots is an expensive and lengthy process, so considerable attention has been given, since the First World War, to improving the selection of these individuals so as to reduce failures in training—the provenance of personnel and training psychology. Similarly, the great cost of aircraft and their loss due to accidents contributed to the development of engineering psychology and human factors. Human interaction with automated systems, now a great concern in the computer age, has been an issue of study for decades in aviation, beginning from the introduction of flight director systems and in recent years the advanced glass cockpits. Much of the research developed in an aviation setting for these advanced systems is equally germane to the advanced displays and controls that will soon appear in automobiles and trucks.

In addition, studies of the interaction of crew members on airliner flight decks and the problems that ensue when one of the other crew members does not clearly assert his or her understanding of a potentially hazardous situation have led to the development of a class of training interventions termed crew resource management (CRM). After a series of catastrophic accidents, the concept and techniques of CRM were developed by the National Aeronautics and Space Administration (NASA) and the airline industry to ensure that the crew operates effectively as a team. Building upon this research base from aviation psychology, CRM has been adapted for other settings, such as air traffic control centers, medical operating rooms, and military command and control teams. This is a topic we will cover in much more detail in Chapter 6.

1.2 WHAT IS RESEARCH?

Before we delve into the specifics of aviation psychology, however, it may be worthwhile to consider in somewhat greater detail the general field of psychology. As noted above, psychology is the science of behavior and mental process. We describe it as a science because psychologists use the scientific method to develop their knowledge of behavior and mental process. By agreeing to accept the scientific method as the mechanism by which truth will be discovered, psychologists bind themselves to the requirements to test, using empirical methods, their theories and they modify or reject those which are not supported by the results. The APA defines scientific method as, "The set of procedures used for gathering and interpreting objective information in a way that minimizes error and yields dependable generalizations.*"

For a discussion of the "received view" of the philosophy of science, see Popper (1959) and Lakatos (1970). According to this view, science consists of bold theories that outpace the facts. Scientists continually attempt to falsify these theories but can never prove them true. For discussions on the application of this philosophy of science to psychology, see Klayman and Ha (1987); Poletiek (1996); and Dar (1987).

At a somewhat less lofty level, scientific method consists of a series of fairly standardized steps, using generally accepted research procedures. These steps are the following:

- Identify a problem and formulate a hypothesis (sometimes called a theory).
- Design an experiment that will test the hypothesis.
- Perform the experiment, typically using experimental and control groups.
- Evaluate the results from the experiment to see if the hypothesis was supported.
- Communicate the results.

For example, a psychologist might observe that a large number of pilot trainees fail during their training (the *problem*). The psychologist might form a hypothesis, possibly incorporating other observations or information, that the trainees are failing because they are fatigued, and that the source of this fatigue is a lack of sleep. The psychologist might then formally state his or her hypothesis that the probability of succeeding in training is directly proportional to the number of hours of sleep received (the *hypothesis*). The psychologist could then design an experiment to test that hypothesis. In an ideal experiment (not likely to be approved by the organization training the pilots), a class of incoming trainees would be randomly divided into two groups. One group would be given X-hours of sleep, and the other group would be given Y-hours of sleep, where Y is smaller than X (*design* the experiment). The trainees would be followed through the course, and the numbers of failures in each group recorded (*perform* the experiment). The results could then be analyzed using statistical methods (*evaluate* the results) to determine whether, as predicted by the psychologist's hypothesis, the proportion of failures in group X was smaller than the proportion of failures in group Y. If the difference in failure rates between the two groups was in the expected direction and if it met the generally accepted standards for statistical significance, then the psychologist would conclude that his or her hypothesis was supported and would indicate as such in his or her report (*communicate* the

---

* http://www.psychologymatters.org/glossary.html#s

results). If the data he or she collects from the experiment did not support the hypothesis, then he or she will have to reject his or her theory or modify it to take the results of the experiment into account.

Like research in other fields, psychological research must meet certain criteria in order to be considered scientific. The research must be

Falsifiable: The hypothesis or theory must be stated in a way that makes it possible to reject it. If the hypothesis cannot be tested, then it does not meet the standards for science.

Replicable: Others should be able to repeat a study and get the same results. It is for this reason that reports of studies should provide enough detail for other researchers to repeat the experiment.

Precise: Hypotheses must be stated as precisely as possible. For example, if we hypothesize that more sleep improves the likelihood of completing pilot training, but only up to some limit (i.e., trainees need 8 hours of sleep, but additional hours beyond that number do not help), then our hypothesis should explicitly state that relationship. To improve precision, operational definitions of the variables should be included that state exactly how a variable is measured. Improved precision facilitates replication by other researchers.

Parsimonious: Researchers should apply the simplest explanation possible to any set of observations. This principle, sometimes called Occam's razor, means that if two explanations equally account for an observation, then the simpler of the two should be selected.

1.3   GOALS OF PSYCHOLOGY

Describe: Specify the characteristics and parameters of psychological phenomena more accurately and completely. For example, studies have been conducted of human short-term memory, which very accurately describe the retention of information as a function of the amount of information to be retained.

Predict: Predicting what people will do in the future, based on knowledge of their past and current psychological characteristics, is a vital part of many aviation psychology activities. For example, accurately predicting who will complete pilot training, based on knowledge of their psychological test scores, is important to the organization performing the training. Likewise, predicting who is more likely to be in an aircraft accident, based on psychological test scores, could also be valuable information for the person involved.

Understand: Being able to specify the relationships among variables; in plain language, knowing the "how" and "why" drives both psychologists and nonpsychologists alike. Once we understand, we are in a position to predict and to influence.

Influence: Once we have learned why a person fails in training or has an accident, for example, we may be able to take steps to change the outcome. From our earlier example, if we know that increasing the amount of sleep that trainees receive improves their likelihood of succeeding in training, then we almost certainly will wish to change the training schedule to ensure that everyone gets the required amount of sleep every night.

Psychology can also be broken down into several different general approaches. These approaches reflect the subject matter under consideration and, to a large degree, the methods and materials used. These approaches include the following:

Behaviorist approach looks at how the environment affects behavior.
Cognitive approach studies mental processes and is concerned with understanding how people think, remember, and reason.
Biological approach is concerned with the internal physiological processes and how that influences behavior.
Social approach examines how we interact with other people and emphasizes the individual factors that are involved in social behavior, along with social beliefs and attitudes.
Developmental approach is primarily interested in emotional development, social development, and cognitive development, including the interactions among these three components.
Humanistic approach focuses on individual experiences, rather than on people in general.

The delineation of these six approaches may suggest more homogeneity than actually exists. Although there are some psychologists who remain exclusively within one of those approaches (physiological psychologists are perhaps the best example), for the most part psychologists take a more eclectic view—borrowing concepts, methods, and theories from among the six approaches as it suits their purpose. Certainly, it would be very difficult to classify aviation psychologists into one of those six approaches.

1.4   MODELS AND PSYCHOLOGICAL CONSTRUCTS

The rules of science are met in other disciplines (e.g., chemistry, physics, or mathematics) through the precise delineation of predecessors, actions, conditions, and outcomes. In chemistry, for example, this is embodied in the familiar chemical equation, depicting the reaction between two or more elements or compounds. The chemical equation for the generation of water from hydrogen and oxygen is unambiguous: $2H + O = H_2O$.

That is, two hydrogen atoms will combine with one oxygen atom to form one molecule of water. This is a simple but powerful model that lets chemists understand and predict what will happen when these two elements are united. It also provides a very precise definition of the model, which allows other scientists to test its validity. For example, a scientist might ask, are there any instances in which H_3O is produced? Clearly, the production of a model such as this is a very desirable state and represents the achievement of the goals, in the chemical domain, that were listed for psychology earlier. While psychology cannot claim to have achieved the same levels of specificity as the physical sciences, great progress has nevertheless been made in specifying the relationships among psychological variables, often at a quantitative level. However, the level of specificity at present generally is inversely related to the complexity of the psychological phenomenon under investigations.

Some of the earliest work in psychology dealt with psychophysics—generally including issues such as measurement of just noticeable differences (JNDs) in the tones of auditory signals or the weights of objects. In Leipzig, Germany, Ernst Weber (1795–1878) discovered a method for measuring the internal mental events and quantifying the JND. His observations are formulated into an equation known as *Weber's law*, which states that the "just noticeable difference" is a constant fraction of the stimulus intensity already present (Corsini, 2001).

More recent efforts have led to the development of several equations describing psychological phenomena in very precise models. These include Fitts' law (Fitts 1954), which specifies that the movement time (e.g., of a hand to a switch) is a logarithmic function of distance when target size is held constant, and that movement time is also a logarithmic function of target size when distance is held constant. Mathematically, Fitts' law is stated as follows:

$$MT = a + b \log_2\left(\frac{2A}{W}\right)$$

where *MT* is the time to complete the movement, *a* and *b* are parameters which vary with the situation, *A* is the distance of movement from start to target center, and *W* is the width of the target along the axis of movement.

Another such example is Hick's law, which describes the time it takes a person to make a decision as a function of the possible number of choices (Hick 1952). This law states that given *n* equally probable choices, the average reaction time (*T*) to choose among them is

$$T = b \log_2(n+1)$$

This law can be demonstrated experimentally by having a number of buttons with corresponding light bulbs. When one light bulb is lit randomly, the person must press the corresponding button as quickly as possible. By recording the reaction time, we can demonstrate that the average time to respond varies as the log of the number of light bulbs. Although a seemingly trivial statements of relationships, Hick's and Fitts' laws are considered in the design of menus and submenus used in a variety of aviation and nonaviation settings (Landauer and Nachbar 1985).

WHAT IS A MODEL?

A model is a simplified representation of reality. It can be a physical, mathematical, or logical representation of a system, entity, phenomenon, or process. When we talk about a psychological model, we are usually referring to a statement, or a series of statements, about how psychological constructs are related or about how psychological constructs influence behavior. These models can be very simple and just state that some things seem to be related. For an example, see the description of the SHEL model.

On the other hand, the model could be quite complex and make specific quantitative statements about the relationships among the constructs. For an example of this type of model, see the Weather Modeling study in which a mathematical modeling technique is used to specify how pilots combine weather information.

Other models, such as those of human information processing or aeronautical decision-making (ADM), make statements about how information is processed by humans or how they make decisions. A good model allows us to make predictions about how changes in one part of the model will affect other parts.

Clearly, from some psychological research, very precise models may be constructed of human sensory responses to simple stimuli. Similarly, early work on human memory established with a fairly high degree of specificity the relationship between the position of an item in a list of things to be remembered and the likelihood of its being remembered (Ebbinghaus 1885, as reprinted in Wozniak 1999).

In addition to highly specific, quantitative models, psychologists have also developed models that specify qualitative or functional relationships among variables. Some models are primarily descriptive and make no specific predictions about relationships among variables other than to suggest that a construct exists and that, in some unspecified way, it influences another construct or behavior. Some models propose a particular organization of constructs or a particular flow of information or events. The predicted relationships and processes of those models may be subject to empirical tests to assess their validity—a very worthwhile characteristic of models. Of particular interest[*] to the field of aviation psychology are those models that deal with

- General human performance
- Skill acquisition and expertise development
- Human information processing
- Accident etiology
- Decision-making (specifically, ADM)

1.5 HUMAN PERFORMANCE MODELS

One of the most widely used models of human performance is the SHEL model, originated by Edwards (1988), and later modified by Hawkins (1993). The SHEL model consists of the following elements:

---

[*] These are but a sampling of the many models currently available. For more information, consult Foyle et al. (2005); Wickens et al. (2003), or Wickens and Holland (2000). An extensive review of human performance models is also available from Leiden et al. (2001) who include task network, cognitive, and vision models. Table 1 in the report by Isaac et al. (2002) also provides a comprehensive listing of models.

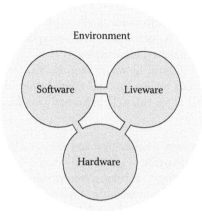

FIGURE 1.1   SHEL model.

- *Software*: Procedures, manuals, checklists, and literal software
- *Hardware*: The physical system (aircraft, ship, operating suite) and its components
- *Environment*: The situation in which the other elements (L, H, and S) operate, including working conditions, weather, organizational structure, and climate
- *Liveware*: The people (pilots, flight attendants, mechanics, etc.)

This model is typically depicted as shown in Figure 1.1, which highlights the interrelationships of the S, H, and L components, and their functioning within the Environment (E).

Although this model is useful at an overall conceptual level, it is pedagogic rather than prescriptive. That is, it serves to help educate people outside the disciplines of psychology and human factors about the interactions and dependencies of the SHEL elements. However, it makes no specific statements about the nature of those interactions and no quantifiable predictions about the results of disruptions. Clearly, this is a simple model of a very complex situation. As such, it has very little explanatory power, although it does serve a general descriptive function.

Despite, or perhaps because of, its simplicity, the SHEL model has proven to be a very popular model within human factors and is frequently used to explain concepts relating to the interdependencies of those four elements. It is cited, for example, by the Global Accident Information Network (GAIN 2001) in their chapter on human factors to illustrate the continuous interaction among the elements. It is also referenced in the U.K. Civil Aviation Authority (CAA 2002) publication on human factors in aircraft maintenance. The SHEL model has also been used extensively outside of aviation, particularly in the field of medicine (cf. Bradshaw 2003; Molloy and O'Boyle 2005).

1.5.1   DEVELOPMENT OF EXPERTISE

How a pilot develops from a novice to an expert is clearly an issue of keen interest to psychologists, since there is general agreement that experts are safer than novices (an assumption that should not be accepted without question). Accordingly, several models have been utilized to help understand this process. Some of these models are taken from the general psychological literature on expertise development, and some are specifically adapted to the aviation setting.

One model from the general literature on expertise development specifies five developmental levels from novice to expert, reflecting an increasing capacity to internalize, abstract, and apply rules (Dreyfus and Dreyfus 1986). These levels are the following:

Novice: Learns basic facts, terminology, and rules and how they are applied in well-defined circumstances.

Advanced Beginner: Begins to develop a feel for rules through repeated practical application. The student begins to understand the use of concepts and rules in situations that are similar to those in prior examples.

Competence: Has a deep-enough understanding of the rules to know when they are applicable and how to apply them in novel situations.

Proficiency: Has a refined and internalized sense of the rules.

Expert: Produces increasingly abstract representations and is able to map novel situations to the internalized representations.

This model is primarily descriptive, in that it makes no specific predictions regarding the transitions between states, other than the general suggestion that there is an increasing capacity to internalize, abstract, and apply rules. It leaves unanswered questions such as how the process might be accelerated, or specifically how to measure competence at each of the hypothesized stages.

According to Fitts (1964) and Fitts and Posner (1967), there are three phases to skill acquisition:

- *Cognitive Phase*: Characterized by slow, declarative learning of primarily verbal information.
- *Associative Phase*: Characterized by the detection and elimination of errors in performance, and the strengthening of connections.
- *Autonomous Phase*: Characterized by automated and rapid performance, requiring less deliberate attention and fewer resources.

Arguably, this model, like that of Dreyfus and Dreyfus (1986), is primarily descriptive. However, Anderson (1982) has provided a quantitative formulation of the three-phase skill acquisition model. This quantitative model (ACT-R) can be used to make specific quantitative predictions, and as such is subject to more rigorous evaluation than the simply descriptive models. In addition, although originally intended to apply to motor learning, the model is also applicable for cognitive skill acquisition (VanLenh 1996), thus broadening its applicability.

1.6 MODELS OF HUMAN INFORMATION PROCESSING

Perhaps, the best known of the human information-processing models is that proposed by Wickens (Wickens and Holland 2000), which draws heavily upon previous research on human memory (Baddeley 1986), cognition (Norman and Bobrow 1975), and attention (Kahneman 1973). The Wickens model is characterized by the presence of discrete stages for the processing of information, the provision of both a working memory and a long-term memory, and a continuous feedback stream. The provision of an attention resource component is also notable, since it implies the notion of a limited attention store, which the human must allocate among all the ongoing tasks. Hence, the attention has a selective nature.

Clearly, this model is more sophisticated in its components and proposed interrelationships than the more descriptive models considered earlier. This level of sophistication and the wealth of detail provide ample opportunity for the evaluation of the validity of this model experimentally. It also makes it a useful tool for understanding and predicting human interaction with complex systems.

1.7 MODELS OF ACCIDENT CAUSATION

The predominant model of accident causation is the Reason (1990) model, or as it is sometimes called, the "Swiss-cheese" model. Because it is so widespread in regard to aviation safety, it will be described at length in Chapter 11, and hence will not be described in detail here. For present, let us simply note that the Reason model might be properly described as a process model, somewhere midway between the purely descriptive models, like Dreyfus and Dreyfus, and the highly structured model of Wickens. It describes the process by which accidents are allowed or prevented, but also hypothesizes a rather specific hierarchy and timetable of events and conditions that lead to such adverse events.

Moving away from the individual person, there are also models that treat the relationships of organizations and the flow of information and actions within organizations. The current term for this approach is Safety Management Systems, and it has been adopted by the International Civil Aviation Organization (ICAO 2005) and by all the major western regulatory agencies (including, e.g., the U.S. Federal Aviation Administration, the U.K. Civil Aviation Authority [CAA 2002], Transport Canada [2001], and the Australian Civil Aviation Safety Authority [CASA 2002]).

1.8 MODELS OF ADM*

Following a study by Jensen and Benel (1977) in which it was found that poor decision-making was associated with about half of the fatal general aviation accidents, a great deal of interest developed in understanding how pilots make decisions and how that process might be influenced. These interests lead to the development of a number of prescriptive models that were based primarily on expert opinion. One such example is the "I'M SAFE," a mnemonic device, which serves to help pilots remember to consider the six elements indicated by the IMSAFE letters: illness, medication, stress, alcohol, fatigue, and emotion.

The DECIDE (detect, estimate, choose, identify, do, evaluate) model (Clarke 1986) could be considered both descriptive and prescriptive. That is, it not only

---

* O'Hare (1992) provides an in-depth review of the multiple models of ADM.

describes the steps that a person takes in deciding on a course of action, but it can also be used as a pedagogic device to train a process for making decisions. The DECIDE model consists of the following steps:

- *D—Detect*: The decision maker detects a change that requires attention.
- *E—Estimate*: The decision maker estimates the significance of the change.
- *C—Choose*: The decision maker chooses a safe outcome.
- *I—Identify*: The decision maker identifies actions to control the change.
- *D—Do*: The decision maker acts on the best options.
- *E—Evaluate*: The decision maker evaluates the effects of the action.

In an evaluation of the DECIDE model, Jensen (1988) used detailed analyses of accident cases to teach the DECIDE model to 10 pilots. Half of the pilots received the training, while the other half served as a control group. Following the training, the pilots were assessed in a simulated flight in which three unexpected conditions occurred, requiring decisions by the pilots. A review of the experimental flights indicated that all of the experimental group members who chose to fly (four of five) eventually landed safely. All of the control group members who chose to fly (three of five) eventually crashed. Although the very small sample size precluded the usual statistical analysis, the results suggest some utility for teaching the model as a structured approach to good decision-making. As a result of this and other studies conducted at The Ohio State University, Jensen and his associates (Jensen 1995, 1997; Kochan, et al. 1997) produced the general model of pilot expertise shown in Figure 1.2.

This overall model of pilot expertise was formulated based on four studies of pilot decision-making. These studies began with a series of unstructured interviews of pilots who, on the basis of experience and certification, were considered as experts in the area of general aviation. These interviews were used to identify and compile characteristics of these expert pilots. Successive studies were used to further identify the salient characteristics, culminating in the presentation to the pilots of a plausible general aviation flight scenario using a verbal protocol methodology. The results from the final study, in combination with the earlier interviews, suggested that, when compared to competent pilots, expert pilots tended to (1) seek more quality information in a more timely manner, (2) make more progressive decisions to solve problems, and (3) communicate more readily with all available resources (Kochan et al. 1997).

In a different approach to understanding how pilots make decisions, Hunter et al. (2003) used a linear modeling technique to examine the weather-related decision-making processes of American, Norwegian, and Australian pilots. In this study, which is described in more detail in Chapter 10, data from pilots' risk assessments of 27 weather scenarios were used to develop individual regression equations* for each pilot. These equations described how each individual pilot combined information about weather conditions (cloud ceiling, visibility, and amount and type of precipita-

---

* *Regression Equation*: This is a mathematical equation that shows how information is combined by using weights assigned to each salient characteristic. The general form of the equation is $Y = b_1x_1 + b_2x_2 + \cdots + c$, where b_1, b_2, etc., are the weights applied to each characteristic. Most introductory texts on statistics will include a discussion on linear regression. For a more advanced, but still very readable, description of the technique, see Licht (2001).

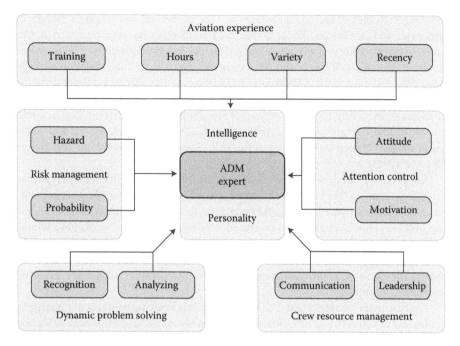

FIGURE 1.2 ADM expertise model. (Adapted from Kochan et al. 1997. *A New Approach to Aeronautical Decision-Making: The Expertise Method.* Technical report DOT/FAA/ AM-97/6. Washington, DC: Federal Aviation Administration.)

tion) to make his or her risk assessment. Examination of the weights that the pilots used in combining the information allowed the researchers to compare the weather decision models that the pilots used. Some pilots favored a compensatory model, in which a high score on one of the variables (ceiling, for example) could compensate for a low score on another of the variables (visibility, for example). In practical terms, this means that pilots might take-off on a flight under potentially hazardous conditions (low visibility, but high ceiling) because of the way the information was combined. In contrast, other pilots used a noncompensatory model, in which each condition was judged independently—the preferred, safer model.

Typically, psychological models become less quantitative and more qualitative as they attempt to account for more complex behavior. For example, contrast the very precise equations that relate response time to number of choices to the models that attempt to account for human information processing. However, the study by Hunter et al. (2003) demonstrates that in some cases we can establish quantitative relationships for relatively complex behavior and stimuli.

Although linear modeling provides a powerful technique for establishing quantitative models, even more powerful statistical modeling techniques are now available. Structural equation modeling (SEM) allows psychologists to specify variables and the quantitative relationships among those variables, and then to test the veracity of that model. Although a discussion of SEM is well beyond the scope of this book, let us simply say that it allows researchers to create models, such as those of Wickens,

Jensen, or Hunter et al., and to assign specific numerical relationships among the processes and conditions. These numerical parameters may then be tested statistically, and the validity of the hypothesized model tested empirically. The interested reader may consult Raykov and Marcoulides (2006) for an introduction to SEM; however, texts on Lisrel, AMOS, and EQS, three of the common implementations of SEM, are also widely available. There are also a few examples of the use of SEM in aviation, including mental workload of student pilots (Sohn and Jo 2003), mental workload and performance in combat aircraft (Svensson et al. 1997), and analysis of the psychometric properties of the U.S. Navy Aviation Selection Test Battery (Blower 1998).

All of these models present a view of reality from a different perspective. Arguably, none of them are true in some absolute sense. Rather, they all present a simplified abstraction of reality. Although the results of the mathematical modeling process (Hunter et al. 2003) produced very reliable results, we would certainly not argue that humans actually have a small calculator in their head that they use to evaluate such judgments. Rather, we would suggest that whatever is happening during the decision-making process can be predicted rather accurately using our mathematical model.

The distinction is important, because later in this book we will discuss many psychological constructs and describe research that shows relationships between a construct and some outcome of interest. For example, we might look at how intelligence relates to successfully completing training. Or, we could examine how a person's internality (the degree to which they believe themselves in control of their destiny) relates to accident involvement. Both intelligence and internality are psychological constructs—convenient titles given to hypothesized underlying psychological traits and capacities. A psychological construct is an abstract theoretical variable that is invented to explain some phenomenon of interest to scientists. The issue of constructs, in particular their measurement, is like most of the topics introduced in this book, also the subject of many articles and books in its own right. (For more information, see Campbell and Fiske [1959] regarding the measurement of constructs. Also, for a contemporary problem in construct definition, see the discussion on emotional intelligence by Mayer and Salovey [1993].)

The reader should be aware of the nebulous nature of these constructs and the models that psychologists have devised to describe the relationships among constructs and external events. The insights that the constructs provide and the predictions that may be made from the models are potentially useful, even though the utility of a psychological construct or model is no guarantee of its underlying physical reality.[*] The reader should dismiss neither the constructs as mere "psychobabble" nor the models as gross oversimplifications of a complex world. Both can be taken as a means of helping us understand the world by framing it in familiar terms.

---

[*] This is a situation that is not unique to psychological science. The *Bohr model* of the atom, proposed by Niels Bohr in 1915, is not completely correct, but has many features that are approximately correct and that make it useful for some discussions. At present, the generally accepted theory of the atom is called *quantum mechanics*; the Bohr model is an approximation to quantum mechanics that has the virtue of being much simpler. Perhaps in 100 years, the quantum mechanical model will be considered a quaint approximation to reality.

Before we leave the discussion of models, constructs, and theories, let us make one last point. Although specifically addressed to the role of Fitts' law, the comments of Pew and Baron (1983, p. 664) regarding models and theories are broadly applicable:

> There is no useful distinction between models and theories. We assert that there is a continuum along which models vary that has loose verbal analogy and metaphor at one end and closed-form mathematical equations at the other, and that most models lie somewhere in-between. Fitts' law may be placed in this continuum. As a mathematical expression, it emerged from the rigors of probability theory, yet when transplanted into the realm of psychomotor behaviour it becomes a metaphor.

1.9 SUMMARY

In this chapter, we have tried to introduce the student to some of the concepts and goals of psychology, and to delineate some of the domain of aviation psychology. We have also outlined some of the dominant models of human performance that are currently applied to further our understanding of how humans perform in an aviation setting.

Aviation psychology represents an amalgamation of the various approaches and subdisciplines within psychology. In the following chapters, we will repeat and expand upon the topics introduced here as we delve more deeply into the design and development of aviation systems, the selection and training of pilots, and efforts to improve safety from a psychological perspective. Like the rest of the aviation community, aviation psychologists share the ultimate goals of improving safety, efficiency, and comfort. Practitioners of aviation psychology bring to bear the tools and techniques of psychology to describe, predict, understand, and influence the aviation community to achieve those goals.

REFERENCES

Anderson, J.R. 1982. Acquisition of cognitive skill. *Psychological Review* 89: 369–406.

Baddeley, A.D. 1986. *Working Memory*. Oxford, UK: Oxford University Press.

Blower, D.J. 1998. *Psychometric Equivalency Issues For the APEX System*. Special Report 98-1. Pensacola, FL: Naval Aerospace Medical Research Laboratory.

Bradshaw, B.K. 2003. The SHEL model: Applying aviation human factors to medical error. *Texas D.O.* 60: 15–17.

CAA. 2002. *Safety Management Systems For Commercial Air Transport Operations*. CAP 712. Gatwick, UK: Civil Aviation Authority, Safety Regulation Group.

Campbell, D.T. and Fiske, D.W. 1959. Convergent and discriminant validation by the multitrait-multimethod matrix. *Psychological Bulletin* 56: 81–105.

Civil Aviation Safety Authority. 2002. *Safety Management Systems: Getting Started*. Canberra, Australia: Author.

Clarke, R. 1986. *A New Approach to Training Pilots in Aeronautical Decision Making*. Frederick, MD: AOPA Air Safety Foundation.

Colman, A.M. 2001. *Dictionary of Psychology*. Oxford, UK: Oxford University Press.

Dar, R. 1987. Another look at Meehl, Lakatos, and the scientific practices of psychologists. *American Psychologist* 42: 145–151.

Dreyfus, H. and Dreyfus, S. 1986. *Mind over machine: The Power of Human Intuition and Expertise in the Era of the Computer*. New York, NY: Free Press.

Edwards, E. 1988. Introductory overview. In Weiner, E.L., and Nagel, D.C. (Eds.), *Human Factors in Aviation* (pp. 3–25). San Diego, CA: Academic Press.

Fitts, P.M. 1954. The information capacity of the human motor system in controlling the amplitude of movement. *Journal of Experimental Psychology* 47: 381–391. (Reprinted in *Journal of Experimental Psychology: General* 121: 262–269, 1992).

Fitts, P.M. 1964. Perceptual skill learning. In Melton, A.W. (Ed.), *Categories of Skill Learning* (pp. 243–285). New York, NY: Academic Press.

Fitts, P.M. and Posner, M.I. 1967. *Learning and Skilled Performance in Human Performance*. Belmont, CA: Brock-Cole.

Foyle, D.C., Hooey, B.L., Byrne, M.D., Corker, K.M., Duetsch, S., Lebiere, C., Leiden, K., and Wickens, C.D. 2005. Human performance models of pilot behavior. In *Proceedings of the Human Factors and Ergonomics Society 49th Annual Meeting*, (pp. 1109–1113). Orlando, FL: Human Factors and Ergonomics Society.

GAIN. 2001. *Operator's Flight Safety Handbook. Global Aviation Information Network*. Chevy Chase, MD: Abacus Technology.

Hawkins, F.H. 1993. *Human Factors in Flight*. Aldershot, UK: Ashgate.

Hick, W.E. 1952. On the rate of gain of information. *Quarterly Journal of Experimental Psychology* 4: 11–26.

Hunter, D.R., Martinussen, M., and Wiggins, M. 2003. Understanding how pilots make weather-related decisions. *International Journal of Aviation Psychology* 13: 73–87.

International Civil Aviation Organization. 2005. ICAO Training Page. Retrieved on September 15, 2007 from: http://www.icao.int/anb/safetymanagement/training%5Ctraining.html

Isaac, A., Shorrock, S.T., Kennedy, R., Kirwan, B., Andersen, H., and Bove, T. 2002. *Short Report on Human Performance Models and Taxonomies of Human Error in ATM (HERA)*. Report HRS/HSP-002-REP-02. Brussels, Belgium: European Organization for the Safety of Air Navigation.

Jensen, R.S. 1988. Creating a '1000 hour' pilot in 300 hours through judgement training. In *Proceedings of the Workshop on Aviation Psychology*. Newcastle, Australia: Institute of Aviation, University of Newcastle.

Jensen, R.S. 1995. *Pilot Judgment and Crew Resource Management*. Brookfield, VT: Ashgate.

Jensen, R.S. 1997. The boundaries of aviation psychology, human factors, aeronautical decision making, situation awareness, and crew resource management. *International Journal of Aviation Psychology* 7: 259–267.

Jensen, R.S. and Benel, R.A. 1977. *Judgment Evaluation and Instruction in Civil Pilot Training*. Technical Report FAA-RD-78-24. Washington, DC: Federal Aviation Administration.

Kahneman, D. 1973. *Attention and Effort*. Englewood Cliffs, NJ: Prentice-Hall.

Klayman, J. and Ha, Y.W. 1987. Confirmation, disconfirmation, and information in hypothesis-testing. *Psychological Review* 94: 211–228.

Kochan, J.A., Jensen, R.S., Chubb, G.P., and Hunter, D.R. 1997. *A New Approach to Aeronautical Decision-Making: The Expertise Method*. Technical report DOT/FAA/AM-97/6. Washington, DC: Federal Aviation Administration.

Lakatos, I. 1970. Falsification and the methodology of scientific research programmes. In Lakatos, I. and Musgrave, A. (Eds.), *Criticism and the Growth of Knowledge* (pp. 91–196). New York, NY: Cambridge University Press.

Landauer, T.K. and Nachbar, D.W. 1985. Selection from alphabetic and numeric menu trees using a touch screen: Breadth, depth, and width. In *Proceedings of CHI '85*, (pp. 73–78). New York, NY: ACM.

Leiden, K., Laughery, K.R., Keller, J., French, J., Warwick, W., and Wood, S.D. 2001. *A Review of Human Performance Models for the Prediction of Human Error.* Technical Report. Boulder, CO: Micro Analysis and Design.

Licht, M.H. 2001. Multiple regression and correlation. In Grimm, L.G., and Yarnold, P.R. (Eds.), *Reading and Understanding Multivariate Statistic* (pp. 19–64). Washington, DC: American Psychological Association.

Mayer, J.D. and Salovey, P. 1993. The intelligence of emotional intelligence. *Intelligence* 17: 433–442.

Molloy, G.J. and O'Boyle, C.A. 2005. The SHEL model: A useful tool for analyzing and teaching the contribution of human factors to medical error. *Academy of Medicine* 80: 152–155.

Norman, D. and Bobrow, D. 1975. On data-limited and resource-limited processing. *Cognitive Psychology* 7: 44–60.

O'Hare, D. 1992. The 'artful' decision maker: A framework model for aeronautical decision making. *International Journal of Aviation Psychology* 2, 175–191.

Pew, R.W. and Baron, S. 1983. Perspectives on human performance modeling. *Automatica* 19: 663–676.

Poletiek, F.H. 1996. Paradoxes of falsification. *Quarterly Journal of Experimental Psychology Section A: Human Experimental Psychology* 49: 447–462.

Popper, K.R. 1959. *The Logic of Scientific Discovery.* New York, NY: Harper and Row.

Raykov, T. and Marcoulides, G.A. 2006. *A First Course in Structural Equation Modeling.* Mahway, NJ: Erlbaum.

Reason, J. 1990. *Human Error.* New York, NY: Cambridge University Press.

Sohn, Y. and Jo, Y.K. 2003. A study on the student pilot's mental workload due to personality types of both instructor and student. *Ergonomics* 46: 1566–1577.

Svensson, E., Angelborg-Thanderz, M., Sjöberg, L., and Olsson, S. 1997. Information complexity—Mental workload and performance in combat aircraft. *Ergonomics* 40: 362–380.

Transport Canada. 2001. *Introduction to Safety Management Systems.* TP 13739E. Ottawa, Canada: Transport Canada.

VanLenh, K. 1996. Cognitive skill acquisition. *Annual Review of Psychology* 47: 513–539.

Wickens, C.D., Goh, J., Hellebert, J., Horrey, W., and Talleur, D.A. 2003. Attentional models of multi-task pilot performance using advanced display technology. *Human Factors* 45: 360–380.

Wickens, C.D. and Holland, J.G. 2000. *Engineering Psychology and Human Performance*, 3rd ed. Upper Saddle River, NJ: Prentice-Hall.

Wozniak, R.H. 1999. *Classics in Psychology, 1855–1914: Historical Essays.* Bristol, UK: Thoemmes Press.

2 Research Methods and Statistics

2.1 INTRODUCTION

The purpose of research is to gain new knowledge that may be used to improve both decisions and practice. In order to be a good consumer of research, it is important to have some knowledge about the research process and how research findings are analyzed. One could argue that learning some of the concepts and tools used by researchers will make it possible to gain a better understanding of research findings, and also possible shortcomings associated with the studies. Some basic knowledge about how research is conducted in aviation psychology and human factors may be seen as a can opener to understanding empirical findings and also reading the rest of the book.

In order to be able to trust new findings, it is important that scientific methodology is used. The tools that researchers use to conduct research should be described in sufficient detail so that other researchers may conduct and replicate the study. In other words, an important principle is that the findings should be replicable, which means that they are confirmed in new studies and by other researchers. There are several scientific methods available depending on the research area, and the most important aspect is that the methods are well suited for exploring the research question. Sometimes, the best choice is to use an experiment, whereas at other times a survey may be the best choice.

Research ideas may come from many sources. Many researchers work within an area or research field, and a part of their research activity will be to keep updated on unresolved questions and unexplored areas. Other times, the researcher will get ideas from his or her own life or things that happen at work, or the researcher may be asked to solve a specific applied problem.

Research can be categorized in many ways—for example, basic and applied research. In basic research, the main purpose is to understand or explain a phenomenon without knowing that these findings will be useful for something. In applied research, it is easier to see the possibilities for using the research findings for something. Frequently, the boundaries between these two types of research will be unclear, and basic research may later be important as a background for applied research and for the development of products and services. As an example, basic research about how the human brain perceives and processes information may later be important in applied research and in the design of display systems or perhaps for developing tests for pilot selection.

Research should be free and independent. This means that the researcher should be free to choose research methods and to communicate the results without any form of censorship. To what extent the researcher is free to choose the research problem is partly dependent upon where the researcher works; however, frequently one important practical limitation is lack of funding. Even though the researcher may have good ideas for a project and have chosen appropriate methods, the project may not receive any funding.

2.2 THE RESEARCH PROCESS

The research process normally consists of a series of steps (Figure 2.1) that the researcher proceeds through from problem description to final conclusion.

The first step is usually a period in which ideas are formulated and the literature on the topic reviewed. The first ideas are then formulated in more detail as problems and hypotheses. Some may be very descriptive—for example, to estimate the prevalence of fear of flying in the population. At other times, the purpose may be to determine the cause of something—for example, whether a specific course aimed at reducing fear of flying is in fact effective in doing so.

The next step will be to choose a method well suited for studying the research problem. Sometimes, aspects other than the nature of the problem or hypothesis will influence the choice of method—for example, practical considerations, tradition, and ethical problems. Within certain disciplines, some methods are more popular than others, and the choice of methods may also depend on the training that the researcher has received. In other words, there will likely be many aspects involved when choosing research methods and design in addition to the nature of the research question. The next step in the research process involves data collection. Data may be

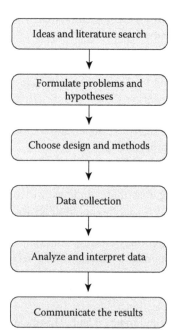

FIGURE 2.1 Research process.

quantitative, implying that something is measured or counted that may be processed using statistical methods, or that data may be qualitative, often involving words, observations, or text. The majority of research conducted within aviation is based on quantitative data, and this chapter will focus on how to collect, process, and interpret such data.

2.3   LITERATURE REVIEWS AND RESEARCH QUESTIONS

The start of any research project is usually a systematic review of relevant studies already conducted and published. There are a large number of scientific journals in psychology, and some of them publish aviation-related research. One example is the *International Journal of Aerospace Psychology*, which is an American journal published by Taylor & Francis. Another journal published by Hogrefe is *Aviation Psychology and Applied Human Factors*, which is also the official organ of the European Association for Aviation Psychology (EAAP). In addition, a medical journal called *Aerospace Medicine and Human Performance* is published by the Aerospace Medical Association. A number of other psychology journals will publish articles in aviation psychology and other related areas of work and organizational psychology—for example, *Human Factors*, *Safety Science*, *Journal of Applied Psychology*, and *Military Psychology*. Articles from these journals may be accessed through a library or by contacting the author of the article. One can also visit the journal's Web site, but it may be necessary to purchase the article unless it is published as open access. Open access means that the article is free to read for everyone and may be downloaded without any cost. In addition, the Federal Aviation Administration (FAA) has produced a large number of reports over the years that are available online, free of charge. A general literature search using a regular search engine may also result in relevant articles and reports, but it is important to evaluate the source and quality of the information critically.

Before they are published, scientific articles have been through a peer-review system. This means that two or three other researchers in the field will review the article. The author then receives the feedback from the reviewers and the editor, and in most cases, the article will have to be revised before it is published. Sometimes, the quality of the article is too poor compared to the standards of the journal, and the author is not given the option to revise and resubmit. The journals vary in relation to the proportion of submitted articles that are accepted and how often articles from the journal are cited by other authors.

Research in aviation psychology is also presented at conferences. One of the organizers of such conferences is EAAP. EAAP is an association of aviation psychologists now more than 60 years old that organizes conferences every 2 years. In addition, the International Symposium on Aviation Psychology is organized every 2 years and is usually held in Dayton, Ohio. Approximately every 3 years, the Australian Association for Aviation Psychology organizes a conference in Sydney. Proceedings are usually published after the conferences, and they include the papers presented at the conference, usually in the form of short articles. These are available for those attending the conference and sometimes also through the Web sites of the organizers. Researchers* often present their results at a conference before the results appear in a journal, so attending conferences may provide a snapshot of the latest news in the area.

2.4 RESEARCH PROBLEMS

Not all questions can be answered through research, and even if the questions or problems can be examined by scientific methods, it is often necessary to restrict the study to some selected questions. One type of research problem can be categorized as *descriptive*. This term is used when the purpose is to describe a phenomenon or how things covary. An example of a descriptive research problem would be to assess the level of stress among air traffic controllers or to examine whether a test can be used to select cabin crew members. Sometimes, in addition to an overall research problem, more specific questions may be formulated as hypotheses. Suppose a survey on job stress is conducted among air traffic controllers. The researcher might want to examine the hypothesis that there is an association between lack of social support and experienced stress. Such hypotheses are usually based on a theory or on earlier research findings.

If a correlation between two variables—for example, between social support and stress—is discovered in a survey, it does not necessarily mean that a causal relationship exists between the two variables. It may be a causal link, but a correlation is not sufficient to determine this. In addition, we need to know that social support precedes the feeling of stress, and preferably, we should know something about the mechanism behind or how social support reduces or acts as a buffer to stress. Perhaps, a third variable affects both variables studied and is the real cause of variations in both social support and stress. If a causal relationship is the main focus of the study, then the research question will have to be formulated differently than in descriptive research, and it will also require a different research design from that used in descriptive research. The best way to examine causal problems is usually by means of an experiment.

2.5 VARIABLES

Variables are aspects or attributes of a person or phenomenon studied; they may have different values depending on what is being measured. Some examples include the age of a person or the number of hours of flying experience. Alternatively, we may be interested in personal characteristics such as personality traits—for example, extroversion or whether the person has completed a CRM (crew resource management) course. Variables manipulated by the researcher are usually labeled independent variables (e.g., whether a person receives a course or not). The variables studied afterward (e.g., improved communication skills or fewer operational mistakes) are called dependent variables.

---

* Researchers are usually thrilled to get a request for their publications, so if an article cannot be found through a library or on the Web, try sending a note to the author and asking for a copy. Many of the researchers in this area can be contacted through social networking sites such as ResearchGate, Academia, or LinkedIn.

Variables also differ in how they are measured or assessed. Some variables are easy to assess; for example, age could be measured in years (at least for adults) or salary measured in dollars or euros. Both age and salary are continuous variables measured on a scale with equal intervals between the values. Many psychological variables are measured using a five-point scale or a seven-point scale where the person is asked to indicate how much she or he agrees with a statement. Sometimes, fewer categories are used, and it can be argued whether such scales can be seen as continuous or not; this has implications for the statistical methods that may be used for analyzing the data.

Some variables are categorical; for example, gender has two categories (man/woman), whereas masculinity could be measured on a continuous scale. Numbers may also be used for categorical variables, but would only say something about group membership (e.g., men are given the value 1 and women the value 2) and simply serve as labels. The number would only indicate that they are different, and the letters A and B could be used instead. Variables may, in other words, have many values and the numbers would contain different types of information depending on the type of variable and what is being measured.

As a general rule, it is better to measure a variable using a continuous scale than as a categorical variable (e.g., age in years, rather than in categories young vs. old). This applies as long as the variable may be seen as a continuous variable in its nature and not categorical like country or airline. More statistical analyses are available for continuous variables, and it is easier to detect findings when variables are continuously measured compared to categorical (see Chapter 5 on how to correct for this artifact).

2.6 DESCRIPTIVE METHODS AND MEASUREMENT

Research usually requires measurement or some form of categorization. Some variables are easy to assess, and others are not. Many psychological constructs are not easily observed—for example, intelligence, anxiety, or personality traits. These constructs will have to be operationalized before they can be measured. Psychological tests are one way of measuring these constructs, in addition to interviews and observations.

2.6.1 PSYCHOLOGICAL TESTS

A psychological test is a standardized device or procedure for assessing the amount or magnitude of a person's behavior or other characteristic in a specific domain. The test results are scored and interpreted using a standardized procedure. It could involve a handful of questions or an extensive procedure involving equipment and computers. Psychological tests may be used for many different purposes, including clinical use, personnel selection, and research. Regardless of purpose, it is important that the tests be of high quality, which usually involves three requirements: reliability, validity, and appropriate norms. Each of these concepts will be discussed in detail on the following pages. Sometimes, other names than tests are used such as scales, measures, or instruments, but regardless of the labels, the same rules for measurement apply.

There are many requirements for tests and test users. The European Federation of Psychologists' Associations has published a common set of guidelines for how tests should be evaluated (EFPA 2013), and the American Educational Research Association (AERA 2014) has published similar guidelines in a book called *Standards for Educational and Psychological Testing*. These professional guidelines explain important constructs such as reliability and validity, in addition to providing guidelines for how tests should be used appropriately, professionally, and in an ethical manner.

2.6.2 CLASSICAL TEST THEORY

In psychology, we usually assume that a person's test score consists of two components that together constitute what is called the observed score. One component is the person's true score, while the other is the error term. This can be expressed as follows: observed score = true score + error part. If the same person is tested several times under the same conditions, we would expect a similar, but not identical, test score every time. The observed scores will vary slightly from time to time. If the error term is small, then the variations will be smaller than those if the error term is large. In addition, we make the assumption that the error is unsystematic—for example, that the error does not depend on a person's true score. This model of measurement is called *classical test theory* (Magnusson 2003) and is the starting point for many of the psychological tests used today. It is possible to have more advanced models for test scores and the error component (e.g., assuming that not all the error is random but that part of it is systematic).

A more recent development is *item response theory* (Embretson and Reise 2000), which represents a different way of studying test scores. It is the starting point of so-called adaptive testing, in which the degree of difficulty on tasks is tailored to the individual level. The theory is based on the assumption that the probability of answering correctly is a function of a latent trait or ability. Item response theory makes stronger assumptions than classical test theory, but the advantage is a more detailed analysis of the items. One disadvantage is the lack of user-friendly software to conduct the analyses compared to the analyses performed in classical test theory, which may be performed with most statistical programs. In the years to come, more tests will certainly be developed based on this theory.

2.6.3 RELIABILITY

Within classical test theory, reliability is defined as the correlation between the two parallel tests—that is, two similar, but not identical, tests. The correlation coefficient is a statistical measure of covariation between two variables. This index will be further discussed in Section 2.8 on statistics. In other words, if we test a group of people twice using two parallel tests, a large correlation is expected between the test scores if the error term is small. However, it is often difficult and time consuming to create parallel tests, so a different approach to examining the reliability of the test scores is needed.

One way to estimate reliability is to test the same group of people twice with the same test (e.g., after a few months). This is called *test–retest reliability*. For tests with time constraints (e.g., most cognitive ability tests), test–retest reliability is an appropriate way of estimating the test reliability. Another common approach is to divide the test into two parts—for example, by taking every other question in each section (split-half reliability). Then, a group of people is tested and two scores are calculated for each person, one for each part of the test. Finally, the correlation is calculated between the two parts. However, this approach will result in an estimate of the reliability of a test with only 50% of the items or half the length of the original test. It is possible to correct the reliability estimate for this using a formula that provides an estimate of the reliability for the entire test.

Of course, we can divide the test into two parts in many ways, depending on how the questions or items are split. One form of reliability that is frequently used for personality traits is the Cronbach's alpha, which is a kind of average split-half reliability of all the possible split-half reliability estimates for a given measure. The various types of reliability will provide different types of information about the test scores. Test–retest reliability will say something about the stability over time, and the other forms of reliability will provide information about the internal consistency (split-half and Cronbach's alpha). The calculated correlations should be as high as possible, preferably 0.70 or higher, but sometimes lower values may be accepted (see, e.g., EFPA 2013). One factor affecting test reliability is the number of questions: the more questions there are, the higher the reliability is. In addition, it is important that the test conditions and scoring procedures be standardized, which means that clear and well-defined procedures are used for all the subjects. Sometimes, the scoring of a test may require some judgment, and then inter-rater reliability should be assessed, for example, by having two or more raters score the same sample of subjects and then assess the degree of consistency between them.

How reliability is estimated depends on the nature of the test and the intended use. If a test is used for making important decisions about an individual, for example, who should be accepted into pilot training, then high reliability is needed. If the test is used in a research project and not to make decisions about individuals, then a lower reliability may be accepted.

2.6.4   VALIDITY

The most important form of test validity is *construct validity*. This refers to the extent to which the test measures what it purports to be measuring. Does an intelligence test measure intelligence or is the test only a measure of academic performance? There is no simple solution to the problem of documenting adequate construct validity. Many strategies may be used to substantiate that the test actually measures what we want it to measure. If, for example, we have developed a new intelligence test, then one way to examine construct validity would be to investigate the relationship between the new test and other well-established intelligence tests.

Another form of validity is *criterion-related validity*. This refers to the extent to which the test predicts a criterion. If the criterion is measured about the same time as the test is administered, then the term "concurrent validity" is used, in contrast to "predictive validity," which is used when a certain time period has passed between testing and measurement of the criterion. Predictive validity asks the question: can the test scores be used for predicting future work performance? The predictive validity is usually examined by calculating the correlation between the test scores and a measure of performance (criterion).

Content validity, which is the third type of validity, concerns the extent to which the test items or questions are covering the relevant domain to be tested. Do the exam questions cover the area to be examined or are some parts left out?

These three forms of validity may seem quite different, and the system has received some criticism (Guion 1981; Messick 1995). An important objection has been that it is not the test itself that is valid; rather, the conclusions that we draw on the basis of test scores must be valid. Messick (1995) has long argued that the examination of test validity should be expanded to include value implications inherent in the interpretation of a test score as well as social consequences of testing. This would involve an evaluation to see whether the use of a particular test may have unfortunate consequences—for example, that special groups are not selected in connection with the selection of a given job or education.

2.6.5   Test Norms and Cultural Adaptation

In addition to reliability and validity, it is often desirable that the test be standardized. This means that the test scores for a large sample of subjects are known so that a person may be compared with the mean of these scores. Sometimes, it may be appropriate to use a random sample of the population when establishing test norms, whereas at other times more specialized groups are more relevant. Imagine a situation where a person is tested using an intelligence test and the result is calculated as the number of correct responses. Unless we compare the result with something, it is hard to know whether the person performed well or not. The result could be compared to the average number of correct responses based on other adults in the same age group and from the same country. The tests should be administered in the same way for all who have been tested. Everyone receives the questions in the same order, with the same instructions, and with specific scoring procedures.

This is an important principle in order to be able to compare performance. If a test is not developed and norms established in the country where the test will be used, then it is necessary to translate and adapt the test to the new conditions. For example, when a test developed in the United States is used in Norway, the test needs to be translated to Norwegian. A common procedure is first to translate the test into Norwegian and then for another bilingual person to translate the work back to the original language. This procedure may reveal problems in the translation that should be resolved before the test is used. Even if we can come up with a good word-for-word translation, test reliability and validity should be examined again, and national norms should be established. In situations where national norms or norms for a specific occupational group are not available, then caution needs to be taken when interpreting the test scores based on norms from other countries or other target groups.

2.6.6   Questionnaires

A questionnaire is an efficient way to collect data from large groups. It is also easier to ensure that the person feels that he or she can respond anonymously (e.g., compared to an interview). A questionnaire may consist of several parts or sections (e.g., one section on background information such as age, gender, education, and experience). The questionnaire will include specific questions designed for the purpose and may also include more established scales that, for example, measure personality characteristics such as extroversion. The answers can be open ended or with closed options. Sometimes, a five-point or seven-point scale is used where people can indicate their opinion by marking one of the options. If the questionnaire involves using established scales—for example, to measure satisfaction in the workplace—it is important to keep the original wording and the response options of these scales identical to the original measurement instrument. Changes may alter the psychometric properties of the instrument and make comparisons with other studies difficult.

To formulate good questions is an art, and often there will be a lot of work behind a good questionnaire. It is important to avoid formulating leading or ambiguous questions, to use a simple language, and avoid professional terminology and expressions. A questionnaire that looks appealing and includes clear questions increases the response rate. The length of the questionnaire is also related to the response rate, so shorter questionnaires are preferred; thus, designers must think carefully about whether all the questions really are necessary. A good summary of advice when formulating questions and conducting a survey is provided by Fink and Kosecoff (1998).

Researchers would like the response rate (the proportion of people who actually complete the survey and/or send back the questionnaire) to be as high as possible. Some methods books claim that it should be at least 70%, but this proves difficult to achieve in practice, even after a reminder has been sent to all the respondents. A meta-analysis of studies in clinical and counseling psychology summarized 308 surveys and found an average response rate of 49.6% (Van Horn et al. 2009). The survey showed that the response rate increased by an average of 6% after the first reminder. Response rate also declined over the 20-year period covered by the meta-analysis (1985–2005).

2.6.7 INTERNET

Many surveys are conducted via the Internet, and various programs can be used to create Web-based questionnaires. Some of the programs must be purchased, but other applications can be freely downloaded via the Web. Participants in Internet surveys may be recruited by sending them an e-mail or by making the address of the Web site known to the audience in many ways. It is often difficult to determine what the response rate is in online surveys. This is due in part to the fact that e-mail addresses change more frequently than residential addresses, and thus it is difficult to know how many people actually received the invitation. In cases where participants are recruited through other channels, it may also be difficult to determine how many people were actually informed about the survey. Some findings have indicated lower response rates for Web-based surveys compared to equivalent mail surveys (Solomon 2001). A meta-analysis of Web-based surveys identified different ways to increase the response rate with follow-up contacts, using a personalized introduction letter, and by contacting sampled people prior to the study (Cook et al. 2000). Another interesting finding from this study was that providing incentives did not increase the response rates as expected, but instead slightly higher response rates were found for studies that did not provide any incentives (Cook et al. 2000).

Internet surveys are becoming very popular because they are efficient and save money on printing, postage, and also punching of data. However, these surveys may not be the best way to collect data for all topics and all participant groups. Not everyone has access to a PC, and not all people will feel comfortable using it for such purposes.

2.6.8 INTERVIEW

An interview can be used for personnel selection and as a data collection method. The interview may be more or less structured in advance, that is, the extent to which the questions are formulated and the order can be determined in advance. When exploring new areas or topics, it is probably best for the questions to be reasonably open; at other times, specific questions should be formulated, and, in some instances, both the questions and answering options will be given. If the questions are clearly formulated in advance, it will probably be sufficient for the interviewer to write down the answers. During extensive interviews, it may be necessary to record the interview, and the interview is transcribed later. An interview is obviously more time consuming to process than a questionnaire, but probably more useful when complex issues have to be addressed or new themes explored.

Before the interview begins, an interview guide with all the questions is usually constructed, and if multiple interviewers are used, they should all receive the necessary training so that the interviews are conducted in the same way. It is also important that interviewers are aware of the possible sources of error in the interview and how the interviewer may influence the informants with his or her behavior.

2.6.9 OBSERVATION

Like the interview, observation of people may be more or less structured. In a structured observation, the behavior to be observed is specified in advance, and there are clear rules for what should be recorded. An example would be an instructor who is evaluating pilots' performance in a simulator. Then, different categories should be specified and what constitutes good and poor performance should be outlined in advance. The observers may be a part of the situation, and the observed person may not even be aware that he or she is observed. This is called hidden observation.

An obvious problem with observation is that people who are observed may be influenced by the fact that an observer is present. A classic experiment that illustrates this is the Hawthorne study, where workers at a U.S. factory producing telephone equipment were studied. The purpose was to see whether various changes in lighting, rest hours, and other working conditions increased the workers' production. Irrespective of the changes implemented—increased lighting or less light—production increased. One interpretation of these findings was that being observed and receiving attention affected individuals' job performances. The study is described in most introductory textbooks in psychology. The fact that people change behavior when being observed has subsequently been given the term "Hawthorne effect" after the factory where these original studies were conducted in the 1920s.

The study has since been criticized because the researchers failed to consider a number of other factors specific to the workers who participated in the study. One difference was that women who took part in the study gained feedback on their performance and received economic rewards compared to the rest of the factory workers (Parsons 1992). This shows that studies may be subject to renewed scrutiny and interpretation more than 60 years after they have been conducted. Regardless of what actually happened in the Hawthorne plant, it is likely that people are influenced by the fact that they are observed. One way to prevent this problem is to conduct a so-called hidden observation. This is not ethically unproblematic, especially if one is participating in the group observed. The situation is different if large groups are observed in public places and the individuals cannot be identified. For example, if the researcher is interested in how people behave in a security check, this may be an effective and ethical research method.

Often, in the beginning of a study, those who are observed are probably aware of the fact that an additional person is present in the situation. After some time, however, the influence is probably less as the participants get used to having someone there and get busy with work tasks to be performed.

2.7 EXPERIMENTS, QUASI-EXPERIMENTS, AND CORRELATION RESEARCH

In a research project, it is important to have a plan for how the research should be conducted and how the data should be collected. This is sometimes called the design of the study; we will describe three types of design.

2.7.1 EXPERIMENTS

Many people probably picture an experiment as something that takes place in a laboratory with people in white coats. This is not always the case, and the logic behind the experiment is more crucial than the location. An important feature of an experiment is the presence of a control group. The term "control group" is used for one of the groups that receives no treatment or intervention. The control group is then compared to the treatment group, and the differences between the groups can then be attributed to the treatment that one group received and the other did not. This requires that the groups be similar, and the best way to ensure this is by randomly assigning subjects to the two conditions.

Another important feature of an experiment is that the researcher can control the conditions to which people are exposed. Sometimes, several experimental groups receive different interventions. For example, a study may include two types of training, both of which will be compared to the control group that receives no training. Alternatively, there may be different levels of the independent variable; for example, a short course may be compared to a longer course.

2.7.2 Quasi-Experiments

A compromise between a true experiment and correlational studies is a so-called quasi-experimental design. The purpose of this design is to mimic the experiment in as many ways as possible. An example of a quasi-experiment is to use a comparison group and treatment group to which the participants have not been randomly assigned. It is not always possible to allocate people at random to experimental and control conditions. Perhaps, those who sign up first for the study will have to be included in the experimental group, and those who sign up later will have to be included in the comparison group. Then, the researcher has to consider the possibility that these groups are not similar.

One way to explore this would be to do some pretesting to determine whether these groups are more or less similar in relation to important variables. If the groups differ, this may make it difficult to draw firm conclusions about the effect of the intervention. There are other quasi-experimental designs, such as a design without any control or comparison group. One example would be a pretest/posttest design where the same people are examined before and after the intervention. The problems associated with this design are addressed in Section 2.9.

2.7.3 Correlational Research

It is not always possible to conduct a real experiment for both practical and ethical reasons. For example, it may not be possible to design an experiment in which the amount of social support employees receive from the leader is manipulated. This approach will be viewed as unethical by most people, but studying natural variation in this phenomenon is possible. Research in which working conditions are studied will often include a correlational design. The purpose may be to map out various work demands such as workload and burnout. After these variables have been studied, various statistical techniques may be used to study the relationship between these variables. Also, more complex models of how multiple variables are connected with burnout can be studied, in addition to examining the extent to which burnout can be predicted from work-related factors and personal characteristics.

2.8 STATISTICS

An important part of the research process occurs when the results are processed. If the study includes only a few subjects, then it is easy to get an overview of the findings. However, in most studies, a large number of participants and variables are included, so a tool is clearly needed to get an overview. Suppose that we have sent out a questionnaire to 1000 cabin crew members to map out what they think about their working environment. Without statistical techniques, it would be almost impossible to describe the opinions of these workers.

Statistics can help us with three things:

- Sampling (how people are chosen and how many people are required)
- Describing the data (graphical, variation, and the most typical response)
- Drawing conclusions about parameters in the population

In most cases, we do not have the opportunity to study the entire population (e.g., all pilots and all passengers), and a smaller group needs to be sampled. Most statistical methods and procedures assume a random selection of subjects, which means that all participants initially have equal chances to be selected. There are also other ways to sample subjects; for example, stratified samples may be employed where the population is divided into strata and then subjects are randomly selected from each stratum. These sampling methods are primarily used in surveys where one is interested in investigating, for example, how many people sympathize with a political party or the extent of positive attitudes toward environmental issues. An application of statistics is thus to determine how the sampling should be done and, not least, how many people are needed in the study.

After the data are collected, the next step is to describe the results. There are many possibilities, depending on the problem and what types of data have been collected. The results may be presented in terms of percentages, rates, means, or perhaps a measure of association (correlation). Graphs or figures for summarizing the data could also be used.

The third and last step is the deduction from the sample to the population. Researchers are usually not satisfied with just describing the specific sample, but rather want to draw conclusions about the entire population. Conclusions about the population are based on findings observed in a sample. One way to do this is through hypothesis testing. This means that a hypothesis about the population is formulated that can be tested using results from the sample.

The second procedure involves estimating the results in the population on the basis of the results in the sample. Suppose we are interested in knowing the proportion of people with fear of flying. After conducting a study measuring this attitude about flying, we will have a concrete number: the proportion of our subjects who said they were afraid of flying. Lacking any better estimates, it would then be reasonable to suggest that, among the population at large, approximately the same proportion as we have observed in the sample has a fear of flying. In addition, we might propose an interval that is likely to capture the true proportion of people with fear of flying in the population. These intervals are called confidence intervals. If many people are included in the sample, then these intervals are smaller; that is, the more people who are in our sample, the more accurate is our estimate.

2.8.1 DESCRIPTIVE STATISTICS

The most common measure of central tendency is the arithmetic mean. This is commonly used when something is measured on a continuous scale. The arithmetic mean is usually denoted with the letter M (for "mean") or $\bar{X}$. An alternative is the median, which is the value in the middle, after all the values have been ranked from lowest to highest. This is a good measure if the distribution is skewed—for example, if the results include some very high or very low values. The mode is a third indicator of central tendency, which simply is the value with the highest frequency. Thus, it is not necessary that the variable be continuous to use this measure of central tendency.

In addition to a measure of the most typical value in the distribution, it is also important to have a measure of variation. If we have calculated the arithmetic mean, it is common to use the standard deviation as a measure of variation. Formulated a little imprecisely, the standard deviation is the average deviation from the mean. If results are normally distributed—that is, bell shaped—and we inspect the distribution and move one standard deviation above and one standard deviation below the average, then about two-thirds of the observations fall within that range. Including two standard deviations on both sides of the mean, then about 95% of the observations will be included. The formulas for calculating the arithmetic mean and standard deviation are

$$\bar{X} = \frac{\sum\limits_{i=1}^{N} X_i}{N}$$

$$SD = \sqrt{\frac{\sum\limits_{i=1}^{N} (X_i - \bar{X})^2}{N-1}}$$

where N is the sample size, X_i is the test score, and $\bar{X}$ is the mean score.

As an example, we have created a simulated data set for 10 people (Table 2.1).

Assume that people have answered a question in which they are asked to specify on a scale from 1 to 5 the degree of fear of flying. In this case, the higher the score is, the greater is the discomfort. In addition, age and gender are recorded. Remember that these data have been fabricated. Suppose we are interested in describing the group in terms of demographic variables and the level of fear of flying. Both age and fear can be said to be continuous variables, and then the arithmetic mean and standard deviation are appropriate measures of central tendency and variation. If a statistical program is used to analyze the data, each person must be represented as a line in the program. The columns represent the different variables in the study. If a widely used statistics program in the social sciences and medicine (Statistical Package for the Social Sciences [SPSS]) is applied, the output would look like the one in Table 2.2.

TABLE 2.1
Constructed Data Set

Person	Fear of Flying	Age	Gender
1	5	30	Female
2	4	22	Female
3	4	28	Male
4	3	19	Male
5	3	20	Female
6	2	21	Female
7	2	22	Male
8	1	24	Male
9	1	23	Male
10	1	21	Male

TABLE 2.2

SPSS Output

Descriptive Statistics

	N	Range	Minimum	Maximum	Sum	Mean	Std. Deviation
Fear of flying	10	4.00	1.00	5.00	26.00	*2.6000*	*1.42984*
Age	10	11.00	19.00	30.00	230.00	*23.0000*	*3.49603*
Valid N (listwise)	10						

Gender

		Frequency	Percentage	Valid Percentage	Cumulative Percentage
Valid	F	4	40.0	40.0	40.0
	M	6	60.0	60.0	100.0
	Total	10	100.0	100.0	

The figures in italics are the computed means and standard deviations for fear of flying and age, respectively. In addition, the minimum and maximum scores for each of the variables are presented. For the variable gender, it is not appropriate to calculate the mean score, and the best way to describe gender would be to specify the number of women and men included in the study. If the sample is large, it would be wise to give this as a percentage.

The researcher may also be interested in exploring the relationship between age and fear of flying. Because both variables are continuous, the Pearson product-moment correlation may be used as an index of association. The correlation coefficient indicates the strength of the relationship between two variables. It is a standardized measure that varies between -1.0 and $+1.0$. The number indicates the strength of the relationship and the sign indicates the direction. A correlation of 0 means that there is no association between the variables, while a correlation of -1.0 or $+1.0$ indicates a perfect correlation between variables in which all points form a straight line. Most correlations that we observe between two psychological variables will be considerably lower than 1.0. (See Table 2.4 for a description of what can be labeled a small, medium, or high correlation.)

Whenever a correlation is positive, it means that high values on one variable are associated with high values on the other variable. A negative correlation means that high values on one variable are associated with low values for the other variable. Correlation actually describes the extent to which the data approximate a straight line, and this means that if there are curvilinear relationships, the correlation coefficient is not an appropriate index. It is therefore wise to plot the data set before performing the calculations.

In the example in Figure 2.2, the plot indicates a tendency for higher age to be associated with a higher score in fear of flying (i.e., a positive correlation).

According to the output, the observed correlation is 0.51, which is a strong correlation between the variables. In addition, a significance test of the correlation is performed and reported in the output, but we will return to this later.

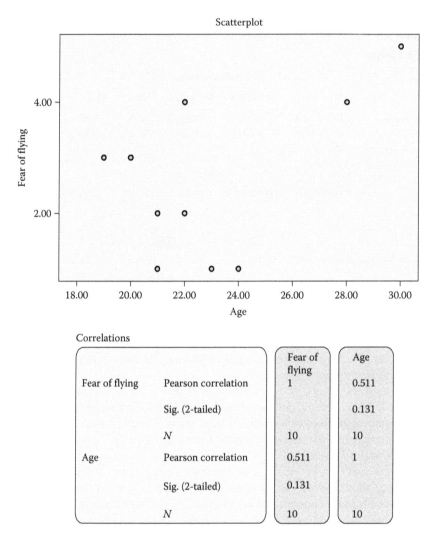

FIGURE 2.2   Correlation: scatterplot and calculations.

Sometimes, we want to examine in more detail the nature of the relationship between the two variables beyond the strength of the relationship. For example, we may want to know how much fear of flying would increase when increasing the age by 1 year (or perhaps 10 years). Using a method called regression analysis, we can calculate an equation for the relationship between age and fear of flying that specifies the nature of the relationship. Such a regression equation may have one or more independent variables. The purpose of the regression analysis is to predict as much as possible of the variation in the dependent variable, in this case fear of flying.

The correlation coefficient is the starting point for a series of analyses—among other things, factor analysis. The purpose of factor analysis is to find a smaller number of factors that explain the pattern of correlations among many variables. Suppose we have tested a group of people with a range of ability tests that are then correlated with each other. Some of the tests will be highly correlated with each other while others will be less correlated. Using factor analysis, it is possible to arrive at a smaller number of factors than the number of tests that will explain the pattern in the correlation matrix. Perhaps, the tests can be grouped into two groups: one including tests that measure mathematical abilities and one consisting of tests that measure verbal abilities. The results of the factor analysis may be the identification of two underlying factors that might be named after tests that are intertwined with each of them. Here, one could perhaps say that the tests measure the two abilities—namely, linguistic and mathematical skills.

There are two main strategies when performing a factor analysis: exploratory factor analysis and confirmatory factor analysis. In the first case, a factor structure is suggested by the statistical program based on the specific intercorrelations in the data set. In confirmatory factor analysis, the researcher suggests the number of factors and the structure among these. The model is then compared to the actual data and the correspondence between model and data is examined.

Returning to our data set, we may want to determine whether any gender differences exist. On the basis of the SPSS output in Table 2.3, we see that women score higher on fear of flying compared to men in this group, although the standard deviations are very similar.

Sometimes, it can be difficult to evaluate whether such a difference can be said to be big or small. This obviously depends on how well one knows the scale used. An alternative is to transform the difference between the means to a more familiar

TABLE 2.3
SPSS Output: *t*-Test of Differences between Means

Group Statistics

	Gender	N	Mean	Std. Deviation	Std. Error Mean
Fear of flying	Female	4	3.5000	1.29099	0.64550
	Male	6	2.0000	1.26491	0.51640

Independent Samples Test

	Levene's Test for Equality of Variances		*t*-Test for Equality of Means					95% Confidence Interval of the Difference	
	F	Sig.	t	df	Sig. (Two-Tailed)	Mean Difference	Std. Error Difference		
Fear of Flying								Lower	Upper
Equal variances assumed	0.000	1.000	1.823	8	0.106	1.50000	0.82285	−0.39750	3.39750
Equal variances not assumed			1.815	6.477	0.116	1.50000	0.82664	−0.48715	3.48715

scale—for example, in the form of a standard deviation. These standardized mean difference scores can be calculated in different ways depending on which standard deviation that is used. The most common approach is to use the pooled standard deviation based on both groups. This index-labeled Hedges' g is calculated as $g = (\bar{X} - \bar{Y})/SD_{pooled}$ (see, e.g., Hunter and Schmidt 2003). In this calculation, the difference between means is divided by a pooled standard deviation. The standard deviations in this example are approximately equal for the groups and we can use $SD_{pooled} = 1.3$. Hedges' g is then $(3.5 - 2.0)/1.3 = 1.15$. This can be described as a large difference, and it means that the difference between women and men is slightly more than one standard deviation. In addition, the confidence interval for the difference is large, ranging from -0.398 to 3.398. The confidence interval is estimated to capture the actual difference between women and men in the population with a high certainty.

The range also includes zero, which means that we cannot rule out the possibility that the difference between women and men in the population is zero.

2.8.2 INFERENTIAL STATISTICS

We have now described the variables and also the associations between some of these variables for the sample. The next step would be to draw conclusions about the population from which these individuals were randomly picked. Several interesting hypotheses can be tested. For one, we found a positive correlation between age and fear of flying. The question is, will there also be a correlation in the population? This question is restated in the form of a null hypothesis (H_0). The null hypothesis in this example is that the correlation is zero in the population. The alternative hypothesis (H_1) would be that the correlation is greater than zero or less than zero. It is now possible to calculate a number (a test statistic) that will help us decide whether our current results support the null hypothesis or the alternative hypothesis. In Figure 2.2, the results from this significance test are presented. The number in Figure 2.2 indicates the probability of observing the correlation we have obtained, or a stronger correlation when the true correlation in the population is zero (i.e., H_0 is true). The probability in this case is 0.13, and this is higher than what we usually would accept. As a rule, the calculated probability should be lower than 0.05 and preferably 0.01. This limit is chosen in advance and is called the significance level. By choosing a given significance level, we decide on how "strict" we will be. To put it in a slightly different way, how much evidence is required before the null hypothesis can be discarded? In this example, we cannot reject the null hypothesis because $0.13 > 0.05$. It is important to remember that the sample in this case is very small (only 10 people); for most purposes, this is too small a sample when conducting a study.

If we want to test whether the difference between women and men is significant, we also need to formulate a null hypothesis. The null hypothesis in this case will be that the difference between the mean scores for women and men is zero in the population (H_0 = mean score for women in population − mean score for men in the population = 0). This is another way of saying that the two means are equal. In addition, we need an alternative hypothesis if the null hypothesis is rejected. This hypothesis would be that the difference between the means is different from zero.

Sometimes, we choose a specific direction for the alternative hypothesis based on previous findings or theory. Suppose previous studies have shown that women score higher than males on measures of anxiety and depression. We could then formulate an alternative hypothesis that indicates that the difference is greater than zero (H_1 = mean score for women in population − mean score for men in the population > 0). In this case, a so-called one-tailed significance test could be performed; if we do not have a specific hypothesis in advance, both options would have to be specified, and this is called a two-tailed test. This represents a more conservative approach and is therefore used more frequently. Most statistics programs therefore use a two-tailed test as the default option.

An example of a significance test is presented in Table 2.3. In the top part of the table, the mean scores for men and women are presented. For women, it is 3.5; men score lower and achieve 2.0. Is this difference large enough for the result to be significant? In Table 2.3, a t-value ($t = 1.82$) and the corresponding probability (0.106) are presented. The calculations are based on the assumption that the difference really is zero in the population (H_0 is true). This is a higher probability than is commonly used as a limit (e.g., 0.05), and thus the null hypothesis cannot be rejected. A prerequisite for such tests, at least if the samples are small, is that the variations in the two groups are equal. The table also shows a test that can be used if this assumption does not hold.

There are a number of different significance tests depending on the hypotheses and how data are collected. In our example, the appropriate test is called a t-test for independent data because two independent groups were examined. If a different design had been used and, for example, the same person had been examined twice, a slightly different version of this significance test is appropriate (dependent samples t-test). When several groups are investigated, there will be many group means. Comparing multiple group means can be done with analysis of variance (ANOVA). The basic principles involved in the significance testing, however, are the same:

- Formulate H_0 and H_1.
- Select the significance level (0.01 or 0.05).
- Perform calculations. What is the probability of getting the observed results if H_0 is true?
- Conclude. Can H_0 be rejected?

2.8.3 TYPE 1 AND TYPE 2 ERRORS

When a significance test is conducted, several decisions can be made—two correct and two incorrect. Correct decisions are to reject the null hypothesis when it is wrong and keep it when it is correct. Wrong decisions are to retain the null hypothesis when it is incorrect (Type 2 error) or reject it when it is correct (Type 1 error). The probability of making a Type 1 error is set by the significance level. If the researcher wants to be very confident that such a mistake is avoided, a more stringent significance level should be chosen. To avoid Type 2 error, it is important that the study be conducted with a sufficient number of people so that true correlations or differences between groups are discovered.

TABLE 2.4
What Is the Required Sample Size?

Correlation	Effect	N (One-Tailed Test)	N (Two-Tailed Test)
Small effect	$r = 0.10$	600	770
Medium effect	$r = 0.30$	60	81
Large effect	$r = 0.50$	20	25
Differences between Two Groups			
Small effect	$g = 0.20$	310 (in each group)	390 (in each group)
Medium effect	$g = 0.50$	50 (in each group)	63 (in each group)
Large effect	$g = 0.80$	20 (in each group)	25 (in each group)

Note: Significance level $= 0.05$; statistical power $= 0.80$; r, correlation; g, standardized mean difference.

Somewhat imprecisely, one can say that significance is a function of both the size of the effect and the sample size. The findings from a study may be reported as a correlation or a standardized mean difference (Hedges' g); both are examples of effect sizes. This means that if we study a very strong association (high correlation), a small sample may be sufficient. If the relationship is weaker (a smaller correlation), a much larger sample is needed to detect this. It can sometimes be difficult to determine the necessary sample before the survey is conducted if the size of the effect is unknown. If similar studies have already been published, these results can be used to calculate the sample size needed. In Table 2.4, some calculations have been performed for small, medium, and large effects in order to estimate the sample sizes needed. It is, of course, desirable that the study should have sufficient statistical power. This means that the probability should be high (e.g., 0.80) for correctly rejecting the null hypothesis.

Different programs can be used to perform such calculations; the calculations in Table 2.4 are performed with a program called "Power and Precision" (Borenstein et al. 2001). When the calculations are performed, it is necessary to specify the size of the effect, significance level (one-tailed or two-tailed test), and the desired statistical power.

2.9   DESIGN AND VALIDITY

Every research design will have advantages and disadvantages, and the researcher needs to consider every option and possible methodological problem carefully before choosing the study design. In addition, practical, ethical, and economic factors will have to be considered. An important aspect when choosing design is the impact this will have on validity. A very short and simple explanation of validity is that it relates to how well we can trust the conclusions that are drawn from a study.

There are different forms of validity related to study design, such as *statistical validity, internal validity, external validity,* and *construct validity.* In short, statistical validity is related to obtaining a significant effect, internal validity is about causality, construct validity has to do with measuring constructs, and external validity has to do with generalizing findings over time, places, and people. This validity system was first introduced by Cook and Campbell in 1979; a revised edition of their classic book was published in 2002 (Shadish et al. 2002). The system is particularly intended for research addressing causal problems, although some types of validity may also be relevant to more descriptive research.

2.9.1 STATISTICAL VALIDITY

This type of validity relates to the extent to which we can trust the statistical conclusions from a study. Is there a significant difference between the two groups studied (experimental and control groups), and is the difference of a certain magnitude? To investigate this, we usually perform a significance test. There are several threats to the statistical validity, such as low statistical power, which typically results from having too few participants in the study. Another threat to this type of validity is that inappropriate statistical methods are used or that mathematical assumptions are not met. All types of statistical analyses have certain requirements that may relate to how the variables are measured or the design of the study. One requirement could be that the variables are continuously measured and normally distributed. If a statistically significant difference between the groups is detected, it is possible to move on to discuss other forms of validity. Thus, statistical validity is a prerequisite for the other types of validity. If the experimental and control groups show no significant differences, then there is little point in discussing whether the findings can be generalized to other subjects.

2.9.2 INTERNAL VALIDITY

Internal validity has to do with causality. Is it possible to draw firm conclusions about cause and effect based on the study? The best way to ensure this is to have an experimental design with a control group. Participants are distributed randomly between the two conditions; this allows us to conclude that any difference observed between the groups can be attributed to the treatment or intervention. One problem in many studies is dropout, especially if more people choose to drop out from the control condition compared to the treatment condition. Sometimes, it may not be possible to assign participants randomly to two conditions, and another solution could be to use a comparison group. If a CRM course is already implemented in an airline, it may not be possible to perform a true experiment with randomized groups to examine the effectiveness of the course. Another option would be to recruit a comparison group from another airline company or to use pilots who have not participated in the CRM course yet. The problem would then be that the comparison group may differ from the experiment group in ways that the researcher cannot control. One way of managing this problem would be to ensure that the groups are as similar as possible initially, and also do some pretesting to measure that they are indeed similar on important variables before the CRM course is administered.

If a design with a control or comparison group is not possible and instead a pretest/posttest design is used (participants are tested before and after the course), the internal validity is threatened because one cannot exclude other causes that may have produced or caused the change. It is possible that at the same time that they invited the employees to participate in the course, the airline also implemented other changes that contributed to the observed effect. The longer the time period between the two test periods is, the more likely it is that other things can occur and produce a change. There may be situations where a pretest/posttest design can be justified—for example, as a preliminary study of a new intervention before the intervention is implemented and examined in a larger experimental study.

Even though a true experiment is optimal, it may sometimes be possible to use other designs—so-called quasi-experimental designs—to conduct valid research. It is then important to remember that the further away you move from the ideal experiment with control and randomization, the weaker the internal validity will be.

2.9.3 CONSTRUCT VALIDITY

If both statistical validity and internal validity have been addressed, it is possible to examine construct validity and external validity. Construct validity addresses whether one can generalize the relationship between cause and effect from the measured variables to the constructs. Suppose that we have implemented a CRM course for air traffic controllers, and the researcher is interested to see whether the course has increased job engagement in this group. An experimental design is used and the researcher has detected a significant difference in job engagement between the two groups after the course is completed. Both statistical validity and internal validity are considered to be sufficient and no major threats to internal validity and statistical validity have been detected. The question is then whether the findings can be generalized to the constructs—that is, to CRM courses in general and to the construct of job engagement, which would involve that the specific measurement instrument actually measured job engagement.

In addition, we must ensure that the CRM course has been conducted according to the course plan and with the specified content because we want to conclude that the specific training of the CRM course gives the effect, rather than just any course. Many interventions, such as a course, could include many effective ingredients. To investigate this further, we could also evaluate other training courses that focus only on safety in aviation and do not have a focus on collaboration and communication, such as most CRM courses do. If both types of courses are effective in relation to increasing the engagement, then the specific academic content in the CRM course is not the effective ingredient, but rather attending a course in general. Another possible outcome is that there is a difference between the two courses and that the CRM group had the highest score on engagement, and the control group and the other group (safety course) scored lower on engagement. Then, it would be safe to assume that the specific CRM course is the effective treatment, rather than just any course.

Construct validity in relation to study design is similar to construct validity in testing. The difference is that test validity is usually related to how well one construct is measured. However, when we talk about construct validity in study design, it is usually two (or more) constructs that are operationalized. We want to be able to make conclusions regarding the causal relationship between them rather than the measurement of one construct.

2.9.4 EXTERNAL VALIDITY

External validity is the extent to which we can generalize the results to other groups, to other situations, and over time. For example, will the effect of participating in a course last over time? Could the course be applied in a different airline and perhaps for other professions? Often, not all of these questions can be answered in a single study, for a variety of reasons:

- The study may have been limited to one group.
- The study may have been conducted in a single organization or country.
- There are limits to how long participants may be followed after the study is completed.
- The experiment may have been conducted in a laboratory setting.

An example would be determining how long it takes for a group of people to evacuate an airplane cabin under two conditions (high or low reward). If we observe differences between the groups, the question is whether this difference will also apply in a critical situation with actual passengers. Probably, some factors will be the same, but there will also be differences. It is a paradox that if one is using a design where good internal validity is ensured (i.e., a randomized controlled experiment in a laboratory setting), then the external validity may suffer (i.e., it may be more difficult to generalize the findings to a real-life situation). In other words, a design will therefore often represent a compromise between different concerns, and it is rare that a design is optimal in relation to all forms of validity.

In order to document that the findings can be generalized to different settings, to different persons, and over time, it is necessary to perform many studies where these aspects are varied. An effective way to systematize and compare several studies is through a meta-analysis.

2.10 META-ANALYSIS

Meta-analysis involves using statistical techniques to combine results from several studies that address the same problem. Suppose a researcher is interested in examining whether psychological tests measuring spatial abilities can be used to select pilots. How can this problem be investigated? One solution is to perform a so-called primary study. This means that a study that examines this problem is conducted. For example, a group seeking flight training is tested using a measure of spatial ability, and then later these results are combined with information on performance. If the research hypothesis is correct, then those with the highest test scores would receive the highest ratings by the instructor.

Another possibility would be to review other studies that have previously examined this issue. For most topics, published studies addressing the research question range from a handful to many hundreds of studies. If the number of studies is large, it can be difficult to get a clear picture of the overall results. In addition, studies probably vary in terms of samples used and measurement instruments, and it may therefore be difficult to summarize everything simply by reading through the articles.

An alternative to a narrative review of the studies would be to do a meta-analysis. In this approach, all the studies are coded and an overall measure of effect is recorded (such as *g* or *r*) from each article or report. In this example, it will probably be a correlation between test results and instructor ratings. The meta-analysis would involve calculating a mean correlation based on all studies, and the next step would be to study variation between studies. In some studies, a strong correlation may be detected, but in others no correlation between test results and performance will be found.

A meta-analysis consists of several steps similar to the research process in a primary study:

- Formulating a research problem
- Locating studies
- Coding studies
- Meta-analysis calculations
- Presenting the results

2.10.1   LITERATURE SEARCH AND CODING OF ARTICLES

Locating studies for a meta-analysis usually starts with a literature search using available electronic databases. This can be PsychInfo, which includes most of the articles published in psychology, or Medline, which contains the medical literature. They are many different databases depending on the discipline in which one is interested. It is thus important to use the right keywords so that all relevant studies are retrieved. In addition to searching in these databases, studies that are published in the form of technical reports or conference presentations may also be used. Often these can be found on the Web—for example, via the Web sites of relevant organizations. In addition, reference lists of articles that have already been obtained could provide further studies. Basically, as many studies as possible should be collected, but it is, of course, possible to limit the meta-analysis to recent studies or where a particular occupational group is examined.

Then, the work of developing a coding form starts, and the form should include all relevant information from the primary studies. Information about the selection of participants, age, gender, effects, measurement instruments, reliability, and other study characteristics may be included. The coding phase is usually the most time-consuming part of a meta-analysis; if many studies need to be encoded, more than one coder is usually needed. Coder reliability should be estimated by having a sample of studies coded by two or more coders.

2.10.2   STATISTICAL SOURCES OF ERROR IN STUDIES AND META-ANALYSIS CALCULATIONS

Hunter and Schmidt (2003) have described a number of factors or circumstances that may affect the size of the observed correlation (or effect size). One such factor is the lack of reliability in measurements. This will cause the observed correlations to be lower than if measurements had been more reliable. These statistical error sources or artifacts will cause us to observe differences between the studies in addition to variations caused by sampling error. When a meta-analysis is conducted, the effect sizes should be corrected for statistical errors; in addition, the observed variance between studies should be corrected for sampling error. Some of these error sources will be addressed in greater detail in Chapter 5 on selection. For simplicity, we will further limit this presentation to a "bare-bones" meta-analysis where only sampling error is taken into account.

The average effect size is calculated as a sample-size-weighted mean correlation. A similar mean effect size may be calculated for other types of effect sizes such as percentages or standardized mean differences (Hedges' g) with the same type of sample size weighting. Thus, studies based on a large number of people are given more weight than those based on smaller samples. The formula for calculating the sample-size-weighted mean correlation is

$$\bar{r} = \frac{\sum N_i r_i}{\sum N_i}$$

where N is the sample size and r is the correlation.

True variance between the studies is calculated as the difference between the observed variance between effect sizes and the variance due to sampling error—that is, random errors caused by studying a sample and not the entire population.

The formula for estimating the population variance between the studies is

$$\sigma_\rho^2 = \sigma_r^2 - \sigma_e^2$$

where σ_ρ^2 is the population variance between correlations, σ_r^2 is the observed variance between correlations, and σ_e^2 is the variance due to sampling error.

2.10.3 META-ANALYSIS EXAMPLE

Suppose a researcher wants to sum up studies examining the relationship between an ability test and job performance for air traffic controllers. Suppose 17 studies reporting correlations and the corresponding sample sizes are available (see Table 2.5).

The data set is fictitious, but not completely unrealistic. The most important part will be to calculate the mean weighted correlation as a measure of the test's predictive validity. In addition, it will be interesting to know whether there is some variation between studies, or, to put it in a slightly different way, to what extent can the predictive validity be generalized across studies?

The calculations (presented in Figure 2.3) show that the average validity is 0.35 (unweighted), while a sample-size-weighted mean is slightly lower (0.30). This means that there is a negative correlation between sample size and the correlation, which implies that studies with small sample sizes have somewhat higher correlations

TABLE 2.5
Data Set with Correlations

Study	N	r
1	129	0.22
2	55	0.55
3	37	0.44
4	115	0.20
5	24	0.47
6	34	0.40
7	170	0.22
8	49	0.40
9	131	0.20
10	88	0.37
11	59	0.28
12	95	0.26
13	80	0.42
14	115	0.25
15	47	0.38
16	30	0.40
17	44	0.50

than those with higher n. If we correct the observed variance for sampling error, the remaining variance almost equals zero (based on the output in Figure 2.3: $0.01110 - 0.01092 = 0.00019$). This means that there is no true variation between studies. Thus, the average correlation is a good measure of the predictive validity of this test.

2.10.4 CRITICISM OF THE META-ANALYSIS METHOD

Currently, the several traditions within meta-analysis employ somewhat different techniques to sum up and compare studies (see, e.g., Borenstein et al. 2009). The main difference concerns how the various studies are compared and whether inferential statistics are used to examine differences between studies. The alternative to this is the procedure suggested by Hunter and Schmidt (2003) in which emphasis is put on estimating variance between studies.

A problem that has been raised in relation to meta-analysis is whether the published studies can be said to be a representative sample of all studies conducted. Perhaps, there is a bias in which published studies are systematically different from unpublished studies. It is reasonable to assume that studies with significant findings have a higher likelihood of being published than studies with no significant results. Because a meta-analysis is largely based on published studies, it is reasonable to assume that we overestimate the actual effect to some extent. Statistical methods can calculate the number of undiscovered studies with null effects that would have to exist in order to reduce the mean effect to a nonsignificant level. If this number is very large

Bare-bones meta-analysis calculations:

Number of substudies	: 17
Number of correlations	: 17
Mean number of cases in substudies	: 76
Mean number of cases in corr.	: 76
Total number of cases	: 1302
R mean (weighted)	: 0.30260
R mean (simple)	: 0.35059

Observed variance	: 0.01110
Std.dev of	: 0.10538

Sampling variance	: 0.01092
Std.dev of	: 0.10449

Lower endpoint 95% CRI	: 0.27580
Upper endpoint 95% CRI	: 0.32939
Credibility value 90%	: 0.28510

Population variance	: 0.00019
Std.dev of	: 0.01367

Percentage of observed variance accounted for by sampling error	98.32%

95% confidence interval (homogeneous case)	
Lower endpoint	: 0.5293
Upper endpoint	: 0.35227

95% confidence interval (homogeneous case)	
Lower endpoint	: 0.25250
Upper endpoint	: 0.35269

Analysis performed with Metados
(Martinussen and Fjukstad 1995)

FIGURE 2.3 Bare-bones meta-analysis calculations.

(e.g., 10 times the number of retrieved studies), then it is unlikely that such a large number of undiscovered studies would exist, and the overall effect can be trusted.

Another criticism of meta-analysis has been that studies that are not comparable are summarized together or that categories that are too global are used for the effects. The research problem should be considered when making coding decisions including which categories and methods should be used. For example, if we are interested in the effect of therapy in reducing PTSD (posttraumatic stress disorder), then combing different types of treatment would make sense; however, if the researcher is interested in discovering whether cognitive behavioral therapy works better than, for example, group therapy, then obviously categories for each therapy form will be needed. This problem is known in the literature as the "apple and orange" problem. Whether it is a good idea to combine apples and oranges depends on the purpose. If one wants to make fruit salad, it can be a very good idea; on the other hand, if one likes only apples, the oranges are best avoided.

2.11   RESEARCH ETHICS

Research has to comply with many rules and regulations in addition to scientific standards—for example, research ethics. Research ethics include how participants are treated and the relationship between the researcher and other researchers, as well as relationships with the public. International conventions, as well as national regulations and laws, govern research ethics. Each country and sometimes even large organizations have their own ethics committees where all projects are evaluated. One such international agreement is the Helsinki Declaration, which includes biomedical research conducted on humans. According to the declaration, research should be conducted in accordance with recognized scientific principles by a person with research competence (e.g., a PhD), and the subjects' welfare, integrity, and right to privacy must be safeguarded. Informed consent to participate in the study should be obtained from the subjects before the study begins.

In general, there is substantial agreement on the basic principles that should govern research, although the formal approval procedures to which projects are subjected may vary slightly from country to country. People who participate in research projects should be exposed to as little discomfort or pain as possible, and this must be carefully weighed against the potential benefits of the research. These two perspectives—society's need for knowledge and the welfare of the participants—need to be balanced. Participation should be voluntary, and special care needs to be taken when people are in a vulnerable position or in a special position in relation to the researcher (e.g., a subordinate or a client).

An important principle in relation to research ethics is *informed consent*. This means that the person asked to participate should have information about the purpose of the study, the methods to be used, and what it will involve in terms of time, discomfort, and other factors to participate in the study. The person should also receive information about opportunities for feedback and who can be contacted if additional information is needed. It should also be emphasized that participation is voluntary and that information is treated confidentially. For many studies involving an experiment or an interview, it is common for people to sign a consent form before the study begins. If the study is an anonymous survey, then a consent form is not usually attached; instead, the person gives consent to participate implicitly by submitting the questionnaire. The person should also receive information that he or she may at any time withdraw from the study and have his or her data deleted.

In some studies, perhaps especially from social psychology, subjects have been deceived about the real purpose of the study. An example is experiments where one or more of the research assistants act as participants in the experiment; the purpose is to study how the test subjects are influenced by what other people say or do. The most famous experiment in which subjects were deliberately misled about the true purpose of the experiment was the Milgram studies on obedience conducted in the 1960s. This study was presented as an experiment in learning and memory, but it was really an experiment to study obedience. Subjects were asked to punish with electrical shocks a person who in reality was a research assistant. Many continued to give electric shock even after the person screamed for help. Many of the subjects reacted with different stress responses and showed obvious discomfort in the situation, but nevertheless continued to give shocks.

These studies violate several of the ethical principles outlined in this section. These include lack of informed consent, the fact that people were pressured to continue even after they indicated that they no longer wanted to participate, and exposing people to significant discomfort even though they were informed about the purpose of the study afterward.

Such experiments would probably not be approved today, and a researcher would need to make a strong argument for why it would be necessary to deceive people on purpose. If the researcher did not inform the participants about the whole purpose of the project or withheld some information, the participants would need to be debriefed afterward. A common procedure in pharmaceutical testing is to provide a group of people with the drug while the other group (control) receives a placebo (i.e., tablets without active substances). Such clinical trials would be difficult to perform if the subjects were informed in advance about their group assignment. Instead, it is common to inform the subjects that they will be in the experimental group or in the placebo group and that they will not be informed about the group to which they belonged until the experiment ended.

2.12   CHEATING AND FRAUD IN RESEARCH

Research dishonesty can take many forms. One of the most serious forms of fraud is tampering with or direct fabrication of data. Several examples have been published in the media, both from psychology and from other disciplines where scientists have constructed all or parts of their data. The Dutch social psychologist Diederik Stapel has written an interesting autobiography about how he faked his own data and then desperately tried to hide this when students and colleagues became suspicious (Stapel 2014). The book resembles in many ways an accident report, which describes system failures, predisposing events, and finally some personality traits that may have contributed to the derailment. Another form of dishonesty is to withhold parts of a data set and selectively present the data that fit with the hypothesis. Other types of dishonest behavior include stealing other researchers' ideas or text without quoting or acknowledging the source, or presenting misleading representations of others' results.

It should be possible to verify a researcher's results, so the raw data should be stored for at least 10 years after the article has been published, and the data should be made available to others in the event of any doubt about the findings. Many countries have permanent committees that will investigate fraud and academic dishonesty whenever needed.

2.13   SUMMARY

During the Crimean War, far more British soldiers died in field hospitals than on the battlefield due to various infections and poor hygienic conditions. Florence

Nightingale discovered these problems and implemented several reforms to improve health conditions in the field hospitals. To convince the health authorities about the benefits of hygiene interventions, she used statistics, including pie charts, to demonstrate how the mortality rates of the hospitals changed under different conditions (Cohen 1984). She also demonstrated how social phenomena could be objectively measured and analyzed and that statistics were important tools to make a convincing argument for hospital reforms.

The main topic of this chapter has been related to how we can gain new knowledge and about important research requirements concerning methods, design, analyses, and conclusions. Research methods and statistics are important tools when a phenomenon is investigated and the results are presented to others. Without methodology and statistics, it would be very difficult to present a convincing argument for the statements one wished to make, and the example set by the Florence Nightingale is still valid today.

2.14 OUTSIDE ACTIVITIES

- Go online and find one research article in your area of interest. You could check some of the aviation journals mentioned earlier in this chapter or use ResearchGate to discover articles published by a researcher you would like to know more about. Try to identify the research questions that were examined. What type of design and methods were used to examine the research questions? Try to read the tables in the results section, and figure out what the findings are. Are there any limitations or problems associated with the study? All in all, what did you learn from reading the article and what are the practical implications?
- If you would like to know more about how statistical analyses are done, Search YouTube for tutorials and lectures (e.g., by Andy Field).

RECOMMENDED READINGS

Cooper, H., Hedges, L.V., and Valentine, J.C. 2009. *The Handbook of Research Synthesis and Meta-Analysis*, 2nd ed. New York, NY: Russel Sage Foundation.

Field, A. 2013. *Discovering Statistics Using IMB SPSS Statistics*, 4th ed. Thousand Oaks, CA: Sage Publications Ltd.

Hunt, M. 1997. *How Science Takes Stock. The Story of Meta-Analysis*. New York, NY: Russel Sage Foundation.

Lipsey, M.W. and Wilson, D.B. 2001. *Practical Meta-Analysis*. Applied Social Research Methods Series, Vol. 49. London, UK: Sage Publications.

Murphy, K.R. and Davidshofer, C.O. 2005. *Psychological Testing. Principles and Applications*, 6th ed. Upper Saddle River, NJ: Pearson Education.

Wiggins, M.W. and Stevens, C. 1999. *Aviation Social Science: Research Methods in Practice*. Aldershot, UK: Ashgate Publishing Ltd.

REFERENCES

American Educational Research Association (AERA). 2014. *Standards for Educational and Psychological Testing*. Washington, DC: Author.

Borenstein, M., Hedges, L.V., Higgins, J.P.T., and Rothstein, H.R. 2009. *Introduction to Meta-Analysis*. New York, NY: Wiley.

Borenstein, M., Rothstein, H., and Cohen, J. 2001. *Power and Precision: A Computer Program for Statistical Power Analysis and Confidence Intervals*. Englewood Cliffs, NJ: Biostat Inc.

Cohen, I.B. 1984. Florence Nightingale. *Scientific American* 250: 128–137.

Cook, C., Heath, F., and Thompson, R. 2000. A meta-analysis of response rates in web or Internet-based surveys. *Educational and Psychological Measurement* 60: 821–836.

Embretson, S.E. and Reise, S. 2000. *Item response theory for psychologists*. Mahwah, NJ: Lawrence Erlbaum Associates.

European Federation of Psychologists' Association (EFPA). 2013. *EFPA Review Model for the Description and Evaluation of Psychological and Educational Tests: Test Review Form and Notes for Reviewers, v 4.2.6*. Retrieved from: http://www.efpa.eu/professional-development

Fink, A. and Kosecoff, J. 1998. *How to Conduct Surveys. A Step by Step Guide*. Newbury Park, CA: Sage Publications, Inc.

Guion, R.M. 1981. On Trinitarian doctrines of validity. *Professional Psychology* 11: 385–398.

Hunter, J.E. and Schmidt, F.L. 2003. *Methods of Meta-Analysis: Correcting Error and Bias in Research Findings*. Newbury Park, CA: Sage.

Magnusson, D. 2003. *Testteori [Test Theory]*, 2nd ed. Stockholm, Sweden: Psykologiförlaget AB.

Martinussen, M. and Fjukstad, B. 1995. *Metados: A Computer Program for Meta-Analysis Calculations*. Tromsø, Norway: University of Tromsø.

Messick, S. 1995. Validity of psychological assessment. *American Psychologist* 50:741–749.

Parsons, H.M. 1992. Hawthorne, an early OBM experiment. *Journal of Organizational Behavior Management* 12: 27–43.

Shadish, W.R., Cook, T.D., and Campbell, D.T. 2002. *Experimental and Quasi-experimental Designs*. Boston, MA: Houghton Mifflin Company.

Solomon, D. J. 2001. Conducting web-based surveys. *Practical Assessment, Research & Evaluation* 7(19). Retrieved from: http://PAREonline.net/getvn.asp?v=7&n=1

Stapel, D. 2014. *Faking Science: A True Story of Academic Fraud* (Brown, N.J.L., Trans.). Retrieved from: https://errorstatistics.files.wordpress.com/2014/12/fakingscience-2014 1214.pdf

Van Horn, P., Green, K., and Martinussen, M. 2009. Survey response rates and survey administration in clinical and counseling psychology: A meta-analysis. *Educational and Psychological Measurement* 69: 389–403.

3 Aviation Physiology

3.1 INTRODUCTION

Physiology is defined as "a branch of biology that deals with the functions and activities of life or of living matter … and of the physical and chemical phenomena involved" (Merriam-Webster Ninth New Collegiate Dictionary 1985). Aviation physiology is the study of human systems' integrated functions and the processes by which they maintain the body functions—how the body and mind work in the flying environment. This chapter addresses the various physiological factors that can degrade the mental and physical performance of pilots, and countermeasures to those factors.

In a normal environment (i.e., at sea level and without any unusual forces acting upon it), the human body does a good job of acquiring and processing information. However, when placed in an environment for which it is not adapted (e.g., an airplane at altitude, with *g*-forces exerting loads in unusual directions), that functioning may be degraded. Functioning may also be affected by drugs such as caffeine or marijuana, nutritional state, and fatigue arising from lack of sleep, among other factors. The acquisition and processing of information may also be affected by visual illusions arising from the characteristics of the environment and by somatic illusions arising from the organs of balance. All of these are important considerations, but our discussion will begin with what is arguably the most important aspect of flying from a physiological standpoint—as you go up, the pressure and oxygen go down. If you do not think this is the most pressing problem, try holding your breath while you read the rest of this chapter.

3.2 ALTITUDE EFFECTS: LACK OF OXYGEN AND LACK OF PRESSURE

Physiologically, the most important concern of a pilot is hypoxia. At the surface of the Earth, the atmosphere contains about 78% nitrogen and 21% oxygen. These ratios remain fairly constant up to about 100 km due to turbulent mixing. However, the pressure decreases steadily with an increase in altitude. As the partial pressure of oxygen decreases, your body has increasing difficulty in absorbing sufficient oxygen to maintain body functions. This is reflected in the concept of *time of useful consciousness*. This describes the maximum time that a pilot has to make and carry out decisions at a given altitude without supplemental oxygen. As altitude increases above 10,000 feet, the symptoms of hypoxia increase in severity and the time of useful consciousness decreases (Table 3.1).

While we usually associate hypoxia with increased altitude, it can actually occur at any altitude. For example, even at or near sea level a pilot can experience hypoxia due to poor blood circulation, anemia, recent blood donation, or exposure to toxic substances, such as the cyanide released from a fire. Hypoxia can even occur on the

TABLE 3.1
Effect of Altitude on Time of Useful Consciousness

Altitude	Time of Useful Consciousness
45,000 feet MSL	9–15 s
40,000 feet MSL	15–20 s
35,000 feet MSL	30–60 s
30,000 feet MSL	1–2 min
28,000 feet MSL	2.5–3 min
20,000 feet MSL	3–5 min
22,000 feet MSL	5–10 min
20,000 feet MSL	30 min or more

Source: Federal Aviation Administration. (2008). *Pilot's Handbook of Aeronautical Knowledge.* FAA-H-8083-25A. Washington, DC: Author.

ground. In one incident reported to the Aviation Safety Reporting System (ASRS), an air carrier crew became hypoxic during preflight because 10,000 lb of dry ice was loaded on the aircraft, but ventilation was poor because the Auxiliary Power Unit (APU) was inoperative while air start carts were being used for ventilation. As the dry ice evaporated, the gaseous carbon dioxide displaced the air in the aircraft, resulting in a lack of available oxygen. Fortunately, the crew noticed the symptoms of hypoxia and subsequently evacuated the aircraft without lasting ill effects.

More common are incidents like the following, also taken from the ASRS:

> It is clear to me that I encountered an advanced case of hypoxia in my VFR descent. I had been cruising for about 4 hours with flight following at 12,500 feet, and the flight at that altitude had been progressing uneventfully…I think I may have heard wrong or selected a wrong frequency, but my attempts at contact [with ATC] went nowhere, and somehow I was unable to return to my previous controller. This seems incredible for a pilot with my level of experience, but, while flying the airplane was no problem, handling even the most simple mental tasks became almost impossible. (ASRS, ACN: 666262)

There are numerous such reports in the ASRS of pilots becoming partially disabled due to the effects of hypoxia. Often, these come from pilots who had been flying for some time at or just above 10,000 feet without supplemental oxygen. In addition, there are many reports from pilots who experienced hypoxia due to a malfunction or misuse of a supplemental oxygen system. Clearly, hypoxia is a serious matter and something each pilot must bear in mind, and be alert for the symptoms listed below:

- Cyanosis (blue fingernails and lips)
- Headache
- Decreased reaction time
- Impaired judgment
- Euphoria

- Visual impairment
- Drowsiness
- Lightheaded or dizzy sensation
- Numbness

We usually think of hypoxia as being caused by flight at high altitude. However, there are four types of hypoxia, and all of these individually and collectively may affect pilots and degrade their performance.

3.2.1   HYPOXIC HYPOXIA

This is the hypoxia typically associated with high altitude flight. Your body cannot absorb adequate oxygen because there is not enough pressure to force the oxygen molecules through membranes of the respiratory system.

There are four stages of hypoxic hypoxia: indifferent, compensatory, disturbance, and critical. Table 3.2 shows the variance of stages according to the altitude and severity of symptoms. Since the majority of pilots, at least in the early stages of their aviation careers, tend to operate at fairly low altitudes, the indifferent and compensatory stages of hypoxic hypoxia may be of greatest concern. Recall the example taken earlier of the ASRS report of a pilot who had been cruising for some time at 12,500 feet and subsequently found himself experiencing symptoms of hypoxia. Most pilots are aware of the need for supplemental oxygen at higher altitudes, but may decide that they can manage without it at altitudes around or just over 10,000 feet. While these operations may be legal, pilots should be aware of the wide variation in individual

---

TABLE 3.2
Stages of Hypoxic Hypoxia

Stages	Blood Oxygen Concentration (%)	Altitude (thousands of feet)	Symptoms
Indifferent	98–90	0–10	Decreased night vision
Compensatory	89–80	10–15	Drowsiness, poor judgment, impaired coordination, and efficiency
Disturbance	79–70	15–20	Impaired flight control, handwriting, speech, vision, intellectual function and judgment; decreased coordination, memory, and sensation to pain
Critical	69–60	20–25	Circulatory and central nervous system failure; convulsions, cardiovascular collapse; death

Source: U.S. Army. 2009. *Aeromedical Training for Flight Personnel.* Training Circular 3-04.93. Washington, DC: Author.

responses to flight at these altitudes. Smoking, poor circulatory health, and a number of other factors can reduce a pilot's capacity to absorb oxygen, such that a flight at seemingly benign altitudes may result in hypoxic hypoxia and the onset of the symptoms listed in Table 3.2.

3.2.2 HYPEMIC HYPOXIA

Hypemic hypoxia occurs when the oxygen-carrying capacity of the blood is reduced. Sufficient oxygen at adequate pressure is present in the inhaled air, but the oxygen molecules do not bind to the hemoglobin in the blood. Carbon monoxide poisoning is a common cause of this condition. Carbon monoxide binds to the blood hemoglobin about 200 times more easily than oxygen and prevents the oxygen molecules from attaching. Exhaust fumes from the engine or from a cabin heater are the most common source of carbon monoxide in the cabin. Carbon monoxide is colorless and odorless, and thus is difficult to detect. Fortunately, inexpensive carbon monoxide detectors are now readily available that will alert the pilot to the presence of this dangerous gas.

Hypemic hypoxia may also be caused by blood donation. In that case there are simply not enough red blood cells present in the blood stream to pick up the oxygen. The effects of blood donation may last several weeks.

3.2.3 STAGNANT HYPOXIA

Stagnant hypoxia occurs when there is an oxygen deficiency due to impaired circulation. Stagnant hypoxia can result from high g-loading during flight, and more commonly from diseases of the blood vessels, such as a constricted artery.

3.2.4 HISTOTOXIC HYPOXIA

In some cases, the cells comprising body tissues may become unable to use oxygen. In this case, the blood stream is delivering a sufficient supply of oxygen to the cells, but the oxygen is not being transferred from the hemoglobin of the red blood cells to the tissues. Impaired cellular respiration of this sort is typically caused by alcohol or other drugs, such as narcotics and poisons. The effects of alcohol, in particular, will be discussed in detail later in this chapter.

3.2.5 PERFORMANCE EFFECTS OF HYPOXIA

There have been numerous studies of pilots under conditions of mild hypoxia—such as might be found when flying from 5000 to 10,000 feet. Generally, researchers have found little effect on performance under typical conditions. However, under more demanding conditions, or when pilots were fatigued, performance decrements were observed. A study by Mertens and Collins (1985) illustrates these results. They found that when the pilots in their study were rested, altitude (12,500 feet) had no effect. However, when the pilots were sleep-deprived (loss of one night of sleep), performance was significantly lower. Increasing the pilots' workload further exacerbated the effects of sleep deprivation.

This interaction of task demand and hypoxia was also found by Nesthus et al. (1997). In their study, pilots who had flown for 2 hours at altitudes of 10,000 and 12,500 feet exhibited unsafe and high-risk piloting behaviors during the final phases of flight. By comparison, pilots in the control group (rested) generally exhibited deliberate and cautious behaviors during the last critical phases of flight. This study is particularly relevant, since it approximates actual flight by general aviation pilots who may make complicated instrument approaches after an extensive period of mild hypoxia. Similarly, a study by Legg et al. (2014) found that mild hypoxia might impair working memory and complex logical reasoning involving difficult conflicts.

In addition to the effects of hypoxia, flight at higher altitudes can also present problems simply due to the low atmospheric pressure. Usually, these problems are associated with gases trapped inside the body at sea level (relatively high pressure). When exposed to low-pressure environments, the high-pressure gas expands, leading to some potentially painful and distracting conditions.

3.2.6 BLOCKED EUSTACHIAN TUBE

The expansion of gas trapped in the middle ear can produce ear and sinus pain, in addition to a temporary reduction in the ability to hear. The typical cause of this condition is a blocked Eustachian tube. This is the tube (shown in Figure 3.1) that allows for equalization of pressure between the middle ear and the outside world. Usually closed, this tube opens during chewing, yawning, or swallowing. Should the pilot experience the symptoms of an ear block, those are the first actions the pilot should take to alleviate the situation. Should those fail to equalize the pressure, then the pilot should close their mouth, pinch the nostrils closed, and make a moderately forceful attempted exhalation, as if blowing up a balloon. (This is commonly called the Valsalva procedure.)

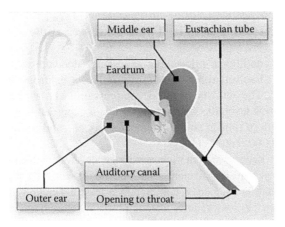

FIGURE 3.1 Anatomy of the ear. (Reproduced from Federal Aviation Administration. 2008. *Pilot's Handbook of Aeronautical Knowledge.* FAA-H-8083-25A. Washington, DC: Author.)

3.2.7 SINUS BLOCK

If the sinuses are congested, then air trapped there can also produce a painful condition. This sinus block occurs most frequently during descent. Slowing or stopping the descent until the pressure inside the sinus equalizes with the external pressure is the best course of action once this condition occurs. Of course, not flying when the pilot has a congested sinus is even better.

3.2.8 GASTRIC DISTRESS

Gases in the gastrointestinal tract produced by food, drinks, or illness can be very uncomfortable at sea level, and even more so at altitude. Pilots in larger aircraft with a copilot may find some relief from a visit to the onboard toilet. However, for single-pilot situations, judicious venting, a slowing of the ascent rate, or even a descent may be required to relieve the pain.

3.2.9 DENTAL PAIN

Reduction in atmospheric pressure may also result in barodontalgia—tooth pain. This may be caused by a number of dental conditions including (a) dental disease, (b) dental caries (a cavity), (c) defective tooth restoration, (d) pulpitis, (e) cysts, and (f) impacted teeth. This condition may be avoided by avoiding flying for 48–72 hours following a major dental work. As with the other problems associated with lower atmospheric pressure, descending to a lower altitude (and correspondingly higher atmospheric pressure) is often the best antidote.

3.2.10 DECOMPRESSION SICKNESS

Nitrogen (78% of atmosphere) is forced into solution in the blood when we breathe. Because the nitrogen is less diffusible than oxygen, the body is not able to equilibrate it at the same rate with outside air. This occurs at sea level. It also occurs more markedly when breathing under higher pressures, such as those experienced when scuba diving.

Under those conditions, pilots may experience decompression sickness. This occurs when the dissolved nitrogen gas is released resulting from a decrease in atmospheric pressure. The severity of the decompression sickness may be affected by the pilot's hydration level, the number and extent of exposures (number of dives and depths), the length of time at altitude, the rate of ascent, and the altitude (especially altitudes over 18,000 feet).

Symptoms of decompression sickness range in severity from bends to severe central nervous system impairment. The Federal Aviation Administration (FAA; Airman's Information Manual) recommends at least a 4-hour waiting period after scuba diving, which has not required decompression before flying to a cabin altitude of 8000 feet or less, and 24-hour wait after dives requiring decompression. They further recommend 24-hour wait for all flights above 8000 feet. If a pilot (or passenger) begins to experience symptoms of decompression sickness, administration of 100% oxygen and descent (if possible) are recommended.

3.3 FATIGUE

3.3.1 WHAT IS FATIGUE?

Like happiness, fatigue can be a hard thing to define. The dictionary (Merriam-Webster Ninth New Collegiate Dictionary 1985) defines fatigue as "weariness or exhaustion from labor, exertion, or stress." The FAA defines fatigue as "… a condition characterized by increased discomfort with lessened capacity for work, reduced efficiency of accomplishment, loss of power or capacity to respond to stimulation, and is usually accompanied by a feeling of weariness and tiredness" (Salazar 2007, p. 2).

Many people associate fatigue with sleepiness, but fatigue is not just being sleepy. This distinction is made by Shen et al. (2006) who noted that "Sleepiness and fatigue are two interrelated, but distinct phenomena" (p. 63). Arguably, pilots seldom become fatigued in the same way as a person who has just completed a 10-km race. However, other aviation workers, such as aviation maintenance technicians, might well experience fatigue with no sleepiness component after completing some physically-demanding tasks. Nevertheless, fatigue and sleepiness are often used interchangeably, and the research literature, at least that dealing with aviation, has largely ignored aspects of fatigue other than sleepiness. Therefore, while the distinction between fatigue and sleepiness is recognized, the discussion in this section is limited to sleepiness.

3.3.2 WHY IS FATIGUE IMPORTANT?

In 1990, the National Transportation Safety Board (NTSB) added "Reduce Accidents and Incidents Caused by Human Fatigue" to its list of most wanted safety recommendations. This arose out of a series of accidents in which fatigue (usually, lack of sufficient, timely sleep) was indicated as a factor in the crash. This was typified by the crash of a cargo DC-8 on approach to Guantanamo Bay, Cuba on August 18, 1993. The NTSB found that the probable cause of the accident was, "The impaired judgement, decision-making, and flying abilities of the captain and flight crew due to the effects of fatigue" (NTSB 1994, p. 78). In this case, the flightcrew had experienced a disruption of circadian rhythms and sleep loss, after being on duty for 18 hours and having flown 9 hours at the time of the accident.

Following that recommendation, many air carriers implemented policies to improve the rest of their crew. However, pilot fatigue continues to appear as a factor in accidents as illustrated by the fatal Colgan Air crash in Buffalo, New York on February 12, 2009. In that case, the NTSB concluded that "… the pilots' performance was likely impaired because of fatigue" (National Research Council 2011, p. 12). This crash also highlighted the importance of considering not just the time a pilot is on duty, but also what they are doing in the hours leading up to a flight. In the case of the Colgan crash, pilots' commuting practices may have contributed significantly to fatigue. For a detailed examination of the pilot commuting issue, see the report by the National Research Council.

In a review of commercial pilot work practices, Goode (2003) found that 20% of human factors accidents involved pilots who had been on duty for 10 or more hours.

However, only 10% of pilot duty hours occurred during that time. Similarly, 5% of human factors accidents involved pilots who had been on duty for 13 or more hours, although only 1% of pilot duty hours occur during that time. These results clearly demonstrate a pattern of increased probability of an accident as the duty time for pilots increases, and are consistent with the extensive literature on the effects of fatigue (operationalized as lack of sleep) and human performance.

There is a massive research literature on the effects of fatigue/sleepiness on human performance, including many studies involving aircrew. Reviews of this literature have been produced by Battelle Memorial Institute (1998), Lim and Dinges (2008), Caldwell et al. (2012), and Avers and Johnson (2011). The review by Caldwell et al. is particularly interesting in that it addresses differences between chronic and acute sleep deprivation. Chronic sleep deprivation refers to the accumulative effects of restricting sleep to less than 8 hours daily over an extended period. Acute sleep deprivation is typically characterized by a single period of enforced wakefulness (perhaps 24–36 hours). Both types of deprivation will result in performance decrements in cognitive performance. In the case of acute sleep deprivation, decrements become noticeable fairly rapidly, while in the case of chronic sleep deprivation, they accumulate more slowly. Recovery from each of these situations reflects, to some degree, the duration of sleep deprivation. For individuals suffering from acute sleep deprivation, recovery is fairly rapid, while recovery from chronic sleep debt occurs at a much slower rate. Some researchers (Belenky et al. 2003) have reported that recovery did not occur on numerous cognitive measures even after three nights of 8 hours of sleep. These results are illustrated in Figure 3.2, which shows the mean

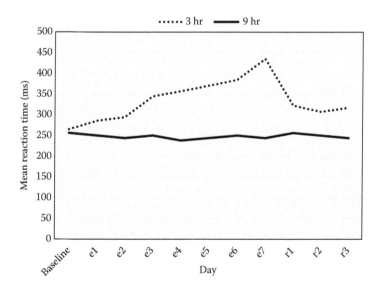

FIGURE 3.2 Mean reaction time for psychomotor vigilance task. (Belenky, G. et al. Patterns of performance degradation and restoration during sleep restriction and subsequent recovery: A sleep dose-response study. *Journal of Sleep Research*. 2003. 12: 1–12. Copyright Wiley-VCH Verlag GmbH & Co. KGaA. Reproduced with permission.)

reaction time on a vigilance task for subjects who were restricted to 3 hours of sleep over a 7-day period, and then allowed to recover (sleep 8 hours per night) for 3 days. As the graph shows, even after 3 days of recovery, those subjects who had suffered chronic sleep loss still performed poorer than the subjects who had 9 hours of sleep.

Fatigue caused by chronic or acute loss of sleep can produce a variety of physical, mental, and emotional symptoms. Slowed reaction time (as shown in Figure 3.2) is one physical symptom, as well as lack of energy, repeated yawning, heavy eyelids, headaches, and microsleeps. Mental symptoms include difficulty concentrating on tasks, lapses in attention, failure to anticipate events, forgetfulness, and poor decision-making. The emotional symptoms associated with fatigue are irritability, withdrawal, lack of motivation, and heightened emotional sensitivity (Avers and Johnson 2011).

In addition to the traditional, narrative reviews of the fatigue literature, several researchers (cf. Pilcher and Huffcutt 1996; Griffith and Mahadevan 2006) have used meta-analysis to mathematically summarize the results from large numbers of individual studies. These studies have found strong relationships between sleep deprivation and performance degradation. For example, Pilcher and Huffcutt cumulated the results from 19 individual research studies and found that overall there was a substantial (−1.37 standard deviations) effect of sleep deprivation on performance. They also demonstrated that the largest negative effects were on subjects' mood, and that partial sleep deprivation (defined as fewer than 5 hours of sleep in a 24-hour period for 1 or more days) produced more decrements in performance than either short-term or long-term sleep deprivation. These results are illustrated in Figure 3.3.

An interesting study by Lamond and Dawson (1999) demonstrated the relationship between sleep loss and blood alcohol content. The issues associated with

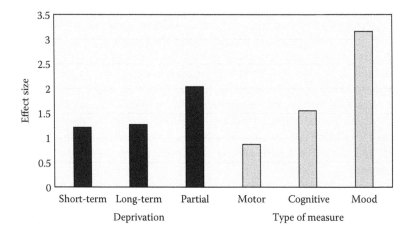

FIGURE 3.3 Meta-analysis of sleep deprivation studies. (Based on Pilcher, J.J. and Huffcutt, A.I. 1996. *Sleep* 19: 318–26, Table 2.)

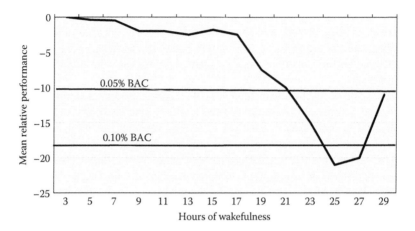

FIGURE 3.4   Response latency and fatigue. (Lamond, N. and Dawson, D. Quantifying the performance impairment associated with fatigue. *Journal of Sleep Research.* 1999. 8: 255–262. Copyright Wiley-VCH Verlag GmbH & Co. KGaA. Reproduced with permission.)

alcohol usage and performance will be considered later, but for now consider the degree to which loss of sleep produces the same level as performance decrement as a blood alcohol level that would render drivers and pilots ineligible to operate. In the United States, the legal limit for commercial drivers in all 50 states is 0.04% BAC (blood alcohol concentration). That is also the level established as the limit for pilots (FAR 91.17). As shown in Figure 3.4, the level of performance decrement associated with that level of intoxication is reached after only about 20 hours of wakefulness. This rather clearly demonstrates that moderate levels of fatigue can produce levels of performance decrement equivalent to or greater than those associated with unacceptable levels of intoxication. So, if you would not fly if you were drunk, why would you fly if you were tired?

The effects of sleep deprivation on the performance of pilots have been demonstrated in several studies. Figure 3.5 shows the effects of sleep deprivation on the cognitive performance of a group of U.S. Air Force pilots in a simulated flight (Lopez et al. 2012). Clearly, their vigilance suffered as they became more sleep deprived—particularly in the period around 2:00 to 4:00 a.m. Later, in the discussion of circadian rhythms, the importance of this particular period will be explored in more detail. For now, just consider the fourfold increase in lapses that occurred between 4:00 p.m. on the first day and 4:00 p.m. on the second day. In an operational context, an increase in missed signals of this magnitude might well have serious consequences.

Significant effects of sleep loss on performance in an aviation environment have also been demonstrated by von Dongen et al. (2006) and Previc et al. (2009). In the latter study, flight performance deficits began in the early morning hours and peaked at 9:30 a.m. before waning by noon on the second day. Interestingly, instrument scanning was remarkably unaffected by the pilots' sleep deprivation, suggesting that the pilots were redirecting resources toward the most important tasks. Overall, the

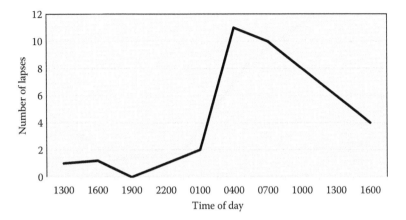

FIGURE 3.5 Lapses on psychomotor vigilance test. (Reprinted from *Journal of Applied Research in Memory and Cognition*, 1, Lopez, M. et al. Effects of sleep deprivation on cognitive performance of United States Air Force pilots, 27–33, Copyright 2012, with permission from Elsevier.)

magnitude of the flight performance deterioration was not large, even at its peak (only about 15%). This was less than that in some previous studies, which have shown deficits of as much as 45% (Caldwell et al. 2003).

Caldwell et al. evaluated the effects of 37 hours of continuous wakefulness on U.S. Air Force F-117 pilots. They found substantial decrements in flight skills, reaction times, mood, and brain activation after only 26 hours of wakefulness. However, the greatest decrements in flight performance occurred after 27–33 hours of wakefulness. Figure 3.6 shows the effects of wakefulness on a combined flight maneuver performance measure. Since the subjects arose at 6:00 a.m. on the first day of the study, performance is clearly declining after 17 hours of wakefulness (corresponding to 11:00 p.m. on Figure 3.6), while the nadir of performance corresponds to 32 hours of wakefulness.

3.3.3 Circadian Rhythms

No, "circadian rhythms" is not the name of a new Latin dance band. But, if you stay up dancing the night away, you may experience some of its effects. The problem with fatigue associated with sleeplessness is not just the number of hours of wakefulness, but also when those hours occur. Humans are subject to circadian rhythms that influence their levels of alertness and performance. Consider the relationship between time of day and driving accidents shown in Figure 3.7 (Horne and Reyner 1995). Clearly, there is a large spike in accident likelihood around 1:00 a.m., tapering off to an average level of likelihood around 8:00 a.m. For most people who are accustomed to sleeping at night and working during the day, these peaks and valleys are characteristic of their circadian rhythms. Sleep is regulated by two body systems. These systems are sleep/wake homeostasis and the circadian biological clock. The sleep/wake system tells the body that a need for sleep is accumulating, and that it is

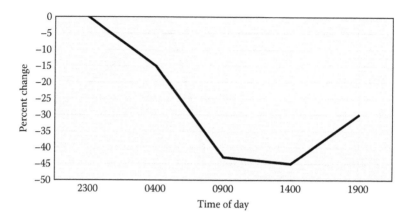

FIGURE 3.6 Effect of sleep loss on flight maneuver performance. (Adapted from Caldwell, J.A. et al. 2003. *The Effects of 37 Hours of Continuous Wakefulness on the Physiological Arousal, Cognitive Performance, Self-Reported Mood, and Simulator Flight Performance of F-117A Pilots.* AFRL-HE-BR-TR-2003-0086. Brooks City-Base, TX: U.S. Air Force Research Laboratory.)

time to sleep. The internal circadian biological clock regulates the timing of periods of sleepiness and wakefulness throughout the day. Generally, the strongest drive for sleep occurs between 2:00 and 4:00 a.m., and again in the afternoon around 1:00 to 3:00 p.m.

Circadian rhythms are produced by natural factors within the body, but they are also affected by signals from the environment. Light is the main cue influencing circadian rhythms, turning on or turning off genes that control an organism's internal

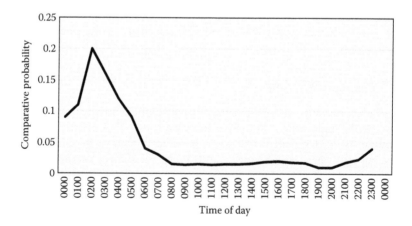

FIGURE 3.7 Driving accidents and time of day. (Horne, J.A. and Reyner, L.A. Driver sleepiness. *Journal of Sleep Research.* 1995. 4: 23–29. Copyright Wiley-VCH Verlag GmbH & Co. KGaA. Reproduced with permission.)

clocks. The well-known "jet lag" phenomenon (also known as circadian rhythm disruption) occurs when the internal circadian rhythm gets out of synch with the external world. Transmeridian flights disrupt the synchronization of internal circadian time and external clock time. The challenge of multiple time-zone flights is the time required for the body to adjust to the new time zone. The body will eventually adjust to the new time zone, but the period of adjustment depends on the direction of travel, and the number of time zones transited. Generally, adjustment appears to be faster after westward flights than for eastward flights (Klein and Wegmann 1980). For the westward flights, the body resynchronizes at a rate of about 1.5 hours per day. For eastward flights, the adjustment rate is about 1 hour per day (Aschoff et al. 1975). For tips on how to deal with circadian rhythm disruption, see the informative pamphlet produced by FAA (2009).

Fatigue, and the effects of circadian rhythm disruption, may be a significant concern for pilots operating outside their normal wake–sleep cycle times, and especially for pilots during extended transmeridian flights. Petrie and Dawson (1997) surveyed international pilots regarding their symptoms experienced during flights and their coping mechanisms. They found that the symptoms could be grouped into five factors: sleepiness, cognitive dysfunction, emotional disturbance, boredom, and physical effects. Similarly, the coping strategies used by pilots could be grouped into five factors: planning energy use, active coping, mental withdrawal, communicating with other crew, and coffee drinking.

Fatigue becomes a particularly important concern on ultra-long-range flights—those greater than 16 hours. Holmes et al. (2012) examined sleep and sleepiness of 44 pilots who completed multiple ultra-long-range flights between Doha, Qatar and Houston, Texas. On the basis of the activity records of the crew and sleep diaries, they were able to produce a timeline that provided guidance on when to ideally nap. They also advised crew to sleep as long as possible, when to avoid or use caffeine, and when to avoid or seek light and exercise. A manual on alertness management was also produced by Flower (2001) for use by British Airways crews. Generally, the guides produced by these authors follow the coping strategies listed in Table 3.3. In addition to those coping strategies, strategic napping on extended flights has also been recommended. A 45-minute nap was shown to improve alertness and sustained attention during the approach and landing phases; however, napping (bunk sleep) is available only for augmented crews, so that a crewmember may nap only while not on duty. While the FAA prohibits in-seat napping, some non-U.S. carriers utilize the practice.

Regardless of current prohibitions, in a NASA survey of regional airline operations, 56% of flightcrew respondents reported having been on a flight in which the flightcrew came to an agreement to allow one of the pilots to nap in-seat (Co et al. 1999). For corporate/executive flightcrew, the number was 39% (Rosekind et al. 2000). (There are also anecdotal reports of both pilots falling asleep, so perhaps the next generation of aircraft will include an alarm clock.)

Long-haul pilots are not alone in suffering the effects of sleep loss. While short-haul pilots are not subjected to circadian rhythm disruption associated with transmeridian flights, they may have duty periods that approach those of the long-haul

TABLE 3.3
Coping Strategies Used to Manage Fatigue

Description

Take things one step at a time
Keep up a conversation with other crew
Have a cold drink
Get up and walk around
Try and be as organized as possible
Keep busy and active
Keep my mind busy and active
Make an extra effort to fight fatigue
Eat more
Tell other crew how I feel

Source: Petrie, K.J. and Dawson, A.G. 1997. *The International Journal of Aviation Psychology* 7: 251–258.

pilots, with arguably a greater workload due to the more frequent departures and landings. In addition, the time at which pilots start their duty day may have an effect. Roach et al. (2012) studied duty periods to examine the impact of early start times on the amount of sleep obtained prior to duty and on fatigue levels at the start of duty. They had 70 short-haul pilots use self-report duty/sleep diaries and wrist activity monitors to collect data on their duty schedule and sleep/wake behavior. Consistent with the information given on sleep and circadian patterns, the greatest fatigue was reported for early start times (4:00 a.m.) and the least fatigue was reported for later times (9:00 a.m.).

3.3.4 THERMAL STRESS

Before leaving the topic of fatigue, some consideration should also be given to factors other than sleep loss that may contribute to fatigue, or at least to a loss in performance. Both hot and cold ambient temperatures impact performance on a wide range of cognitive tasks. Pilcher et al. (2002) conducted a meta-analysis of 22 studies of the effects of temperature variation on performance and found that both hot temperatures (90°F/32°C) and cold temperatures (50°F/10°C) produced a decrement of about 14%–15% relative to a temperature of 15–75°F (–9.4–23.9°C). Further, task performance was degraded the longer a person was exposed to the temperature prior to task performance.

Substantial effects of temperature on monitoring performance were noted by Mackworth (1950) and Pepler (1958) (cited in Hancock 1984). Mackworth reported that missed signals fell from about 28% at 65°F (18°C) to 18% at 82°F (28°C), and then rose again to 28% for a temperature of 92°F (33°C). Similar effects were found by Pepler.

3.4 NUTRITION

Just as the brain needs oxygen to function, it also needs fuel to combine with the oxygen and produce energy. That fuel is blood glucose, which is carried by the bloodstream and easily passes the blood–brain barrier. Glucose is a simple sugar and serves as an immediate source of energy for cells. The brain cannot store glucose and requires a continuous supply to function properly. All foods containing carbohydrates will raise blood glucose levels. Failure to eat properly may result in a shortage of glucose (hypoglycemia), which will produce decrements in cognitive functioning. Figure 3.8 shows one of the results from a study by Evans et al. (2000), in which they induced hypoglycemia in subjects and recorded their performance on a variety of tasks. Compared with the control subjects who were maintained at normal blood glucose levels (euglycemia, labeled EU in the figures), the performance of the hypoglycemic subjects (HYPO in the figures) declined substantially on both reaction time and the number of words correctly identified in the Stroop Color–Word Test (shown in Figure 3.9). Interestingly, Evans et al. found that hypoglycemia may not be noticeable by the affected individual for up to 20 minutes.

This lack of awareness of impairment was also found by Cox and associates in two studies of performance in a driving simulator (Cox et al. 1993; Cox et al. 2000). They found that even moderate hypoglycemia could produce a variety of errors in driving, including more swerving, driving over the midline or off the road, failing to stop at stop signs, and crashes. The effect of poor nutrition was also demonstrated in a study by Chaplin and Smith (2011) who surveyed over 800 nurses on their breakfast consumption. They found that the frequency of breakfast consumption (mainly cereal—a good source of carbohydrates that can be easily converted to glucose) was associated with lower stress, fewer cognitive failures, and fewer injuries and accidents at work. They also reported that unhealthy snacking (chocolate, chips, cookies, etc.) more than three times a week was associated with more accidents and minor

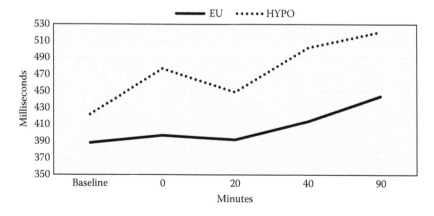

FIGURE 3.8 Effects of diet on choice reaction time. (Based on Evans, M.L. et al. 2000. *Diabetes Care* 23: 893–898.)

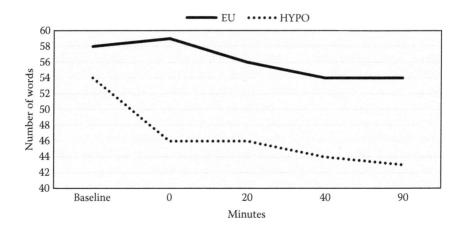

FIGURE 3.9 Effects of diet on cognitive processing. (Based on Evans, M.L. et al. 2000. *Diabetes Care* 23: 893–898.)

injuries. So, it seems your mother was right all this time: eat a healthy breakfast and do not snack between meals.

In a study that looked specifically of the effects of diet on pilot performance, Lindseth et al. (2011) examined the effects of three different diets on flight performance in a GAT-2 full-motion flight simulator. The diets were (a) a high-carbohydrate diet, (b) a high-protein diet, and (c) a high-fat diet. Each pilot was exposed to each of the three experimental diets (plus a control diet) for a 4-day period. They found that the pilots who consumed high-fat and high-carbohydrate diets had better cognitive flight performance scores than the pilots who consumed the high-protein diets. Although the authors did not address the underlying biochemical reasons for the findings, it might be argued that consumption of the fats and carbohydrates resulted in better performance because they are more readily converted to glucose than proteins. Regardless, pilots trying to lose weight may wish to avoid one of the currently popular high-protein diets, in favor of a more balanced approach to nutrition.

The decrements in performance associated with low blood glucose illustrated in Figures 3.8 and 3.9 are typical of the effects noted in a variety of studies of a large range of cognitive functions vital for pilots, air traffic controllers, and maintenance technicians. A summary of some of those studies is found in Table 3.4. For much more detail on the effects of blood glucose on human performance, the extensive summary of the literature compiled by NASA researchers (Feldman and Barshi 2007) is an excellent resource. On the basis of their review of hundreds of studies, they concluded, "Research clearly supports the notion that hypoglycemia significantly compromises performance, resulting in longer response times and lower scores on cognitive tests" (Feldman and Barshi 2007, p. 68).

Finally, besides watching what and when they eat, pilots should also be aware of the effects of dehydration. One study that examined the effect of fluid intake and possible dehydration on cognitive flight performance of pilots found that flight

TABLE 3.4
Summary of Effects of Low Glucose Levels on Human Performance

Function Impaired

Spatial memory
Decision-making and reaction time
Fine motor skill and divided attention
Verbal fluency
Visual processing
Auditory processing
Sustained attention

Source: Feldman, J. and Barshi, I. 2007. *The Effects of Blood Glucose Levels on Cognitive Performance: A Review of the Literature.* Technical report NASA/TM-2007-214555. Ames Research Center, Moffett Field, CA: National Aeronautics and Space Administration.

performance and spatial cognition test scores were significantly poorer for pilots who had low fluid intakes and experienced dehydration compared to hydrated pilots (Lindseth et al. 2013).

3.5 CHEMICAL AGENTS

The NTSB's Most Wanted List for 2015 includes, "End substance impairment in transportation." The list of chemical agents that can impair performance of pilots, air traffic controllers, and just about anyone else is extensive. However, this section addresses only three agents with generally negative effects (alcohol, marijuana, and nicotine) and one agent with generally positive effects (caffeine). A later section will discuss some over-the-counter and prescription drugs with similar negative and positive effects.

3.5.1 ALCOHOL

Since humans discovered how to make beer about 7000 years ago, alcoholic beverages have become almost universally available and popular. In North America (the United States, Canada, and Cuba), about 65% of the adult population consume alcoholic beverages (Rehm et al. 2003), and the average annual consumption is about 14 L. European consumption is similar. The deleterious effects of alcohol on human performance seem unquestionable, at least at more than the most modest levels. Hence, almost every nation has established limits for the consumption of alcohol and the operation of moving vehicles (e.g., cars, boats, airplanes). In all jurisdictions of the United States, the legal limit for driving under the influence of alcohol (DUI) is 0.08% BAC for noncommercial drivers. Most western countries have lower limits (e.g., Sweden and Norway have a limit of 0.02% BAC) for noncommercial drivers, while only one (the Cayman Islands) has a higher limit. In the United States, the limit for commercial drivers is 0.04% BAC (Drink Driving Limits n.d.). Pilots are also held to that standard and are prohibited from acting or attempting to act as a crewmember of a civil aircraft: (1) within 8 hours of consuming any alcoholic beverage and (2) while having an alcohol concentration of 0.04% BAC or greater (14 CFR 91.17).

Notwithstanding the prohibitions, postmortem examinations of fatally injured civil pilots conducted at 5-year internals by the Civil Aerospace Medical Institute (CAMI) of the FAA (Chaturvedi et al. 2015) have shown that alcohol has been present in about 7% of the cases. Further, this rate of detection is fairly consistent over the period from 1989 to 2013. Studies of alcohol among military pilots have also shown cases in which alcohol may have been involved (Zeller 1975); however, the methodologies used are quite different from those used by the civil studies, making comparisons difficult.

There have been hundreds of studies of the effects of varying levels of BAC on performance, with dozens of reviews and summaries. For examples, see Levine et al. (1973); Holloway (1994); Newman (2004); and Levine et al. (1975). Arguably, the best of these reviews (or at least the most current) is that conducted by Newman (2004) for the Australian Transportation Safety Board (ATSB). A summary of the findings from Newman's review is given in Table 3.5.

Clearly, the list of dreadful effects of alcohol on performance shown in Table 3.5 should deter any sane, reasonable person from drinking and flying (or driving, or trying to do most anything that requires much cognitive effort). As the study on postmortem alcohol mentioned above indicates, some people still drink and fly, just as some people drink and drive. In a later chapter, the concept of self-serving bias will be discussed, which may explain to some extent why people (and pilots) think

---

TABLE 3.5
Summary of Findings of Effects of Alcohol

Alcohol has widespread general effects on human behavior and performance

It has detrimental effects on cognitive functions and psychomotor abilities

Risk-taking behavior may result

A full appreciation of the consequences of a planned action may not be possible

Almost all forms of cognitive function have been shown to be affected adversely

Alcohol has a particularly serious effect on information processing and memory, particularly short-term memory

Alcohol interferes with the integration of incoming information

Alcohol significantly impairs attention

Psychomotor performance is adversely affected by alcohol, in a dose-dependent way

Alcohol has its greatest performance-impairing effect on demanding and complex cognitive tasks

Alcohol has been shown to have adverse effects on both the visual and vestibular systems, and is a contributory factor to the development of spatial disorientation

Source: Newman, D.G. 2004. *Alcohol and Human Performance from an Aviation Perspective: A Review.* Unnumbered research report. Canberra, Australia: Australian Transport Safety Bureau.

that they will not be harmed, even when they are doing something that, by most objective standards, is clearly hazardous. At present, let us examine some studies that illustrate the effects of alcohol on performance by pilots, beginning with a study by Billings et al. (1973), in which 16 instrument-rated pilots flew ILS (instrument landing system) approaches at night in a light plane with BAC levels ranging from 0% (control) to 0.12% BAC.

Billings et al. (1973) found that procedural errors (e.g., selecting the wrong approach frequency, failing to select carburetor heat) increased significantly in frequency and potential seriousness with each increase in BAC, as shown in Figure 3.10. At the highest level (0.12% BAC), the pilots lost control of the aircraft 16 times on 30 flights. Even at the lowest BAC (0.04%), a pilot lost control during one flight. The composite performance scores (based on the pilots' tracking accuracy) also showed substantial decrements from baseline (Figure 3.11). Interestingly, the alcohol degraded performance of inexperienced and experienced pilots equally (as indicated by the parallel lines in both charts).

A study (Davenport and Harris 1992) of simulated landings (both visual and ILS) in a twin-engine aircraft demonstrated the greater effect alcohol may have in a more demanding situation. As shown in Figure 3.12, alcohol contributed to a disproportionately larger decline in performance in a high cognitive workload situation (the asymmetric thrust situation). This demonstrates a general finding with respect to the effect of alcohol (and other factors, such as cannabis) on performance—the more demanding the situation, the greater is the degrading effect. This study also shows that even at BAC levels considerably below the legal threshold of 0.04% BAC, alcohol can have a significant impact. Saliva samples taken from the pilots in this study showed that the mean BAC for the pilots in the experimental trials was 0.01% BAC. The effects of BAC levels less than 0.04% were also examined by Ross et al. (1992) who had pilots fly flight scenarios of varying difficulty in a Frasca 141 simulator. They found that alcohol impacted performance in the most demanding of the two scenarios and concluded that "Results of present study do not support the idea that

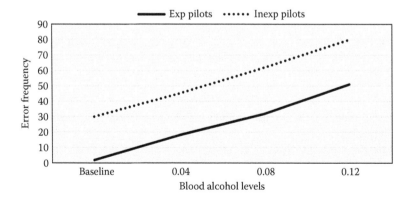

FIGURE 3.10 Effect of alcohol on major pilot errors. (Adapted with permission from Billings, C.E. et al. 1973. *Aviation, Space, and Environmental Medicine* 44: 379–382.)

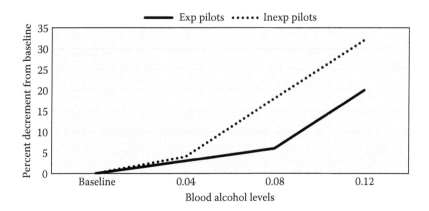

FIGURE 3.11 Effect of alcohol on composite pilot performance. (Adapted with permission from Billings, C.E. et al. 1973. *Aviation, Space, and Environmental Medicine* 44: 379–382.)

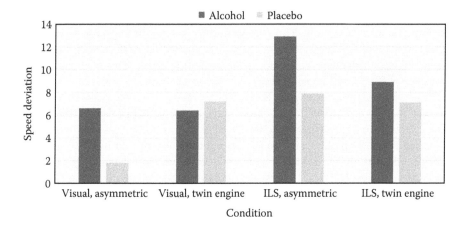

FIGURE 3.12 Effects of alcohol on complex task performance. (Adapted from Davenport, M. and Harris, D. 1992. *The International Journal of Aviation Psychology* 2: 271–280, Table 2.)

BAC levels under 0.04% are safe in flight … Even a quite low BAC can result in pilot errors" (p. 956).

While the study by Ross et al. (1992) suggests that the BAC limit of 0.04% may be too lenient, the results from a study by Petros et al. (2003) call into question the policy of flying after only waiting 8 hours following the consumption of an alcoholic beverage (as prescribed by 14 CFR 91.17). Petros et al. had 36 IFR-rated pilots fly two, 75-minute scenarios in a Frasca 241 simulator 11 hours after ingestion of alcohol. In this study, either a placebo, 2 mL/kg, or 3 mL/kg of 100

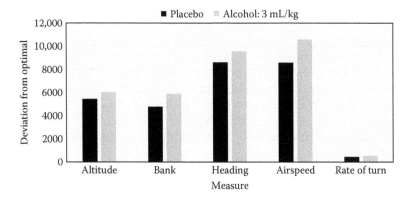

FIGURE 3.13 Hangover effects on pilot performance measured 11 hours after ingestion. (Adapted from Petros, T. et al. 2003. *The International Journal of Aviation Psychology* 13: 287–300, Table 3.)

proof vodka were administered the evening before a flight.* At the time of the test flights, all participants had a BAC of 0%. Performance deficits were observed on measures of rate of turn and bank for the group who ingested the largest dose of alcohol. This group also carried out fewer directives from air traffic control than the placebo or 2 mL/kg groups. The performance of the placebo and 3 mL/kg group at 11 hours after ingestion of the alcohol is shown in Figure 3.13. From that figure, it is clear that, at least for the group with the higher dose of alcohol, there is a lingering performance decrement even though alcohol is no longer detectible in the blood stream. This begs the question then of how much alcohol is too much and how soon is too soon to fly? Further, how may alcohol abuse be avoided? One study took the question to actual aircrew. Harris and Maxwell (2001) surveyed 472 private and professional pilots concerning effectiveness of various countermeasures to reduce likelihood of drinking and flying. They found that "Punitive sanctions and tougher enforcement of the regulations were regarded as the most effective countermeasures, although offenders and professional pilots thought these actions less effective than private pilots and nonoffenders" (p. 237). Of course, one might argue that sanctions are already in place, and when offenders are discovered, the laws are enforced. Perhaps, a more nuanced approach based upon an understanding of the psychology of alcohol abusers would be more productive.

---

* To give you an idea of what that dose means, 200 lb equals about 91 kg, so a dose of 3 mL/kg would amount to 273 mL, or roughly 3 cups (24 oz) of vodka. Since a typical drink (e.g., a bloody mary) contains 4 oz of vodka, the participants would have consumed the equivalent of roughly 6 cocktails— typical of a fairly heavy, but not improbable, evening of drinking. A 12 oz beer contains the equivalent of 1.4 oz of 100 proof vodka, so you would need to drink about 17 bottles of beer (6%) to get an equivalent dose.

3.5.2 CANNABIS

Cannabis (marijuana) is by most measures the most popular illicit drug. A recent study of drug trends in aviation was conducted by the NTSB. The NTSB (2014) noted a generally increasing trend in the use of illicit drugs that have no medical use, and the illicit use of prescription drugs. They cited a study by the Substance Abuse and Mental Health Services Administration, U.S. Department of Health and Human Services (SAMHSA 2013) that showed an overall use rate for illicit drugs of 9.2% for the U.S. population ages 12–64. Marijuana was the most commonly used illicit drug.

To examine drug use trends among pilots, the NTSB matched their accident database against the toxicology database from the CAMI for all domestic civil accidents from 1990 to 2012 in which the flying pilot died. Evidence of illicit drug use was found only in a small number of cases; however, the percentage of study pilots who tested positive for marijuana increased from 1.6% in the 1990–1997 period to 3.0% in the most recent 5-year period 2008–2012.

This trend is worrisome, since even small doses (5–15 mg) of delta-9-tetrahydrocannabinol (D-THC; active ingredient of marijuana) can cause significant impairment of performance in complex or demanding tasks (Ashton 1999). Also worrisome is the trend toward increased potency of marijuana. From 1993 to 2008, the content of D-THC in confiscated cannabis preparations increased from 3.4% to 8.8% (Mehmedic et al. 2010). An even greater contrast is between the D-THC content of marijuana cigarettes from the 1960s and 1970s, which averaged 1%–3% (Ashton 1999). Since a cigarette with 1%–3% D-THC delivers approximately 10 mg of D-THC, clearly the modern reefer can deliver a drug dose more than capable of substantially impairing performance.

To appreciate the extent of that impairment, consider the results from two studies that examined the performance of pilots following ingestion of D-THC. In a study by Janowsky et al. (1976), 10 pilots smoked a social dose of marijuana (0.09 mg/kg) and flew a specified flight sequence on an ATC-510 flight simulator. The flight scenario included holding patterns, and other maneuvers typically encountered in instrument flight. All the pilots flew a 16-minute flight sequence 30 minutes after ingestion of the D-THC. Six of the pilots also flew the 16-minute scenarios at 2, 4, and 6 hours after ingestion. The results showed that D-THC caused a gross decrement in flying performance with an increased prevalence of major errors (shown in Figure 3.14). Effects were also evident for course control (Figure 3.15) and altitude control (Figure 3.16). The authors suggest that the most significant effect was marijuana's ability to affect short-term memory and time sense. They report that subjects often forgot where they were in a flight sequence or had difficulty recounting how long they had been performing a given maneuver. Clearly, this sort of effect has profound implications for maintenance of situational awareness on the part of the pilot. Indeed, the authors note that "... at times subjects exhibited a complete loss of orientation with respect to the navigational fix" (p. 127).

Recall that in the earlier discussion regarding the effects of alcohol it was suggested that highly demanding tasks were most impacted by alcohol. A study by Leirer et al. (1989) addressed much the same question by evaluating the effects

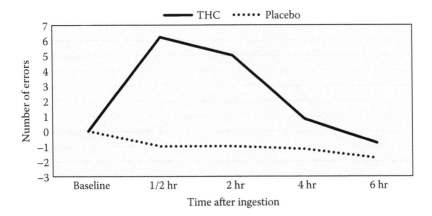

FIGURE 3.14 Effect of D-THC on major pilot errors. (Adapted with permission from Janowsky, D.S. et al. 1976. *Aviation, Space, and Environmental Medicine* 47: 124–128.)

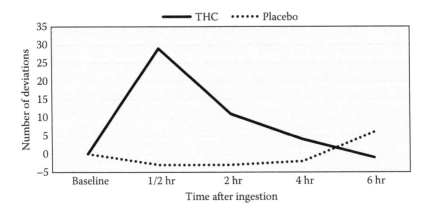

FIGURE 3.15 Effect of D-THC on course control. (Adapted with permission from Janowsky, D.S. et al. 1976. *Aviation, Space, and Environmental Medicine* 47: 124–128.)

of marijuana, aging, and task difficulty on pilot performance. They had groups of young and old pilots complete both calm and turbulent flights in a light plane simulator after smoking cigarettes containing 0, 10, or 20 mg of D-THC. Marijuana was found to significantly affect performance at 1 and 4 hours after ingestion in the turbulent flights, but not in the calm flights. They concluded that "... effects of aging, marijuana use, and increased task difficulty are cumulative. Performance progressively declines with the addition of each variable" (p. 1151).

Finally, it should be noted that residual levels of D-THC are maintained in the body for a long time following ingestion. The half-life (the time it takes for 50% of the D-THC to be metabolized) for an infrequent user is 1.3 days, while for frequent

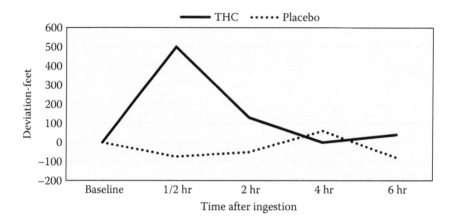

FIGURE 3.16 Effect of D-THC on altitude control. (Adapted with permission from Janowsky, D.S. et al. 1976. *Aviation, Space, and Environmental Medicine* 47: 124–128.)

users it is 5–13 days (Sharma and Ravi 2010). On the basis of the D-THC content of modern reefers and the decay rate, consider the following scenario. If pilots who are infrequent users of marijuana smoke one marijuana cigarette of average potency, they ingest approximately 75 mg of D-THC. After 1.3 days, they will have a load of approximately 37 mg of D-THC remaining unmetabolized (50% of the original 75 mg). After a further 1.3 days, they will have 18 mg of D-THC (50% of the 37 mg). After a further 1.3 days (for a total elapsed time of about 4 days after smoking the single cigarette), they will still have 9 mg of D-THC (50% of the 18 mg) remaining—well within the bounds that Ashton (1999) indicates can impair performance of complex tasks. Although many may argue that marijuana is no more dangerous than alcohol, in this regard at least it presents a unique hazard since it is metabolized so much more slowly than alcohol.

The degree of impairment associated with carryover effects of marijuana has been examined in a series of studies. In a preliminary study, Yesavage et al. (1985) evaluated the performance of 10 pilots who flew a landing task in a flight simulator 24 hours after smoking a cigarette containing 19 mg of D-THC (equivalent to a strong social dose). The pilots' mean performance showed impairment on all flight tasks, with significant impairment in the number and size of aileron changes, the size of elevator changes, the distance off-center on landing (illustrated in Figure 3.17), and vertical and lateral deviation on approach to landing. In addition, the pilots reported no awareness of their impaired performance, as shown in Figure 3.18.

In a follow-up study (Leirer et al. 1991), pilots were again evaluated on a complicated six-leg pattern flown in a Frasca 141 flight simulator 24 hours after smoking a cigarette containing 20 mg of D-THC. As in the preliminary study, significant impairment was observed on performance measures 24 hours after ingestion of D-THC, as shown in Figure 3.19, and pilots were unaware of their impairment.

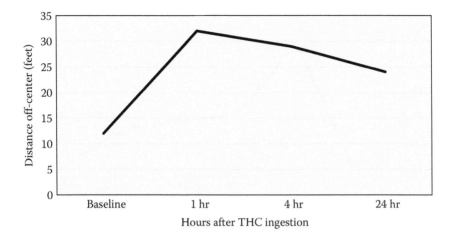

FIGURE 3.17   Effect of D-THC on landing performance. (Adapted from Yesavage, J.A. et al. 1985. *American Journal of Psychiatry* 142: 1325–1329, Table 1.)

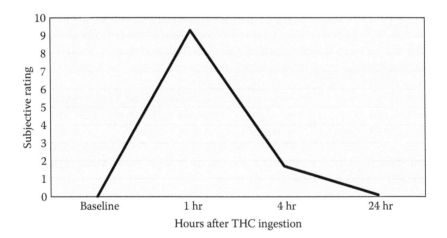

FIGURE 3.18   Subjective rating of D-THC high. (Adapted from Yesavage, J.A. et al. 1985. *American Journal of Psychiatry* 142: 1325–1329, Table 1.)

3.5.3   TOBACCO

Leaving aside any considerations of cancer or heart disease, the "… most significant impact of smoking … lies in the concomitant introduction of carbon monoxide into the pilot's bloodstream" (Garland et al. 1999, p. 322). This has, at least, two immediate negative effects. First is the production of a state of hypemic hypoxia caused by the binding of carbon monoxide to the hemoglobin of the pilot's blood. This reduces the capacity of the blood to acquire oxygen from the atmosphere and transport it to the body's cells. Engstrom (2003) indicates that tests have shown a person's tolerance for altitude reduced by 5000–6000 feet due to the carbon monoxide from

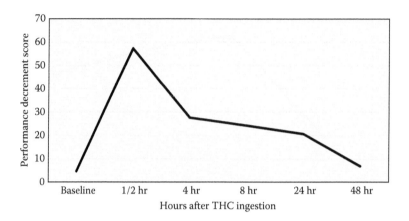

FIGURE 3.19   Pilot performance following D-THC ingestion. (Adapted from Leirer, V.O. et al. 1991. *Aviation, Space, and Environmental Medicine* 62: 221–227, Table 1.)

tobacco. Secondly, carbon monoxide will also reduce visual acuity. In a study of U.S. Army aviators (Sharma and Ravi 2010), the visual acuity and field of view (FOV) of nonsmokers, light smokers, and heavy smokers were compared. The Snellen visual acuity was found to be significantly lower in the light and heavy smokers, compared to the nonsmokers in all illumination conditions. FOV was also found to be significantly reduced.

Smoking reduces night vision as a function of the altitude. The increased levels of carbon monoxide in the blood result in reductions in the ability of the eye to adjust to reduced illumination. A person who smokes an average of one pack of cigarettes per day will experience an 8%–10% increase in the level of carbon monoxide in his blood. This increase corresponds to reductions in night vision at the different altitudes, as shown in Table 3.6.

TABLE 3.6
Effect of Smoking on Night Vision

Percent Reduction in Night Vision

Altitude (feet)	Nonsmoker	Smoker
4000	0	20
6000	5	25
10000	20	40
14000	35	55
16000	40	60

Source: U.S. Army, n.d. *Aviation Medicine*, Sub-course AV0593. Washington, DC: U.S. Army Institute for Professional Development.

3.5.4 OVER-THE-COUNTER AND PRESCRIPTION DRUGS

Although alcohol and illicit drugs, such as marijuana, may play a role in some accidents as shown by the study conducted by the NTSB (2014), there are many drugs, available on prescription or over-the-counter, that can have debilitating effects on pilot performance. Table 3.7 shows some of the many drugs found in the study of fatalities by the NTSB (2014). Of particular concern are those drugs that cause sedation (sleepiness). Principal among those drugs is diphenhydramine (Benedryl™), commonly administered to control the effects of allergies. A single dose of diphenhydramine has been found to significantly impair performance in a driving simulator (Weiler et al. 2000). However, the relationship between this drug and performance decrement is unclear. A recent meta-analysis (Bender et al. 2004) found that diphenhydramine impaired performance relative to placebos and second-generation antihistamines (the nonsedating antihistamines in Table 3.7), but the effects were quite varied and the sedating effect of diphenhydramine was modest. On the other hand, a study by Valk et al. (2004) conducted at an altitude of 8000 feet showed that diphenhydramine caused significantly more sleepiness than a placebo as well as impaired performance on a tracking task and an increased number of omissions. Given the variety of results, perhaps the best characterization of the effects of diphenhydramine is "it depends." The degree of impairment may depend on the biochemistry of a particular individual, the altitude, the nature of the task, the degree of fatigue, or any of many other factors. So, unless a pilot wishes to become an experimental test subject, the best advice is to avoid taking diphenhydramine before any flight.

In addition to the many drugs that can cause sedation or otherwise impair performance, there are also some drugs that have been shown to improve performance.

TABLE 3.7
Drugs Detected in Deceased Pilots from 1990 to 2012

Drug Category	1990–1997	1998–2002	2003–2007	2008–2012	Total Study Period
Sedating antihistamines	5.6%	8.2%	8.3%	9.9%	7.5%
Nonsedating antihistamines	4.6%	6.8%	6.2%	7.3%	5.9%
Nonsedating over-the-counter drugs	2.4%	4.2%	8.0%	12.4%	5.7%
Cardiovascular drugs	1.0%	4.5%	5.8%	5.3%	3.5%
Antidepressants	2.3%	2.9%	2.9%	3.8%	2.8%
Sedating pain relievers	1.0%	2.4%	2.6%	4.4%	2.2%
Diet aids	1.2%	2.4%	2.0%	1.2%	1.6%
Benzodiazepines[a]	1.3%	1.1%	1.1%	2.0%	1.3%

Source: NTSB (National Transportation Safety Board). 2014. *Drug Use Trends in Aviation: Assessing The Risk of Pilot Impairment.* Safety Study NTSB/SS-14/01. Washington, DC: Author.

[a] Benzodiazepines—a class of drug known as tranquilizers (e.g., Valium™, Xanax™), usually prescribed for anxiety, panic attacks, or insomnia.

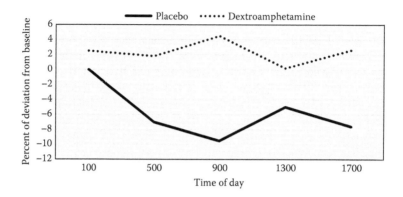

FIGURE 3.20 Effect of dextroamphetamine on straight and level flight. (Reprinted from *Transportation Research Part F*, 4, Caldwell, J.A. Efficacy of stimulants for fatigue management: The effects of Provigil® and Dexedrine® on sleep-deprived aviators, 19–37, Copyright 2001, with permission from Elsevier.

In addition to caffeine (to be discussed later), these drugs include nicotine, Dexedrine® (dextroamphetamine sulfate), Provigil® (modafinil), and Aricept® (donepezil). In a study of U.S. Army pilots, Caldwell (2001) evaluated the effects of dextroamphetamine and modafinil relative to placebo. Both of these drugs worked to improve alertness and performance. Figures 3.20 and 3.21, which illustrate the differences between a placebo and treatment groups for straight-and-level performance, are typical of the results from this study. The effects of both drugs are evident in the increased performance levels, relative to the placebo.[*]

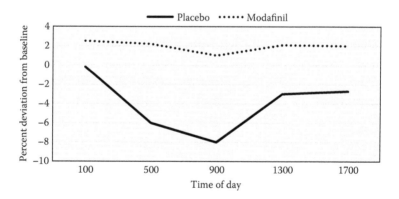

FIGURE 3.21 Effect of modafinil on straight and level flight. (Reprinted from *Transportation Research Part F*, 4, Caldwell, J.A. Efficacy of stimulants for fatigue management: The effects of Provigil® and Dexedrine® on sleep-deprived aviators, 19–37, Copyright 2001, with permission from Elsevier.)

---

[*] This discussion of performance-enhancing drugs is intended to inform readers of their potential effects, but should definitely *not* be considered an endorsement of their use by pilots, maintainers, or other aviation professionals, except under the direction of a qualified flight surgeon.

The effect of dextromethamphetamine on pilot performance was also investigated by Weigmann et al. (1996). They administered either 5 or 10 mg/70 kg body weight of dextromethamphetamine to 40 naval aviation candidates awaiting initial flight training. They then assessed the effects of the drug on performance on computer-based tests of running memory and compensatory tracking in a 13.5-hour sustained-performance session that included one night of sleep loss. Consistent with Caldwell (2001), they found that the drug improved performance.

Donepezil is a member of the class of drugs known as acetylcholinesterase inhibitors. It acts upon the cholinergic system of the body and improves mental function (such as memory, attention, ability to interact with others, speak, think clearly, and perform regular daily activities). It is commonly prescribed to improve cognition and behavior of people with Alzheimer's. Its effect on pilot performance was investigated by Yesavage et al. (2002). In this study, pilots received either a placebo or a 5-mg dose of donepezil each day for 30 days. They then examined the change in performance for the placebo and drug treatment groups from baseline (before drug administration) at Day 1 to the flight tests conducted at Day 30. The results suggest that donepezil increases the ability to retain the capacity to perform complex simulator tasks. The authors concluded that "Donepezil appears to have beneficial effects on retention of training on complex aviation tasks" (Yesavage et al. 2002, p. 123).

Another drug that acts upon the cholinergic system is nicotine, which has a method of action different from donepezil. Nicotine has been shown to improve information processing and enhance sensorimotor performance (Sherwood et al. 1992). Since those abilities are particularly relevant to flying an airplane, the effect of nicotine administration on performance by pilots in a flight simulator was tested by Mumenthaler et al. (2003) who found that it had a positive effect on several measures of pilot performance.

Both of the cholinergic drugs (nicotine and donepezil) showed positive effects on flight tasks requiring sustained visual attention. Methamphetamine also has been shown to improve performance. However, these drugs have potential side effects that render them unacceptable for use, except for a few military applications—hence the preponderance of military pilots in the studies cited. Most civil aviation authorities forbid the use of unapproved drugs by civil aircrew, and these compounds are definitely not approved. Taking a few meth tabs before flying is a great way to get grounded for a very long time if caught, besides being inherently risky. So, if pilots cannot take these pills to improve performance, what can they do? Fortunately, the answer, covered next, may be as close as the nearest Starbucks®.

3.5.5 CAFFEINE

Caffeine, usually consumed in the form of coffee, tea, or cola, is arguably the most popular licit stimulant drug in the world. Leading the world in consumption (in the form of coffee) is Finland, where the annual per capita consumption is 9.6 kg, or about 3 cups per day. By comparison, the consumption of coffee in Germany, the United States, Australia, and the United Kingdom are 5.2, 3.1, 2.6, and 1.7 kg per capita, respectively (Caffeine [Coffee] Consumption by Country n.d.). Coffee accounts for about 54% of the consumption of caffeine, while tea accounts for about 43%.

Caffeine is considered a moderately effective stimulant that acts as an adenosine receptor antagonist. Adenosine promotes sleepiness, and caffeine blocks the adenosine receptor to prevent feeling sleepy. It works best when taken on an intermittent basis. Because the body builds up a tolerance for caffeine, habitual consumers must take larger doses in order to achieve the same alerting effects. A typical dose of caffeine is in the range of 50–200 mg. Although there is a large range of caffeine content dependent upon the method of brewing, a cup (8 oz) of brewed coffee typically contains about 100 mg of caffeine while a cup of black tea contains about 55 mg. Some beverages marketed as "high energy" drinks contain 150–180 mg of caffeine (Fredholm et al. 1999). In addition to beverages (and some foods such as chocolate), caffeine is also available in a powdered form. Ingesting caffeine in this form can be hazardous, since a lethal amount of caffeine is contained in less than a tablespoon (15 mL). The LD_{50} (the amount of caffeine that is fatal to 50% of the population) for caffeine is about 150–200 mg/kg of body weight (Peters 1967). Therefore, ingesting 12.25 grams (0.43 oz) of powdered caffeine would be fatal about half the time for an adult weighing 70 kg (150 lb). That amount of caffeine is contained in about 75–100 cups of coffee, so it is unlikely that an adult would consume enough to be potentially lethal by drinking coffee. However, even sublethal doses of caffeine can cause cardiac arrhythmia, particularly in individuals with some preexisting cardiac condition. So, do not overdo it.

Caffeine is readily absorbed from the gastrointestinal track and can reach its peak levels in the bloodstream in 15–45 minutes. The half-life of caffeine is 2.5–4 hours, but the half-life is reduced by 30%–50% for smokers compared to nonsmokers (Fredholm et al. 1999). These are important numbers for those who need maximum alertness at a particular time. For example, toward the end of a long night flight, a pilot might wish to have a cup of coffee about 30–45 minutes before beginning the descent and approach to landing. These activities will significantly increase cognitive workload compared to cruise flight, so it would be prudent to assure that the pilot is operating at the highest level of alertness possible. The question then is, just how much effect will the caffeine have?

There have been many studies of the effects of caffeine on human behavior and affective state. Some studies find a beneficial effect on performance, and some do not. The outcomes seem to depend very much on just what behavior is being assessed, the characteristics of the experimental test subjects (e.g., whether they are habitual coffee drinkers), the exact nature of the task (e.g., whether it is primarily a psychomotor task or a complex reasoning task), and the timing of the study (i.e., whether it starts in the morning and ends in the evening). A study by Lieberman (2003) is an example of a study that showed a positive effect for caffeine. In that study, subjects (military personnel) were tested on their detection of a target while on a simulated sentry duty task after receiving either a placebo or 200 mg of caffeine. The results from this study are illustrated in Figure 3.22.

Since sleepiness is often implicated as a cause in motor vehicle accidents, there have been many studies that have evaluated the effects of caffeine on driving performance. Figures 3.23 and 3.24 show the results from a study (Brice and Smith 2001) that compared the performance of subjects who had received 3 mg/kg caffeine or a placebo. Some subjects completed a battery of computer tests, while others completed a 60-minute drive in a simulator. As shown in the figures, the placebo and

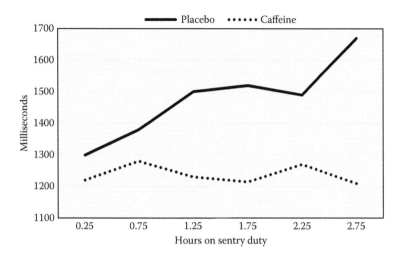

FIGURE 3.22 Effects of caffeine on target detection time. (Reprinted from *Appetite*, 40, Liebermann, H.R. Nutrition, brain function and cognitive performance, 245–254, Copyright 2003, with permission from Elsevier.)

caffeine groups differed (significantly) both on their self-reported alertness (Figure 3.24) and on steering variability (Figure 3.25) in the driving simulator. More variability is a sign of poor control.

As noted earlier, however, a large portion of studies of caffeine and performance fail to find significant effects. In a study of Finnish military pilots who were tested during 37 hours of sleep deprivation, researchers found that caffeine did not improve flight performance (Kilpeläinen et al. 2010). Caska and Molesworth (2007) investigated the effects of low doses of caffeine and found that the performance of pilots who received 0, 1, or 3 mg/kg of caffeine was not significantly different. However, they did find a significant interaction between the caffeine dosage groups and sleep. This suggests that the caffeine had the greatest effect on pilots who had slept the

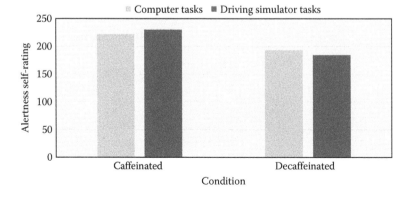

FIGURE 3.23 Effects of caffeine on alertness. (Adapted from Brice, C. and Smith, A.P. 2001. *Human Psychopharmacology Clinical and Experimental* 16: 523–531, Table 2.)

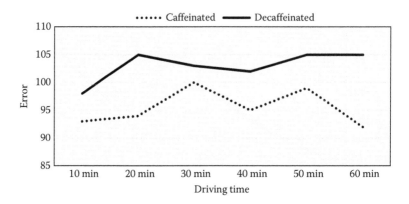

FIGURE 3.24 Effects of caffeine on steering variability. (Adapted from Brice, C. and Smith, A.P. 2001. *Human Psychopharmacology Clinical and Experimenta*l 16: 523–531, Table 3.)

least in the preceding 24 hours. The authors concluded that, for a normal, well-rested person, caffeine at relatively low doses has no measurable effect on performance. However, for a person who is not well rested, caffeine in low doses can noticeably improve performance.

A study (Jouni et al. 2007) that used a larger dose of caffeine (200 mg) administered 1 hour before simulated flights by military pilots with 37 hours of sleep deprivation also failed to find differences in flight performance between the pilots who took the caffeine and a control group who received a placebo. In an even more extreme

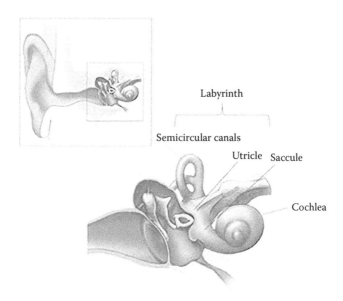

FIGURE 3.25 Anatomy of the vestibular system. (From National Institutes of Health. *National Institute on Deafness and Other Communication Disorders.* https://www.nidcd. nih.gov/health/menieres-disease)

sleep deprivation study, Kilgore et al. (2007) subjected pilots to 75 hours of sleep deprivation and measured their risky decision-making using the Iowa Gambling Task. Even in such a sleep-deprived condition, caffeine had no significant effects on the pilots' risk-taking behavior.

From the studies described above, it seems evident that the effects of caffeine are not clear. In the doses contained in one or two cups of coffee, caffeine seems to act as a mild stimulant, particularly for those who do not regularly consume large amounts of caffeine. Having a cup or two late in a flight may well provide a slight boost to pilots, but the effects will not entirely compensate for the fatigue associated with a long night flight. In an extensive review of the literature on the effects of caffeine on human behavior, Smith (2002) examined hundreds of studies with positive and negative results. His evaluation of the effects of caffeine provides a succinct summary of the present knowledge on this complex topic:

- Caffeine, in doses that would be obtained in normal consumption of caffeinated products, improves performance of vigilance tasks and simple tasks which benefit from a high level of alertness.
- The beneficial effects of caffeine can be most easily demonstrated in low arousal situations. However, improved performance has been shown when reduced alertness is not involved.
- Caffeine improves performance of artificial tasks and simulations of driving and industrial work. These findings suggest that it will be of benefit in safety-critical situations and will improve operational efficiency.
- Effects on more complex cognitive tasks are less clear cut, probably because of the moderating influence of factors such as personality and time of day. However, even this area shows few costs of caffeine consumption.
- It has been claimed that the positive effects of caffeine really reflect removal of negative effects of caffeine withdrawal. This view cannot account for effects observed in non-consumers or non-deprived individuals. In addition, there is little evidence of caffeine withdrawal impairing tasks which show improvements following ingestion of caffeine. (Reproduced with permission from Smith 2002, p. 1250.)

3.6 SENSORY ILLUSIONS

The topics addressed up to this point have largely been concerned with matters of biochemistry and the internal functioning of the human body. The body needs oxygen and glucose to function. It also needs regular rest and sleep to function well, and its functioning can be negatively or positively impacted by a number of chemicals, including carbon monoxide from tobacco smoke, and a variety of licit and illicit drugs. But, the body can also be fooled by outside stimuli—both visual and kinesthetic (movement sense).

3.6.1 Spatial Disorientation

Accidents due to spatial disorientation occur with alarming frequency; and, they do not just happen to general aviation pilots who fly into an area of instrument meteorological conditions. They also happen to experienced aircrew flying modern transport aircraft. One example of such an accident is the crash of a Boeing 737-300 minutes after takeoff from Sharm el-Sheikh, Egypt in January, 2004. On departure on a dark night over the Red Sea, the captain (the pilot flying) became disoriented and eventually rolled the aircraft to about 110° to the right. Subsequent control inputs were too late to avoid a crash into the Red Sea. Two similar 737 accidents occurred in 2007. In both cases, the pilot flying made control inputs away from a wings level condition, resulting in loss of control and a crash (Mumaw et al. n.d.).

Fortunately, such events are rare among air carriers; however, they are all too common among military and general aviation pilots. McGrath et al. (2002) reported that spatial disorientation accounted for 26% of total mishaps and 50% of fatalities for the U.S. Navy during 2001, and that those proportions are consistent with those of previous years and other services. Various studies of general aviation accidents over the past several decades have found that spatial disorientation was a common causal factor in fatal accidents. The percentages ranged from 16% during the period 1976–1992 (Kirkham et al. 1978) to 11% of fatal accidents during the period 1976–1991 (Collins and Dollar 1996). Some authors, however, have argued that the actual percentages are much larger. Gibb et al. (2011) conducted an extensive review of accident reports and spatial disorientation research and concluded that it contributes to nearly 33% of all mishaps with a fatality rate of almost 100%.

The human ear contains the vestibular system that provides us with our sense of balance. This system has two main components: the semicircular canals that detect changes in angular acceleration, and the otolith organs (the utricle and the saccule) that detect changes in linear acceleration and gravity (see Figure 3.25). Both of these components send information to the brain regarding the body's position and movement.

Each ear has three semicircular canals that are filled with a viscous liquid and are lined with tiny hairs (cilia). Each of these canals is aligned with one primary axis of motion: pitch, roll, and yaw. When the head moves, the fluid in the canals presses against the cilia that line the canals. The cilia translate this movement into an electrical signal that is then transmitted to the brain.

The vestibular system also contains two otolith organs: the saccule and the utricle. These organs are set at right angles to each other. The utricle detects changes in linear acceleration in the horizontal plane, while the saccule detects gravity changes in the vertical plane. In combination with a variety of body proprioceptors, including tendons, joints, vision, touch, and pressure, the semicircular canals and the otolith organs allow the body to sense position and motion in three-dimensional space.

The structure of the vestibular system gives rise to two types of vestibular illusions. Somatogyral illusions involve the semicircular canals. Somatogravic illusions involve the otolithic organs.

3.6.2 Somatogyral Illusions

These illusions involve the semicircular canals of the vestibular system and occur primarily under conditions of unreliable or unavailable external visual references, resulting in false sensations of rotation. These include the leans, the graveyard spin and spiral, and the coriolis illusion (FAA 2003; Flight Safety Foundation n.d.).

3.6.2.1 Leans

This is the most common illusion. The "leans" corresponds to a false sensation of roll attitude. Several situations can lead to the leans, but the most common is a recovery from a coordinated turn to level flight when flying by instruments. Spatial disorientation can occur when movement is below the sensory threshold for the semicircular canal (0.2–8.0°/s), especially during slow rotational movement. A pilot will feel as if the aircraft is in a wings-level attitude while, in fact, it is banked. If recovery from the turn is made abruptly, the semicircular canal in the plane of the rotation is stimulated. Thus, the pilot may feel that the aircraft is flying one wing low when the attitude display indicates the wings are level. These perceptions may lead a pilot to align his or her body with the apparent vertical. Alternatively, a pilot may roll the aircraft into an incorrect attitude to neutralize the false sensation of bank. The leans disappear as soon as the pilot has a strong visual reference to the horizon or ground.

3.6.2.2 Graveyard Spiral

The graveyard spiral (illustrated in Figure 3.26) is a high-speed, tight, descending turn. Since any rate of roll of less than 2°/s is not perceived, the wing can drop and the aircraft may begin a turn without the pilot realizing it. As the aircraft spirals downward and its rate of descent accelerates, the pilot senses the descent but not the turn. With the bank angle having gradually increased, any control input only tightens the turn and increases the descent rate. This condition may develop when an aircraft begins to bank in cloud or dark night conditions. Under those conditions,

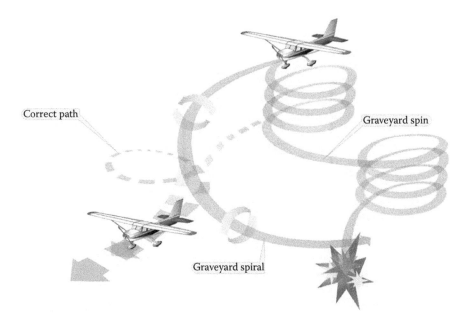

FIGURE 3.26 Graveyard spiral and spin. (From Federal Aviation Administration. 2016. *Pilot's Handbook of Aeronautical Knowledge*. H-8083-25B. Washington, DC: Author.)

a constant rate of bank will be undetectable by the vestibular system, and no visual clue will be available unless the pilot is monitoring the attitude indicator. The pilot may hear the rushing of slipstream indicative of increasing airspeed of a dive in what otherwise appears to be straight-and-level flight. Subsequent attempts to pull out of the dive serve only to tighten the unrecognized turn. If left uncorrected, this may cause the aircraft to break up in flight.

3.6.2.3   Graveyard Spin

This occurs when a pilot enters a spin and initially has a sensation of spinning in the same direction as the aircraft because the motion of the liquid in the semicircular canals bends the hair cells accordingly. If the pilot applies opposite rudder and stops the spin, the liquid will abruptly flow in the opposite direction. That will bend the hair cells in the opposite direction, which gives the pilot the illusion of a spin when in reality the aircraft is flying straight and level. If the pilot applies the rudder to correct this perceived spin, the pilot will unknowingly reenter the original spin. If the pilot believes the body sensations instead of trusting the instruments, the spin will continue. This maneuver is also illustrated in Figure 3.26.

3.6.2.4   Coriolis Illusion

This illusion generally occurs when a pilot is in a turn and bends the head downward or backward (e.g., to look at a chart or the overhead panel). This angular motion of the head and of the aircraft on two different planes can cause problems. The turn activates one semicircular canal and the head movement activates another (shown in Figure 3.27). The simultaneous stimulation of two semicircular canals produces an almost unbearable sensation that the aircraft is rolling, pitching, and yawing all at the same time and can be compared with the sensation of rolling down a hillside.

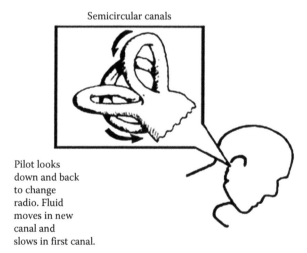

Semicircular canals

Pilot looks down and back to change radio. Fluid moves in new canal and slows in first canal.

FIGURE 3.27   Fluid movement in the semicircular canals during a turn. (From U.S. Army. 2009. *Aeromedical Training for Flight Personnel.* TC 3-04.93. Washington, DC: Author. Chapter 9.)

This specific spinning sensation is called vertigo. It can quickly disorient a pilot and cause a loss of aircraft control.

3.6.3 SOMATOGRAVIC ILLUSIONS

These illusions involve the utricle and the saccule of the vestibular system and are most likely under conditions with unreliable or unavailable external visual references. They are caused by changes in linear accelerations and decelerations or a change in gravity (G) forces. All involve the body's inability to distinguish pitch changes from acceleration. There are three versions of the somatogravic illusion.

3.6.3.1 Inversion Illusion

The inversion illusion occurs when an abrupt change from climb to straight-and-level flight causes excessive stimulation of the gravity and linear acceleration sensory organs. This combination of accelerations produces an illusion that the aircraft is inverted or tumbling backward. A common response to this illusion is to lower the nose of the aircraft.

3.6.3.2 Head-Up Illusion

This illusion involves a sudden forward linear acceleration during level flight where the pilot perceives that the nose of the aircraft is pitching up. The pilot's response to this illusion would be to push the control forward to pitch the nose of the aircraft down, as shown in Figure 3.28. Night takeoff from a well-lit airport into a dark sky or the application of full power during a missed instrument approach can lead to this illusion.

3.6.3.3 Head-Down Illusion

The head-down illusion involves a sudden linear deceleration (e.g., application of air brakes, lowering flaps, decreasing engine power) during level flight. This may cause the pilot to perceive that the nose of the aircraft is pitching down. The pilot's response would be to raise the nose of the aircraft, which may lead to a stall if executed during a low-speed final approach.

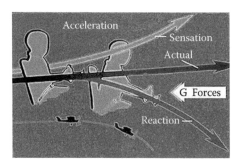

FIGURE 3.28 Head-up illusion. (From Federal Aviation Administration. 2003. *Medical Facts for Pilots: Spatial Disorientation.* AM-400-03/01. Oklahoma City, OK: FAA Civil Aerospace Medical Institute.)

3.6.4 Vision and Visual Illusions

Vision provides the most important sensory information to a pilot during flight. Central vision, known as foveal vision, is involved in the identification of objects and the perception of colors. Peripheral vision, also known as ambient vision, is involved with the perception of movement and provides peripheral cues to maintain spatial orientation. The brain uses information gained from vision to make judgments regarding the distance, speed, and relative movement of objects. The cues used by the visual system include the following:

- Comparative size and shape of known objects at different distances.
- Relative velocity of images moving across the retina. Objects that are close are perceived as moving faster than more distant objects.
- The interposition or layering of known objects. If one object is placed in front of another, it is perceived as being closer.
- The texture and contrast of known objects. These cues are lost as the object moves further away.
- Changes in illumination of objects due to light and shadows.
- Differences in aerial perspective. Distant objects are usually seen as bluish and blurry (FAA 2000).

Although vision is usually a reliable source of information, there are some circumstances in which what the eyes and brain perceive does not correctly interpret the external reality. Visual illusions are believed to play an important part in accidents that occur during night visual landing approaches. Analyses of civilian and military accidents have shown a relatively large number of aircraft crash short of the runway in nighttime accidents, even in the absence of adverse weather. Many of these crashes are thought to have been caused by a lack of visual information or to visual illusions associated with certain geographical characteristics (e.g., sloping runway or sloping terrain around the runway) of the airport vicinity (Mertens and Lewis 1981).

The effects of these illusions have been demonstrated in the laboratory by Mertens and Lewis (1981). They used an aircraft simulator with a computer-generated visual display of the runway scene to measure performance during approaches to runways of constant length but varying width, following practice with a fixed runway width. Subjects flew 20 simulated visual approaches and landings to a runway that was 75, 150, or 300 feet wide. The effect of practice was then measured in 20 additional approaches in which five runway widths (75, 100, 150, 200, and 300 feet) were presented in a random order. The pilots who were trained to make night landings in a flight simulator on a wide runway subsequently had lower approach angles in approaches to narrower runways. Conversely, a narrow practice runway also raised approach angles to wider runways. These effects increased as distance from runway threshold decreased.

The effect of runway width demonstrated by Mertens and Lewis is but one of several visual illusions that may occur under certain conditions of topography and runway configuration.

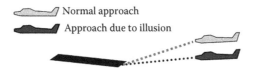

FIGURE 3.29   Approach to an up-sloping runway. (From Federal Aviation Administration. 2000. *Medical Facts for Pilots: Spatial Disorientation: Visual Illusions*. AM-400-00/1. Oklahoma City, OK: FAA Civil Aerospace Medical Institute.)

3.6.4.1   Up-Sloping Runway

A final approach over flat terrain to an up-sloping runway (as shown in Figure 3.29) may produce the illusion of a too-high final approach. The pilot may then respond by lowering the nose of the aircraft to decrease the altitude. If performed too close to the ground, this may result in accident.

3.6.4.2   Down-Sloping Runway

A final approach over flat terrain to a down-sloping runway (Figure 3.30) may produce the illusion of a too-low final approach. In this case, the pilot may respond to raising the nose of the aircraft to increase the altitude. This may then result in a low-altitude stall or a missed approach.

3.6.4.3   Up-Sloping Terrain

A final approach over up-sloping terrain may produce the visual illusion that the aircraft is higher than it actually is. This is shown in Figure 3.31. Under this condition, the pilot may pitch the nose down to decrease the altitude, resulting in a lower

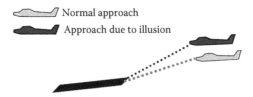

FIGURE 3.30   Approach to a down-sloping runway. (From Federal Aviation Administration. 2000. *Medical Facts For Pilots: Spatial Disorientation: Visual Illusions*. AM-400-00/1. Oklahoma City, OK: FAA Civil Aerospace Medical Institute.)

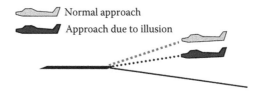

FIGURE 3.31   Approach to a flat runway over up-sloping terrain. (From Federal Aviation Administration. 2000. *Medical Facts for Pilots: Spatial Disorientation: Visual Illusions*. AM-400-00/1. Oklahoma City, OK: FAA Civil Aerospace Medical Institute.)

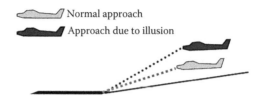

FIGURE 3.32 Approach to a flat runway over down-sloping terrain. (From Federal Aviation Administration. 2000. *Medical Facts for Pilots: Spatial Disorientation: Visual Illusions.* AM-400-00/1. Oklahoma City, OK: FAA Civil Aerospace Medical Institute.)

approach. This can result in landing short of the runway, or flaring short of the runway and experiencing a low-altitude stall.

3.6.4.4 Down-Sloping Terrain

A final approach over down-sloping terrain (shown in Figure 3.32) may produce the visual illusion that the aircraft is lower than it actually is. The pilot may then respond by raising the nose of the aircraft to gain altitude, possibly resulting in landing further down the runway than intended.

3.6.4.5 Narrow or Long Runway

A final approach to an unusually narrow or unusually long runway can produce the visual illusion of being too high. As was the case of the up-sloping runway, this may lead the pilot to pitch the nose down to lose altitude, leading to the same result—a low-altitude stall or a missed approach. This situation is shown in Figure 3.33.

3.6.4.6 Wide Runway

A final approach to an unusually wide runway (as shown in Figure 3.34) may produce the visual illusion of being too low and, just as was the case with the down-sloping runway, may lead the pilot to raise the nose of the aircraft to gain altitude.

3.6.4.7 Black-Hole Approach Illusion

The black-hole illusion can occur during final approach on a dark night over water or unlighted terrain, when a horizon is not visible beyond the lighted runway. The lack of peripheral visual cues makes it difficult for pilots to orient themselves relative to the earth. One particularly dangerous situation occurs when approaching a runway

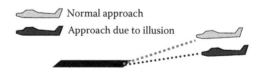

FIGURE 3.33 Approach to a narrow or long runway. (From Federal Aviation Administration. 2000. *Medical Facts for Pilots: Spatial Disorientation: Visual Illusions.* AM-400-00/1. Oklahoma City, OK: FAA Civil Aerospace Medical Institute.)

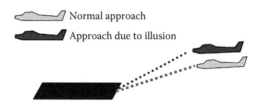

FIGURE 3.34 Approach to an unusually wide runway. (From Federal Aviation Administration. 2000. *Medical Facts for Pilots: Spatial Disorientation: Visual Illusions.* AM-400-00/1. Oklahoma City, OK: FAA Civil Aerospace Medical Institute.)

where there are no lights before the runway and city lights or rising terrain beyond the runway. This may lead the pilot to believe they are too high and to lower their approach slope. When a pilot follows the false visual cues of the black-hole approach, the flight path typically has a bow shape—an initial steep descent that slowly flattens out. Runways in remote locations, or located along the shore of a large body of water, are prone to inducing this illusion. Checking altitude against range and using landing aids, such as visual approach slope indicator (VASI) or the ILS glideslope, where available, will help to avoid descending too low on approach.

3.6.4.8 Autokinetic Illusion

The autokinetic illusion gives the pilot the impression that a stationary object is moving in front of the path of the airplane. It is caused by the pilot staring at a single fixed point of light in an otherwise totally dark and featureless background. Autokinesis occurs primarily at night when ambient visual cues are minimal and a small, dim light is seen against a dark background. After about 6–12 seconds of visually fixating on the light, an individual perceives movement at up to 20° in any particular direction or in several directions in succession, although there is no actual object displacement. This illusion can cause a pilot to mistake the fixated object for another aircraft (U.S. Army 2009).

3.6.4.9 False Visual Reference Illusion

The false visual reference illusion may occur when flying over a banked cloud, night flying over featureless terrain with ground lights that are indistinguishable from the stars, or night flying over a featureless terrain with a clearly defined patter of ground lights and a dark starless sky. Under these conditions, pilots may confuse cloud formations or lights with the horizon or ground. A sloping cloud deck can be difficult to perceive as anything but horizontal if it extends any great distance in the pilot's peripheral vision. The pilot might perceive the cloudbank to be horizontal even if it is not horizontal to the ground, causing the pilot to fly the aircraft in a banked attitude. This condition is often insidious and goes undetected until the pilot recognizes it, transitions to instruments, and makes necessary corrections. This illusion also might occur if the pilot looks outside after having given prolonged attention to a task inside the cockpit. Confusion can result in the pilot placing the aircraft parallel to the cloudbank (U.S. Army 2009).

3.6.4.10   Vection Illusion

This is the sensation of moving backward when a vehicle next to you moves forward. Your peripheral vision detects the forward motion of the other object and interprets it as your movement in the opposite direction. This is commonly experienced when sitting next to another automobile at an intersection. If the other car starts to move forward, you feel that you are moving backward (FAA 2000).

3.7   SUMMARY

All of the factors discussed here—lack of oxygen, availability of nutrients, fatigue, the presence of various chemical substances, and the somatogravic and visual illusions—can influence cognition and behavior in degrees ranging from subtle to dramatic. Arguably, the dramatic effects associated with exposure to more extreme levels of hypoxia, intoxication, or drug use are less worrisome than the more subtle effects found with low levels of exposure. Few pilots, air traffic controllers, or maintenance technicians would report for duty while intoxicated from alcohol, severely fatigued, or high from smoking marijuana. However, as shown earlier, detectable effects on behavior, particularly when under stress, may be found long after the obvious effects of sleep loss, alcohol, marijuana, or other substances are gone. You may feel fine, and you may even be legal, but you may not be capable of performing at your full potential. Usually, that will not matter. You will do your job, and nothing extraordinary will happen to require that you perform at your optimal level. However, as we will discuss in Chapter 11, occasionally multiple events and conditions will converge to demand performance which taxes your capacity. On those occasions, even the subtle effects of drugs taken long ago or sleep missed over several nights may contribute to your failure to meet the demands of the situation.

Of course, some physiological effects are out of your direct control. The somatogyral, somatogravic, and visual illusions are driven by the nature of your physiological systems and the external stimuli acting upon your balance and visual senses. Countering these effects is largely a matter of awareness, training, and a firm belief that the instruments are correct, regardless of what you feel.

With a little care, your body will last a long time and will effectively acquire and process the information needed to fly, repair, or direct aircraft. But, if you take away the nutrients it needs or poison it with licit or illicit substances, do not be surprised if it stops working up to specifications.

3.8   OUTSIDE ACTIVITIES

Now that you have read about hypoxia, drug effects, fatigue, and so on, you may find it interesting and instructive to actually experience some of what you have read.

3.8.1   Hypoxia

Aerospace physiology training is available at the CAMI in Oklahoma City. Besides some classroom work, this also includes exposure to simulated high altitude effects in their pressure chamber, and a ride in their spatial disorientation demonstrator. Physiological training is also available at various aviation events around the United States using a reduced oxygen breathing device that can simulate conditions up to 25,000 feet (7600 m); outside the United States, check with the local civil aviation authority for similar programs. CAMI's Airman Education Programs maintain a current list of training dates available at CAMI and other locations. You can access these dates by calling (405) 954-4837.

If you have a high tolerance for frustration, you can also visit the FAA's training Web site and try to find the scheduled events. Search for "physiology." The Web address is https://www.faasafety.gov/content/TabLanding.aspx?tab=pilots.

3.8.2 Drug and Fatigue Effects

If you want to be your own lab rat, you can test your personal reactions to drugs (legal only, please) and fatigue by doing some simple experiments. Let us say you want to see how fatigue affects your performance. There are several Internet sites (listed below) that measure simple and choice reaction time, and some that also measure number, verbal, and visual memory. You might go to one of those sites in the morning when you are fully rested and take, for example, the simple and choice reaction time tests. Record your scores,* and then go back to the same site (do not switch sites or computers) and complete the tests again late in the evening when you are feeling sleepy. Have your scores changed?

You could do much the same thing to test the effects of caffeine. Complete the tests, drink a cup of caffeinated coffee, wait about an hour, and then do them again. Any difference? What if you drink two cups of coffee?

You could combine the fatigue and caffeine experiment. Test yourself in the morning. Test yourself again in the evening. Then drink some coffee, and after an hour test yourself again.

The same sorts of experiments could be conducted using alcohol. See how much alcohol consumption affects your performance. See if caffeine lessens the performance decrement caused by alcohol (*hint*: it will not). Demonstrate the sedating effects of the older antihistamines, such as diphenhydramine (Benadryl®) impact performance. In those locations where marijuana is legal, you could do the same experiments with that drug. Isn't science fun!

The following are the Web sites for personal assessments†:

- Human Benchmark
  - http://www.humanbenchmark.com/dashboard
  - Number memory
  - Reaction time

---

* Do not just do the reaction time trials one time. To get a fairly reliable estimate of your reaction time, you need to do at least 5, and preferably 10, trials and take the average of all the times. Always start each trial with the same conditions—fingers lightly on the keys, quiet room, same lighting, no distractions.

† These Web sites were valid in November 2016. If they have been taken down, then just search for "reaction time test" and you should find several available.

- • Verbal memory
- • Visual memory
- • Washington University
  - • https://faculty.washington.edu/chudler/java/redgreen.html
  - • Simple reaction time test (nice, gives 5 trials, and shows average)
- • JustPark
  - • https://www.justpark.com/creative/reaction-time-test/
  - • Simple reaction time, in driving context
  - • Gives age equivalence; nice graph showing reaction time versus age
- • Psychological Tool Kit
  - • http://www.psytoolkit.org/lessons/experiment_simple_choice_rts.html
  - • Choice reaction time test and simple reaction time
  - • Multiple trials; displays results

RECOMMENDED READINGS

Breedlove, S.M. and Watson, N.V. 2013. *Biological Psychology: An Introduction to Behavioral, Cognitive, and Clinical Neuroscience*, 7th ed. Sunderland, MA: Sinauer Associates. [A good, broad coverage of biological psychology. Much easier reading than the Gallagher and Nelson text.]

Cacioppo, J.T., Tassinary, L.G., and Berntson, G.G. (Eds.) 2000. *Handbook of Psychophysiology*, 2nd ed. Cambridge, UK: Cambridge University Press.

Caldwell, J.A. Mallis, M.M., Caldwell, J.I., Miller, J., Paul, M., and Neri, D. 2009. Fatigue countermeasures in aviation. *Aviation, Space, and Environmental Medicine* 80: 29–59. [This is an excellent review of fatigue countermeasures. Available free from the Internet.]

Gallagher, M. and Nelson, R.J. 2003. *Handbook of Psychology: Volume 3—Biological Psychology*. Hoboken, NJ: John Wiley and Sons. [For a detailed study of the biological processes and structures underlying behavior and thought, this is a very good source. It is not light reading.]

Hansrote, R.W. and Villaire, N.E. 2006. *Applied Aviation Physiology*. Casper, WY: Endeavor Books.

International Civil Aviation Organization. 2012. *Manual of Civil Aviation Medicine*. Document 8984. Montreal, Canada: Author. [In particular, see Chapter 14, Hazards of medication and drugs. Available from: http://www.icao.int/publications/documents/8984_cons_en.pdf]

Lenne, M., Triggs, T., and Regan, M. 2004. *Cannabis and Road Safety: A Review of Recent Epidemiological, Driver Impairment, and Drug Screening Literature*. Clayton, Australia: Monash University Accident Research Centre. [This is a nice review of the literature on these subjects. Results from drivers are generalizable to pilots for the most part. The Accident Research Centre at Monash University publishes a lot of studies on human factors issues of transportation, and they are all available free from their Web site: http://www.monash.edu/miri/research/research-areas/transport-safety]

Miller, R.E. and Tredici, T.J. 1992. *Night Vision Manual for the Flight Surgeon*. Brooks, TX: U.S. Air Force Armstrong Laboratory. [We did not address all the problems of night vision in the text. If you want more information, this is a good starting place. It is available free from the Defense Technical Information Center, as are almost all other documents produced by the U.S. government. Go to their Web site and search for the title, or use the catalog number for this particular report AD-A257059. The Web address is http://www.dtic.mil/dtic/search/search.html]

Reinhart, R. 2007. *Basic Flight Physiology*. New York, NY: McGraw-Hill Education.
U.S. Army. 2009. *Aeromedical Training for Flight Personnel*. Training circular 3-04.93 [FM 3-04.301]. Washington, DC: Author. Chapter 9, Spatial disorientation. Retrieved from: https://rdl.train.army.mil/catalog-ws/view/100.ATSC/C696BACA-168F-4B4A-9750-BB

REFERENCES

Aschoff, J., Hoffman, K., Pohl, H., and Wever, R. 1975. Re-entrainment of circadian rhythms after phase-shifts of the Zeitgeber. *Chronobiologia* 2: 23–78.
Ashton, C.H. 1999. Adverse effects of cannabis and cannabinoids. *British Journal of Anesthesiology* 83: 637–649.
Avers, K. and Johnson, W.B. 2011. A review of Federal Aviation Administration fatigue research. *Aviation Psychology and Applied Human Factors* 1: 87–98.
Battelle Memorial Institute. 1998. *An Overview of the Scientific Literature Concerning Fatigue, Sleep, and the Circadian Cycle*. Unpublished technical report prepared for the Office of the Chief Scientific and Technical Advisor for Human Factors. Washington, DC: Federal Aviation Administration.
Belenky, G., Wesensten, N.J., Thorne, D.R., Thomas, M.L., Sing, H.C., Redmond, D.P., Russo, M.B., and Balkin, T.J. 2003. Patterns of performance degradation and restoration during Sleep restriction and subsequent recovery: A sleep dose-response study. *Journal of Sleep Research* 12: 1–12.
Bender, B.G., Berning, S., Dudden, R., Milgrom, H., and Tran, Z.V. 2004. Sedation and performance impairment of diphenhydramine and second-generation antihistamines: A meta-analysis. *Journal of Allergy and Clinical Immunology* 111: 770–776.
Billings, C.E., Wick, R.L., Gerke, R.J., and Chase, R.C. 1973. Effects of ethyl alcohol on pilot performance. *Aviation, Space, and Environmental Medicine* 44: 379–382.
Brice, C. and Smith, A.P. 2001. The effect of caffeine on simulated driving, subjective alertness and sustained attention. *Human Psychopharmacology Clinical and Experimental* 16: 523–531.
Caffeine (Coffee) Consumption by Country. n.d. Retrieved on November 14, 2015 from: http://www.caffeineinformer.com/caffeine-what-the-world-drinks
Caldwell, J.A. 2001. Efficacy of stimulants for fatigue management: The effects of Provigil® and Dexedrine® on sleep-deprived aviators. *Transportation Research Part F* 4: 19–37.
Caldwell, J.A., Caldwell, J.L., Brown, D.L., Smythe, N., Smith, J.K., Mylar, J., Mandichak, M., and Schroeder, C. 2003. *The Effects of 37 Hours of Continuous Wakefulness on the Physiological Arousal, Cognitive Performance, Self-Reported Mood, and Simulator Flight Performance of F-117A Pilots*. AFRL-HE-BR-TR-2003-0086. Brooks City-Base, TX: U.S. Air Force Research Laboratory.
Caldwell, J.L., Chandler, J.F., and Hartzler, B.M. 2012. Battling fatigue in aviation: Recent advancements in research and practice. *Journal of Medical Science* 32: 46–57.
Caska, T.J. and Molesworth, B.R.C. 2007. The effects of low dose caffeine on pilot performance. *International Journal of Applied Aviation Studies* 7: 244–255.
Chaplin, K. and Smith, A.P. 2011. Breakfast and snacks: Associations with cognitive failures, minor injuries, accidents and stress. *Nutrients* 3: 515–528.
Chaturvedi, A.K., Craft, K.J., Hickerson, J.S., Rogers, P.B., and Canfield, D.V. 2015. *Prevalence of Ethanol and Drugs in Civil Aviation Accident Pilot Fatalities, 2009–2013*. DOT/FAA/AM-15/13. Washington, DC: Federal Aviation Administration.
Co, E.L., Gregory, K.B., Johnson, J.M., and Rosekind, M.R. 1999. *Crew Factors in Flight Operations XI: A Survey of Fatigue Factors in Regional Airline Operations*. Report No: NASA/TM -1999-208799. Moffett Field, CA: NASA Ames Research Center.

Collins, W.E. and Dollar, C.S. 1996. *Fatal General Aviation Accidents Involving Spatial Disorientation: 1976–1992.* DOT/FAA/AM-96/21. Washington, DC: Federal Aviation Administration.

Cox, D., Gonder-Frederick, L., and Clarke, W. 1993. Driving decrements in type I diabetes during moderate hypoglycemia. *Diabetes* 42: 239–243.

Cox, D.J., Gonder-Frederick, L.A., Kovatchev, B.P., Julian, D.M., and Clarke, W.L. 2000. Progressive hypoglycemia's impact on driving simulation performance. *Diabetes Care* 23: 163–170.

Davenport, M. and Harris, D. 1992. The effect of low blood alcohol levels on pilot performance in a series of simulated approach and landing trials. *The International Journal of Aviation Psychology* 2: 271–280.

Drink Driving Limits. n.d. Retrieved on November 10, 2015 from: http://www.drinkdriving. org/worldwide_drink_driving_limits.php

Engstrom, P. 2003. Smoking: Hazardous to your aviation health. I Fly America Online. https://iflyamerica.org/smoking.asp

Evans, M.L. Pernet, A. Lomas, J. Jones, J., and Amiel, S.A. 2000. Delay in onset of awareness of acute hypoglycemia and of restoration of cognitive performance during recovery. *Diabetes Care* 23: 893–898.

Federal Aviation Administration. 2000. *Medical Facts for Pilots: Spatial Disorientation: Visual Illusions.* Publication AM-400-00/1. Oklahoma City, OK: Civil Aerospace Medical Institute.

Federal Aviation Administration. 2003. *Medical Facts for Pilots: Spatial Disorientation.* Publication AM-400-03/1. Oklahoma City, OK: Civil Aerospace Medical Institute.

Federal Aviation Administration. 2008. *Pilot's Handbook of Aeronautical Knowledge.* FAA-H-8083-25A. Washington, DC: Author.

Federal Aviation Administration. 2009. *Medical Facts for Pilots: Circadian Rhythm Disruption and Flying.* Publication No. AM-400-09/03. Oklahoma City, OK: Civil Aerospace Medical Institute.

Federal Aviation Administration. 2016. *Pilot's Handbook of Aeronautical Knowledge.* H-8083-25B. Washington, DC: Author.

Feldman, J. and Barshi, I. 2007. *The Effects of Blood Glucose Levels on Cognitive Performance: A Review of the Literature.* Technical report NASA/TM-2007-214555. Ames Research Center, Moffett Field, CA: National Aeronautics and Space Administration.

Flower, D.J.C. 2001. Alertness management in long-haul flying. *Transportation Research Part F* 4: 39–48.

Flight Safety Foundation n.d. Operator's guide to human factors in aviation: Vestibular system and illusions. Downloaded on March 31, 2017 from http://www.skybrary.aero/index.php/Vestibular_System_and_Illusions_(OGHFA_BN)

Fredholm, B.B., Battig, K., Holmen, J., Nehlig, A., and Zvartau, E.E. 1999. Actions of caffeine in the brain with special reference to factors that contribute to its widespread use. *Pharmacological Reviews* 51: 84–133.

Garland, D.J., Wise, J.A., and Hopkin, V.D. 1999. *Handbook of Aviation Human Factors.* Mahwah, NJ: Lawrence Erlbaum Associates.

Gibb, R., Ercoline, B., and Scharff, L. 2011. Spatial disorientation: Decades of pilot fatalities. *Aviation Space and Environmental Medicine* 82: 1–8.

Goode, J.H. 2003. Are pilots at risk of accidents due to fatigue? *Journal of Safety Research* 34: 309–313.

Griffith, C.D. and Mahadevan, S. 2006. *Sleep Deprivation Effect on Human Performance: A Meta-Analysis Approach.* Report INL/CON-06-01264. Idaho Falls, ID: Idaho National Laboratory.

Hancock, P.A. 1984. Effect of environmental temperature on display monitoring performance: An overview with practical implications. *Journal of the American Industrial Hygiene Association* 45: 122–126.

Harris, D. and Maxwell, E. 2001. Some considerations for the development of effective countermeasures to aircrew use of alcohol while flying. *The International Journal of Aviation Psychology* 11: 237–252.

Holloway, F.A. 1994. *Low-Dose Alcohol Effects on Human Behavior and Performance: A Review of Post-1984 Research.* DOT/FAA/AM-94/24. Washington, DC: Federal Aviation Administration.

Holmes, A., Al-Bayat, S., Hilditch, C., and Bourgeois-Bourgine, S. 2012. Sleep and sleepiness during an ultra long-range flight operation between the Middle East and United States. *Accident Analysis and Prevention* 45S: 27–31.

Horne, J.A. and Reyner, L.A. 1995. Driver sleepiness. *Journal of Sleep Research* 4: 23–29.

Janowsky, D.S., Meacham, M.P., Blaine, J.D., Schoor, M., and Bozzetti, L.P. 1976. Simulated flying performance after marijuana intoxication. *Aviation, Space, and Environmental Medicine* 47: 124–128.

Jouni, J.L., Huttunen, K.H., Lahtinen, T.M.M., Kilpelainen, A.A., Muhli, A.A., and Leino, T.K. 2007. Effect of caffeine on simulator flight performance in sleep-deprived military pilot students. *Military Medicine* 172: 982–987.

Kilgore, W.D.S., Liipizzi, E.L., Kamimori, G.H., and Balkin, T. 2007. Caffeine effects on risky decision making after 75 hours of sleep deprivation. *Aviation, Space, and Environmental Medicine* 78: 957–962.

Kilpeläinen, A.A., Huttunen, K.H., Lohi, J.J., and Lyytinen, H. 2010. Effect of caffeine on vigilance and cognitive performance during extended wakefulness. *International Journal of Aviation Psychology* 20: 144–159.

Kirkham, W.R., Collins, W.E., Grape, P.M., Simpson, J.M., and Wallace, T.F. 1978. *Spatial Disorientation in General Aviation Accidents.* FAA-AM-78-13. Washington, DC: Federal Aviation Administration.

Klein, E.K. and Wegmann, H.M. 1980. *Significance of Circadian Rhythms in Aerospace Operation.* Technical report AGARD-AG-147. Neuilly-sur-Seine, France: Advisory Group for Aerospace Research & Development, North Atlantic Treaty Organization.

Lamond, N. and Dawson, D. 1999. Quantifying the performance impairment associated with fatigue. *Journal of Sleep Research* 8: 255–262.

Legg, S., Hill, S., GIlbey, A., Raman, A., Schlader, Z., and Mundel, T. 2014. Effect of mild hypoxia on working memory, complex logical reasoning, and risk judgment. *The International Journal of Aviation Psychology* 24: 126–140.

Leirer, V.O., Yesavage, J.A., and Morrow, D.G. 1989. Marijuana, aging, and task difficulty effects on pilot performance. *Aviation, Space, and Environmental Medicine* 60: 1145–1152.

Leirer, V.O., Yesavage, J.A., and Morrow, D.G. 1991. Marijuana carry-over effects on aircraft pilot performance. *Aviation, Space, and Environmental Medicine* 62: 221–227.

Levine, J.M., Greenbaum, G.D., and Notkin, E.R. 1973. *The Effect of Alcohol on Human Performance: A Classification and Integration of Research Findings.* Unpublished report. Washington, DC: American Institutes for Research.

Levine, J.M., Kramer, G.G., and Levine, E.N. 1975. Effects of alcohol on human performance: An integration of research findings based on an abilities classification. *Journal of Applied Psychology* 60: 285–293.

Liebermann, H.R. 2003. Nutrition, brain function and cognitive performance. *Appetite* 40: 245–254.

Lim, J. and Dinges, D.F. 2008. Sleep deprivation and vigilant attention. *Annals of the New York Academy of Science* 1129: 305–322.

Lindseth, G.N., Lindseth, P.D., Jensen, W.C., Petros, T.V., Helland, B.D., and Fossum, D.L. 2011. Dietary effects on cognition and pilots' flight performance. *The International Journal of Aviation Psychology* 21: 269–282.

Lindseth, P.D., Lindseth, G.N., Petros, T.V., Jensen, W.C., and Caspers J. 2013. Effects of hydration on cognitive function of pilots. *Military Medicine* 178, 792–798.

Lopez, M., Previc, F.H., Fischer, J., Heitz, R.P., and Engle, R.W. 2012. Effects of sleep deprivation on cognitive performance of United States Air Force pilots. *Journal of Applied Research in Memory and Cognition* 1: 27–33.

Mackworth, N.H. 1950. *Researches on the Measurement of Human Performance.* Medical Research Council Special Report 268. London, UK: HMSO.

McGrath, B.J., Rupert, A.H., and Guedry, F.E. 2002. Analysis of spatial disorientation mishaps in the US Navy. *The RTO HFM Symposium on Spatial Disorientation in Military Vehicles: Causes, Consequences and Cures,* April 15–17, 2002, RTO-MP-086. Neuilly-sur-Seine Cedex, France: North Atlantic Treaty Organization, Research and Technology Organization.

Mehmedic, Z., Chandra, S., Slade, D., Denham, H., Foster, S., Patel, A.S., Ross, S.A., Khan, I.A., and ElSohly, M.A. 2010. Potency trends of delta-9-THC and other cannabinoids in confiscated cannabis preparations from 1993 to 2008. *Journal of Forensic Sciences* 55: 1209–1217.

Merriam-Webster Ninth New Collegiate Dictionary. 1985. Springfield, MA: Merriam-Webster.

Mertens, H.W. and Collins, W.E. 1985. *The Effects of Age, Sleep Deprivation, and Altitude on Complex Performance.* FAA-AM-85-3. Oklahoma City, OK: Civil Aerospace Medical Institute.

Mertens, H.W. and Lewis, M.F. 1981. *Effect of Different Runway Size on Pilot Performance During Simulated Night Landing Approaches.* FAA-AM-81-6. Washington, DC: Federal Aviation Administration.

Mumaw, R.J., Groen, E., Fucke, L., Anderson, R., Bos, J., and Houben, M. n.d. A new tool for analyzing the potential influence of vestibular illusions. Downloaded on November 15, 2015 from: http://www.isasi.org/Documents/library/technical-papers/2015/Vestibular%20Illusion%20Tool.pdf

Mumenthaler, M.S., Yesavage, J.A., Taylor, J.L., O'Hara, R., Friedman, L., Lee, H., and Kraemer, H.C. 2003. Psychoactive drugs and pilot performance: A comparison of nicotine, donepezil, and alcohol effects. *Neuropsychopharmacology* 28: 1366–1373.

National Research Council. 2011. *The Effects of Commuting on Pilot Fatigue.* Washington, DC: National Academies Press.

Nesthus, T.E., Rush, L.L., and Wreggit, S.S. 1997. *Effects of Mild Hypoxia on Pilot Performance at General Aviation Altitudes.* DOT/FAA/AM-97/0. Washington, DC: Federal Aviation Administration.

Newman, D.G. 2004. *Alcohol and Human Performance from an Aviation Perspective: A Review.* Unnumbered research report. Canberra, Australia: Australian Transport Safety Bureau.

NTSB (National Transportation Safety Board). 1994. *Uncontrolled Collision with Terrain, American International Airways Flight 808.* NTSB/AAR-94/04. Washington, DC: Author.

NTSB (National Transportation Safety Board). 2014. *Drug Use Trends in Aviation: Assessing The Risk of Pilot Impairment.* Safety Study NTSB/SS-14/01. Washington, DC: Author.

Pepler, R.D. 1958. Warmth and performance: An investigation in the tropics. *Ergonomics* 2: 63–88.

Peters, J.M. 1967. Factors affecting caffeine toxicity: A review of the literature. *The Journal of Clinical Pharmacology and the Journal of New Drugs* 7: 131–141.

Petrie, K.J. and Dawson, A.G. 1997. Symptoms of fatigue and coping strategies in international pilots. *The International Journal of Aviation Psychology* 7: 251–258.

Petros, T., Bridewell, J., Jensen, W., Ferraro, F.R., Bates, J., Moulton, P., Turnwell, S., Rawley, D., Howe, T., and Gorder, D. 2003. Postintoxication effects of alcohol on flight performance after moderate and high blood alcohol levels. *The International Journal of Aviation Psychology* 13: 287–300.

Pilcher, J.J. and Huffcutt, A.I. 1996. Effects of sleep deprivation on performance: A meta-analysis. *Sleep* 19: 318–26.

Pilcher, J.J., Nadler, E., and Busch, C. 2002. Effects of hot and cold temperature exposure on performance: A meta-analytic review. *Ergonomics* 45: 682–698.

Previc, F.H., Lopez, N., Ercoline, W.R., Daluz, C.M., Workman, A.J., Evans, R.H., and Dillon, N.A. 2009. The effects of sleep deprivation on flight performance, instrument scanning, and physiological arousal in pilots. *The International Journal of Aviation Psychology* 19: 326–346.

Rehm, J., Rehn, N., Room, R., Monteiro, M., Gmel, G., Jernigan, D., and Frick, U.L. 2003. The global distribution of average volume of alcohol consumption and patterns of drinking. *European Addiction Research* 9: 147–156.

Roach, G.R., Sargent, C., Darwent, D., and Dawson, D. 2012. Duty periods with early start times restrict the amount of sleep obtained by short-haul airline pilots. *Accident Analysis and Prevention* 45S: 22–26.

Rosekind, M.R., Co, E.L., Gregory, K.B., and Miller, O.L. 2000. *Crew Factors in Flight Operations XIII: A Survey of Fatigue Factors in Corporate/Executive Aviation Operations*. NASA/TM-2000-209610. Moffett Field, CA: NASA Ames Research Center.

Ross, L.E., Yeazel, L.M., and Chau, A.W. 1992. Pilot performance with blood alcohol concentrations below 0.04%. *Aviation, Space, and Environmental Medicine* 63: 951–956.

Salazar, G.J. 2007. *Medical Facts for Pilots: Fatigue in Aviation*. OK-07-193. Oklahoma City, OK: FAA Civil Aerospace Medical Institute.

SAMHSA (Substance Abuse and Mental Health Services Administration). 2013. *Results from the 2012 National Survey on Drug Use and Health: Summary of National Findings*. NSDUH Series H-46, HHS Publication No. SMA 13-4795. Rockville, MD: Author.

Sharma, M.D. and Ravi, R. 2010. Visual effects of long term active smoking: Are aircrew flying NVG-aided missions at a disadvantage? *Indian Journal of Aerospace Medicine* 54: 18–25.

Shen, J., Barbera, J., and Shapiro, C.M. 2006. Distinguishing sleepiness and fatigue: Focus on definition and measurement. *Sleep Medicine Reviews* 10: 63–76.

Sherwood, N., Kerr, J.S., and Hindmarch, I. 1992. Psychomotor performance in smokers following single and repeated doses of nicotine gum. *Psychopharmacology* 108: 432–436.

Smith, A. 2002. Effects of caffeine on human behavior. *Food and Chemical Toxicology* 40: 1243–1255.

U.S. Army. n.d. *Aviation Medicine*. Sub-course AV0593. Washington, DC: U.S. Army Institute for Professional Development.

U.S. Army. 2009. *Aeromedical Training for Flight Personnel*. Training circular 3-04.93 [FM 3-04.301]. Washington, DC: Author. Chapter 9, Spatial disorientation. Retrieved from: https://rdl.train.army.mil/catalog-ws/view/100.ATSC/C696BACA-168F-4B4A-9750-BB

Valk, P.J., Van Roon, D.B., Simons, R.M., and Rikken, G. 2004. Desloratadine shows no effect on performance during 6 h at 8,000 ft simulated altitude. *Aviation, Space, and Environmental Medicine* 75: 433–438.

von Dongen, H.P.A., Caldwell, J.A., and Caldwell, J.L. 2006. Investigating systematic individual differences in sleep-deprived performance on a high-fidelity flight simulator. *Behavior Research Methods* 38: 333–343.

Weigmann, D.A., Stanny, R.R., McKay, D.L., Neri, D.F., and McCardie, A.H. 1996. Methamphetamine effects on cognitive processing during extended wakefulness. *The International Journal of Aviation Psychology* 6: 379–397.

Weiler, J.M., Bloomfield, J.R., Woodworth, G.G., Grant, A.R., Layton, T.A., Brown, T.L., McKenzie, D.R., Baker, T.W., and Watson, G.S. 2000. Effects of fexofenadine, diphenhydramine, and alcohol on driving performance: A randomized, placebo-controlled trial in the Iowa driving simulator. *Annals of Internal Medicine* 132: 354–363.

Yesavage, J.A., Leirer, V.O., Denari, M., and Hollister, L.E. 1985. Carry-over effects of marijuana intoxication on aircraft pilot performance: A preliminary report. *American Journal of Psychiatry* 142: 1325–1329.

Yesavage, J.A., Mumenthaler, M.S., Taylor, J.L., Friedman, L., O'Hara, R., and Sheikh, J. 2002. Donepezil® and flight simulator performance: Effects on retention of complex skills. *Neurology* 59: 123–125.

Zeller, A.F. 1975. Joint committee on aviation pathology: IX. Alcohol and other drugs in aircraft accidents. *Aviation, Space, and Environmental Medicine* 46: 1271–1274.

4 Abilities and Personality Traits

4.1 INTRODUCTION

When we describe someone, we often do so in terms of their abilities and personality traits. So, we might say that a person is great on the controls, but has trouble getting along with other crew members. Humans are quite good at detecting the strengths and weaknesses of others—their abilities and the aspects of their personality that will help or hinder task performance and group interaction. This was, and remains, an important survival skill in a species that lives in community groups where survival depends on knowing who can do tasks well and who can be depended upon to perform their tasks. When hunting wooly mammoths, you really need to know who can throw the spear accurately and who will not turn and run at the first sign of danger.

While the wooly mammoths are long gone, abilities and personality traits remain very important in our understanding of how people perform complex activities. Ability and personality constructs* (such as intelligence, psychomotor coordination, and conscientiousness) affect how pilots make decisions, how they interact with other crew members, how they use or misuse licit and illicit drugs, and how well they absorb and retain training, to give but a few examples. This chapter will provide you with an overview of topics that will pervade all of the chapters that follow. You may have a good commonsense understanding of abilities and personality, but in the following pages you may well find there is a great deal more to these concepts than meets the eye.

4.2 INDIVIDUAL DIFFERENCES

Like snowflakes, no two people are identical—at least after the first few days following birth. Even monozygotic (so-called identical) twins who begin life with the same DNA soon begin to develop different abilities, interests, and personality traits. Differences among individuals who share less DNA are even more remarkable. Besides obvious physical differences (e.g., height, weight, gender, hair color), people also differ with respect to their mental abilities and personality traits. In some instances, to be discussed in detail in later chapters, these mental abilities and personality traits may be related to important behavior. For example, differences in psychomotor coordination ability may lead to differences in skill of flying an airplane. Differences in fine motor dexterity may result in differences among individuals in

---

* Constructs are psychological attributes on which people differ from one another. Generally, they refer to something that cannot be directly observed (unlike characteristics such as height or weight) but must be inferred from observations of behavior. Thus, we infer that there is a construct called intelligence because we see differences among individuals in what everyone mostly agrees is intelligent behavior.

the time it takes them to repair a defective engine. Differences in spatial ability may produce differences among individuals in their speed of recognition of an impending conflict between the targets on a radar screen. Having more (or sometimes less) of an ability or trait can sometimes be shown to be related to better (or worse) performance at a task. Which abilities and traits are related to performance, how they are related, and how they are measured are major topics of interest to psychologists and the subject of extensive, continuing research.

Subsequent chapters will discuss many abilities and personality traits and some of the research that has identified important abilities and traits for personnel selection, decision-making, and other aviation activities. For now, let us simply look at these topics in general, with special emphasis on the abilities and traits that have been shown to be important to aviation.

4.3   ABILITIES

To begin, let us start with a definition of an ability. The Dictionary of Psychology (Coleman 2001) defines ability as developed skill, competence, or power to do something, whether mental or physical. This is consistent with the everyday notion of an ability as being more or less synonymous with capacity. If a person has a particular ability, it is usually taken to mean that he or she has a capacity to do something, usually at a moderate to high level of competence. The child who is able to play a musical instrument proficiently is said to have musical ability, while the adult who cannot play even the simplest tune is not.

4.3.1   INTELLIGENCE

Closely related to the idea of ability is the notion of intelligence. Like ability, and so many other human characteristics, everyone thinks they know what intelligence is, but it proves a rather difficult concept to define. When two dozen prominent psychologists were asked to define intelligence, they gave two dozen different definitions (Neisser et al. 1996). Relying on the dictionary for a definition is not totally satisfactory, since it defines intelligence as, "...the ability to learn or understand or to deal with new or trying situations, or the ability to apply knowledge to manipulate one's environment" (Merriam-Webster 2016). The difficulty here is that the dictionary defines intelligence as an ability; however, current theories of intelligence regard abilities as components of intelligence. Hence, the dictionary definition is somewhat circular. For the current purposes, it may be best to simply consider intelligence as the title accorded an aggregate of many different, but interrelated, cognitive processes and capacities.

4.3.1.1   Models of Intelligence

4.3.1.1.1   The Structure of Intellect

One of the earlier researchers to consider the nature of intelligence was J.P. Guilford who proposed what he termed a Structure of Intellect (SI) model. In Guilford's model, an individual's performance on intelligence tests may be attributed to a large number of underlying mental abilities. His SI theory proposed 150 different intellectual abilities organized along three dimensions: operations, content, and products (Guilford 1956).

Guilford's SI model has been criticized, largely because of the statistical techniques used to construct the model. For example, Jensen (1998) noted that Guilford based his SI model on the failure to observe a g-factor* among the many cognitive tests of U.S. Air Force (USAF) personnel that he used as the basis for the model. Later reanalysis of the data from those tests demonstrated that the correlations among the tests in the data sets were positive (Mackintosh 1998).

For the most part, Guilford's SI model of human abilities has been superseded by other models, and today has few supporters. It is mentioned here simply to illustrate one approach to disaggregating the overall concept of intelligence into its component parts, and as a caution to readers who may find textbooks that give the impression that this model is valid, when it is not.

4.3.1.1.2 Fluid and Crystallized Intelligence

The concepts of fluid and crystallized intelligence were put forth by Raymond Cattell and were elaborated by his student John Horn. *Fluid* intelligence is the capacity to reason and solve novel problems, independent of any knowledge from the past. Fluid intelligence includes such abilities as pattern recognition, abstract reasoning, and problem-solving (Cattell 1963; Horn and Cattell 1966; Horn 1968). *Crystallized* intelligence is the capacity to use skills, knowledge, and experience. Crystallized intelligence is demonstrated largely through one's vocabulary and general knowledge and improves to some degree with age (Jaeggi et al. 2008).

Fluid intelligence might be considered as providing the underlying mechanisms and capacity (similar to the hardware in a computer) that supports the acquisition and development of other capacities (similar to the software in a computer). This hardware/software analogy is consistent with findings that fluid intelligence is more affected by brain injury than is crystallized intelligence (Suchy et al. 2007).

There are various measures of fluid and crystallized intelligence. The Raven Progressive Matrices (RPM; Raven et al. 2003) is a nonverbal multiple choice test that is often used to assess fluid intelligence. The RPM has participants complete a series of drawings by identifying relevant features based on the spatial organization of an array of objects. Participants then choose one object that matches one or more of the identified features (see Figure 4.1 for an example†). Since it relies on nonverbal reasoning skills, it is fairly independent of crystallized intelligence.

Crystallized intelligence relies upon specific, acquired knowledge, and hence is measured by a number of scales. For example, the verbal subscale of Wechsler Adult Intelligence Scale (WAIS) is considered a good measure of crystallized intelligence.

Both fluid and crystallized intelligence measures have been found to correlate significantly with academic performance; however, crystallized ability measures have

---

* Psychometric g: Psychologists have found that all mental ability tests are somewhat positively intercorrelated, suggesting that performance on these tests may all be dependent to greater or lesser extent on some common cognitive function or structure. They refer to this common core or general mental capacity as "psychometric g," or sometimes simply "g."
† This is a very easy example. But, if you have trouble, then the answer is D.

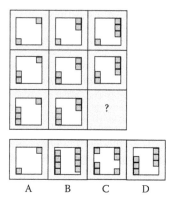

FIGURE 4.1   RPM example item.

been found to be superior to fluid ability measures. The relationships of fluid and crystallized intelligence to academic performance were evaluated in a meta-analysis of over 400 primary studies conducted over a span of 100 years. This meta-analysis showed that although measures of fluid intelligence were predictive of learning, crystallized ability measures were superior to the fluid measures (Postlewaithe 2011).

4.3.1.1.3   Cattell–Horn–Carroll Theory of Cognitive Abilities

At present, the dominant conceptualization of intelligence is that it is hierarchical. More nearly general abilities are higher up in the hierarchy, while more specific abilities are lower in the hierarchy. This view arises to a large degree from the findings of Carroll (1993), who used exploratory factor analysis on over 460 human cognitive ability data sets to arrive at a comprehensive, systematic organization of the published research. Through his meta-factor analysis, Carroll was able to present an empirically based taxonomy of human cognitive ability elements in a single organized framework (McGrew 2009). It also incorporates the fluid and crystallized intelligence concepts of Cattell.

The hierarchy proposed by Carroll consists of three strata:

- *Stratum I*: Includes narrow, specific abilities (e.g., spelling ability, speed of reasoning)
- *Stratum II*: Includes group-factor abilities (e.g., fluid intelligence, crystallized intelligence)
- *Stratum III*: A single general intelligence factor

4.3.1.2   Other Viewpoints on Intelligence

Several alternatives to the hierarchical models of intelligence (such as the C–H–C model) based largely on the dissection of the general intelligence factor (g) have been proposed. Gardner (1983) suggested that there are relatively distinct, independent modules of intelligence. His original multiple intelligences theory proposed seven distinct multiple intelligences: (a) linguistic, (b) logical–mathematical, (c) spatial, (d) musical, (e) bodily kinesthetic, (f) interpersonal, and (g) intrapersonal.

The concept of emotional intelligence (EI), which is the ability to perceive accurately, appraise, and express emotion, to understand emotion and emotional knowledge, and the ability to regulate emotions was introduced by Mayer and Salovey (1993). The concept of EI received widespread popular attention following the publication of *Emotional Intelligence* by Daniel Goleman (1995). Goleman suggested that EI was as important as the general intelligence factor (g) for success in multiple aspects of a person's life. Some studies have shown that people with high EI have better mental health, job performance, and leadership skills. For example, Goleman (1998) reported that EI accounted for 67% of the abilities required for superior performance in leaders; additionally, EI was twice as important as general mental intelligence or technical expertise. However, these results have been challenged by researchers who suggest that when ability and personality are controlled for, the contribution of EI on leadership and managerial performance is nonsignificant (Cavazotte et al. 2012). Further, general intelligence correlates very closely with leadership (Atwater and Yammarinal 1993). Reviews of the studies in support of EI (e.g., Hunt and Fitzgerald 2013) have generally concluded that poor research methodology has exaggerated the significance of EI.

Another definition of human intelligence is offered by Robert Sternberg. Sternberg (1985, p. 45) defines it as a "…mental activity directed toward purposive adaptation to, selection and shaping of, real-world environments relevant to one's life." He suggests that while the basic information-processing components underlying intelligence are the same, different contexts and different tasks require different kinds of intelligence (Sternberg et al. 2001). His triarchic theory of intelligence comprises three parts: componential, experiential, and practical. The componential part is associated with analytical giftedness. This is influential in being able to take apart problems and see solutions overlooked by others. This is the most often tested part of the triarchic model (Sternberg 1997).

The experiential part deals with a task based on its degree of familiarity. Sternberg divides the role of experience into two elements: novelty and automation. A novel situation is one that has not previously been experienced. Individuals who are adept at managing novel situations can find new ways of solving it that would be overlooked by most people. In contrast to the novel task, an automated process is one that has been performed many times and can be completed with little or no thought. Automated processes can run in parallel with other processes.

The third part of intelligence, called contextual or practical intelligence, is often referred to as "street smarts." By adaptation, shaping, and selection, individuals create an ideal fit between their environment and themselves. Adaptation occurs when individuals change themselves to better fit the surroundings. For example, pilots might get a new type rating so that they could fly a newly acquired aircraft. Shaping occurs when individuals change the environment to better fit themselves. An example of shaping would be the addition of a new navigation system to someone's aircraft so that they could perform GPS approaches. Finally, selection occurs when the individual seeks out a completely new environment to replace the previous environment. An example would be someone who moves to a different part of the country (or even a different country) to look for better employment.

Clearly, the triarchic theory of intelligence is a considerable departure from the traditional theories based upon general intelligence. It places much more importance on the ability to achieve success in life based on an individual's personal standards and sociocultural context and seems to capture important aspects of intelligence (or at least intelligent behavior) not addressed by conventional theories. However, it has not been without its critics. For example, Gottfredson (2003) has criticized the unempirical nature of triarchic theory. Because traditional intelligence tests show moderate correlations with income and an even higher correlation with occupational prestige, it cannot be said that they do not measure practical intelligence. Moreover, traditional IQ tests can predict the ability to stay out of jail and remain alive—arguably valid indices of practical intelligence or "street smarts."

Although several alternative theories of human intelligence have been proposed, they have generally not received the level of support accorded the traditional theories based on general mental intelligence and its subsidiary abilities. This has sometimes been due to deficiencies in the research studies that purported to support the new theories, and sometimes because the traditional theories account for observed data as well or better than the new theory. At present, therefore, the tests and other measures used in selection and training of aviation personnel are, to the best of the authors' knowledge, all based on the traditional theories. Perhaps, a test of "air smarts" will someday be used to assess pilots or controllers, but that time has not yet come.[*]

4.3.2 Abilities Relevant to Aviation

What abilities should pilots (or air traffic controllers, or aviation maintenance technicians) have, in what degree, to complete their training, and be competent and safe over a career spanning 40 years or more? This question has occupied psychologists for over a century. Beginning around the start of World War I, the question of what qualities are needed to be a good pilot has been examined by legions of military and civilian researchers. Because most of this research took place in the context of selecting individuals for military (and occasionally civil) flight training, it will be dealt with in detail in the chapter on selection. For the present, let us simply look at the broad range of abilities that have been suggested as relevant.

In some cases, relevant abilities have been identified through the process of job/ task analysis. Typically, in such an analysis, a group of experienced individuals (e.g., senior flight instructors) are asked to identify the abilities required for a job from an extensive list of potential abilities. One such list of 52 human abilities ranging from verbal comprehension to selective attention was developed by Fleishman (Fleishman et al. 1984; Fleishman and Reilly 2001). When conducting a job analysis, subject matter experts review this list of 52 abilities and provide estimates of the importance of each ability when performing various job tasks. For example, they might be asked to estimate the importance of each ability when performing a preflight inspection,

---

[*] One exception might be the Pilot Situational Judgment Test (Driskill et al. 1998; Hunter 2003) that asks pilots to choose the best of four alternative responses to an aviation scenario.

or when performing a nonprecision approach. Although several ability taxonomies have been developed for job analysis (see Knapp et al. 1995), the Fleishman taxonomy is by far the most often used, at least in the area of pilot selection.

In a review of KSAOs (knowledge, skill, ability, other factors) for military pilot selection, Damos (2011) found that of the nine studies she reviewed, only two did not use some version of Fleishman's taxonomy. One of those two (Meyer et al. 1974a,b) used a unique taxonomy, never again used for pilot selection, while the other study (Youngling et al. 1977) did not use any identifiable taxonomy. This is consistent with the findings of a study conducted by Driskill et al. (1989) in which 36 general and special purposed taxonomies were identified from a review of the literature. From that group, seven methods were subjected to further evaluation, and it was determined that Fleishman's Ability Requirements Scales (ARS) method was the most appropriate for the identification of ability requirement for USAF occupational specialties.

Although there is general agreement that the Fleishman taxonomy is the best approach to identifying abilities required for occupations, such as pilots, the results of the application of that analysis tool are notably variable. Table 4.1 lists the abilities,

TABLE 4.1
Average USAF Pilot Ratings of Cognitive Ability Relevance to Pilot Qualification

Ability	Average Rating
Situational awareness	4.88
Spatial orientation	4.83
Task management (multitasking)	4.74
Memorization	4.71
Listening comprehension	4.69
Psychomotor rate control	4.45
Mathematical computation	4.38
Perceptual vigilance	4.37
Psychomotor choice reaction time	4.33
Psychomotor hand/eye coordination	4.31
Reading comprehension	4.24
Psychomotor finger dexterity	4.22
Oral expression	4.12
Visualization	4.11
Deductive reasoning	3.90
Inductive reasoning	3.86
Psychomotor multi-limb coordination	3.86
Pattern recognition	3.62
Mathematical reasoning	3.56
Psychomotor arm–hand steadiness	3.51
Written expression	3.32

Source: Agee, N. et al. 2009. *Air Force Officer Selection Technical Requirements Survey (AFOSTRS), Volume I: Analysis of Quantitative Results.* Randolph AFB, TX: Air Force Personnel Center.

TABLE 4.2

Average USAF Fighter Pilot Rankings and Ratings of Ability Relevance to Major Tasks

Ability	Average Rating
Situational awareness	4.44
Timesharing	4.43
Memorization	4.42
Perceptual speed	4.37
Selective attention	4.29
Divided attention	4.19
Spatial orientation	4.14
Response orientation	4.13
Flexibility of closure	4.12
Information ordering	4.04
Psychomotor coordination	3.95
Control precision	3.59
Oral comprehension	3.37
Oral expression	3.35
Visualization	3.21
Written comprehension	3.00
Number facility	2.70
Rate control	1.54
Written expression	1.23

Source: Carretta, T.R. et al. 1993. *The Identification of Ability Requirements and Selection Instruments for Fighter Pilot Training.* AL/HR-TP-1993-0016. Brooks AFB, TX: Armstrong Laboratory.

ranked in order of importance, reported as relevant by USAF pilots in a study conducted by Agee et al. (2009). In an earlier study conducted by Carretta et al. (1993), a somewhat different listing of abilities (shown in Table 4.2) was found. Although both studies found that the most important ability reported by both sets of subject matter experts was situational awareness, the remaining abilities are rather striking in their variability. They are also notably different from the list of abilities (shown in Table 4.3) rated as important for U.S. Army pilots (Miller et al. 1981). However, in a more recent study of U.S. Army pilots (Kubisiak and Katz 2006), situational awareness was found to be among the most important abilities.

This variation in the lists of relevant abilities for pilots may be due to variation in the exact form of the analysis instrument used. For example, the Fleishman ARS does not contain situational awareness as a distinct ability; researchers amend the scale by adding abilities (such as situational awareness) that they consider important, but which are not contained in the standard instrument. Further, there may be differences among the groups assessed. Arguably, the abilities required for USAF (predominately fixed-wing jet) pilots may not be the same as those required for Army

TABLE 4.3
Attributes Rated Most Important by U.S. Army Aviators

Attributes

Perceptual speed
Speed of closure
Flexibility of closure
Problem sensitivity
Inductive reasoning
Deductive reasoning
Spatial orientation
Visualization
Verbal expression
Divided attention
Selective attention
Multi-limb coordination
Control precision
Rate control
Reaction time
Establish priorities

> *Source:* Miller, J.T. et al. 1981. *Mission Track Selection Process for the Army Initial Entry Rotary Wing Flight Training Program*, Vol. I. St. Louis, MO: McDonnell Douglas Astronautics Co.

(predominately helicopter) pilots. In addition, the nature of the pilot job and hence the abilities required to be a pilot may change over time.

4.3.3 ABILITY REQUIREMENTS FOR REMOTELY PILOTED VEHICLE* OPERATORS

Besides changes in the tasks, and corresponding abilities, required for pilots in traditional aircraft, the growing use of remotely piloted aircraft (more generally, RPVs) gives rise to a whole new set of operator tasks and ability requirements. Howse (2011) surveyed over 200 publications in which eight were found to contain lists of the KSAOs required for RPV operators. Although comparisons among the results from the eight studies were problematic due to the failure by most of the researchers to use a consistent, well-defined taxonomy (such as the Fleishman ARS), Howse was able to identify some ability areas that are likely to become more important in future RPV operations. For example, oral and written comprehension are likely to increase in importance, partly as a function of the increased teaming of manned and remotely

---

* There is a great deal of variability in the terminology used to refer to individuals who control vehicles (both aircraft and other systems) remotely. An early term, still used in some circles, was unmanned aerial vehicle (UAV). More recently, the terms remotely operated or remotely piloted have come into fashion, coupled with either aircraft (as in remotely piloted aircraft) or vehicle (which could be an aircraft-, marine-, or land-based system). We will use the acronyms RPV and UAV synonymously to refer to the devices and to the individuals who control aircraft in which they are not physically located.

operated vehicles. In these operations, communication between the RPV operators, located potentially many miles distant from the conflict zone, and the aircrew flying in close proximity to the target becomes critical—both for the sake of mission completion and for the safety of the aircrew. As Howse (p. 43) notes, "The demand for specific abilities and other attributes in persons entering training as RPA operators is driven by changes occurring in system capabilities, organization, manpower, and missions."

4.3.4 SUMMARY

Intellectual capacity may be broken down into components, labeled abilities. Many of these abilities are related to human performance in aviation. Later chapters will discuss how measures of these abilities may be used to predict how individuals will perform in flight training, and how aviation systems must be designed to accommodate limitations of individuals' abilities. The opinions of subject matter experts differ from study to study on the relative importance of specific abilities. However, at best these opinions can only serve as general guides. Ultimately, the relevance or contribution of each ability becomes an empirical matter that must be determined through well-designed research. Notably, situational awareness, which is the ability most often highly ranked as important for pilots, does not appear on the Fleishman ARS and is not actually an ability in the traditional sense of the word. That is, there is no evidence for a general ability that corresponds to what we term situational awareness. Rather, situational awareness seems to be specific to a particular environment; hence, it may be better regarded as an acquired skill, rather than an innate ability.

4.4 PERSONALITY TRAITS

Like intelligence and ability, everyone knows what they mean by personality, but they have a very difficult time articulating a coherent definition. The Merriam-Webster Dictionary offers several definitions, among which the most relevant seems to be "the totality of an individual's behavioral and emotional characteristics." This is very close to the definition provided by the Dictionary of Psychology (Coleman 2001): "The sum total of the behavioral and mental characteristics that are distinctive of an individual." Both those definitions imply a summing up of a number of characteristics. So, personality might be considered a meta-construct, in the same sense that intelligence is the sum of a large number of related, but independent abilities. Similarly, personality might be considered as the sum of a large number of personality traits, which can be defined as habitual patterns of behavior, thought, and emotion. Traits are relatively stable over time, they differ across individuals, and they influence behavior.

The importance of traits to human interaction is reflected in the large number of trait-names in the English language. A study by Allport and Odbert (1936) showed that there were almost 18,000 trait-names in Webster's Unabridged New International Dictionary. Of that number, about 4500 clearly symbolized personality traits (e.g., aggressive, introverted). The problem for psychologists was how to organize this large number of traits. That is, how are these traits interrelated? Are there really 4500 distinct human personality traits? Or, as is more likely, are there only a few actual traits? If so, how are the trait-names related to these underlying traits?

4.4.1 SEARCHING FOR STRUCTURE IN PERSONALITY

One of the foremost leaders of the search for a more parsimonious understanding of personality was Raymond Cattell. Cattell reorganized the list of adjectives from Allport and Odbert into 171 personality descriptors. These descriptors were used to describe the personality in multiple empirical studies (Cattell 1943). Through the use of factor analysis, he was able to identify 16 personality factors from among the 171 individual descriptors. These 16 factors (listed in Table 4.4) were proposed as the cornerstones upon which personality is built. Each of the 16 factors is bipolar and is called by the name of the positive pole. The personality inventory (16PF™) created by Cattell measures a person's placement along a continuum for each of the 16 personality factors. Thus, a person might be characterized by a high score on the Warmth Factor, an intermediate score on the Reasoning Factor, a low score on the Emotional Stability Factor, and so on.

A somewhat different approach to understanding personality is that of Eysenck (1997, 1992), who suggested that personality is reducible to three major traits: neuroticism, extraversion, and psychoticism. Neuroticism refers to an individual's

---

TABLE 4.4
Cattell's 16 Personality Factors

Low-Range Descriptors	Primary Factor	High-Range Descriptors
Cool, reserved	Warmth	Outgoing, kindly
Concrete thinking, lower intelligence	Reasoning	Abstract thinking, higher intelligence
Affected by feelings, changeable	Emotional stability	Adaptive, mature
Submissive, deferential	Dominance	Forceful, assertive
Sober, serious	Liveliness	Enthusiastic, animated
Expedient, nonconforming	Rule-consciousness	Dutiful, conforming
Shy, timid	Social boldness	Bold, venturesome
Tough-minded, unsentimental	Sensitivity	Tinder-minded, sentimental
Trusting, accepting	Vigilance	Suspicious, skeptical
Practical, grounded	Abstractedness	Imaginative, impractical
Forthright, open	Privateness	Shrewd, discreet
Self-assured, secure	Apprehension	Self-doubting, worried
Conservative, traditional	Openness to change	Experimental, liberal
Group-oriented, affiliative	Self-reliance	Self-sufficient, solitary
Undisciplined, flexible	Perfectionism	Organized, compulsive
Relaxed, tranquil	Tension	High energy, impatient

Source: Cattell, H.E.P. and Mead, A.D. 2008. The sixteen personality factor questionnaire (16 PF). In Boyle, G.J., Matthews, G., and Saklofske, D.H. (Eds.), *The Sage Handbook of Personality Theory and Assessment* (pp. 135–159). Thousand Oaks, CA: Sage Publications.

tendency to become upset or emotional. Extraversion refers to the outward projection of one's personality through gregarious, outgoing, sociable behavior, while psychoticism is a personality pattern typified by aggressiveness and interpersonal hostility. As with Cattell, these factors are bipolar dimensions. Extroversion is the opposite of introversion. Neuroticism is the opposite of emotional stability, while psychoticism is the opposite of self-control.

Eysenck developed his theory based upon observations of patients in a psychiatric hospital in London during the 1940s. On the basis of the observations, he compiled a battery of questions about behavior, which he then administered to 700 soldiers being treated at the hospital (Eysenck 1997). He found that there were linkages among the soldiers' responses to the questions, which suggested that they reflected different personality traits. Using factor analysis, he identified the three major traits, which are sometimes referred to as supertraits because of their placement at the apex of a hierarchical structure ranging from specific responses and behaviors at the bottom up through habits (clusters of specific behaviors, such as generosity), traits (collections of related habits, such as friendliness), to the superfactors (neuroticism, extroversion, and psychoticism).

4.4.2 FIVE-FACTOR MODEL

The models of personality proposed by Cattell and by Eysenck were precursors, to some degree, to the Five-Factor Model (FFM) of personality, which is the dominant model at present. This model was first proposed by Tupes and Christal (1961) who analyzed the intercorrelations among ratings on 35 personality traits, selected as representative of the personality domain, for 8 independent samples. Five recurrent factors emerged from each analysis, which Tupes and Christal labeled as (1) surgency/extroversion, (2) agreeableness, (3) dependability, (4) emotional stability, and (5) culture. The traits comprising those factors are shown in Table 4.5.

Because the results from the work by Tupes and Christal were published in an Air Force technical report, it failed to reach an academic audience until the 1980s. At that time, other researchers, notably Goldberg (1993) and Costa and McCrae (1988), obtained generally the same results as Tupes and Christal, although because they

---

TABLE 4.5
Personality Factors

Surgency (Extroversion)	Agreeableness	Dependability	Emotional Stability	Culture
Talkativeness	Good-natured	Orderliness	Not neurotic	Cultured
Frankness	Not jealous	Responsibility	Placid	Esthetically fastidious
Adventurousness	Emotionally mature	Conscientiousness	Poised	Imaginative

Source: Tupes, E.C. and Christal, R.E., 1961. *Recurrent Personality Factors Based on Trait Ratings.* Technical Report ASD-TR-61-97. Lackland Air Force Base, TX: Personnel Laboratory, Air Force Systems Command.

used somewhat different methods each set of five factors has somewhat different names and definitions. Arguably, the work by Costa and McCrae has had the most influence, perhaps because of the popularity of their instrument for measuring personality: the NEO Personality Inventory—Revised (NEO-PI-R™).

Embodying some of the components and structure of the Cattell and Eysenck models, the FFM is a hierarchical organization of personality traits with five basic dimensions: extraversion, agreeableness, conscientiousness, neuroticism, and openness to

TABLE 4.6
FFM Definitions

Factor	Factor Definers	
Name	Adjectives[a]	NEO-PI-R™ Facet Scales[b]
Extraversion	Active	Warmth
	Assertive	Gregariousness
	Energetic	Assertiveness
	Enthusiastic	Activity
	Outgoing	Excitement seeking
	Talkative	Positive emotions
Agreeableness	Appreciative	Trust
	Forgiving	Straightforwardness
	Generous	Altruism
	Kind	Compliance
	Sympathetic	Modesty
	Trusting	Tender-mindedness
Conscientiousness	Efficient	Competence
	Organized	Order
	Planful	Dutifulness
	Reliable	Achievement striving
	Responsible	Self-discipline
	Thorough	Deliberation
Neuroticism	Anxious	Anxiety
	Self-pitying	Hostility
	Tense	Depression
	Touchy	Self-consciousness
	Unstable	Impulsiveness
	Worrying	Vulnerability
Openness	Artistic	Fantasy
	Curious	Aesthetics
	Imaginative	Feelings
	Insightful	Actions
	Original	Ideas
	Wide interests	Values

Source: McCrae, R.R. and John, O.P. 1992. An introduction to the five-factor model and its applications. *Journal of Personality* 60: 175–215.

[a] From the Adjective Check List.

[b] Revised NEO Personality Inventory facet scales from self-reports.

experience. Table 4.6 lists adjectives that defined each of the five factors from a study of 280 men and women who were rated by 10 psychologists. The table also shows the facet scales for each factor from the NEO-PI-R™ (McCrae and John 1992).

Although early lexical studies of personality-related words in the English language indicated five large groups of personality traits, more recent studies have suggested that there are six large groups rather than five (Ashton et al. 2004). These six groups form the basis of the HEXACO model of personality structure. The factors comprising this model (and its acronym) are humility (H), emotionality (E), extraversion (X), agreeableness (A), conscientiousness (C), and openness to experience (O). Since the HEXACO model was developed using methods similar to those used to develop the other trait taxonomies, it shares several common elements with the other trait models. The model builds on the work of Tupes and Christal (1961), Costa and McCrae (1993, 1988), and Goldberg (1993); therefore, it shares several common elements with other trait models. However, the HEXACO model is unique mainly due to the addition of the honesty–humility factor (Ashton and Lee 2007). The four facets that define the honesty–humility factor are sincerity, fairness, greed avoidance, and modesty.[*] Although the FFM does not include an honesty–humility factor, some of the characteristics belonging to honesty–humility are incorporated into the FFM's agreeableness factor.

Interestingly, although the hierarchical personality models, such as the FFM, help in organizing the vast set of personality descriptors found in the English and other languages, studies have shown that the FFM factors are not as powerful in predicting and explaining actual behavior as are the more numerous facet or primary traits (Mershon and Gorsuch 1988; Paunonen and Ashton 2001). Apparently, giving up the specificity of behavior indexed by the primary traits for the generality of taxonomic organization comes at the price of surrendering some of the predictive utility of the more specific measures.

Nevertheless, the FFM has some significant advantages. Primary among those advantages is the more-or-less general acceptance of the FFM as a parsimonious and reasonably inclusive taxonomy of the personality domain. There are certainly critics (e.g., Block 1995, 2001) who suggest additions of modifications to the FFM (e.g., the addition of an honesty–humility factor). However; in general, the FFM is accepted as an adequate, if not perfect model.

Another advantage of the FFM is the stability of the trait scores. Costa and McCrae (1988, 1994) have argued that personality traits are largely unchanged after age 30. They found that test–retest correlations (0.90 or above) for three of the FFM traits were almost as high over a 6-year period as they were when assessed only 2 weeks apart. Additionally, Sold and Valliant (1999) examined a group of 163 men who were followed prospectively for over 45 years. These men were rated on 25 personality traits at the end of college, and completed the NEO-PI at approximately 67–68 years of age. The college trait ratings were transformed to scales assessing each of the FFM dimensions, and correlated with the corresponding NEO-PI trait scores. Three of the FFM traits (neuroticism, extraversion, and openness) were significantly

---

[*] Honesty–humility factor characteristics: Sincere, honest, faithful, loyal, modest/unassuming *versus* sly, deceitful, greedy, pretentious, hypocritical, boastful, pompous.

correlated across the 45-year interval. Interestingly, conscientiousness in college was the best predictor of later life outcomes.

4.4.3 PERSONALITY TRAITS AND AIRCREW PERFORMANCE

Psychologists have evaluated personality traits and their relationship to aircrew performance in multiple contexts. It is commonly believed that accomplished pilots have "the right stuff"—meaning a combination of both abilities and personality traits. While research has generally shown that some abilities are indeed quite important for pilot (and air traffic controller and aviation maintenance technician) performance, the results for personality traits have been much more varied, beginning with the selection of individuals to receive pilot training.[*]

In meta-analyses of the published research reaching back to World War I, both Hunter and Burke (1994) and Martinussen (1996) concluded that personality measures were not valid predictors of pilot training success. Similar results have been observed in individual studies (e.g., Siem 1990). However, these studies have primarily been concerned with the prediction of pass versus fail in military flight training. It could be argued that during this period when individuals are learning new skills, largely on a one-on-one basis, personality traits may well play a secondary role. It is only after completion of training, when the new pilot begins to function as part of a crew that personality traits become more important. Indeed, Chidester et al. (1991, p. 29) suggest that

> …superior performance in command of jet transport aircraft with multiperson crews relates to high scores on positive, instrumental traits including a need for mastery of new and challenging tasks, and low scores on negative instrumental attributes including traits such as arrogance and hostility… operation of a complex aircraft is a group endeavor, requiring the close coordination of a crew.

Chidester et al. also noted that because of the emphasis on selection training and periodic performance checks, the contribution of technical skills to variation in aircrew performance for major air carriers is restricted. In a sense, this is comparable to a piano competition in which all the contestants are highly trained concert pianists. Among that caliber of group, technical proficiency is a given, and any variability in the performance of some particular piece of music is due to the pianists' interpretation and styling. Similar comparisons could be drawn with professional golfers, for whom course strategy may be the determining factor in winning, since all the competitors are masters of the technical aspects of the game. This view is consistent with the results of a detailed review of 10 years of air transport accidents conducted by Cooper et al. (1979). They found that accidents resulting from a lack of knowledge or technical skill were extremely rare, and that breakdowns in communication and workload distribution were more typically cited as causal factors.

This change in importance of personality factors following training was termed the honeymoon effect by Helmreich et al. (1986). They examined the performance

---

[*] The use of both personality and ability tests will be covered in much more detail in Chapter 5.

of a group of airline ground employees and found that personality measures did not predict performance immediately after training. However, after 6 months on the job, those personality measures were significantly correlated with the employees' job performance. A similar result was observed by Tracey et al. (2010) in a study of restaurant employees. The five personality traits (i.e., conscientiousness, emotional stability, extroversion, openness to experience, and agreeableness) were assessed by the NEO-PI-R™ (Costa and McCrae 1991), and general mental ability (GMA) was assessed using the Wonderlic Personnel Test. For the total sample of 241 employees, the correlation between GMA and performance was 0.23 ($p < 0.05$). For the personality traits, conscientiousness and extroversion were also significantly ($p < 0.05$) correlated with performance ($r = 0.28$ and $r = 0.22$, respectively). When they analyzed new and experienced employees separately, they found that the correlation between GMA and performance for newcomers was 0.39 ($p < 0.01$) and 0.14 ($p < 0.05$) for experienced employees. However, the correlation between the FFM trait of conscientiousness and performance was -0.04 (ns) for newcomers, but 0.34 ($p < 0.01$) for experienced employees, clearly demonstrating a reversal of the relative importance of GMA and personality for new and experienced employees.

The finding by Tracey et al. (2010) that conscientiousness was significantly related to employee performance is consistent with the general research on the FFM (e.g., Barrick and Mount 1991; Salgado 1997; Judge et al. 1999). Conscientiousness is manifested in three related facets—achievement orientation (hardworking and persistent), dependability (responsible and careful), and orderliness (planful and organized). Conscientiousness is thus related to an individual's degree of self-control, as well as their need for achievement, order, and persistence—all of importance for aircrew.

Many studies have attempted to identify the abilities and personality traits required for military pilots and have produced lists of the relevant traits. Damos (2011, p. 25) reviewed the recent work in this area and concluded, with respect to personality traits that, "…traits related to conscientiousness are considered to be very important for success as a pilot. Traits related to emotional stability are considered less important. Risk tolerance, stress tolerance, and leadership show mixed results, but are seen as less important than traits pertaining to conscientiousness." She also noted, however, that for the most part researchers used idiosyncratic approaches to selecting the personality traits to be included in their studies and have made limited use of the FFM personality theory. This limits the utility of studies in this area by making comparisons among the various studies difficult or impossible. Hopefully, the increased popularity of the FFM personality theory and the ready availability of measures that conform to that theory will result in more comparability of studies in the future.

Research over the previous few decades has clarified the structure of personality and has confirmed the commonly held belief that personality traits are important aspects of an individual. By moving away from assessment instruments intended to identify psychopathology into instruments based upon the FFM taxonomy, the validity of measures of personality traits for the prediction of occupational and other activities has been greatly increased.

4.5 SUMMARY

In this chapter, the concepts of abilities and personality traits have been described and some of the research on these constructs has been briefly summarized. Scientific understanding of both abilities and personality traits has been advanced by the development of taxonomies that delineate the hierarchical structure of both abilities and personality traits. In the following chapters, the role of abilities and personality traits in personnel selection, training, aeronautical decision-making, and safety will be discussed. Abilities and personality traits play an important role in determining an individual's performance in all aspects of aviation. It might be said, without too much exaggeration, that to know an individual's abilities and personality traits is to know the essence of who they are and fairly precisely what they may accomplish.

4.6 OUTSIDE ACTIVITIES

After all this discussion about abilities and personality traits, perhaps you would like to see how you shape up. There are a large number of Web sites that offer free online tests of GMA (IQ), specific abilities, and personality traits. Some of these sites also offer more extensive testing if you subscribe. We *do not endorse* the products being offered by the sites, but simply present them as providing examples of assessments of some of the common abilities and traits.

4.6.1 ABILITY TESTS

All of the sites listed below offer at least a sample test of 10–20 items. Some of these sites also offer more extensive testing if you subscribe.

- Practice Aptitude Tests
  - http://www.practiceaptitudetests.com/
  - Numerical reasoning
  - Verbal reasoning diagrammatic reasoning
  - Situational judgment
- Psychometric Institute
  - http://www.psychometricinstitute.com.au/Free-Aptitude-Tests.asp
  - Mechanical aptitude
  - Verbal
  - Abstract
  - Numerical
- AptitudeTests.Com
  - https://www.aptitude-test.com/
  - This site offers multiple tests in each of these categories listed below The 10-item tests are free, but the site tries to sell you on membership to get more extensive tests
  - Mechanical

- Nonverbal reasoning
- Verbal
- Numerical
- Kent University (United Kingdom)
  - https://www.kent.ac.uk/careers/psychotests.htm
  - This site has a large number of practice aptitude tests in multiple categories
- Free IQ Test
  - http://www.free-iqtest.net/
  - This site offers a 20-item IQ test
- IQTest.Com
  - http://www.iqtest.com/
  - This site offers a 38-item IQ test

4.6.2 PERSONALITY TRAITS

As with the ability measures, there are a large number of sites that offer online personality assessments. We recommend that you stick to sites that use the FFM taxonomy, and have listed two such sites below. However, if you want to try something a bit different, we have also provided a link to a site that uses the Briggs–Meyer typology. It is popular in business settings—particularly for team-building exercises—but has generally found to lack validity and reliability. Hence, the Five-Factor measures are more typically used now, especially for personnel selection.

- The Big-Five Project
  - http://www.outofservice.com/bigfive/
  - This appears to be some sort of research project on the FFM—probably conducted out of Europe, since it offers German, Spanish, and Dutch language versions.
  - There are 46 personality questions, plus some biographical questions.
  - The results are shown graphically and with percentile scores.
- Truity Psychometrics, LLC
  - http://www.truity.com/test/big-five-personality-test
  - Administers a 50-item version of the FFM, plus a few biographical questions.
  - Nice output.
- Humanmetrics, Inc.
  - http://www.humanmetrics.com/cgi-win/jtypes2.asp
  - Administers a 64-item version of the Myers–Briggs personality inventory.
  - It produces a four-letter code (type indicator) that indicates
    - Extraversion (E) versus introversion (I)
    - Sensing (S) versus intuition (N)
    - Thinking (T) versus feeling (F)
    - Judging (J) versus perceiving (P)

REFERENCES

Agee, N., Shore, W.C., Alley, W.E., Barto, E., and Halper, M. 2009. *Air Force Officer Selection Technical Requirements Survey (AFOSTRS), Volume I: Analysis of Quantitative Results*. Randolph AFB, TX: Air Force Personnel Center.

Allport, G.W. and Odbert, H.S. 1936. Trait-names: A psycho-lexical study. *Psychological Monographs*, Whole No. 211: 1–38.

Ashton, M.C. and Lee, K. 2007. Empirical, theoretical, and practical advantages of the HEXACO model of personality structure. *Personality and Social Psychology Review* 11: 150–166.

Ashton, M.C., Lee, K., Goldberg, L.R. 2004. A Hierarchical analysis of 1,710 English personality-descriptive adjectives. *Journal of Personality and Social Psychology* 87: 707–721.

Atwater, L. and Yammarinol, F. 1993. Personal attributes as predictors of superiors' and subordinates' perceptions of military academy leadership. *Human Relations* 46: 645–668.

Barrick, M.R. and Mount, M.K. 1991. The big five personality dimensions and job performance: A meta-analysis. *Personnel Psychology* 44: 1–26.

Block, J. 1995. A contrarian view of the five-factor approach to personality description. *Psychological Bulletin* 117: 187–215.

Block, J. 2001. Millennial contrarianism: The five-factor approach to personality description 5 years later. *Journal of Research in Personality* 35: 98–107.

Carretta, T.R., Rodgers, M.N., and Hansen, I. 1993. *The Identification of Ability Requirements and Selection Instruments for Fighter Pilot Training*. AL/HR-TP-1993-0016. Brooks AFB, TX: Armstrong Laboratory.

Carroll, J.B. 1993. *Human cognitive abilities*. Cambridge, UK: Cambridge University Press.

Cattell, R.B. 1943. The description of personality: I. Foundations of trait measurement. *Psychological Review* 50: 559–594.

Cattell, R.B. 1963. Theory of fluid and crystallized intelligence: A critical experiment. *Journal of Educational Psychology* 54: 1–22.

Cavazotte, F., Moreno, V., and Hickmann, M. 2012. Effects of leader intelligence, personality and emotional intelligence on transformational leadership and managerial performance. *The Leadership Quarterly* 23: 443–455.

Chidester, T.R., Helmreich, R.L., Gregorich, S.E., and Geis, C.E. 1991. Pilot personality and crew coordination: Implications for training and selection. *The International Journal of Aviation Psychology* 1: 25–44.

Coleman, A.M. 2001. *A Dictionary of Psychology*. Oxford, UK: Oxford University Press.

Cooper, J.E., White, M.D., and Lauber, J.K. 1979. Resource management on the flight-deck. NASA Conference Publication 2120, NASA—Ames Research Center, Moffet Field, CA.

Costa, P.T. and McCrae, R.R. 1988. Personality in adulthood: A six-year longitudinal study of self-reports and spouse ratings on the NEO personality inventory. *Journal of Personality and Social Psychology* 54: 853–863.

Costa, P.T. and McCrae, R.R. 1991. *NEO Five-Factory Inventory: Form S*. Lutz, FL: Psychological Assessment Resources.

Costa, P.T. and McCrae, R.R. 1993. Bullish on personality psychology. *The Psychologist* 6: 302–303.

Costa, P.T. and McCrae, R.R. 1994. Set like plaster? Evidence for the stability of adult personality. In Heatherton, T.F., and Weinberger, J.L. (Eds.), *Can Personality Change?* (pp. 21–40). Washington, DC: American Psychological Association Books.

Damos, D.L. 2011. *KSAOs for Military Pilot Selection: A Review of the Literature*. AFCAPS-FR-2011-0003. Randolph AFB, TX: Air Force Personnel Center.

Driskill, W.E., Weismuller, J.J., Hageman, D.C., and Barrett, L.E. 1989. *Identification and Evaluation of Methods to Determine Ability Requirements for Air Force Occupational Specialties.* AFHRL-TP-89-34. Brooks AFB, TX: Manpower and Personnel Division, Air Force Human Resources Laboratory.

Driskill, W.E., Weissmuller, J.J., Quebe, J.C., Hand, D.K., and Hunter, D.R. 1998. *Evaluating the Decision-Making Skills of General Aviation Pilots.* DOT/FAA/AM-98/7. Washington, DC: Federal Aviation Administration.

Eysenck, H.J. 1992. The definition and measurement of psychoticism. *Personality and Individual Differences* 13: 757–785.

Eysenck, H.J. 1997. *The Biological Basis of Personality.* Springfield, IL: Thomas. (Original work published in 1947).

Fleishman, E.A., Quaintance, M.K., and Broedling, L.A. 1984. *Taxonomies of Human Performance: The Description of Human Tasks.* Orlando, FL: Academic Press.

Fleishman, E.A. and Reilly, M.E. 2001. *Handbook of Human Abilities.* Potomac, MD: Management Research Institute.

Gardner, H. 1983. *Frames of Mind: The Theory of Multiple Intelligence.* New York, NY: Basic Books.

Goldberg L.R. 1993. The structure of phenotypic personality traits. *American Psychologist* 48: 26–34.

Goleman, D. 1995. *Emotional Intelligence.* New York, NY: Bantum Books.

Goleman, D. 1998. *Working with Emotional Intelligence.* New York, NY: Bantum Books.

Gottfredson, L. 2003. Dissecting practical intelligence theory: Its claims and its evidence. *Intelligence* 31: 343–397.

Guilford, J.P. 1956. The structure of intellect. *Psychological Bulletin* 53: 267–293.

Helmreich, R.L., Sawin, L.L., and Carsmd, A.L. 1986. The honeymoon effect in job performance: Delayed predictive power of achievement motivation. *Journal of Applied Psychology* 71: 1085–1088.

Horn, J.L. 1968. Organization of abilities and the development of intelligence. *Psychological Review* 75: 242–259.

Horn, J.L. and Cattell, R.B. 1966. Refinement and test of the theory of fluid and crystallized general intelligences. *Journal of Educational Psychology* 57: 253–270.

Howse, W.R. 2011. *Knowledge, Skills, Abilities, and Other Characteristics for Remotely Piloted Aircraft Pilot Operators.* AFCAPS-FR-2011-0006. Randolph AFB, TX: Air Force Personnel Center.

Hunt, J. and Fitzgerald, M. 2013. The relationship between emotional intelligence and transformational leadership: An investigation and review of competing claims in the literature. *American International Journal of Social Science* 2: 30–38.

Hunter, D.R. 2003. Measuring general aviation pilot judgment using a situational judgment technique. *International Journal of Aviation Psychology* 13: 373–386.

Hunter, D.R. and Burke, E.F. 1994. Predicting aircraft pilot training success: A meta-analysis of published research. *The International Journal of Aviation Psychology* 4: 297–313.

Jaeggi, S.M., Buschkuehl, M., Jonides, J., and Perrig, W.J. 2008. Improving fluid intelligence with training on working memory. *Proceedings of the National Academy of Sciences of the United States of America* 105: 6829–6833.

Jensen, A.R. 1998. *The G Factor: The Science of Mental Ability.* Westport, CT: Praeger.

Judge, T.A., Higgins, C.A., Thoresen, C.J., and Barrick, M.R. 1999. The big five personality traits, general mental ability, and career success across the life span. *Personnel Psychology* 52:621–652.

Knapp, D.J., Russell, T.L., and Campbell, J.P. 1995. *Building a Joint-Service Classification Research Roadmap: Job Analysis Methodologies.* AL/HR-TP-1994-0027. Brooks AFB, TX: Armstrong Laboratory.

Kubisiak, C. and Katz, L. 2006. *U.S. Army Aviator Job Analysis.* Technical Report 1189. Alexandria, VA: US Army Research Institute for the Behavioral and Social Sciences.

Mackintosh, N.J. 1998. *IQ and Human Intelligence.* Oxford, UK: Oxford University Press.

Martinussen, M. 1996. Psychological measures as predictors of pilot performance: A meta-analysis. *The International Journal of Aviation Psychology* 1: 1–20.

Mayer, J.D. and Salovey, P. 1993. The intelligence of emotional intelligence. *Intelligence* 17: 433–442.

McCrae, R.R. and John, O.P. 1992. An introduction to the five-factor model and its applications. *Journal of Personality* 60: 175–215.

McGrew, K.S. 2009. CHC theory and the human cognitive abilities project: Standing on the shoulders of the giants of psychometric intelligence research. *Intelligence* 37: 1–10.

Merriam-Webster. 2016. *Merriam-Webster Dictionary.* Springfield, MA: Merriam Webster Inc.

Mershon, B. and Gorsuch, R.L. 1988. Number of factors in the personality sphere: Does increase in factors increase predictability of real-life criteria? *Journal of Personality and Social Psychology* 55: 675–680.

Meyer, R.P., Laveson, J.I., Weissman, N.S., and Eddowes, E.E. 1974a. *Behavioral Taxonomy of Undergraduate Pilot Training Tasks and Skills: Taxonomy Refinement, Validation and Operations.* AFHRL-TR-74-33(II). Brooks Air Force Base, TX: Air Force Human Resources Laboratory.

Meyer, R.P., Laveson, J.I., Weissman, N.S., and Eddowes, E.E. 1974b. *Behavioral Taxonomy of Undergraduate Pilot Training Tasks and Skills: Surface Task Analysis, Taxonomy Structure, Classification Rules and Validation Plan.* AFHRL-TR-74-33(III). Brooks Air Force Base, TX: Air Force Human Resources Laboratory.

Miller, J.T., Eschenbrenner, A.J., Marco, R.A., and Dohme, J.A. 1981. *Mission Track Selection Process for the Army Initial Entry Rotary Wing Flight Training Program,* Vol. I. St. Louis, MO: McDonnell Douglas Astronautics Co.

Neisser, U., Boodoo, G., Bouchard, T.J., Boykin, A.W., Brody, N., Ceci, S.J., Halpern, D.F. et al. 1996. Intelligence: Knowns and unknowns. *American Psychologist* 51: 77–101.

Paunonen, S.V. and Ashton, M.S. 2001. Big five factors and facets and the prediction of behavior. *Journal of Personality and Social Psychology* 81: 524–539.

Postlethwaite, B.E. 2011. *Fluid Ability, Crystallized Ability, and Performance Across Multiple Domains: A Meta-Analysis.* Unpublished doctoral dissertation, University of Iowa.

Raven, J., Raven, J.C., and Court, J.H. 2003. *Manual for Raven's Progressive Matrices and Vocabulary Scales.* San Antonio, TX: Harcourt Assessment.

Salgado, J.F. 1997. The five-factor model of personality and job performance in the European Community. *Journal of Applied Psychology* 82: 30–43.

Siem, F.M. 1990. Predictive validity of an automated personality inventory for Air Force pilot selection. *The International Journal of Aviation Psychology* 2: 261–270.

Sold, S. and Vaillant, G.E. 1999. The big five personality traits and the life course: A 45-year longitudinal study. *Journal of Research in Personality* 33: 208–232.

Sternberg, R.J. 1985. *Beyond IQ: A Triarchic Theory of Intelligence.* Cambridge, UK: Cambridge University Press.

Sternberg, R.J. 1997. A triarchic view of giftedness: Theory and practice. In Coleangelo, N., and Davis, G.A. (Eds.), *Handbook of Gifted Education* (pp. 43–53). Boston, MA: Allyn and Bacon.

Sternberg, R.J., Nokes, C., Geissler, W., Prince, P., Okatcha, F., Bundy, D.A., and Grigorenke, E.L. 2001. The relationship between academic and practical intelligence: A case study in Kenya. *Intelligence* 29: 401–418.

Suchy, Y., Eastvold, A., Whittaker, W.J., and Strassberg, D. 2007. Validation of the Behavioral Dyscontrol Scale-Electronic Version: Sensitivity to subtle sequelae of mild traumatic brain injury. *Brain Injury* 21: 69–80.

Tracey, J.B., Sturman, M.C., Shao, L., and Tews, M.J. 2010. The role of personality and general mental ability in predicting performance for new and experienced employees [Electronic version]. Retrieved on November 12, 2016 from Cornell University, School of Hospitality Administration site: http://scholarship.sha.cornell.edu/articles/297

Tupes, E.C. and Christal, R.E. 1961. *Recurrent Personality Factors Based on Trait Ratings.* Technical Report ASD-TR-61-97. Lackland Air Force Base, TX: Personnel Laboratory, Air Force Systems Command.

Youngling, E.W., Levine, S.H., Mocharnuk, J.B., and Weston, L.M. 1977. *Feasibility Study to Predict Combat Effectiveness for Selected Military Roles: Fighter Pilot Effectiveness.* MDC E1634. East St. Louis, MO: McDonnell Douglas Astronautics Co.

5 Personnel Selection

5.1 INTRODUCTION

Highly skilled people are essential for the airlines to operate efficiently, safely, and with satisfied customers. In a military context, the organization will also have other objectives, but skilled workers are still as important. For the individual employee, it is important to have a job that is sufficiently challenging, where the individual is appreciated and rewarded in relation to how well he or she performs the job. To achieve this, it is important to have both a good selection system and an effective training program for candidates who have been selected. A successful selection process will lead to lower dropout rates during training and an increase in the number of students completing the program. In addition, a well-designed selection system will, in the long term, contribute to a more effective and resilient organization; however, this claim may be harder to document compared to lowered dropout rates. Ideally, the selection of personnel should be based on the best available evidence. In medicine, psychology, and other health-care professions, the term "evidence-based practice" has been used for some time (Sackett et al. 1996; Levant 2005). It means that patients or clients should receive treatment, which is based on the best empirical evidence available, and that the health professionals should make a critical evaluation of the evidence in addition to also considering the client's or patient's characteristics, culture, and preference when choosing a treatment. If we adapt this principle to a selection context, then an evidence-based practice should be based on the best available research evidence, expertise in selection in addition to considering both the applicant and the organization in need of aviation personnel. The type of evidence that would be most relevant would be studies linking the selection methods to future work performance. Expertise in selection means that the person is qualified to use the methods, is aware of their limitations, and also knows the legal and professional guidelines for personnel selection.

Most of the research on selection methods in aviation has addressed the selection of pilots and air traffic controllers (ATCs), and in recent years UAV (unmanned aerial vehicle)/RPA (remotely piloted aircraft) pilots also. The selection of military pilots is often based on young people without any previous flying experience; however, selection for civilian airlines includes experienced pilots as well as people without any flying experience (*ab initio*). Most airlines probably prefer to hire experienced pilots and thus avoid a long and expensive period of training. This may change with an estimated increase in need for pilots worldwide (Damos 2014), and also fewer military pilots who transfer to civilian airlines later in their career (Weissmuller and Damos 2014). On the basis of a survey conducted by the International Air Transport Association (IATA) among 66 airlines worldwide, there seems to be large variations in how the selection process is conducted and what type of methods are used (IATA

2010). However, after the Germanwings accident in 2015 where the copilot intentionally crashed the airplane (BEA 2016), there has been an increased interest in pilot selection. A Task Force appointed by EASA (European Aviation Safety Agency) after the accident had as one of the recommendations that commercial pilots should undergo psychological evaluation as part of training or before joining service (EASA 2015). In most cases, the selection of pilots and ATCs is a comprehensive step-by-step process, at least for *ab initio* selection. That is, it usually starts with a large number of applicants who are tested with a range of psychological tests. In addition, applicants must meet a number of formal requirements in the form of medical requirements, no police record, and, sometimes, earlier education (e.g., completed high school or college). These formal requirements, however, may vary from organization to organization, and between countries. After initial testing, the best candidates proceed to further testing and an interview, and often more extensive medical examinations. For both ATC and pilot selection, usually less than 10% of the applicant population will be accepted into the training program.

When choosing methods for the selection process, it is important to start with a thorough review of the job in order to determine what skills, abilities, and qualities are important for the person to possess. Such a systematic review is called a job analysis, and it involves a detailed survey of the tasks involved in the job. There are several ways to do this—for example, by observing workers or interviewing them. In the literature, various techniques are described that can be used to obtain information about the work content and the capabilities or skills needed to perform the tasks.

5.2   JOB ANALYSIS

A job analysis consists mainly of two elements: a job description and a person specification. A job description is an account of the activities or tasks to be performed; a person specification lists the skills, expertise, knowledge, and other physical and personal qualities the person must have to perform these activities. Several methods can be utilized to carry out a job analysis, and a job analysis can have multiple purposes in addition to forming the basis for a selection process (see, e.g., Wilson 2007 for a review). Therefore, some of the job analysis methods emphasize outlining the tasks to be solved or the behaviors that need to be performed, while others focus on the qualities the person should have. A job analysis is therefore both the job requirements and personnel requirements. If the purpose of a job analysis is to determine what should be measured as part of the selection process, more emphasis should be put on the person specification. Figure 5.1 provides an overview of these two perspectives.

One of the most well-known job analysis methods is called the critical incident technique, which was developed by Flanagan during World War II for mapping the job performance of fighter pilots (Flanagan 1954). The main purpose of this method is to identify behavioral examples of good and poor performance. For many tasks, most people would have managed to perform them, so they are of little interest; others will be more demanding and not everyone will be able to perform the tasks successfully (e.g., critical incidents). Critical incidents may be described as occurring

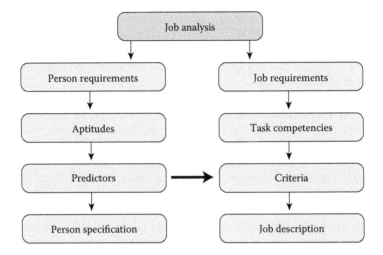

FIGURE 5.1   Two perspectives on job analysis.

frequently, they are important and difficult to perform. The method involves using experienced workers as informants, and they are asked to describe critical tasks and what characterizes both good and bad ways to solve the tasks. It is also important to examine the extent to which these experts agree on what the critical tasks are and the characteristics of good and poor work performance. The work proceeds with some sorting of task descriptions, where the purpose is to create categories. Many tasks may require good communication, and many tasks may require the ability to perform calculations. Finally, a list is constructed of the abilities and skills the person must have to perform these tasks.

Another method, the repertory grid technique, was developed by Kelly (1955). Here, the experts are asked to imagine good, moderate, and poor workers. Then, they are to describe how these workers are similar and different in relation to work performance. A third technique is Fleishman's job analysis survey method (Fleishman 1975; Fleishman and Reilly 2001). Employees are asked to indicate, on a seven-point Likert scale, the extent to which different abilities, personality traits, and skills are relevant to job performance. The person needs to consider seven main areas: cognitive abilities, psychomotor skills, physical demands, sensory capabilities, knowledge and skills, cooperation, and social skills. Each area has a number of subcategories. For example, cognitive ability includes a total of 21 categories, such as spatial orientation, time sharing, and attention.

5.2.1   JOB ANALYSIS FOR PILOTS AND ATCS

Fleishman's job-analysis method was used in a study of civilian pilots ($N = 141$) with a few added categories (Goeters et al. 2004). Many of the cognitive abilities on the list were described as relevant or highly relevant, as were psychomotor and sensory abilities. Within the cooperative/social skills domain, coping with stress, communication, and decision-making were identified as very important.

For military pilots, a revised version of the Fleishman method was used in a NATO study (Carretta et al. 1996) in which pilots from several countries were asked to assess 12 critical tasks specific to the job of fighter pilot. They were then asked to specify the abilities and skills that were important when conducting these tasks. The most important abilities were situational awareness, memory, motivation, and reasoning. Least important were reading comprehension and writing, in addition to leadership. Many of the same cognitive and psychomotor abilities were listed as important for both military and civilian pilots, but leadership received a relatively low rating for military pilots compared to the high ratings that cooperative and social skills had for civilian pilots. A review by Damos (2011) of job analyses of military pilots, including the previously mentioned NATO study, identified a total of nine different studies of military pilots. Spatial orientation and perceptual speed received high ratings in many of the studies included in the review. Numerical ability, mechanical aptitude, multitasking, multi-limb coordination, selective attention, and situational awareness were also mentioned in some of the studies; however, sometimes using differing definitions made it difficult to integrate the findings from the nine studies (Damos 2011).

For UAV/RPA pilots working in a military context, many of the same abilities, skills, and traits as regular military pilots have been assumed to be of importance in order to perform well. A job analysis of UAV operators identified a large number of tasks and the corresponding KSAOs (Knowledge, Skills, Abilities, and Other characteristics). The highest ratings were given to situational awareness, teamwork, communication procedures, work in confined spaces, oral comprehension, vigilance, self-discipline, and adaptability/flexibility. A summary provided by Paullin et al. (2011) identified a total of 21 skills, abilities, and other characteristics relevant to predicting success as an Air Force RPA pilot or sensor operator. The conclusion was that many of these abilities and skills were measured by the current selection tests used for pilots, but two additional measures were developed. This included a measure of time-sharing ability in addition to a scale for assessing person–environment fit to the special RPA work context (Paullin et al. 2011). A review of KSAO studies of RPA pilots also indicated that RPA missions may change in the future, possibly resulting in a shift in demands for the different KSAOs (Howse 2011).

The KSAOs of German ATCs were assessed using the Fleishman method described earlier (Eißfeldt and Heintz 2002). In addition to the original scales from Fleishman, a few more scales were added that included personal characteristics such as cooperation, communication, and the ability to handle stress. The cognitive abilities that received the highest ranking were speed of closure, visualization, and selective attention, in addition to time sharing. Few of the cognitive abilities received a low score. Visualization involves the ability to imagine objects and movements in space; selective attention means that an individual is able to concentrate on a task without being distracted. Time sharing involves the ability to shift attention quickly between different tasks. In addition, several psychomotor skills were rated as important, together with sensory abilities and specific knowledge (e.g., map reading). Several of the social skills were also highly rated, including stress resistance, decision-making, and cooperation. There were some differences in the skills/qualities that were important between ATCs in different functions (area control, approach, airdrome control); however, for the most part, these differences were small.

A large study was conducted by the DLR (Deutsches Zentrum für Luft-und Raumfahrt—German Aerospace Center) where the purpose was to try to determine the future requirements of pilots and ATCs (Eißfeldt et al. 2009). Several subject matter experts were involved in workshops and experiments in order to design future air traffic scenarios, and also determine abilities, skills, and personality traits necessary to operate in the future air space. The findings indicated that many of the current cognitive abilities would also be important or more important in the future scenario in 2030, but some changes were noted; for instance, an increase in the importance of deductive reasoning and a decrease in the importance of number facility (calculations) for pilots. Furthermore, visual color discrimination was expected to be more important in addition to increased resilience (social/personal skills) also for pilots (Eißfeldt et al. 2009). Another study by the FAA (Federal Aviation Administration) on the selection of the next generation of ATC specialists suggested an increased importance of many cognitive aptitudes including perceptual speed, prioritization, and time sharing in addition to two new aptitudes, which were dispositional trust in automation and computer–human interface navigation (Broach 2013).

5.2.2 A Critical Perspective on Job Analysis

An important methodological question is to what extent we can rely on the results from a job analysis. One possibility is that experienced workers who are asked to assess the capabilities needed to perform the job may overestimate the number of skills and qualifications that are necessary. This may be more or less a conscious act, but it is natural that people want to present themselves in a favorable light, including overestimating the complexity of the job they are doing and the abilities and skills needed to perform the job.

In modern job analysis, more emphasis is placed on uncovering the competence needed and less emphasis is put on the specific tasks to be solved (see, e.g., Bartram 2005). This is partly a function of the modern labor market, where many jobs are constantly changing and thus more global assessments and less focus on specific tasks and abilities may be more useful. However, it may be difficult to achieve a reliable assessment of the competence needed because competence is a complex concept often seen as a mixture of skills, knowledge, motivation, and interests. A meta-analysis of reliability coefficients from job analyses concluded that reviews of specific tasks had higher inter-rater reliability than the more general descriptions of the competence needed (Dierdorff and Wilson 2003).

The results from a job analysis may be used to select specific tests to be applied in the selection process, and also to select appropriate criteria of work performance that could be used in a validation study. Many people would therefore argue that a job analysis is an important and necessary first step in a selection process. Meta-analyses have demonstrated, however, that ability tests predict job performance more or less independently of the occupation (Schmidt and Hunter 1998, 2004). One consequence of this may be that a very detailed job analysis may not be needed. On the other hand, job analyses of pilots and ATCs have demonstrated that a number of highly specialized cognitive skills are important, and a test of general intelligence may not provide an adequate measure of such abilities.

5.3 PREDICTORS AND CRITERIA

The methods used to select applicants are identified as predictors, while measures of work performance are labeled criteria. When a psychological test is used to select an ATC, the test is a predictor. To assess how well the test is suitable for this purpose, we have to conduct a validation study—that is, a study in which test results for applicants are compared to actual work performance or academic results. Both work performance and academic grades are examples of criteria.

5.3.1 PREDICTORS IN SELECTION

Predictors should ideally be selected because they measure something relevant for future work performance, possibly identified through a job analysis. A number of different methods can be used in a selection process, and here only the most common will be described. The *interview* as a selection method is applied to most professions, and it may be more or less structured. An interview is highly structured if the questions are formulated in advance and the ordering of the questions is also predetermined. Sometimes, the interview is conducted toward the end of the selection process after the less time-consuming methods have been used. Employers in the process of hiring people probably also feel the need to meet the person face to face through an interview. Many employers believe that they have a unique ability to uncover who is more suited to the job and will fit nicely into the organization.

Unfortunately, this assumption is often wrong. Unstructured interviews often have a very poor predictive validity, and the assumption that this method always identifies the right person is frequently wrong. More structured interviews, however, have a much higher predictive validity than those where random questions are asked (McDaniel et al. 1994). For an interview to be effective, it is important to think through and formulate job-relevant questions to be used with all the applicants. It is also important to train the interviewers, especially if more than one person is conducting the interviews. One advantage of the interview is that it also gives the applicant an opportunity to meet representatives of the organization and ask questions about the job and that it often receives positive applicant reactions (Hausknecht et al. 2004).

Another type of predictor is the *assessment center*, which could be used for more purposes than just selection—for example, in leadership training and promotion. The assessment center method involves the candidate receiving various tasks that are similar or relevant to the job sought. Often, this involves situations in which small groups of people try to resolve a problem together. This makes it possible to study how people interact with each other, their leadership abilities, communication skills, and so on. Several trained observers, who usually make use of standardized forms to rate the performance, observe the applicants. The method is time consuming, and it often takes from half to a whole day or more.

Yet another type of predictor is called the *work sample test*, which represents a less comprehensive approach than an assessment center. This means that the candidate performs a similar task or the same task as the person would do as part of the job. The idea is that the behavior will predict similar behavior at a later date. There are often standardized scoring rules for how the performance should be rated.

A number of *psychological tests* may also be used as predictors, including ability tests and personality tests. Some of these are designed for selection, while others are designed for other purposes—for example, clinical use or diagnostics. Tests that are intended for special groups or designed for completely different purposes may not necessarily be suitable for personnel selection. Psychological tests are frequently used for pilot and ATC selection, but less commonly for other groups in the aviation industry. Many of the tests used in the selection of pilots and ATCs have been developed specifically for these occupational groups.

Past *work experience*, *school grades*, and *biographical data* are also sometimes used for selection purposes. If a person already has some work experience, it would be reasonable to obtain references from former employers and for pilots experience in terms of the total number of flying hours, certificates, and type of aircrafts flown. School grades may also be used in the selection process—in particular, to select people for further education and as a way of reducing a large applicant group to a smaller group where more time-consuming and expensive methods may be used. Biographical data gathered from employment records may also be used to discriminate between successful and unsuccessful employees. This information may be used for future selection of candidates. For example, if the best insurance sellers are married and own their own homes, then applicants who have these characteristics should be preferred. The items and their weighting are based on a purely empirical approach. Some people may argue that the method is unfair because applicants are selected based on factors over which they have little or no control—instead of measuring the relevant abilities and skills directly.

The final and perhaps most exotic method that will be mentioned here is graphology or handwriting analysis. This method involves an analysis of a person's handwriting in order to determine personality characteristics. Several studies have shown that this method is not suitable for selection, even though it is currently used in several European countries for personnel selection decisions (for an overview, see Cook 2009).

The various methods mentioned here have different predictive validity, and they are also different in relation to how costly and time consuming they are. Meta-analysis methods have been used to investigate the various methods' predictive validity, and the best predictors are work sample tests, intelligence tests, and structured interviews, with an average predictive validity of about 0.50. Age and graphology had no predictive validity (Schmidt and Hunter 1998). An overview of the validity of different methods is presented in Figure 5.2.

5.3.2 CRITERIA OF JOB PERFORMANCE

Valid criteria for work performance are as important as good predictors when evaluating the selection process. The selection of criteria can be based on a previous job

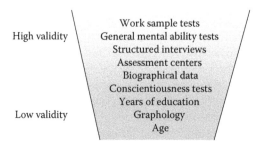

FIGURE 5.2 Validity of different selection methods. (Based on Schmidt, F.L. and Hunter, J.E. 1998. *Psychological Bulletin* 124: 262–274.)

analysis where key tasks and what constitutes good performance have been identified. The easiest way to examine the predictive validity of a method is to use an overall criterion. For many jobs, one can argue that this is not adequate and that it would be more reasonable to apply multiple criteria to describe job performance and the variety of tasks performed. When conducting a validation study, the researcher needs to choose which criteria to use or, more conveniently, combined criteria instead of trying to predict a large number of criteria at the same time, which could be differentially related to the predictors.

In many cases, instructors or superiors are used to assess performance, and it is important that this happens in a systematic and reliable way. One way to assess reliability would be to let two instructors evaluate the same people and then study the degree of agreement between them. There are a number of known errors in such person evaluations; for example, if a person is good at one thing, it is automatically assumed that he or she performs other tasks equally well. It may also be difficult to get the observers to use the entire scale; that is, all performance may be assessed to be average, or there may be little variation between different items rated for each person. It is important that there is variation between individuals and between various tasks that the same person performs whenever the rating will be used as a criterion. If all the candidates perform the task equally well, it is not suitable as a criterion of work performance.

In order to achieve good inter-rater reliability, it is important to train the observers and to specify what constitutes good and poor work performance. In addition, the criterion needs to have good construct validity, which means that it measures the construct in which one is interested—for example, leadership or communication skills. There will frequently be practical limitations to which criteria can be assessed as part of a validation study, and it is also important that these criteria are seen as relevant to the organization.

In relation to pilot selection, most of the criteria are usually obtained during training; in many cases, pass/fail in training is used. Pass/fail is a criterion about which it is easy to collect information that the organization regards as important. One problem with this criterion is that it is a somewhat indirect measure of performance. In some cases, reasons other than poor performance may cause the candidate to fail training, including everything from airsickness to lack of motivation. Nevertheless, in most cases, the criterion of pass/fail seems to work reasonably well. In a study of students at a Norwegian military flight school, the pass/fail criterion was highly correlated with assessments made by flight instructors (Martinussen and Torjussen 2004). In this study, pass/fail was taken as a valid measure of pilot performance.

Another problem with applying the criterion pass/fail is that it is based on performance during training and not actual work performance. However, few studies employ more long-term criteria of pilot performance, and there may be many reasons for this choice. A more long-term criterion would require that the validation study takes longer time to conduct. It may also be difficult to find comparable criteria for different jobs—for example, pilots working in different airlines. In addition, it is obviously more difficult to evaluate workers in a real-life setting than during training, where they expect to be evaluated.

In addition to pass/fail and instructors' ratings, assessments of graduates' performance in a simulator have also been used in validation studies. For ATCs, the situation is similar, and validation studies have largely been conducted using criteria obtained during training or in a simulator. For RPA pilots, training criteria have been used in addition to officer performance reports, which represent work performance (Barron et al. 2016).

5.4 HOW CAN WE KNOW THAT PREDICTORS WORK?

In order to document that predictors are useful in the selection of candidates, one can perform a local validation study or evaluate meta-analysis results that summarize relevant validation studies. Local validation studies are so named because they are conducted in the native setting in which the selection system under evaluation would eventually be employed. Local validation studies are usually performed by correlating test results with a measure of job performance—for example, performance in a simulator or assessments made by an instructor or supervisor. Sometimes, several tests are used in combination or tests are combined with an interview. In such cases, one can apply a combined test score or use regression analysis to find a weighted combination of predictors that gives the highest correlation with the criterion. In many cases, it may be difficult to conduct local validation studies because the organization does not employ a sufficient number of people within a certain time period, or that performance is never assessed after employment.

5.4.1 META-ANALYSIS

An alternative to conducting a local validation study is to combine previous studies in a meta-analysis. In order to merge results from multiple studies, the studies must all supply a common metric or measure of effect. Fortunately, most of the articles reporting results from validation studies include correlation coefficients, which are highly suitable for meta-analysis. Some studies, however, only report the results from multiple regression analyses, and these cannot be combined with correlations from other studies. The meta-analysis calculation requires that a standardized index (e.g., the Pearson correlation coefficient or another measure of effect size) be used, and that the results be reported for each predictor separately. In a regression analysis, the results indicate how well the combined set of tests predicts a criterion; regression coefficients will depend not only on the correlation between the test and the criterion, but also on the inter-correlations among other predictors included in the equation. Because the individual contributions of the predictor measures cannot be separated, the regression coefficients cannot be used in meta-analyses.

There are several meta-analysis traditions, and the most widely used method within the work and organizational psychology was developed by John Hunter and Frank Schmidt in the late 1970s (Schmidt and Hunter 1998). Their method was initially designed to study how well test validity could be generalized across different settings. The method is therefore well suited to perform a meta-analysis of validation studies because it takes into consideration many of the methodological issues relevant in such studies. Hunter and Schmidt (2014) have described a number of factors or circumstances that may affect the size of the observed correlation or validity coefficient. These factors, or statistical artifacts, will influence the size of the correlation coefficients in various degrees from study to study.

Three such statistical sources of errors are lack of reliability, restriction of range, and use of a dichotomous criterion (e.g., pass/fail) instead of a continuous measure. The lower the score reliability is, the lower the observed correlation will be. It is possible to correct for this artifact if the test score reliability is reported in the article (Hunter and Schmidt 2014):

$$r_{cor} = \frac{r_{obs}}{\sqrt{r_{xx}}\sqrt{r_{yy}}}$$

In this equation, r_{cor} is the corrected correlation, r_{obs} is the observed correlation, and r_{xx} and r_{yy} are reliability of the predictor and the criterion, respectively. The corrected correlation is an estimate of the correlation that would have been observed if the variables had been measured with perfect reliability. In some cases, it is appropriate to correct for lack of reliability in only one of the variables (e.g., correction for criterion reliability in validation studies) because the purpose is to evaluate the usefulness of the tests with all the errors and shortcomings that they may have. The correction is then

$$r_{cor} = \frac{r_{obs}}{\sqrt{r_{yy}}}$$

If we assume that the observed correlation between the ability test and a criterion is 0.40 and that criterion reliability is 0.70, then the corrected correlation is $0.40/\sqrt{0.70} = 0.48$. This number represents the correlation that would have been observed if the criterion had been perfectly measured. The lower the score reliability is, the greater will be the correction factor.

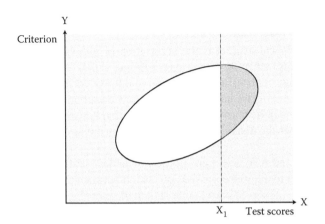

FIGURE 5.3 Illustration of restriction of range.

The second factor that affects the size of the correlation is reduced test score variation (restriction of range) on one or both variables as a result of selection. This occurs if only the relationship between test scores and subsequent performance of those who have been selected on the basis of the test results is studied. If only the better half of the applicant group has been selected, then it will be possible to collect criterion data only for this group. The calculated correlation will be much lower for this group than if we had studied the entire unselected group. The effect on the observed correlation can be dramatic, given that a very small group is selected.

This problem is illustrated in Figure 5.3, where the shaded part represents the selected group included in the study. On the basis of the plot in this figure, we can see that if we calculate the correlation for the selected group, then the correlation would have been much lower than if the calculation had been based on the entire applicant group. If we assume an even stricter selection and move the line (X_1) to the right, then the shaded field will be almost like a round ball, implying zero correlation.

There are few empirical examples of the phenomenon "restriction of range." One of the few examples dates back to World War II, when applicants to the U.S. Air Force were tested and selected. Because of the lack of pilots at that time, all the applicants were admitted into the basic flying program. The predictive validity could then be calculated for the entire group as well as for a selected group. The predictive validity for the total test score (Pilot Stanine) was 0.64. If the normal procedure had been applied and only the top 13% of the candidates had been selected, then the predictive validity would have dropped to 0.18 (Thorndike 1949). This provides a picture of the dramatic effect that calculating the predictive validity on a highly selected group may have. In other words, the problem is that we have excluded the control group by only using the selected applicants in the study. The correction for range restriction is based on information about the test score standard deviation in the whole group, or the proportion of applicants selected (Hunter and Schmidt 2014). In situations where the selection is based on several tests or tests used in combination with other types of information, the situation becomes more complicated and more advanced models for range restriction correction should be applied (Lawley 1943; Johnson and Ree 1994; Sackett and Yang 2000).

The third statistical artifact is the application of a dichotomous criterion (e.g., pass/fail in training) when the performance (flying skills) really can be said to be a continuous variable. This artifact also leads to a lower correlation between the test and the criterion than if we had measured performance on a continuous scale. This statistical artifact can be corrected if the distribution between the pass/fail ratios is known. The farther the distance is from a 50/50 distribution of pass/fail, the greater is the correction.

For both pilot and ATC selection, all these statistical artifacts are frequently present and contribute to a lower observed correlation between the test and the criterion. When possible, the observed correlations should therefore be corrected for these error sources before they are included in a meta-analysis, as well as to provide a better estimate of the true predictive validity. Unfortunately, such corrections are often difficult because the primary studies frequently lack the information needed to perform such corrections. Criterion reliability is rarely examined, and information about the selection ratio is not reported in many articles. The percentage passing or failing training is normally reported; this makes it possible to correct for the effect of using a dichotomous criterion. In studies where such corrections are not implemented, the observed correlations must be viewed as very conservative estimates of the tests' predictive validity. In addition, sampling error will contribute to variation between observed correlations in different studies. However, this error is unsystematic; therefore, the statistical methods described before cannot be used to correct for the error.

5.4.2 When Can Test Validity Be Generalized?

How do we know if the predictive validity of a test can be generalized over different settings? For example, can intelligence tests always be successfully used for selection, regardless of setting and occupation? Hunter and Schmidt (2014) proposed a rule of thumb that states that if at least 75% of the observed variance between the correlations can be attributed to statistical errors and sampling error, then it is reasonable to assume that the remaining variance is due to error sources not corrected for. In such instances, it is safe to assume that the true variance between studies is very small or zero and that the mean correlation is an appropriate estimate of the true validity.

The second situation arises when we have real variance in the population; it is then possible to estimate an interval (credibility interval) that, with a high probability, includes the predictive validity. This interval is calculated based on the corrected average correlation and the estimated population standard deviation (Whitener 1990). If the interval is large and in addition contains zero, it means that the actual variation between studies is considerable and that the test in some cases does not have predictive validity. Other occasions may arise, however, in which the interval is of a certain size, but does not include zero. This means that there is some variation in the predictive validity, but that it is always larger than zero. In that case, the predictive measures can be used as a valid predictor, even though its utility will vary from instance to instance.

It is also possible to perform a significance test of the variation between studies, but this is a less common strategy in the Hunter–Schmidt meta-analysis method, where the estimation of variance is emphasized.

5.5   HISTORICAL OVERVIEW

5.5.1   PILOT SELECTION

Probably, few professions have been tested as much as pilots (see, e.g., Hunter 1989). During World War I, the first tests were developed and validated—not many years after the Wright brothers made their first flight (Dockeray and Isaacs 1921). Many of the first tests were simple constructions simulating tasks or situations with which humans involved in flying would have to cope. One of the earliest test batteries from the United States (Henmon 1919) contained tests that measured emotional stability, reaction time, general cognitive abilities, and sense of equilibrium.

In Europe, similar tests were developed in several countries. In Denmark, Alfred Lehman (Termøhlen 1986) developed methods for pilot selection in his laboratory. He suggested tests that measured emotional stability, evaluation of spatial relationships, attention, reaction time for sound, and sense of equilibrium. The test that measured emotional stability consisted of psychophysiological measurements at the same time as a test administrator fired a shot behind the back of the candidate. Lehman suggested that the test was unsuitable for selection because it was not possible to distinguish those who were really cold blooded from those who reacted to stress induced in the test situation (Termøhlen 1986). There were many similarities between the tests that were used in different countries in this first phase of test development. Paper-and-pencil tests were used together with apparatuses that simulated aspects of a flying machine, in addition to simple measures of reaction time and judging distance and time.

After World War I had ended, there was little research on pilot selection in most countries (Hunter 1989; Hilton and Dolgin 1991). An exception was Germany, where a large number of tests were developed; at the beginning of World War II, the country had a test battery that consisted of 29 tests that measured, among other things, general intelligence, perceptual abilities, coordination, ability, character, and leadership (Fitts 1946). During the war, this test battery was replaced by a less extensive system with fewer tests and more emphasis on references and interview data (Fitts 1946).

In England, the United States, and Canada, the trend was different. At the start of the war, few tests were in use; by the end of the war, a large number of tests had been developed and implemented. In Norway, the Norwegian Air Force used tests first in 1946 (Riis 1986). Since then, the Norwegian test battery has been expanded and validated several times (see, e.g., Martinussen and Torjussen 1998, 2004; Torjussen and Hansen 1999).

After World War II, research declined again, and many countries put emphasis on maintenance rather than on developing new tests. This more or less continued until the first computerized tests were invented in the 1970s and 1980s (Hunter and Burke 1987; Kantor and Carretta 1988; Bartram 1995). As computer technology became cheaper and better, the paper-and-pencil tests were replaced entirely or partially with computerized tests in most Western countries (Burke et al. 1995). Computer-based testing also made it possible to assess more complex abilities and skills, in addition to providing an easy scoring of the test results. However, no technology is flawless, so even with computer-based tests, there may be reliability problems and data loss, often in a very systematic way.

In more recent years, many of the tests initially developed for pilot selection have been used for selecting military UAV/RPA pilots and sensor operators and some new measures have been suggested for this type of aviators (Paullin et al. 2011). So far only a handful of validation studies have been conducted and mostly on military samples (see, e.g., Carretta 2013; Rose et al. 2013).

Early in the history of aviation, personal qualities, as well as cognitive and psychomotor skills, were seen as important in order to become a good pilot. To examine which personality traits were important, both observation of pilots and participant observation were used. After having undergone flight training, Dockeray concluded that "quiet methodical men were among the best flyers, that is, the power and quick adjustment to a new situation and good judgment" (Dockeray and Isaacs 1921). It would still be many years before personality tests were developed and used for pilot selection. In the United States, a comprehensive program to find suitable personality measures for pilot selection was started in the 1950s. The research program was led by Sells (1955, 1956), and a total of 26 personality measures were evaluated. Sells and his colleagues used more long-term criteria of pilot performance in their evaluation, and they concluded that personality tests were better predictors of long-term criteria compared to ability tests, where the predictive validity declined over time.

A number of well-known personality inventories have also been examined in relation to pilot selection over the years. These include the MMPI (Minnesota Multiphasic Personality Inventory) (Melton 1954), Eysenck Personality Inventory (Jessup and Jessup 1971; Bartram and Dale 1982), Rorschach (Moser 1981), and Cattell 16PF (Bartram 1995). The results showed only low-to-moderate correlations with the criterion. One of the few studies on civilian pilots (conducted at Cathay Pacific Airlines) showed that, based on training results, successful pilots scored lower on anxiety compared to less successful pilots (Bartram and Baxter 1996).

In Sweden, a projective test called the "defense mechanism test" (DMT) was developed by Kragh (1960). The purpose was to select applicants for high-risk occupations such as pilots and deep-sea divers. The test material consisted of pictures presented using a special slide projector that displayed images repeatedly. Exposure of each picture was very short, but increased each time the image was presented. The person drew and explained what he or she saw, and the discrepancy between the actual image and what the person reported was then interpreted as various defense mechanisms (Torjussen and Værnes 1991). The test was met with considerable optimism when it was launched, and it was tested on military pilots in several countries such as England, the Netherlands, and Australia, as well as Scandinavia (Martinussen and Torjussen 1993). However, it has been difficult to document the predictive validity of the test for pilots outside the Scandinavian countries, and very few countries, if any, currently use the test.

With the introduction of computers in testing, a number of personality-related concepts have been evaluated. This includes measures of risk taking, assertiveness, field dependency, and attitudes (see Hunter and Burke 1995, for an overview). In the 1990s, trait-based personality tests, especially based on the Five-factor model, became popular and resulted in more optimism regarding the predictive validity of personality measures in general (see, e.g., Barrick and Mount 1991). Such measures were also tried out for pilots and ATCs and are today frequently used as part of the selection system for both civil and military pilots including RPA pilots. Some of these tests have been especially developed for pilot selection (see, e.g., Hörman and Maschke 1996), whereas others are measures developed for assessing personality traits in the general population. How the test results are used may vary between organizations and countries. Sometimes, the test results are used in addition to cognitive ability tests, whereas in other contexts the test results are used in combination with other types of information collected during an interview. One important issue when adding measures of personality measures or other noncognitive abilities to the selection system is whether or not they contribute incremental validity to predictors already in operational use.

5.5.2 SELECTION OF ATCS

Selection of applicants for ATC education occurs in most Western countries by using psychological tests, but research in this area is less extensive compared to that for pilot selection (Edgar 2002). The first psychological tests were put into use early in the 1960s and consisted of paper-and-pencil tests (Hätting 1991). Today, computerized tests are used in many countries, and the selection process is often as comprehensive as that for pilots.

Most validation studies in relation to ATCs have been conducted by the FAA and the U.S. military. The first test batteries adopted in the 1960s had paper-and-pencil tests measuring reasoning (verbal and numerical), perceptual speed, and spatial skills (Hätting 1991). Test results were combined with information about education, age, and experience in the selection process. In the 1970s, the FAA began developing a simulation-based test that would measure the candidates' skills in applying different rules in a simulated airspace. The test was later adapted to a paper-and-pencil format and labeled "multiplex controller aptitude test." It was used together with measures of reasoning ability and professional experience in the selection from the beginning of the 1980s. The development of a computerized test battery began in the 1990s, and it measured, among other things, spatial reasoning, short-term memory, sense of movement, pattern recognition, and attention (Broach and Manning 1997).

In Europe, EUROCONTROL conducted (Hätting 1991) a review of the member states' selection procedures in the late 1970s and discovered that most countries applied tests that measured spatial perception, verbal ability, reasoning, and memory. Few countries used tests to map out the interest or motivation for the profession. An exception was Germany where, in addition to a comprehensive test battery, the DLR also used a measure of personality traits and a simulation-based test to measure cooperation (Eißfeldt 1991, 1998). In addition, all countries had medical requirements and formal requirements concerning age and previous education. In Sweden, a considerable effort was put into developing a situational interview, where the purpose was to map individual abilities and social attitudes (Brehmer 2003). Situation interviews are developed from critical incidents, and the main goal is to determine effective versus ineffective work performance by asking the applicants very specific questions.

In the 1980s, computerized tests were developed in Germany and England, and in 2003 EUROCONTROL launched a common computer-based test battery (called FEAST [First European Air traffic controller Selection Test]) for the selection of ATCs that the member countries could apply. As part of this project, the member countries would also have to supply data to a joint study of the predictive validity of the tests. The current Web-based FEAST battery includes measures of cognitive abilities tests, measuring multitasking, planning ability, learning and applying rules, processing speed and attention, and 3D visualization. In addition, an English test, two work sample tests, and a personality measure (Five-factor) are also included. FEAST is run and managed by the EUROCONTROL, and it may be used alone, or in combination with other tests and interview administered locally (FEAST 2010).

Today, many countries have replaced paper-and-pencil tests entirely or partially by computerized tests. Basic cognitive abilities are measured; in addition, tasks are assigned in which computer technology is used to simulate parts of the work as an ATC.

Some personality tests have also been investigated, but the results have generally been discouraging, with weak correlations between measures and the criterion. Studies based on the Five-factor model, however, have found more positive results (Schroeder et al. 1993; King et al. 2003), and incremental validity was found in a recent study of emotional IQ (Chappelle et al. 2015).

5.6   HOW WELL DO THE DIFFERENT METHODS WORK?

Fewer validation studies have been conducted for ATCs compared to pilots. In 2000, a meta-analysis of available studies found a total of 25 articles and reports that documented validation results for ATC selection based on a total of 35 different samples (Martinussen et al. 2000). These studies were published between 1952 and 1999, and the majority of them were based on applicants and students (92%). Most of the studies were conducted in the United States (77%), and the criteria used were mostly collected during training (e.g., pass/fail, instructor evaluations, simulators).

The results from these 25 articles were combined in a meta-analysis where the average predictive validity was calculated, and the population variance of the tests was estimated. The total samples ranged between 224 and 11,255 persons for the different categories of predictors. Virtually none of the studies reported information that made it possible to correct for lack of reliability in the criterion and restriction of range. The average correlations are therefore an underestimate of the true predictive validity. Correlations were corrected for the use of a dichotomous criterion (pass/fail). The various tests and predictors were grouped into categories, and a summary of these results is presented in Figure 5.4.

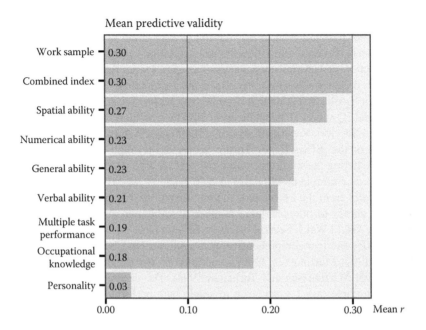

FIGURE 5.4   Meta-analysis results for ATC selection.

For all but two of the predictors (verbal skills and multitasking), there was some true variance between studies.

A study of the predictive validity of the FEAST battery was based on a sample of 225 students from five different nations against pass/fail in training and standardized observations (FEAST 2010). The FEAST battery at that point included six Web-based tests and a work sample test measuring multiple task performance. The overall FEAST test score was significantly correlated with ATC performance early in training, $r = 0.32$ ($r_c = 0.53$, corrected for range restriction and criterion reliability), and the corresponding results for the work sample test were not significant ($r = 0.12$). The results were similar for performance assessed later in training but based on a smaller sample of candidates ($n = 64$). The correlations with pass/fail in training were 0.24 ($r_c = 0.37$, corrected for range restriction) for the FEAST total score and 0.36 ($r_c = 0.47$) for the work sample test based on a sample of 106 students (FEAST 2010).

A similar validation study of one of the work sample tests included in FEAST (The Dynamic ATC Radar Test [DART]) indicated predictive validity for training criteria. The overall DART score predicted performance assessments early in training based on a sample of 171 students ($r = 0.21$; $r_c = 0.44$) (Dehn et al. 2016). The DLR has conducted a validation study of the selection system for German ATCs based on a sample of 430 candidates (Pecena et al. 2013). Three groups of cognitive ability tests were validated against training criteria in addition to a work sample score and an assessment center score. The tests measuring attention and processing speed predicted most of the criteria with correlations between 0.09 and 0.18

(r_c between 0.16–0.30) whereas the work sample score and assessment center ratings did not predict pass/fail in training, but did predict some of the other continuous training criteria (Pecena et al. 2013). Several validation studies have been conducted for the selection of U.S. military and civilian ATCs over the years (Broach et al. 2013). More recent studies have examined the incremental validity of adding the AT-SAT (Air Traffic Selection and Training test battery) (Carretta and King 2008), and emotional IQ scores (Chappelle et al. 2015) to the more basic cognitive ability tests (Armed Services Vocational Aptitude Battery [ASVAB]). The inclusion of one of sub-tests of the AT-SAT (Air Traffic Scenarios) resulted in incremental validity when predicting pass/fail in training ($R^2 = 0.13$, $R_C^2 = 0.45$) (Carretta and King 2008) based on a sample of 448 enlisted ATC students, as did the inclusion of some of the subscales from the Emotional Quotient Inventory (Chappelle et al. 2015).

When it comes to pilots, a large number of validation studies have been conducted since World War I. Several literature reviews (see, e.g., Hunter 1989; Carretta and Ree 2003) and two comprehensive meta-analyses have been published (Hunter and Burke 1994; Martinussen 1996) in addition to two small-scale meta-analyses (Damos 1993; Martinussen and Torjussen 1998). The earlier study (Damos 1993) compared multiple task performance to single task performance based on 14 and 12 different studies, respectively. Both types of measures were predictive of flight performance with mean uncorrected validities of 0.23 (multiple task performance) and 0.18 (single task). The later study (Martinussen and Torjussen 1998) integrated validation studies from the Norwegian Air Force. The two large-scale meta-analyses included all available literature at that time, and for both military and commercial pilots. In spite of a slightly different database and some procedural differences in the way the meta-analyses were conducted, the two meta-analyses resulted in very similar findings. An overview of the average correlations for the different test categories from Hunter and Burke (1994) is presented in Figure 5.5.

A total of 68 studies published between 1940 and 1990 were included with a total sample of 437,258 participants. The average correlation was not corrected for any statistical artifacts because the primary studies did not include the necessary information to make this possible. For all test categories, there was some true variation between studies, and for some test categories, the credibility interval included zero, implying that the predictive validity in some situations was zero. This applied to the categories of general intelligence, verbal skills, fine motor ability, age, education, and personality. This means that, for the other categories, the predictive validity was greater than zero even though there was some true variance between studies. More recent validation studies have confirmed the predictive validity of various cognitive and aptitude tests, including providing support for the use of computer-based tests. A study of the computer-based assessment system for the Norwegian Air Force (Martinussen and Torjussen 2004) found that the combined test score (unit-weighted) was significantly correlated with pass/fail in training ($r = 0.26$, $N = 108$). Another study by DLR of approximately 400 applicants indicated that the correlations between individual tests and pass/fail in training varied from 0.01 to 0.12 (uncorrected), some significantly, and that the multiple R was 0.14 (uncorrected) for all eight tests (Zierke 2014).

Carretta and colleagues have conducted several validation studies for predicting military pilot performance in the United States (Carretta 2000, 2011; Carretta

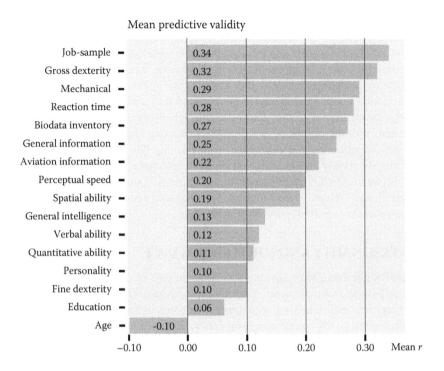

FIGURE 5.5   Meta-analysis results for pilot selection.

et al. 2014). The selection for the U.S. Air Force is based on a weighted composite (Pilot Candidate Selection Method [PCSM] score), which includes the results of the Air Force Officer Qualifying Test (AFOQT), the Test of Basic Aviation Skills (TBAS), and prior flying experience (Carretta 2011). The TBAS is a computer-administered test battery with a total of eight cognitive and perceptual-motor tests designed for pilot selection. A validation study ($N = 883$) examined the predictive validity of both the different parts of the selection system and combinations of predictors against pass/fail in training. The TBAS was correlated 0.22 with pass/fail ($r_c = 0.45$, fully corrected for range restriction and dichotomization). Personality tests in general have demonstrated a relatively modest predictive validity when used for pilot selection, whereas a more recent meta-analysis based on eight studies examining trait-based measures for military pilot selection found mean uncorrected correlations of -0.15 and 0.13 for neuroticism and extroversion, respectively (Campbell et al. 2009). These findings were supported in a study of U.S. Air Force pilot trainees where some of the Five-factor traits predicted training outcomes. However, the uncorrected correlations were generally small ($r < 0.11$) (Carretta et al. 2014), as in a study of over 3000 U.S. Air Force pilots where the highest correlation was between conscientiousness and supervisor ratings ($r = 0.08$) (Barron et al. 2016).

A few validation studies have been conducted on UAV/RPA military pilots including a study by Carretta (2013) of 139 RPA pilot trainees where test results were compared to pass/fail in undergraduate training. The AFOQT pilot composite score predicted pass/fail ($r = 0.38$), and the predictive validity increased to 0.48 when the results of psychomotor tests and flying experience were added. Another study used more long-term criteria in terms of training outcomes, which indicated, in general, much lower correlations between the AFOQT and psychomotor tests than when using pass/fail in undergraduate training (between 0.01 and 0.19) (Rose et al. 2014). A Five-factor measure was also examined, and only openness was significantly correlated with training outcomes ($r = -0.23$), indicating that those candidates who scored low on openness performed better in training (Rose et al. 2014). Another study using supervisor ratings as a criterion ($N = 330$) found a significant correlation of 0.18 between AFOQT pilot composite and ratings. Two Five-factor dimensions were significantly related to the criterion. This included neuroticism ($r = -0.14$) and conscientiousness ($r = 0.14$) (Barron et al. 2016).

5.7   PERSONALITY AND JOB PERFORMANCE

Meta-analysis results (Martinussen 1996; Martinussen et al. 2000) for both pilots and ATCs have shown that cognitive ability tests can be used effectively in the selection process, but the results are less impressive when it comes to personality measures. This finding may be due to several factors and does not imply that personality is not important for work performance. On the contrary, job analyses for both pilots and ATCs have listed personality characteristics as important in order to do a good job. For ATCs, cooperation, good communication skills, and ability to cope with stress were emphasized (Eißfeldt and Heintz 2002). For military pilots, qualities such as achievement motivation and ability to make decisions and act quickly, in addition to emotional stability, have been seen as particularly important (Carretta et al. 1996). In another study, American fighter pilots ($N = 100$) were asked to rate 60 personality traits in relation to various aspects of the job. The most important of these dimensions was conscientiousness (Siem and Murray 1994).

How can we then explain the lack of predictive validity? One possibility is that the personality tests used have not been suitable for selection purposes. For example, clinical instruments originally designed to diagnose problems or pathology may not be appropriate for personnel selection. Another possibility is that many of these tests are self-reported; applicants choose the more socially desirable response and thus it is easy for applicants to present themselves in a favorable light. A meta-analysis of personality measures based on the Five-factor model showed that although the applicants to some degree presented themselves in a favorable light, this had little effect on the predictive validity of the measures (Ones et al. 1996).

Another factor is that the criteria used are often obtained during training, and it is reasonable that some cognitive abilities are more important in this educational setting compared to personality traits. This is in line with the findings of Sells (1955, 1956), suggesting that personality tests were better predictors in the longer term. However, few validation studies have used actual job performance providing empirical evidence for this statement.

In a study of 1301 U.S. pilot students, the results indicated that the male candidates were more outgoing and scored lower on agreeableness compared to the norm. When examining the subscales of the Five-factor inventory, several differences between pilots compared to the normal population can be found: they are less vulnerable (neuroticism); they are active, outgoing, and seek new experiences (openness); and they are coping oriented and competent (conscientiousness). Female pilots showed many of the same characteristics compared to a normative sample of women; in addition, they scored higher on openness to new experience. In other words, they like to try out new things (Callister et al. 1999).

In another study of 112 pilots from the U.S. Air Force, female pilots were compared with male pilots and with a random sample of women. Female pilots scored higher than their male colleagues on the dimensions agreeableness, extroversion, and conscientiousness. They were also more emotionally stable and scored higher on openness (King et al. 1998).

A study of U.S. military pilot students showed that, compared with normative data, these pilots could be described as people who set themselves high goals and engaged in constructive activities to achieve these goals. The goals often included new and unfamiliar experiences and also the quest for increased status, knowledge, and skills. They appeared often as calm, less inhibited, and more willing to tolerate risk compared to a normative sample (Lambirth et al. 2003). Another study of Slovanian Air Force pilots by Meško et al. (2013) found better emotional control, a higher level of emotional stability, extroversion, and higher impulse control among military pilots compared to the general population and other control groups. Personality traits have also been linked to team performance in aviation as well as to accident involvement (for an overview, see Ganesh and Joseph 2005).

In studies that have compared ATCs with other professions, it has been found that ATC students scored lower than other students on anxiety (Nye and Collins 1993). In another study using the Five-factor taxonomy, they scored higher on openness to new experience and conscientiousness and lower on neuroticism than a norm group (Schroeder et al. 1993).

There is, however, little evidence to support the notion of a fixed pilot personality or ATC personality. Pilots and ATCs vary on a number of personality characteristics in the same way that people in the general population vary. At the same time, there are some differences between the pilots and ATCs as a group and the general population, probably as a function of the selection process and self-selection before people enter these professions.

5.8 COMPUTER-BASED TESTING

The first computerized tests were developed in the 1970s and 1980s (Hunter and Burke 1987; Kantor and Carretta 1988; Bartram 1995). As computer technology has become both cheaper and more efficient, paper-and-pencil tests have entirely or partially been replaced with computerized tests in most Western countries (Burke et al. 1995). The introduction of computerized testing has led to simplifications in test administration and scoring. But both computers and software need to be updated, so this type of testing also requires maintenance and revisions. The computerized tests may be administered locally or through the Web. With computerized tests the installation and usually the data remain on the machines whereas with Web-based testing the test content and data are stored in a secure external environment. The Web-based testing may be done from home or under supervision in a controlled environment, which makes it easier to ensure that the correct candidate is completing the test and that the candidate does not receive any help during the test session.

An advantage of the use of computerized testing is that it has made it possible to test more complex psychological abilities and skills than before. It is now possible to measure reaction time and attention, both alone and as part of a more complex task. It is also possible to simulate parts of future work tasks and to present information both on the screen and through headphones. A problem associated with such complex dynamic testing is that the test may progress differently for different applicants. Options and priorities taken at an early stage could have consequences for both the workload and complexity of the task later.

In addition, it may be that applicants use different skills and strategies for problem solving. For example, someone may give priority to speed rather than safety and accuracy. This makes the scoring of such tests more complicated than with simpler tests, where the number of correct answers will usually be sufficient indices of performance. Another aspect of such dynamic tests is that they often require longer instruction and introduction periods before the testing can begin. This makes them time consuming. They are therefore often used at a later stage in the selection process, when the applicant group has already been tested with simpler tests and only the strongest candidates are permitted to enter the final phase of the selection process.

Computers have made it possible to apply more adaptive testing. That is, the degree of difficulty of the tasks is determined by how the candidate performs the first tasks in the test. This type of test is based on item response theory (see, e.g., Embretson and Reise 2000) in which the purpose is to estimate the person's ability level. These tests are expensive in the developmental stage, and most tests used today are based on classical test theory.

With the Internet, it is now possible to test applicants located anywhere in the world. This is financially beneficial to the organization because it saves travel expenses. It is likely that the use of the Internet to conduct such pretesting will be adopted by more organizations. Testing of applicants in their homes over the Internet allows organizations to prescreen applicants, eliminating from consideration those who are clearly unsuitable. This is financially beneficial and it allows applicants to investigate whether this is something for them to pursue. In the next step in the selection process, the best applicants will be invited to participate in further testing and whether the correct person actually took the tests can be checked. Some organizations provide applicants with information about the tests, and they are also given the opportunity to practice some of the tests before the selection process begins.

5.9 THE UTILITY OF SELECTION METHODS

Utility refers to how much an organization saves by applying specific methods in the selection process rather than using a more random selection process (for an overview of the topic, see Hunter 2004). Several models may be used in order to estimate this, and one critical factor in these models is, of course, the value of a good employee relative to a less efficient employee. A rule of thumb that has proven to hold for many occupations is that the best employees produce about twice as much as the worst. In utility calculations, the expenses associated with the selection process and testing have to be included, but this amount is often much smaller compared to that for a poor performing employee or a candidate who fails to complete an expensive training program. In addition, it is to be hoped that increased safety is also an outcome, but this is harder to document empirically because serious accidents are rare in aviation and those who could constitute the control group are normally not hired.

Calculations performed by the DLR in 2000 showed that the selection of *ab initio* candidates costs €3900 per candidate, while the training costs €120,000. If the candidate fails training, the expenditure is estimated to be €50,000 (Goeters and Maschke 2002). The corresponding figure from the U.S. Air Force is between $50,000 and $80,000 for candidates who fail training (Hunter and Burke 1995). In other words, the test costs are relatively low compared to the costs for those who do not complete pilot training.

A simple model that may also be used to calculate the utility of the selection procedure is based on Taylor and Russel's (1939) tables. Their model assumes a dichotomous criterion, which is illustrated in Figure 5.6. According to the model, two correct decisions can be made:

1. Select those who would perform the job successfully.
2. Do not hire those who would not perform the job satisfactorily.

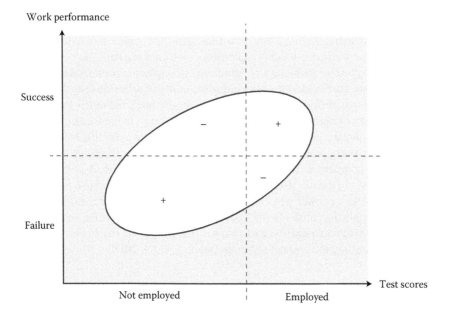

FIGURE 5.6 Right and wrong selection decisions.

Two erroneous decisions can also be made:

1. Employ those who will not be successful (candidates who clearly pose the greatest problem for the organization).
2. Reject those who would manage the job.

The correct decisions are marked with (+) in the figure and the erroneous are marked with (−). The larger the correlation (in other words, the predictive validity) is, the more often correct decisions are made. To calculate the increase in correct decisions by using a given selection method, we need to know the predictive validity, the selection ratio, and how many would perform the job successfully in the applicant group (base rate).

For example, assume that the aviation authorities want to hire 20 people to perform security checks at a smaller airport. Assume that there are 100 applicants and that approximately 50% would be able to perform the job. If we do not use any form of selection process, but rather pick randomly, approximately half of the candidates would do the job satisfactorily. Suppose that we also use an ability test and the predictive validity is 0.40. To sum up, the selection rate is 20/100 = 0.20, base rate is 0.50, and the predictive validity is 0.40. What is the utility of using the test? By inspecting the table, we find that we increase the number that would succeed in the job from 50% to 73%. If the predictive validity is lower—for example, 0.20—the increase would be from 50% to 61%. If the selection rate is lower, fewer people are selected (e.g., only the top 5% of the applicants), and the proportion would increase from 50% to 82% (with $r = 0.40$). In other words, the lower the selection rate and the higher the validity are, the more advantage is provided by using the test.

The effect of changes in the base rate is somewhat more complicated, and the farther away from a base rate of 0.50, the smaller the increase in successful applicants is. Imagine a rather extreme situation (e.g., with no qualified applicants); it does not matter how high the predictive validity is because it will not improve the outcome; that is, no one would be able to do the job. Additional examples are presented in Table 5.1.

More sophisticated models for calculating the utility of selection tests do not make the assumption that performance is twofold (success/failure), but rather that it can be assessed on a more continuous scale. The most difficult part in these calculations is to estimate the monetary value of different workers. One way to do this is to assume a dollar value for a very productive employee—for example, by estimating how much it would cost the company to hire someone to perform the same job. A good employee means one who is in the top layer (i.e., the 85th percentile compared to a poor worker, who is at the 15th or lower percentile). In addition, the predictive validity and the quality of the applicants must also be known. These estimates can then be used to calculate how much the organization will earn per year per person employed. Included in these calculations are the costs of selection (see, e.g., Cook 2009).

5.10 FAIRNESS IN SELECTION

Many countries have laws that prohibit discrimination on the basis of gender, race, and political or religious convictions when hiring. Some countries, such as the

TABLE 5.1
Utility of Selection Methods

Base Rate		Selection Rate		
(%)	*r*	**0.10**	**0.30**	**0.50**
10	0.10	0.13	0.12	0.11
10	0.30	0.22	0.17	0.14
10	0.50	0.32	0.22	0.17
50	0.10	0.57	0.55	0.53
50	0.30	0.71	0.64	0.60
50	0.50	0.84	0.74	0.67

Source: The examples are from Taylor, H.C. and Russel, J.T. 1939. *Journal of Applied Psychology* 32: 565–578.

United States, also have laws against discrimination because of age or disability. Many countries have also adopted guidelines on the use of tests in employment where there are specified requirements for the test user and the methods.

A topic that has been discussed for a long time is how the concept of fairness should be understood. Is a method fair if it has the same predictive validity for different applicant groups, or is it only fair if the method will result in an equal number of people hired as they are represented in the applicant group or perhaps in the population? If, for example, women constitute 30% of the applicant group and a company only hires 5% of women applicants, then the selection method is unfair, that is, it is said to have adverse impact.

Opinions differ on which group should be used for comparison. Is it the total adult population in a country, or is it the group of qualified candidates that should be considered? The latter is probably the most reasonable choice when calculating the adverse impact. In the United States, the employer must ensure that the method used does not have an adverse impact. The solution is then to be sure to hire a certain proportion of the groups that would have been underrepresented. Alternatively, the employer must argue that the test or method is job related and has predictive validity. That other equally valid methods do not have such a negative impact must also be ruled out. The legal practice on this topic appears to be far stricter in the United States (where many lawsuits have been instrumental in shaping today's practice) than in Europe.

5.10.1 DIFFERENTIAL PREDICTIVE VALIDITY

Two hypotheses are concerned with the claim that a test is valid for one group only (often white men), but not for others (e.g., different ethnic groups). One is that the test predicts job performance for one of the groups, but not for the other. The second hypothesis is that the tests are valid for both groups, but have a higher validity for one of the groups (differential validity). It has been difficult to document this, however, probably because the primary studies that have examined the predictive validity for the two groups have often included very small samples of minorities. Meta-analyses have not found support for the hypothesis of differential validity for white versus nonwhite, beyond what one might expect as a result of chance (Hunter et al. 1979).

Similarly, in a meta-analysis where validity coefficients for women were compared with those for men, there was no overall support for differential test validity (Rothstein and McDaniel 1992). However, it turned out that for jobs that required little education and where there was a very high proportion of women or of men, some support for differential predictive validity was discovered. A study of U.S. Air Force applicants found no gender difference in tests' predictive validity in relation to flight performance (Carretta 1997).

All in all, little evidence supports the idea of differential validity, but this does not imply that all groups necessarily will have the same mean test score on all tests. Fair methods imply that the test predicts job performance equally accurately in the different groups, rather than that groups have the same average test score.

5.11 APPLICANT REACTIONS

Most of the research in personnel selection has studied the development and validation of selection methods. It is easy to understand that an organization wants to focus on these areas in order to ensure that the methods with the highest predictive validity are used for selection. Another related perspective is to consider the selection process from the applicant's perspective. How does the person experience the selection methods and what kind of impression does he or she get from the organization on the basis of the selection process? The methods that applicants prefer are not necessarily the methods with the highest predictive validity.

Nevertheless, we should be concerned about the applicant's perspective for several reasons. First, applicants' perceptions of the methods' validity and fairness could influence their motivation to perform well on the tests. If the methods appear strange and unrelated to the job, applicants may be reluctant to do their best and perform well. This may also affect the chances that they will accept a future offer of employment from the organization. In a situation where young people have many opportunities for education and employment, it is important to attract the best applicants.

Several studies have examined what applicants or volunteers (often students) think about different methods, such as ability tests, personality tests, or interview. What applicants prefer depends to some extent on the context (i.e., the job sought) and whether they feel they have some control over what is going on. The content of the test or questions in the interview are also critical, and applicants in general prefer job-relevant questions.

Two studies of pilot applicants examined what the candidates thought about the selection process. One was based on the selection of pilots for Lufthansa (Maschke 2004), and the second study consisted of selection of pilots for the Air Force in Norway (Lang-Ree and Martinussen 2006). In both cases, the applicants were satisfied with the selection process and the procedures were considered to be fair. The applicants were also asked to rate different tests and methods used, and the computerized tests received the highest ratings. In the survey, the relationship between applicants' responses and test performances was also examined (Lang-Ree and Martinussen 2006). The results showed that those who had the most positive attitudes toward the selection system performed slightly better on tests, perhaps not surprisingly.

5.12 SUMMARY

This chapter has dealt with important principles in personnel selection and how selection methods, including tests, should be evaluated. Development of a selection system should start with a job analysis where the abilities and personal characteristics needed to accomplish the job should be specified. Then, methods suited to precise measurement of those capabilities or characteristics should be chosen. It is important to have evidence that the methods have predictive validity, either from local validation studies or from meta-analyses. Other important aspects of the selection process are the applicants' reactions and attitudes and that the methods used are fair. The utility of the selection can be calculated in dollars or in terms of correct decisions. Often, the costs associated with conducting a selection process are small relative to the costs of employees who are not performing well or who are unable to complete training.

5.13 OUTSIDE ACTIVITIES

- How would you select personnel to your position (or a similar)? Try to describe five critical tasks that a person would have to do in order to complete the job successfully. After describing the tasks, what type of abilities and personality traits would be needed to solve the tasks? How can these abilities and traits be measured, and how would you document that the selection procedure works successfully?

RECOMMENDED READINGS

Cook, M. 2009. *Personnel Selection. Adding Value Through People*, 5th ed. Chichester, UK: John Wiley & Sons.
Hunter, D.R. and Burke, E.F. 1995. *Handbook of Pilot Selection*. Aldershot, UK: Avebury Aviation.

REFERENCES

Barrick, M.R. and Mount, M.K. 1991. The Big Five personality dimensions and job performance: A meta-analysis. *Personality Psychology* 44: 1–26.
Barron, L.G., Carretta, T.R., and Rose, M.R. 2016. Aptitude and trait predictors of manned and unmanned aircraft pilot job performance. *Military Psychology* 28: 65–77.
Bartram, D. 1995. Validation of the MICROPAT battery. *International Journal of Selection and Assessment* 3: 83–94.
Bartram, D. 2005. The great eight competences: A criterion-centric approach to validation. *Journal of Applied Psychology* 90: 1185–1203.
Bartram, D. and Baxter, P. 1996. Validation of the Cathay Pacific Airways pilot selection program. *International Journal of Aviation Psychology* 6: 149–169.
Bartram, D. and Dale, H.C. 1982. The Eysenck personality inventory as a selection test for military pilots. *Journal of Occupational Psychology* 55: 287–296.

BEA. 2016. *Final report accident on 24 March 2015 at Prads-Haute-Bléone (Alpes-de-Haute-Provence, France) to the Airbus A320-211 registered D-AIPX operated by Germanwings.* Retrieved from: https://www.bea.aero/uploads/tx_elyextendttnews/BEA2015-0125.en-LR_03.pdf

Brehmer, B. 2003. Predictive validation of the MRU battery. *Proceedings of the Second EUROCONTROL Selection Seminar. HRS/MSP-002-REP-07.* Brussels, Belgium: EUROCONTROL.

Broach, D. 2013. *Selection of the Next Generation of Air Traffic Control Specialists: Aptitude Requirements for the Air Traffic Control Tower Cab in 2018.* DOT/FAA/AM-13/5. Washington, DC: Federal Aviation Administration, Office of Aviation Medicine.

Broach, D., Byrne, C., Manning, C., Pierce, L., McCauley, D., and Bleckley, M.K. 2013. *The Validity of the Air Traffic Selection and Training (AT-SAT) Test Battery in Operational Use.* DOT/FAA/AM-13/3. Washington, DC: Federal Aviation Administration Office of Aerospace Medicine.

Broach, D. and Manning, C.A. 1997. *Review of Air Traffic Controller Selection: An International Perspective.* DOT/FAA/AM-97/15. Washington, DC: Federal Aviation Administration Office of Aviation Medicine.

Burke, E., Kokorian, A., Lescreve, F., Martin, C.J., Van Raay, P., and Weber, W. 1995. Computer-based assessment: A NATO survey. *International Journal of Selection and Assessment* 3: 75–83.

Callister, J.D., King, R.E., and Retzlaff, P.D. 1999. Revised NEO personality inventory profiles of male and female U.S. Air Force pilots. *Military Medicine* 164: 885–890.

Campbell, J.S., Castaneda, M., and Pulos, S. 2009. Meta-analysis of personality assessments as predictors of military aviation training success. *The International Journal of Aviation Psychology* 20: 92–109. doi: 0.1080/10508410903415872

Carretta, T.R. 1997. Male–female performance on U.S. Air Force pilot selection tests. *Aviation, Space and Environmental Medicine* 68: 818–823.

Carretta, T.R. 2000. US Air Force pilot selection and training methods. *Aviation, Space and Environmental Medicine* 71: 950–956.

Carretta, T.R. 2011. Pilot Candidate Selection Method. Still an effective candidate predictor for US Air Force pilot training performance. *Aviation Psychology and Applied Human Factors* 1: 3–8.

Carretta, T.R. 2013. Predictive validity of pilot selection instruments for remotely piloted aircraft training outcome. *Aviation, Space and Environmental Medicine* 84: 47–53.

Carretta, T.R. and King, R.E. 2008. Improved military air traffic controller selection methods as measured by subsequent training performance. *Aviation, Space, and Environmental Medicine* 79: 36–43.

Carretta, T.R. and Ree, M.J. 2003. Pilot selection methods. In Tsang, P.S. and Vidulich, M.A. (Eds.) *Principles and Practice of Aviation Psychology* (pp. 357–396). Mahwah, NJ: Lawrence Erlbaum Associates.

Carretta, T.R., Rodgers, M.N., and Hansen, I. 1996. *The Identification of Ability Requirements and Selection Instruments for Fighter Pilot Training.* Technical Report No. 2. Euro–NATO Aircrew Human Factor Working Group. Brooks Air Force Base, TX: Air Force Materiel Command.

Carretta, T.R., Teachout, M.S., Ree, M.J., Barto, E.L., King, R.E., and Michaels, C.F. 2014. Consistency of the relations of cognitive ability and personality traits to pilot training performance. *The International Journal of Aviation Psychology* 24: 247–264.

Chappelle, W., Thompson, W., Godman, T., Bryan, C.J., and Reardon, L. 2015. The utility of testing non-cognitive aptitudes as additional predictors of graduation from US Air Force air traffic controller training. *Aviation Psychology and Applied Human Factors* 5: 93–103.

Cook, M. 2009. *Personnel Selection. Adding Value Through People,* 5th ed. Chichester, UK: John Wiley & Sons.

Damos, D.L. 1993. Using meta-analysis to compare the predictive validity of single- and multiple-task measures to flight performance. *Human Factors* 35: 615–628.

Damos, D. 2011. *KSAOs for Military Pilot Selection: A Review of the Literature.* Report number AFCAPS-FR-2011-0003. Randolf AFB, TX: Air Force Personnel Center Strategic Research and Assessment.

Damos, D.L. 2014. Editor's preface to the special issue on pilot selection. *The International Journal of Aviation Psychology* 24: 1–5. doi: 10.1080/10508414.2014.860839

Dehn, D., Diaz, U.G., Vasilisca, I., and Damitz, M. 2016. *DART—Validation of the Dynamic ATC Radar Test.* Report 1.0. Luxembourg: EUROCONTROL.

Dierdorff, E.C. and Wilson, M.A. 2003. A meta-analysis of job analysis reliability. *Journal of Applied Psychology* 88: 635–646.

Dockeray, F.C. and Isaacs, S. 1921. Psychological research in aviation in Italy, France, England, and the American Expeditionary Forces. *Journal of Comparative Psychology* 1: 115–148.

EASA. 2015. Action plan for the implementation of the Germanwings Task Force recommendations. Retrieved from: http://www.easa.europa.eu/download/various/GW_action-plan_final.pdf

Edgar, E. 2002. Cognitive predictors in ATCO selection: Current and future perspectives. In Eißfeldt, H., Heil, M.C., and Broach, D. (Eds.), *Staffing the ATM System. The Selection of Air Traffic Controllers* (pp. 73–83). Aldershot, UK: Ashgate.

Eißfeldt, H. 1991. DLR selection of air traffic control applicants. In Farmer, E. (Ed.), *Human Resource Management in Aviation* (pp. 37–49). Aldershot, UK: Avebury Technical.

Eißfeldt, H. 1998. The selection of air traffic controllers. In Goethers, K.M. (ed.), *Aviation Psychology: A Science and a Profession* (pp. 73–80). Aldershot, UK: Ashgate.

Eißfeldt, H., Grasshoff, D., Hasse, C., Hoermann, H.-J., Kissing, D.S., Stern, C., Wenzel, J., and Zierke, O. 2009. *Aviator 2030. Ability Requirements in Future ATM Systems II: Simulations and Experiments.* Hamburg, Germany: Deutsches Zentrum für Luft- und Raumfahrt e. V. Institut für Luft- und Raumfahrtmedizin, Luft- und Raumfahrtpsychologie. Retrieved from: http://www.dlr.de/me/Portaldata/25/Resources/dokumente/Aviator_2030_Report_FB_2009-28.pdf

Eißfeldt, H. and Heintz, A. 2002. Ability requirements for DFS controllers: Current and future. In Eißfeldt, H., Heil, M.C., and Broach, D. (Eds.), *Staffing the ATM System. The Selection of Air Traffic Controllers* (pp. 13–24). Aldershot, UK: Ashgate Publishing Limited.

Embretson, S.E. and Reise, S.P. 2000. *Item Response Theory for Psychologists.* Mahwah, NJ: Lawrence Erlbaum Associates.

FEAST. 2010. *Validation of the First European Air Traffic Controller Selection Tests (FEAST).* Brussels, Belgium: Eurocontrol.

Fitts, P.M. 1946. German applied psychology during World War 2. *American Psychologist* 1: 151–161.

Flanagan, J.C. 1954. The critical incident technique. *Psychological Bulletin* 51: 327–358.

Fleishman, E.A. 1975. Toward a taxonomy of human performance. *American Psychologist* 30: 1127–1149.

Fleishman, E.A. and Reilly, M.E. 2001. *Handbook of Human Abilities.* Potomac, MD: Management Research Institute, Inc.

Ganesh, A. and Joseph, C. 2005. Personality studies in aircrew: An overview. *Indian Journal of Aerospace Medicine* 49: 54–62.

Goeters, K.M. and Maschke, P. 2002. Cost-benefit analysis: Is the psychological selection of pilots worth the money? *The 25th Conference of EAAP*, Warsaw, Poland, September 16–20.

Goeters, K.M., Maschke, P., and Eißfeldt, H. 2004. Ability requirements in core aviation professions: Job analysis of airline pilots and air traffic controllers. In Goeters, K.M. (Ed.), *Aviation Psychology: Practice and Research* (pp. 99–119). Aldershot, UK: Ashgate Publishing Limited.

Hätting, H.J. 1991. Selection of air traffic control cadets. In Galand, R.A. and Mangelsdorff, A.D. (Eds.), *Handbook of Military Psychology* (pp. 115–148). Chichester, UK: John Wiley & Sons.

Hausknecht, J.P., Day, D.V., and Thomas, S.C. 2004. Applicant reactions to selection procedures: An updated model and meta-analysis. *Personnel Psychology* 57: 639–683.

Henmon, V.A.C. 1919. Air service tests of aptitude for flying. *Journal of Applied Psychology* 2: 103–109.

Hilton, T.F. and Dolgin, D.L. 1991. Pilot selection in the military of the free world. In Gal, R. and Mangelsdorff, A.D. (Eds.), *Handbook of Military Psychology* (pp. 81–101). New York, NY: John Wiley & Sons.

Hörmann, H. and Maschke, P. 1996. On the relation between personality and job performance of airline pilots. *International Journal of Aviation Psychology* 6: 171–178.

Howse, W.R. and Damos, D. 2011. *Historical Scientific Analysis of Aviator Selection.* AFCAPS-FR-2011-0008. Randolf Air Force Base, TX: Air Force Personnel Center.

Hunter, D.R. 1989. Aviator selection. In Wiskoff, M.F. and Rampton, G.F. (Eds.), *Military Personnel Measurement: Testing, Assignment, Evaluation* (pp. 129–167). New York, NY: Praeger.

Hunter, D.R. and Burke, E.F. 1987. Computer-based selection testing in the Royal Air Force. *Behavior Research Methods, Instruments, & Computers* 19: 243–245.

Hunter, D.R. and Burke, E.F. 1994. Predicting aircraft pilot-training success: A meta-analysis of published research. *International Journal of Aviation Psychology* 4: 297–313.

Hunter, D.R. and Burke, E.F. 1995. *Handbook of Pilot Selection.* Aldershot, UK: Avebury Aviation.

Hunter, J.E. and Schmidt, F.L. 2014. *Methods of Meta-Analysis: Correcting Error and Bias in Research Findings,* 3rd ed. Beverly Hills, CA: Sage.

Hunter, J.E., Schmidt, F.L., and Hunter, R. 1979. Differential validity of employment tests by race: A comprehensive review and analysis. *Psychological Bulletin* 86: 721–735.

Hunter, M. 2004. Kapittel 11, Personalekonomiska aspekter [Chapter 11, Personnel and economical aspects]. In Hunter, M. (Ed.), *Arbetspsykologisk Testning [Psychological Testing in the Work Place],* 2nd ed. (pp. 355–386). Stockholm, Sweden: Psykologiforlaget AB.

International Air Transport Association (IATA). 2010. Guidance material and best practices for pilot aptitude testing. Montreal: Author. Retrieved from https://www.iata.org/publications/Documents/pilot-aptitude-testing-guide.pdf

Jessup, G. and Jessup, H. 1971. Validity of the Eysenck personality inventory in pilot selection. *Occupational Psychology* 45: 111–123.

Johnson, J.T. and Ree, M.J. 1994. Rangej: A Pascal program to compute the multivariate correction for range restriction. *Educational and Psychological Measurement* 54: 693–695.

Kantor, J.E. and Carretta, T.R. 1988. Aircrew selection systems. *Aviation, Space, and Environmental Medicine* 59: A32–A38.

Kelly, G. 1955. *The Psychology of Personal Constructs.* New York, NY: Norton.

King, R.E., Retzlaff, P.D., Detwiler, C.A., Schroeder, D.J., and Broach, D. 2003. *Use of Personality Assessment Measures in the Selection of Air Traffic Control Specialists.* DOT/FAA/AM-03/20. Oklahoma City, OK: FAA Civil Aerospace Medical Institute.

King, R.E., Retzlaff, P.D., and McGlohn, S.E. 1998. Female United States Air Force pilot personality: The new right stuff. *Military Medicine* 162: 695–697.

Kragh, U. 1960. The defense mechanism test: A new method for diagnosis and personnel selection. *Journal of Applied Psychology* 44: 303–309.

Lambirth, T.T., Dolgin, D.L., Rentmeister-Bryant, H.K., and Moore, J.L. 2003. Selected personality characteristics of student naval aviators and student naval flight officers. *International Journal of Aviation Psychology* 13: 415–427.

Lang-Ree, O.C. and Martinussen, M. 2006. Applicant reactions and attitudes towards the selection procedure in the Norwegian Air Force. *Human Factors and Aerospace Safety* 6: 345–358.

Lawley, D.N. 1943. A note on Karl Pearson's selection formulae. *Proceedings of the Royal Society of Edinburgh, Series A* 62: 28–30.

Levant, R.F. 2005. *Report of the 2005 Presidential Task Force on Evidence-Based Practice.* Washington, DC: American Psychological Association. Retrieved from: http://www. apa.org/practice/resources/evidence/evidence-based-report.pdf

Martinussen, M. 1996. Psychological measures as predictors of pilot performance: A meta-analysis. *International Journal of Aviation Psychology* 1: 1–20.

Martinussen, M., Jenssen, M., and Joner, A. 2000. Selection of air traffic controllers: Some preliminary findings from a meta-analysis of validation studies. *Proceedings of the 24th EAAP (European Association for Aviation Psychology) Conference.* Crieff, Scotland, September 4–8, 2000.

Martinussen, M. and Torjussen, T. 1993. Does DMT (defense mechanism test) predict pilot performance only in Scandinavia? In Jensen, R.S. and Neumeister, D. (Eds.), *Proceedings of the Seventh International Symposium on Aviation Psychology* (pp. 398–403). Columbus, OH: Ohio State University.

Martinussen, M. and Torjussen, T. 1998. Pilot selection in the Norwegian Air Force: A validation and meta-analysis of the test battery. *International Journal of Aviation Psychology* 8: 33–45.

Martinussen, M. and Torjussen, T. 2004. Initial validation of a computer-based assessment battery for pilot selection in the Norwegian Air Force. *Human Factors and Aerospace Safety* 4: 233–244.

Maschke, P. 2004. The acceptance of ab initio pilot selection methods. *Human Factors and Aerospace Safety* 4: 225–232

McDaniel, M.A., Whetzel, D.L., Schmidt, F.L., and Maurer, S.D. 1994. The validity of employment interviews: A comprehensive review and meta-analysis. *Journal of Applied Psychology* 79: 599–616.

Melton, R.S. 1954. Studies in the evaluation of the personality characteristics of successful naval aviators. *Journal of Aviation Medicine* 25: 600–604.

Meško, M., Karpljuk, D., Štok, Z.M., Videmšek, M., Bertoncel, T., Bertoncelj, A., and Podbregar, I. 2013. Motor abilities and psychological characteristics of Slovene military pilots. *The International Journal of Aviation Psychology* 23: 306–318.

Moser, U. 1981. Eine Methode zure Bestimmung Wiederstandsfähigkeit gegenüber der Konfliktreaktiverung unter Verwendung des Rorschachtests, dargestellt am Problem der Pilotenselektion. *Schweizerische Zeitschrift für Psychologie* 40: 279–313.

Nye, L.G. and Collins, W.E. 1993. Some personality and aptitude characteristics of air traffic control specialist trainees. *Aviation Space and Environmental Medicine* 64: 711–716.

Ones, D.S., Viswesvaran, C., and Reiss, A.D. 1996. Role of social desirability in personality testing for personnel selection: The red herring. *Journal of Applied Psychology* 81: 660–679.

Paullin, C., Ingerick, M., Trippe, D.M., and Wasko, L. 2011. *Identifying Best Bet Entry-Level Selection Measures for US Air Force Remotely Piloted Aircraft (RPA) Pilot and Sensor Operator (SO) Occupations.* AFCAPS_FR-2011-0013. Randolph AFB, TX: Air Force Personnel Center, Strategic Research and Assessment Branch.

Pecena, Y., Keye, D., Conzelmann, K., Grasshoff, D., Maschke, P., Heintz, A., and Eißfledt, H. 2013. Predictive validity of a selection procedure for air traffic controller trainees. *Aviation Psychology and Applied Human Factors* 3: 19–27.

Riis, E. 1986. Militærpsykologien i Norge [Military Psychology in Norway]. *Journal of the Norwegian Psychological Association* 23(Suppl. 1): 21–37.

Rose, M.R., Arnold, R.D., and Howse, W.R. 2013. Unmanned aircraft systems selection practices: Current research and future directions. *Military Psychology* 25: 413–427.

Rose, M.R., Barron, L.G., Carretta, T.R., Arnold, R.D., and Howse, W.R. 2014. Early iden-
tification of unmanned aircraft pilots using measures of personality and aptitude. *The International Journal of Aviation Psychology* 24: 36–52.

Rothstein, H.R. and McDaniel, M.A. 1992. Differential validity by sex in employment settings. *Journal of Business and Psychology* 7: 45–62.

Sackett, D.L., Rosenberg, W.M., Gray, J.A., Haynes, R.B., and Richardson, W.S. 1996.
Evidence based medicine: What it is and what it isn't. *British Medical Journal* 312(7023): 71–72.

Sackett, P.R. and Yang, H. 2000. Correction for range restriction: An expanded typology.
Journal of Applied Psychology 85: 112–118.

Schmidt, F.L. and Hunter, J.E. 1998. The validity and utility of selection methods in personnel psychology: Practical and theoretical implications of 85 years of research findings.
Psychological Bulletin 124: 262–274.

Schmidt, F.L. and Hunter, J. 2004. General mental ability in the world of work: Occupational
attainment and job performance. *Journal of Personality and Social Psychology* 86: 162–173.

Schroeder, D.J., Broach, D., and Young, W.C. 1993. *Contribution of Personality to the Prediction of Success in Initial Air Traffic Control Specialist Training.* DOT/FAA/AM-93/4. Washington, DC: Federal Aviation Administration, Office of Aviation Medicine.

Sells, S.B. 1955. Development of a personality test battery for psychiatric screening of flying
personnel. *Journal of Aviation Medicine* 26: 35–45.

Sells, S.B. 1956. Further developments on adaptability screening for flying personnel.
Aviation Medicine 27: 440–451.

Siem, F.M. and Murray, M.W. 1994. Personality factors affecting pilot combat performance: A
preliminary investigation. *Aviation, Space and Environmental Medicine* 65: A45–A48.

Taylor, H.C. and Russel, J.T. 1939. The relationship of validity coefficients to the practical
effectiveness of tests in selection. *Journal of Applied Psychology* 32: 565–578.

Termøhlen, J. 1986. Flyvepsykologiens udvikling [The development of Aviation Psychology].
In Moustgaard, I.K. and Petersen, A.F. (Eds.), *Udviklingslinier i dansk psykologi: Fra Alfred Lehmann til i dag [Historical trends in Danish psychology: From Alfred Lehmann until today]* (pp. 169–181). Copenhagen, Denmark: Gyldendal.

Thorndike, R.L. 1949. *Personnel Selection: Test and Measurement Techniques.* New York, NY: John Wiley & Sons.

Torjussen, T.M. and Hansen, I. 1999. The Norwegian defense, best in test? The use of apti-
tude tests in the defense with emphasis on pilot selection. *Journal of the Norwegian Psychological Association* 36: 772–779.

Torjussen, T.M. and Værnes, R. 1991. The use of the defense mechanism test (DMT) in
Norway for selection and stress research. In Olff, M., Godaert, G., and Ursin, H. (Eds.), *Quantification of Human Defense Mechanisms* (pp. 172–206). Berlin, Germany: Springer-Verlag.

Weissmuller, J.J. and Damos, D.L. 2014. Improving the pilot selection system: Statistical
approaches and selection processes. *The International Journal of Aviation Psychology* 24: 99–118.

Whitener, E.M. 1990. Confusion of confidence intervals and credibility intervals in meta-
analysis. *Journal of Applied Psychology* 75: 315–321.

Wilson, M. 2007. A history of job analysis. In Koppes, L. (Ed.), *Historical Perspectives in Industrial and Organizational Psychology* (pp. 219–241). Mahwah, NJ: Lawrence Erlbaum Associates.

Zierke, O. 2014. Predictive validity of knowledge tests for pilot training outcome. *Aviation Psychology and Applied Human Factors* 4: 98–105. doi: 10.1027/2192-0923/a000061

6 Training

6.1 INTRODUCTION

In the earliest days of aviation, there were no instructor pilots. The first aviators such as Orville and Wilbur Wright, Octave Chanute, Otto Lilienthal, and the Norwegian Hans Fleischer Dons* (originally a submarine officer) trained themselves. They were simultaneously test pilots and student pilots, with the inevitable consequence that many (including Lilienthal who died in a glider crash in 1896) died during the process of discovering how to maintain control of their aircraft. Aspiring modern pilots are fortunate to be the beneficiaries of the experiences of those pioneers, along with several succeeding generations of pilots who have also made their contributions to the art and science of aviation training. However, not all advances in aviation training have come from pilots. Researchers, most of them nonpilots, in the fields of psychology and education have also helped shape the format, if not the content, of current aviation training. Principles of how humans learn new skills developed in the laboratories have been applied advantageously to pilot training. In this chapter, we examine some of those principles and how they are applied in an aviation setting, along with the general process of training development.

Training is a broad term that covers a number of activities conducted in a variety of settings. Training can be categorized according to when it occurs, for example, initial training required to impart some new skill set, as opposed to remedial training required to maintain those skills. It can also be categorized according to where it occurs, for example, whether it takes place in the classroom, in the simulator, or in an aircraft. Training can also be categorized according to the content, for example, whether it addresses purely technical issues, such as the computation of weight and balance, as opposed to nontechnical issues, such as crew coordination. Regardless of how one chooses to categorize training, the goals of these activities are common— the development of a set of skills and knowledge in the trainee, to some specified level of competency.

> *Training*: The systematic process of developing knowledge, skills, and attitudes; activities leading to skilled behavior.
>
> *Skill*: Expertise or accomplishment in any field; specifically, any complex, organized pattern of behavior acquired through training and practice, including cognitive, perceptual, motor, and social skills.

---

* For more information on this and other early Norwegian aviators, consult the very interesting book, *100 Years of Norwegian Aviation* (Norsk Luftfartsmuseum 2005).

6.2 LEARNING AND FORGETTING

The processes and methods that are used to achieve the desired training goals are informed and shaped by the scientific research dealing with human learning. Beginning with the late nineteenth century work of Ebbinghaus (1885), a great deal of research has been directed at understanding the conditions that influence human learning. Using himself as a subject, Ebbinghaus investigated two key features associated with training: learning and forgetting.

Ebbinghaus created nonsense syllables consisting of two consonants separated by a vowel that did not spell anything. (In English, ZOV would be an example.) He constructed 2300 of these items and then memorized them in sets of about 20. He learned each set of these nonsense syllables until he achieved perfect recall, and then recorded how many he was able to retain after various time intervals.

The learning curve (Figure 6.1) shows how much retraining is required to achieve perfect performance. So, after initially learning a set of syllables, about 50% of them are retained the next day, when they are again memorized to perfect recall. The next day, about 65% of the items are recalled, and on the next day 75% are retained. The sharpest increase in the curve, indicating the fastest learning, occurs after the first try and then gradually evens out, meaning that more information is being retained after each repetition of relearning. This curve, like the forgetting curve, shown in Figure 6.2, is exponential. While the learning curve indicates how quickly information is acquired, the forgetting curve indicates how quickly information is lost. As in the learning curve, the sharpest change (in this case, the most rapid decline) occurs in the first few minutes and the decay is significant through the first hour, leveling off after about 1 day.

The learning and forgetting curves described by Ebbinghaus were based on verbal materials (nonsense syllables), and while they certainly apply to many aspects of aviation training (e.g., learning the names of all those clouds in meteorology), learning patterns of complex motor tasks follow a slightly different pattern. For the most part, progress in skill learning commonly follows an S-shaped curve. As shown in

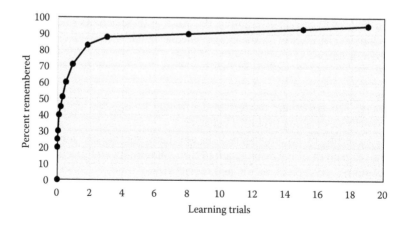

FIGURE 6.1 Learning curve.

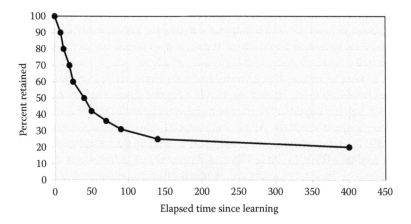

FIGURE 6.2 Forgetting curve.

Figure 6.3, progress is slow at first, and then learners experience a burst of learning, producing a rapid rise on the graph. For some very complex tasks, progress may be characterized as a series of these S-shaped changes in performance. Fitts and Posner (1967) found that gradual improvement with practice occurred in almost all motor skills. Although the pace of improvement may slacken, there is never a true plateau in which no improvement occurs. For pilots, this means that while they may think they are not making progress on learning some new skill (e.g., an ILS approach), in truth they are simply not able to accurately assess their own small increments in improvement. Learning is slow at first as the person becomes familiar with the basic components of a skill, and then rapidly increases as the more basic components become automatic. In our ILS approach example, during the early stages of learning, the pilot must actively think about how to control the aircraft to align the glideslope and localizer indicators. In time, these actions become more automatic, and

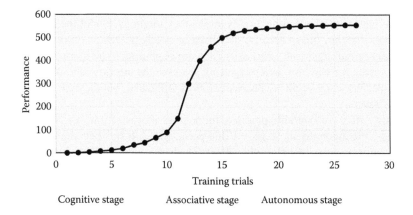

FIGURE 6.3 Motor skill learning curve.

the pilot can devote more attention and effort to fine-tuning the approach by leading the indicators so as to avoid overshooting (chasing the needles) during the approach. Ultimately, performance levels off as the pilot approaches perfect performance of the approach.

This process of motor skill learning has been characterized by Fitts and Posner (1967) as involving three distinct stages: (1) a cognitive stage in which the beginner focuses on solving cognitively oriented problems (Trials 1–10 in Figure 6.3); (2) an associative stage in which the person has learned to associate cues from the environment with the requirement actions, and works to refine performance in order to be more consistent (Trials 11–20 in Figure 6.3); and (3) an autonomous stage in which performance of the skill is automatic, in terms of attention demanded (Trials 21–30 in Figure 6.3).

When pilots begin to acquire a new skill, such as performing an ILS approach, they are confronted with some very specific cognitively oriented problems. What is the basic task? How do I know when to start the descent? What rate of descent (and associated power settings) will keep me aligned with the glide slope? How big a heading correction is needed when the localizer needle is three dots to either side? Each of these questions indicates the basic cognitive level at which the pilot is operating, which is why Fitts and Posner labeled the first stage of learning the cognitive stage. This stage is marked by a large number of errors in performance, and the errors committed tend to be gross. For example, the pilot may turn the wrong way (away from the localizer needle) in order to make a correction. Performance also tends to be quite variable. The pilot may know that he or she is doing something wrong, but they do not yet know exactly how it should be done differently. Hence, they need very specific feedback that will assist them in correcting their errors.

During the second, associative, stage of skill learning, the cognitive activity characteristic of the first stage changes. The learner has now acquired many of the basic fundamentals of the skill to some extent, and no longer has to devote as much cognitive effort to understanding the basic requirements of the task. They are now concentrating on refining their skills and have developed an ability to recognize some of their own errors. Now they know what they did wrong, and are generally aware of what they should have done. For example, they might overshoot the localizer, but they know that they did so because they became overly fixated on correcting the rate of descent or making some radio call. They are beginning to be more proactive and can anticipate the need for actions (getting ahead of the aircraft), and the variability of their performance begins to decrease. Errors still occur, but they are less frequent and less severe.

Finally, after considerable practice, the learner moves on into the final stage of learning—the autonomous stage. At this point, the skill has become almost automatic, requiring very little cognitive effort. The basic motor skill has been mastered, and the learner can devote cognitive effort at making small adjustments (e.g., allowing for a very strong cross-wind during the ILS approach), or attending simultaneously to other activities (such as dealing with an engine problem). Small variations in performance will still occur as will slight improvements; however, the overall level of performance is very near the upper limit.

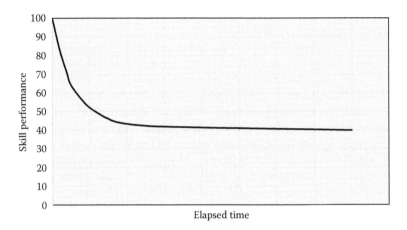

FIGURE 6.4 Motor skill retention.

In contrast to declarative knowledge, such as the nonsense syllables used by Ebbinghaus, motor skills decay very slowly and are typically remembered for months or years. Schendel, Shields, and Katz (1978) reviewed the retention of motor skills and found that

- The single most important determinant of retention was level of original learning.
- Procedural tasks are forgotten in days, weeks, or months, whereas continuous control tasks typically are remembered for months or years.
- The retention of motor skills depends on the length of the no-practice period, the type of task, and the practice of interfering activities, among other factors.
- Retention is improved by overtraining—that is, training to levels beyond the minimum required levels of proficiency.

The overall shape of the curve that describes retention of motor skills (shown in Figure 6.4) is similar to the curve for declarative knowledge. However, for motor skills, most of the loss in proficiency occurs immediately following the cessation of practice, and then quickly levels off to remain stable for a considerable period, subject to the factors listed previously.

6.3 RECURRENT TRAINING AND SKILL DECAY

The purpose of recurrent or refresher training is to maintain skills that have been acquired through some initial training process. As noted earlier, memories and cognitive skills tend to be lost much faster than motor skills. So, a pilot coming back to aviation after a long absence may find that he or she can still fly the plane, but cannot remember how to get taxi and takeoff clearance, and has not a clue as to how to compute density altitude. This phenomenon is known as skill decay. Skill decay "refers to the loss or decay of trained or acquired skills (or knowledge) after periods of nonuse" (Arthur et al. 1998, p. 58).

Difficulties associated with skill decay are exacerbated by the current genera-tion of cockpit automation that tends to place pilots in a passive, monitoring mode. However, at the time something fails, pilots must immediately take positive control of the aircraft and, in some instances, perform tasks that they have only infrequently or never been trained to accomplish. Amalberti and Wibaux (1995) point out that in many cases manual procedures are no longer taught. The example they cite is the use of the brake system during rejected takeoff (RTO) on the Airbus A320. In that aircraft, use of the auto brake is mandatory. Hence, pilots are not trained to use the manual brake. It is interesting to speculate what will happen when, as all things must, the auto brake system fails and manual braking must be used.

Prophet (1976) conducted an extensive review of the literature on the long-term retention of flying skills. His review covered some 120 sources for which abstracts or annotations were available, predominantly from military sources. His results suggest that basic flight skills can be retained fairly well for extended periods of nonflying. However, significant decrement occurs, particularly for instrument and procedural skills. He notes a consistent finding that continuous control (i.e., tracking) skills are retained better than the skills involved in the execution of discrete procedures. One such example is the finding by Wright (1973) that basic visual flight skills remained generally acceptable for up to 36 months, while instrument flight skills fell below acceptable levels within 12 months for about half of the pilots.

In a controlled study of the retention of flying skills (Childs et al. 1983), a group of 42 employees of the Federal Aviation Administration (FAA) received training necessary to qualify them for the private pilot certificate. Their proficiency was then reassessed 8, 16, and 24 months, following award of their certificates using a standardized assessment procedure. The authors reported a decline in the mean percentage of correctly performed measures, beginning with 90% and declining steadily to approximately 50% at the 24-month check. Figure 6.5 illustrates some representative tasks and the decay in performance levels. From these results, Childs et al. concluded that "Recently certified private pilots who do not fly regularly can be expected to undergo a relatively rapid and significant decrement in their flight skills" (p. 41).

Childs and Spears (1986) reviewed the studies dealing with the problem of flight-skill decay. They suggested that cognitive/procedural skills are more prone than control-oriented skills to decay over periods of disuse. This is consistent with the findings noted earlier that cognitive and procedural knowledge decays much more rapidly than motor skills.

Casner et al. (2006) examined pilot's retention of aeronautical knowledge in a series of four experiments in an attempt to discover characteristics of the pilots, and their flying experiences that influence remembering and forgetting. They used ques-tions from the FAA private pilot written examination.

In the first experiment, the average score for the 10-item multiple choice test was 74.8%. Of the 60 pilot participants, 12 had scores in the range of 30%–60%, sub-stantially below the minimum score (70%) required to pass the FAA certification examination. Of the 20 pilots who held a private pilot license and were not pursing

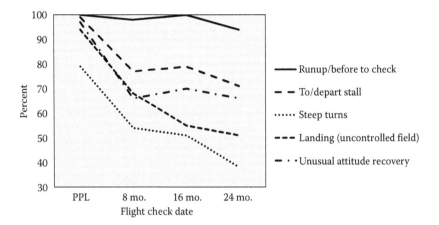

FIGURE 6.5   Percentage of correctly performed flight tasks. (Adapted from Childs, J.M. et al. 1983. *Private Pilot Flight Skill Retention 8, 16, and 24 Months Following Certification.* Technical report DOT/FAA/CT-83/34. Washington, DC: Federal Aviation Administration, Table 5, p. 22.)

any more advanced rating, the average score was 69.5%. Since the national average score for the FAA private pilot written examination is 85%, clearly some substantial forgetting of the material had occurred. The 20 certified flight instructors (CFIs), however, had an average score of 79%, suggesting that they rehearsed their knowledge more often than the other pilots.

Although there was little observed correlation between the test scores and total flight time, significant correlations were obtained between recent flight experience (previous 3 and 6 months) and test scores. Most of this association may be attributed, however, to the strong correlations obtained for the CFIs ($r = 0.34$ and $r = 0.52$, for 3 and 6 months, respectively).

In their second experiment, Casner et al. asked 24 active pilots who had only flown one make and model of aircraft to perform weight and balance calculations for that aircraft and for another aircraft in which they had no prior experience. They found that whereas the pilots retained the knowledge of how to make the computations for their own aircraft, they did considerably poorer with the unfamiliar aircraft. Specifically, they were able to recognize a "no go" situation only 50% of the time.

Casner et al. (p. 93) concluded that "the certificates and ratings held by pilots have little influence on how well those pilots retain what they have learned during training." They suggest that there is a need for more explicit standards for ongoing aeronautical knowledge proficiency and suggest some alternative methods for ensuring that pilots maintain their knowledge. In addition, they suggest that the current practices of aviation education, specifically the emphasis on abstract facts, remote from practical application, may be implicated in this failure to retain important aeronautical knowledge.

Arthur et al. (1998) used meta-analytic techniques to review the skill retention and skill decay literature. They noted that the skill decay literature has identified several factors that are associated with the decay or retention of trained skills. Echoing the findings of Schendel et al. (1978), noted earlier, they found that the most important of those factors were the following:

- *The length of the retention interval*: Longer intervals produce more decay.
- *The degree of overlearning*: Overlearning aids retention and the amount of overlearning is the single most important determinant of retention.
- *Task characteristics*: Open-loop tasks like tracking and problem-solving are better retained, compared to closed-loop tasks, such as preflight checks.

From their analysis of 53 articles, they found that "physical, natural, and speed-based tasks were less susceptible to skill loss than cognitive, artificial, and accuracy-based tasks" (p. 85).

These conclusions are reflected in the findings of a study on the forgetting of instrument flying skills (Mengelkoch et al. 1971). In that study, two groups of 13 subjects with no prior flight experience were given academic training and instrument flying instruction in a simulator. One group received 5 training trials while the other group was given 10 training trials. Both groups were able to successfully complete a program of maneuvers and flight procedures at the conclusion of the training, although the group with the additional training performed substantially better than the other group (95% and 78% correct performance for the 10-trial and 5-trial groups, respectively). After a 4-month interval, the 10-trial group had a 16.5% loss in performance of procedures, while the 5-trial group had a 20.1% loss. Retention loss of the flight control parameters was generally much less, with only altitude and airspeed having a significant loss over the retention interval for both groups.

In a study by Ruffner and Bickley (1985), 79 U.S. Army aviators participated in a 6-month test period in which they flew zero, two, four, or six contact and terrain flight tasks in the UH-1 aircraft. Their results indicated that average level of performance in helicopter contact and terrain flight tasks was maintained after 6 months of no practice. Further, intervening practice flights (up to six) did not significantly improve the average level of performance. These findings were true regardless of total career flight hours or whether the tasks are psychomotor or procedural.

This is an immense body of work on training, or more generally, learning, which is far beyond the scope of this chapter. A large number of introductory volumes on human learning are available for the student who desires more information. Recent examples include Hergenhahn and Olson (2005), Ormrod (2007), and Mazur (2006). In addition to these general works, there are also works dedicated primarily to the issues of training in aviation. Some examples here include Henley (2004), O'Neil and Andrews (2000), and Telfer and Moore (1997). However, it is important to note that training, like the design of the physical apparatus, should be thought of as a system. The design of effective training, particularly when such training will be used by multiple students and instructors over an extended period, requires a careful consideration of a number of interrelated factors. Therefore, we should also examine these factors, and the techniques that have been developed to ensure successful training system development.

6.4 TRAINING SYSTEM DESIGN

The rigor that is applied to the design of a training system reflects the planned application of the training system. That is, very little rigor is typically placed on the design of training that will be used with only one or two people for a job of little significance. Most people have experienced training of this sort. For example, a new employee is shown, in a training program lasting about 1 minute, how to operate the office copier. There is no formal training plan. There is no formal evaluation of student retention of the material. Furthermore, there is no assurance that this employee will receive the same instruction as the next employee. Standardization is lacking because standardization and the planning that entails are expensive, and the result of failure to perform the task successfully is simply a few sheets of wasted paper. Contrast that with the consequences of failure to properly train a pilot to execute an instrument approach or to execute a RTO. Here, the task is complex, and the consequences are potentially severe, both in terms of money and in terms of human life. Clearly, the latter situation requires a more formal approach to the design of a training program to ensure that all the necessary elements are addressed and that the student achieves a satisfactory level of performance. The expense of a rigorously developed training program is justified by the consequence of failure, and, for many organizations such as the military services, by the large numbers of personnel to be trained over an extended period.

6.4.1 SYSTEMS APPROACH TO TRAINING

One method for ensuring that rigor is applied is the use of the Systems Approach to Training (SAT), also known as Instructional System Development (ISD).* This set of procedures to be used for the development of training systems originated with the American military in the mid-1970s. It is described in detail in a multiple-volume military handbook (U.S. Department of Defense, 2001) and in manuals produced by each of the individual services. There is, for example, a manual produced by the U.S. Air Force (1993) that adapts the general guidance given in the Department of Defense handbook to the specific needs of the Air Force. Similarly, individualized documents exist for both the U.S. Navy (NAVEDTRA 130A, 1997) and U.S. Army (TRADOC Pamphlet 350-70). This structured approach to the development of training has also been embraced by civil aviation. For example, its principles are included in the Advanced Qualification Program (AQP) promoted by the FAA and in the Integrated Pilot Training program established by Transport Canada. These advances reflect the general approach of embedding the SAT that is reflected in the International Civil Aviation Organization Convention on International Civil Aviation—Personnel Licensing (ICAO, n.d.).

---

* Much of this discussion of SAT/ISD is derived from Air Force Manual 36-2234 (U.S. Air Force 1993), to which the interested reader is directed for more detailed information. Meister (1985) is also a good source of general information.

To put it simply, SAT/ISD is a process that provides a means to determine the following:

- Who will be trained
- What will be trained
- When the training will take place
- Where the training will take place
- Why the training is being accomplished
- How the training is accomplished

The first reaction of many pilots and nonpilots when seeing such a list is, "why all the fuss?" Why is an elaborate system needed for such simple questions? Surely, the answers to these questions are obvious:

- Whoever wants to be a pilot will get training.
- We will show them how to fly the airplane.
- We will fly in the morning or afternoon.
- The training will take place in the aircraft.
- We are doing the training so that the person can fly the plane.
- The instructor will show them how it is done, and then they will do it themselves.

The other reaction is, "why not just keep on doing what we have always done? After all, we have been training pilots for years."

These concerns are understandable and may even have merit in some situations; however, they reflect a generally limited view of the world. If one is considering only a single instructor and a few aspiring student pilots, then the training will take place more-or-less as outlined in the second set of bullets. It is a casual approach to a situation that does not demand high efficiency of training or rigorous quality control of the product. Consider, however, the situation faced by almost every military service and by many air carriers. The military take large numbers of recruits with no previous military experience and, in most cases, who lack the technical skills and knowledge required to perform the duties of their military specialty. In a relatively short time, these recruits must receive military and technical training that will enable them to function as part of a military unit, where the consequences of failure to perform are often very high. Clearly, their training cannot be left to chance. If for no other reason than to minimize the enormous costs associated with large-scale military training (e.g., the cost of producing one helicopter pilot in the U.S. Army is approximately one million U.S. dollars [Czarnecki 2004]), the training programs must be designed so as to deliver exactly what is needed in a format and at a time that ensures the trainees achieve a satisfactory level of competence. To achieve this goal requires careful analysis and planning, and is precisely what SAT/ISD provides.

The five stages of the SAT/ISD process are the following:

- Analyze
- Design

- Develop
- Implement
- Evaluate

> *Task*: "A single unit of specific work behavior, with clear beginning and ending points, that is directly observable or otherwise measurable. A task is performed for its own sake, that is, it is not dependent upon other tasks, although it may fall in a sequence with other tasks in a mission, duty, or job" (U.S. Department of Defense 2001, p. 47).

6.4.1.1 Analyze

The SAT/ISD process begins with an analysis of the job for which a person is to be trained. The objective is to develop a complete understanding of what it takes to perform the job. During this stage, a task inventory is compiled, in which all the tasks associated with the job are listed. In addition, the standards, conditions, performance measures, and any other criteria that are needed to perform each of the tasks on the task inventory must also be identified.

This job analysis is typically performed by observing personnel (job incumbents) on the job and by making note of what they do or by interviewing incumbents about what they do. In the military services in particular, more formal occupational survey and analysis procedures may be used. One example of an instrument used to capture such information is the Critical Incident Technique (CIT; Flanagan 1954). Once a list of the tasks performed as part of a job is compiled, the CIT procedures can be used to identify those tasks that are preeminent in terms of their frequency, difficulty, and failure consequence. Clearly, more attention should be devoted in the training process to tasks that are difficult, that occur frequently, and that have dire consequence if not performed properly, than to tasks that are seldom completed, are easy, and have little impact. However, until this comprehensive list of the tasks that comprise a job has been compiled and each task analyzed, there is no basis for deciding which tasks are important tasks and which are insignificant.

In addition to examining the job and its constituent tasks, attention must also be paid to the eventual recipients of the training. This is referred to as the target audience—the people who will complete the training and then go on to do the job. Just as the design of the hardware must consider the capabilities and limitations of the users, so must the training system be designed with the eventual users in mind. During the analysis phase, these users must be identified and described in detail, and this information will be critical in the design phase. Consider, for example, the importance of knowing whether the training system is to be designed to accommodate student pilots with no prior flying experience, or whether it will be used by experienced commercial pilots who already have mastered the basics. An extreme example, perhaps; but, the point is that training designers cannot make assumptions about the characteristics of those who will use the training.

As a further example, in the international world of aviation, a minimum command of the English language is required. Training designers would be ill advised to assume that all the students participating in some new training course have a satisfactory command of English or even that they all have the same level of fluency. Clearly, there are substantial national and regional differences in the teaching of English. A thorough analysis would therefore assess this issue to determine whether remedial instruction in English is required for a specified target audience before the technical training may commence. Similar comments could be made with regard to computer literacy, experience in driving automobiles, prior mechanical experience, and intellectual level, to name but a few of the many possible examples. All of these predecessor, or enabling conditions, must be identified during the analysis phase.

6.4.1.2 Design

In this phase, the instructional strategies are determined and the instructional methods and media are selected. One instructional strategy might be to not provide formal training at all. Rather, one might elect to use some sort of apprenticeship and have all learning take place as on-the-job training. This is actually a rather common strategy, particularly for jobs requiring lower skill levels. Consider, for example, the training program for a carpenter's helper. This might be as simple as telling the new helper to follow the carpenter and do what he or she says to do. Admittedly, this is a rather extreme example and not likely to be found in aviation settings. However, a strategy that combines some formal training with on-the-job training is fairly common. This is particularly true for tasks that are seldom performed.

The occupational analysis procedures used in the analysis phase may result in the identification of some tasks that are rarely performed. These may even be tasks with significant consequences, but these occur so infrequently that any training provided during initial qualification would be lost by the time it became necessary to actually perform the task. (Recall the issue of skill decay discussed earlier in this chapter.) The instructional system designers are thus placed in a quandary. Do they include instruction on the performance of a task that they know will be forgotten, on average, long before the task must be performed? Do they rely upon refresher training to maintain task proficiency? Or, do they utilize some sort of just-in-time training scheme, so that when the need for the task arises, the incumbent can quickly learn the required skills?

There are some instances in which the latter approach is satisfactory, particularly when dealing with maintenance of highly reliable electronic systems. The reader may reflect upon the last (if any) time they were called upon to install or replace the disk drive in their personal computer (PC). Without the benefit of any technical training, computer owners are called upon to accomplish this task by the manufacturers of computer disk drives. They are able to do so (usually without injury to themselves or their PC) due, in large part, to the well-designed, step-by-step instructions, with accompanying graphics, provided by disk manufacturers. The instructions provide just-in-time training to enable the PC owner to accomplish the required task. Thus, a person who has never accomplished this task before and has received no training can, during the course of the hour or so required to read and follow the directions, successfully complete the installation, and then promptly forget everything they just learned until the next occasion arises, at which time the abbreviated training, task performance, and skill decay cycle will be repeated.*

Of course, there are some instances in which the task demands require that even rarely performed tasks be trained to a high level of performance, and that frequent refresher training be given to maintain skill levels. In aviation, the RTO is a prime example of such a task. In such a time-critical situation, task performance must be immediate and flawless. During the 2 seconds or so in which the RTO decision must be reached and an appropriate action initiated, there is no time available to even consult the ubiquitous checklist; let alone pull out the abnormal procedures handbook and learn how to perform the task.

During the SAT/ISD analysis phase, these tasks and their performance constraints should have been identified, so that appropriate instructional strategies may be selected. In each case, the strategy should be appropriate for the task being trained.

In addition to the instructional strategy, the instructional developer must also select the instructional methods and media during this phase. Some of the instructional methods are as follows:

- Lecture
- Demonstration
- Self-study
- Computer-based training
- On-the-job training

The media available include

- Printed media
- Overhead transparencies
- Audio tape recordings
- 35-mm slide series
- Multimedia presentations
- Video and film
- Interactive courseware

The selection of the instructional method and media form part of the plan of instruction (POI) developed during this phase. This plan is focused on learning objectives. These are statements of what is expected to be accomplished at each stage of the training program, and proceed in such a sequence that at each stage the skills and knowledge required for successful completion of the new learning objective have already been put into place by the previous learning activities. So, if the objective of a certain set of instruction is for the student to successfully complete an instrument approach, then at some earlier stage the student must have learned how to tune the radio, how to maintain aircraft attitude by reference to the attitude indicator, and how to initiate and control a descent, along with many other skills. Thus, the

---

* Purchasers of furniture from IKEA™ will no doubt familiar with this just-in-time assembly training process.

order in which new material is presented is critical to success and must be considered carefully in the POI. The analysis phase will have resulted in the identification of these predecessor skills and knowledge, and the instructional designer must ensure that during the design phase these restrictions are considered.

6.4.1.3   Develop

Once the objectives have been established and the training strategies and activities have been planned, it is time to implement the design by creating a formal course syllabus, writing lessons, producing the instructional materials, and, if necessary, developing interactive courseware. The key document to be created is the POI or course syllabus. It is this document that serves to control the planning, organization, and conduct of the instruction. It is the blueprint for providing instruction in a course and is used to develop the individual lesson plans used by instructors in the delivery of instruction.

Perhaps, the most visible, or at least the most voluminous, product of this phase is the actual instructional material. During this phase, the books, pamphlets, student guides, videotapes, slides, transparencies, simulators, mock-ups, and everything else identified during the design phase and listed in the POI are produced.

Also constructed during this phase are the tests that will determine whether the students have achieved the mastery levels specified in the POI. This is a very important component, and the development of these tests must adhere to sound psychometric principles. Since these issues will be covered at some length later in this book, they will not be addressed here, other than to note that the care given to tests used to select personnel for pilot training must also be applied to the tests that determine whether, at the end of training, they are now qualified to be pilots.

As one final activity in this phase, it is always wise to try out the new training program on a limited basis to ensure that everything proceeds according to plan. It is said that "No battle plan survives the first contact with the enemy." Similarly, even in the best-planned training program, it is almost inevitable that some things will have been overlooked, which will become glaringly obvious when the full course is administered to real students. Implicit assumptions may have been made about student capabilities that turn out to be faulty. Estimates of the time or number of trials required to learn some new skills to criterion levels may have been too optimistic. Language that seemed perfectly clear to the developers and subject matter experts may prove hopelessly confusing to naive students.

Even though each of the individual sections and training components may have been tried out with students as they were being developed, one final test of the entire system is prudent. It is here that the effects of dependencies among the training elements may be revealed which were not evident when each of the elements was evaluated in isolation. Success in this trial provides the trigger to move to the next phase with confidence.

6.4.1.4   Implement

It is at this stage that the new training program becomes operational. If all the preceding stages have been accomplished successfully, then the expected students will arrive at the proper locations. The instructional materials will be on hand in sufficient quantities, and all hardware, such as simulators, will be operational. The instructors and support personnel be in-place and ready to begin instruction. This marks the boundary, then, between the largely technical activities of the preceding phase, and what is now largely a management or administrative activity.

6.4.1.5 Evaluate

When conducted properly, evaluation is ongoing during the SAT/ISD process. Each of the preceding phases should include some sort of evaluation component. For example, during the analysis phase, some method is needed to ensure that all the tasks comprising the job have been included in the analysis and that appropriate, rigorous task analytic methods have been applied to ensure a quality result. During the design phase, the selection of methods and media should be evaluated against the learning objectives to ensure that they are appropriate. During the development phase, the instructional material being created must be checked carefully for validity. For example, the radio phraseology that is taught during flight training must be checked against the phraseology prescribed by the civil or military authority, since departures from standard phraseology lead to confusion and errors. Finally, at the implementation phase, several evaluation components, such as the quality of the graduates, are possible. Overall, these evaluation activities can be divided into three general types:

- Formative evaluation
- Summative evaluation
- Operational evaluation

The formative evaluation process extends from the initial SAT/ISD planning through the small-group tryout. The purpose is to check on the design of the individual components comprising the instructional system. It answers the question, "Have be done what we planned to do?"

That is, if the plan for achieving a specified learning objective called for the use of a partial simulation in which the student would be taught to operate the flight management system (FMS) to a specified level of competence, did that actually occur. Does the instructional system include the use of the partial simulation to achieve that particular learning objective? Do students who complete this particular training component demonstrate the level of competence required?

When this sort of evaluation is conducted early on, it allows the training developers to improve the training program while the system is still being developed, and changes can be made for the least cost. For example, discovery that students completing the FMS training cannot perform all the tasks to a satisfactory level could lead to changes in the training design to either modify the training content or provide additional time for practice on the simulator. However, if this deficiency was not discovered until late in the training development process, then the relatively simple and inexpensive changes might no longer be possible. For example, the simulator might have been scheduled for other training components, so that additional practice on the existing simulators is no longer a possibility. This means that either major change must be made to the training program or additional simulation assets must be purchased. Both of these alternatives have negative cost implications.

The summative evaluation involves trying out the instructional program in an operational setting on students from the target population. The basic question answered by this evaluation is "does the system work?" That is, does the instructional system work under operational conditions? Typically, the summative evaluation examines the training program during the operational tryout of two or three classes. This provides enough data to identify such issues as lack of adequate resources, changes needed to the schedules, inadequacies of the support equipment, need for additional training of instructors, or modifications to the training materials to improve clarity. The summative evaluation also addresses the key question of graduate performance. That is, it should show whether the graduates of the training program can perform the jobs for which they are being trained. Clearly, the graduates of a medical college should be able to pass the medical licensing examination, and the graduates of a pilot training school should be able to pass the licensing authority's written and practical tests. If a significant number of graduates cannot meet these standards, then there is almost certainly something wrong in the training school.

Operational evaluation is a continuous process that should be put into place when the new training system is placed into operation. This form of evaluation is used to gather and analyze internal and external feedback data to allow management to monitor the status of the program. At a minimum, it should provide for monitoring of the status of graduates of the training course, to ensure that they continue to meet job performance requirements. Changes in the proportion of graduates who pass licensing examinations, for example, should signal the need to reevaluate the training program. Perhaps, some changes have taken place in the operational environment, which dictate changes in the training program. In an aviation context, the use of GPS navigation provides such an example. As GPS begins to supplement or eventually even replace Very High Frequency Omni-Directional Range (VOR) radio navigation, pilot training programs must be modified to provide instructions on GPS navigation techniques, perhaps at the cost of decreased instruction on VOR navigation. An alert training institution might make these changes proactively. However, the use of an ongoing operational evaluation component, particularly one that examined more than gross pass/fail rates, should signal the need for change, even if the changing technology was not otherwise noticed.

6.4.1.6 Conclusion

The use of SAT/ISD provides a framework for the development of training. It does not prescribe methods or modes, a feature for which it is sometimes criticized,* but which others argue is a strength of the technique. Its use is ubiquitous in the military, including military aviation. Hence, some familiarity with its basic concepts is desirable, even for those who may not be directly involved in the development of a large-scale training program. An adherence to its general precepts and procedures will inform and guide any training development, even at a modest level. The casual flight instructor may not utilize a formal SAT/ISD process in planning how he or she will teach student pilots, but at least some consideration of learning objectives,

---

* SAT/ISD has also been criticized on other grounds. For example, Gordon and Zemke (2000) suggest that SAT/ISD has an overly bureaucratic, lock-step approach, which makes it slow and clumsy.

choice of teaching modes, evaluation, and the other SAT/ISD components would almost certainly result in an improved training delivery and a better-trained student.

Cockpit/crew resource management (CRM): The effective use of all available resources—people, weapon systems, facilities and equipment, and environment—by individuals or crews to safely and efficiently accomplish an assigned mission or task (U.S Air Force definition).

6.5   CREW RESOURCE MANAGEMENT

The preceding section has dealt in some length on a generalized system for developing training, without regard for the specific elements to be trained. Typically, training is thought of in conjunction with the technical skills of operating an aircraft. These include such skills as reading a map, reading and interpreting weather forecasts, accurately calculating weight and balance, and proper movement of the controls so as to accomplish a desired maneuver. However, there are other skills that are also valuable. These skills are typically referred to under the general heading of cockpit/crew resource management (CRM), although in Europe they may also be termed nontechnical skills (NOTECHS). This area includes such things as getting along with crewmembers, knowing when and how to assert one's self effectively in critical situations, and maintaining situational awareness. For the most part, training in CRM presupposes competency in all the technical skills required to operate an aircraft. However, a well-developed training program for *ab initio* pilots, particularly one that has been developed in accordance with the precepts of SAT/ISD, may well include CRM as either a stand-alone element or as part of the technical skill training.

The need for CRM training was identified in the 1980s as a result of studies of the causes of, predominately, civilian airliner accidents. Christian and Morgan (1987) reviewed the causes of aircraft accidents and found the following human factors that contributed to mishaps:

- Preoccupation with minor mechanical irregularities
- Inadequate leadership and monitoring
- Failure to delegate tasks and assign responsibilities
- Failure to set priorities
- Failure to communicate intent and plans
- Failure to utilize available data
- Failure to adequately monitor other crewmembers in the cockpit

Perhaps, the seminal article on this subject, however, is that of Foushee (1984), in which he applied the techniques and terminology of social psychology to the environment of an air carrier cockpit. From that point, interest in CRM has mushroomed. The evolution of CRM in commercial aviation is documented by Helmreich et al. (1999). However, there is now a vast literature on this subject, which extends beyond aviation to such settings as the hospital operating theater (cf. Fletcher et al. 2003) and the control rooms of offshore drilling platforms (cf. Salas et al. 2001).

A major proponent of CRM has been the FAA in the United States. The FAA has sponsored an extensive program of research on CRM, most notably by Robert Helmreich and his colleagues at the University of Texas. On the basis of the results of the research of Helmreich, and many others, the FAA has produced publications that provide guidance and definitions to air carriers and others regarding the desired characteristics of CRM training. According to the CRM Advisory Circular produced by the FAA, CRM training is one way of addressing the challenge of optimizing the human/machine interface and accompanying interpersonal activities. These activities include team building and maintenance, information transfer, problem-solving, decision-making, maintaining situation awareness, and dealing with automated systems. CRM training is composed of three components: initial indoctrination/awareness, recurrent practice and feedback, and continual reinforcement (FAA 2004, p. 2) (CRM Advisory Circular).

That same FAA Advisory Circular provides a listing of the characteristics of effective CRM:

- CRM is a comprehensive system of applying human factors concepts to improve crew performance.
- CRM embraces all operational personnel.
- CRM can be blended into all forms of aircrew training.
- CRM concentrates on crewmembers' attitudes and behaviors and their impact on safety.
- CRM uses the crew as the unit of training.
- CRM is training that requires the active participation of all crewmembers. It provides an opportunity for individuals and crews to examine their own behavior, and to make decisions on how to improve cockpit teamwork.

6.5.1 Generations of CRM

In their review of the evolution of CRM, Helmreich et al. (1999) identified five distinct generations of CRM, beginning with the first comprehensive CRM program begun by United Airlines in 1981. Helmreich et al. (p. 20) characterize first generation courses as, "psychological in nature, with a heavy focus on psychological testing and such general concepts as leadership." Perhaps not surprisingly, some of these courses were resisted by some pilots as attempts to manipulate their personalities.

The second generation of CRM courses is characterized as having more of a focus on specific aviation concepts that were related to flight operations. In addition, the training became more modular and more team oriented. This is reflected in the change of names from cockpit resource management in the first generation to crew resource management. This training featured much more emphasis on team building, briefing strategies, situation awareness, and stress management. Although participant acceptance was greater for these courses, some criticism of the training and its use of psychological jargon remained. Helmreich et al. note that second-generation courses continue to be used in the United States and elsewhere.

In the third generation of CRM courses, beginning in the early 1990s, the training began to reflect more accurately and holistically the environment in which the aircrews operate. Thus, organizational factors such as organization culture and climate begin to be included. This may reflect to some degree the writings by Reason (1990) that appeared at about that time, in which he described the multiple-layer concept of accident causality. In that model (to be described in more detail in Chapter 11), organizational factors are clearly identified as possible contributors to accidents.

The initiation of the AQP (Birnbach and Longridge 1993; Mangold and Neumeister 1995) by the FAA in 1990 marked the beginning of the integration and proceduralization of CRM that define the fourth generation. AQP allows air carriers to develop innovative training to meet their particular needs. However, the FAA requires that both CRM and line-oriented flight training (LOFT) be included as part of the AQP for an air carrier. Because of the advantages that AQP provided an air carrier in terms of customizing their training so as to reduce costs while maintaining a satisfactory product, most air carriers have adopted AQP. Accordingly, they have also developed comprehensive CRM programs based on detailed analyses of training requirements and human factors issues.

Finally, Helmreich et al. suggest that a fifth generation of CRM training may be characterized by an explicit focus on error management. They suggest that the ultimate purpose of CRM, which should be reflected in the training syllabus and the training exercises, is to develop effective means to manage risks. This philosophy reflects the Reason (1990, 1997) model of accident causality referred to earlier, in which it is acknowledged that perfect defenses against accidents do not exist. That is, despite the best-laid plans and best-designed systems, there will inevitably be failures, mistakes, and errors. It is prudent, therefore, to train to expect, recognize, and manage those risks.

Thus, CRM has progressed from an early emphasis on teaching good interpersonal relations to its current focus on effectively utilizing all the resources at the disposal of a flight crew (other flight-deck crew, cabin attendants, dispatchers, air traffic control, ground maintenance staff, etc.) to manage risk. In making this transition, CRM has moved from a program with sometimes only vaguely defined goals to a more sharply defined program with well-defined behavioral markers and well-established assessment procedures. Even so, there remains a continuing debate over whether CRM works. That is, does CRM actually result in improved safety?

6.5.2   EVALUATION OF CRM EFFECTIVENESS

The effectiveness of CRM has been debated in the scientific literature, and on the flight deck, since its inception. As noted previously, some early participants in the training resisted it because of its predominantly psychological nature, which they perceived as an attempt to manipulate their personalities. Changes in the training format and, to some extent, its content have largely eliminated those criticisms. Baubien and Baker (2002) surveyed 30,000 airline pilots on perceptions of and experiences with CRM. They found that pilots were generally satisfied and find it useful. However, even training that is well received and liked by participants may or may not achieve the desired effect.

The effectiveness of CRM has been investigated by many researchers, and is summarized in a study by Salas and his associates at the University of Central Florida. Salas et al. (2001) reviewed 58 published studies of CRM training in an aviation setting to establish its effectiveness. They used Kirkpatrick's (1976) typology for training evaluation as their framework to evaluate the effectiveness of the CRM training. The Kirkpatrick typology organizes the data obtained after training into the categories of reactions, learning, behaviors, and results (impact on organization). Of these categories, reactions to training are the easiest to collect and typically consist of the responses of participants to Likert scale statements, such as "I found the training interesting." Participants indicate the strength of their agreement or disagreement with the statement by choosing one of (typically) five alternatives: *strongly agree*, *agree*, *undecided*, *disagree*, and *strongly disagree*. Collections of such questions can be analyzed to assess the reactions of the participants to the training for any of several dimensions (e.g., interest, relevance, effectiveness, utility). Of the 58 studies reviewed by Salas et al., 27 involved the collection of reaction data. Their results showed that participants generally liked the CRM training, and that the training that utilized role play was better liked than the lecture-based training. In addition, participants also felt that CRM training was worthwhile, useful, and applicable.

Assessments at the second level (learning) have also shown that CRM generally has a positive impact. This has been evidenced in studies of changes in both attitudes and knowledge. Attitudes toward CRM (specifically a positive attitude regarding CRM training) have been shown to be more positive following CRM training. In addition, increased knowledge of human factors issues, crew performance, stressors, and methods of dealing with stressors have also been observed following CRM training.

Of the 58 studies reviewed by Salas et al., 32 included some assessment of behavioral change following CRM training. Most commonly, this was assessed through the measurement of CRM-related behaviors while participants engaged in a simulated flight, although, in some instances (11 out of 32), an online assessment of behavior was used. Most of these studies showed that CRM training had a positive impact on behavior, in that CRM-trained crews exhibited better decision-making, mission analysis, adaptability, situation awareness, communication, and leadership. These findings provide strong support for the impact of CRM on crew behavior.

While the studies of crew behavior indicate that CRM training has an impact, the effects of those changes in behavior have yet to be clearly demonstrated at an organizational level. Only six studies collected some form of evaluation data at this level, and as Salas et al. (p. 651) note, "The predominant type of evidence that has been used to illustrate CRM's impact on aviation safety consists of anecdotal reports ...." Thus, a clear relationship between CRM and the desired outcome of increased safety, and corresponding decrease in accidents, has yet to be demonstrated. It is not surprising, then, that Salas et al. end their review by calling for more and better evaluations to assess the safety impact of CRM training.

In a subsequent study, Salas et al. (2006) reviewed 28 studies of CRM training to determine its effectiveness, within aviation, medicine, offshore oil production and maintenance, shipping/maritime, and nuclear power domains. Although the CRM training produced generally positive reactions from trainees, results were mixed with respect to the impact of training on learning and behavioral changes. As in the previous study, they could not determine whether CRM had an impact on the safety of an organization.

That additional evaluations of CRM in terms of both its method of implementation and its content are needed is made evident by continuing evidence of CRM-related contributions to accidents. In a military context, Wilson-Donnelly and Shappell (2004) reported on a study whose objective was to determine which of the CRM skills included in the U.S. Navy CRM training program matched CRM failures identified in naval aviation accidents. The seven critical skills of CRM included in U.S. Navy training were the following:

- Decision-making
- Assertiveness
- Mission analysis
- Communication
- Leadership
- Adaptability/flexibility
- Situational awareness

Of the 275 Navy/Marine Corps accidents involving some CRM failure during the period 1990–2000, a lack of communication was identified as the number one CRM failure, occurring in over 30% of the accidents. Inadequate briefing was the second most prevalent CRM failure, occurring in slightly over 20% of the accidents. Since a previous study (Wiegmann and Shappell 1999) found that CRM failures contributed to more than half of all major (Navy Class A) accidents, this suggests that failures associated with the materials being specifically addressed in the Navy/Marine Corps CRM training continue to be a major factor in accidents in the Navy/Marine Corps. Wilson-Donnelly and Shappell recognized the unsatisfactory nature of this situation, but suggested that before the current CRM training program is modified or scrapped, similar analyses should be conducted of civilian accident data to see if the same situation holds there.

In a paper presented at the meeting of the International Society of Air Safety Investigators, Diehl (1991) summarized what may be the best evidence for a measurable impact of CRM training on organizational safety. Diehl reviewed data from the military services, with particular respect to rotary-wing aircraft, which tend to have higher accident rates than fixed-wing aircraft. He reported that the global human error accident rate for rotary-wing aircraft fell 36% during the 4-year period following the introduction of CRM training, compared to the preceding 4-year period. He further notes that following the introduction of CRM training at the largest commercial helicopter operator in the United States, the accident rate fell by 54% in the subsequent 2 years. By comparison, the accident rate for this organization had been stable for the six preceding years. In addition, Diehl reported that in 1985 the U.S. Air Force Military Airlift Command (MAC) introduced a CRM-style program. In the following 5-year period, accident rates fell by 52% and serious flight-related mishaps fell by 51% compared to the preceding 5-year period.

On the basis of these analyses and investigations of the contributing factors in civilian accidents, it seems clear that not all CRM issues have been successfully resolved by CRM training, at least in its current implementation. Moreover, the nagging question of the effectiveness of the current generation of CRM training on individual safety behaviors and organizational safety remains open.

6.6 SIMULATOR TRAINING

Every military pilot, every airline pilot, and many instrument-rated private pilots have had some exposure to flight simulators. They are used for a number of reasons, not the least of which is the cost savings they provide over in-flight instruction. For example, the U.S. Air Force estimates that an hour of training in a C-5 aircraft costs $10,000 while an hour in a C-5 simulator is $500 (Moorman 2002 as cited in Johnson 2005).

Particularly for the military and air carrier pilots, simulators also have the great advantage of allowing pilots to practice maneuvers and respond to events that are far too hazardous to practice in a real aircraft. The RTO decision due to the loss of an engine on takeoff is an obvious example from civil aviation.

However, the utility of simulation for training is not a given. It has to be established that the training provided on a device will influence behavior in the real environment. Will what is learned in the simulator carry over into the aircraft? This is the question usually referred to as *transfer of training*, and it has been the subject of much research. Clearly, the preponderance of results shows that what pilots learn in a simulator is carried over to the aircraft.

> Training transfer is the "extent to which the learned behavior from the training program is used on the job" (Phillips 1991).

There have been two major reviews of the transfer of training effectiveness in flight simulation. The first study (Hays et al. 1992) reviewed the pilot training literature from 1957 to 1986. Using meta-analysis, Hays et al. found that simulators consistently led to improved training effectiveness for jet pilots, relative to training in the aircraft only. However, the same results were not found for helicopter pilots.

In the second major review, Carretta and Dunlap (1998) reviewed the studies conducted from 1987 to 1997. In particular, they focused on landing skills, radial bombing accuracy, and instrument and flight control. In all three of these areas, Carretta and Dunlap concluded that simulators had been shown to be useful for training pilot skills.

In one of the studies of landing skills cited by Carretta and Dunlap (1998), Lintern et al. (1990) examined the transfer of landing skills from a flight simulator to an aircraft in early flight training. They compared one group of pilots who were given two sessions of practice on landings in a simulator prior to the start of flight training to a control group that was given no practice prior to the start of training in the aircraft. They found that the experimental group that had received the 2 hours of simulator training required 1.5 fewer hours prior to solo than the control group. For this group, 2 hours of simulator time were equivalent to 1.5 hours of aircraft time. Comparisons of this sort are usually given in terms of the transfer effectiveness ratio (TER).

6.6.1 THE TRAINING EFFECTIVENESS RATIO

Originated by Roscoe (1980), the TER expresses the degree to which hours in the simulator replace hours in the aircraft, and is defined as

$$TER = \frac{\text{Control group time} - \text{Experimental group time}}{\text{Time of total training}}$$

For example, if private pilot training normally requires 50 flight hours, and the use of a 10-hour simulator training program reduces the requirement to 40 in-flight hours, then

$$TER = \frac{50 - 40}{10} = 1$$

In other words, one hour of simulator times saves one hour of flight time.

For a more realistic example, if the simulator training took 10 hours, and then 45 additional hours of in-flight training were required, then:

$$TER = \frac{50 - 45}{10} = 0.5$$

This is interpreted to mean that 1 hour of simulation saves one-half hour of flight time.

Simulators are widely used for training instrument skills, and Carretta and Dunlap (1998) concluded that "simulators provide an effective means to train instrument procedures and flight control" (p. 4). They cite Pfeiffer et al. (1991), who found a correlation of $r = 0.98$ between simulator performance and actual flight performance.

Flight simulators can vary substantially in their fidelity to the actual flight environment in terms of motion, control dynamics, visual scene, and instrumentation. Some simulators are designed for whole-task training, whereas others are designed as part-task trainers, intended, for example, to only train students in the use of the FMS or the aircraft pressurization system. In general, the reviews such as Carretta and Dunlap (1998) have shown that high-fidelity simulators are not necessary for successful transfer of training.

Vaden and Hall (2005) conducted a meta-analysis to examine the true mean effect for simulator motion with respect to fixed-wing training transfer. Working with a rather small sample of only seven studies, they found a small $(d = 0.16)$[*] positive effect for motion. Thus, while their study shows that motion does promote a greater transfer of training, the relatively small effect may not be worth the considerable

---

[*] The effect size (d) is a quantitative measure of the strength of some treatment. It is defined as the difference between two means divided by a standard deviation for the data. An effect size of 0.20 is considered small, meaning, in this case, that simulator motion did not have much of an effect.

expense that motion-based simulators entail, over and above a fixed-based simulator. Indeed, the ultimate reason for using a motion-base simulator may not be greater transfer of training but decreased simulator sickness. (For a review of simulator sickness research, see Johnson 2005.)

In four quasi-experiments, Stewart et al. (2002) investigated the potential of simulators to replace a portion of the primary phase of U.S. Army rotary-wing training. In their studies, positive TERs were observed for most flight maneuvers from the simulator to the UH-1 training helicopter. Generally, student pilots who received simulator training required less training than controls to reach proficiency on flight maneuvers. For example, the TERs for the maneuver Takeoff to Hover ranged from 0.18 to 0.32 for the four experiments, while TERs for Land from Hover ranged from 0.25 to 0.72. Because the simulator was undergoing continual refinement during the course of the four experiments, Stewart et al. were able to show that improvements in the visual scene and aerodynamic flight model could result in improvements to the TER.

In a subsequent study (Stewart and Dohme 2005), the use of an automated hover trainer was investigated. This system utilized the same simulator as was used in the Stewart et al.'s (2002) series of experiments and incorporated a high-quality visual display system. A simple two-group design was used with 16 pilot trainees receiving the experimental training and 30 trainees serving as controls. For the five hovering tasks that were practiced in the simulator, there were no instances of negative transfer of training. In all cases, fewer iterations of the tasks were required for the simulator-trained subjects than for the control subjects. Stewart and Dohme conclude that these results show the potential for simulation-based training in traditionally aircraft-based primary contact tasks, in addition to its traditional role in instrument training.

In a similar experiment (Macchiarella et al. 2006) using civilian student pilots at Embry-Riddle University, 20 student pilots received their initial training in a Frasca flight training device (FTD) configured to match the Cessna 172S in which 16 control subjects were trained. Positive TERs were obtained for 33 out of 34 tasks in this study. This is particularly interesting since the Frasca, in contrast to the simulators used in the Army studies, is a nonmotion-base simulator.

6.6.2 Training Using PCs

In contrast to traditional simulators that generally replicate to a fair degree of realism the flight deck, instruments, and controls of a particular aircraft, several recent studies have assessed the use of PCs for training. Although some studies of, by current standards, crude PC-based training devices were conducted as early as the 1970s, the major impetus for this work begin in the early 1990s, with the work of Taylor and his associates at the University of Illinois at Urbana-Champaign. As with traditional simulators, the initial studies were primarily concerned with the use of personal computer aviation training devices (PCATDs) for the training of instrument skills. Taylor et al. (1999) evaluated the extent to which a PCATD could be used to teach instrument tasks and the subsequent transfer of those skills to an aircraft. Taylor et al. constructed a PCATD out of commercially available software and hardware and administered portions of two university-level aviation courses to students. Following instruction in the PCATD, the students then received instruction and evaluation in an aircraft. TERs ranged from a high of 0.28 to a low of 0.12, depending on the specific task. An interesting finding from this study was that the PCATD was more effective for the introduction of new tasks than for the review of tasks previously learned to criterion level.

In a subsequent study, Taylor et al. (2001) demonstrated again that these devices can be used successfully to teach instrument skills, with an overall TER of 0.15, or a savings of about 1.5 flight hours for each 10 hours of PC-based training. An earlier study by Ortiz (1994) demonstrated a TER of 0.48 for PC-based training of instrument skills to students with no previous piloting experience.

In addition to their use in acquiring initial instrument flight skills, PCATDs might also be of use in maintaining those skills. As we note in the following section of this chapter, complex cognitive skills are subject to loss over extended periods with no practice. Whether PCATDs could provide that practice was the question addressed by Talleur et al. (2003) in their study of 106 instrument-rated pilots. They randomly assigned pilots to one of four groups who, following an initial instrument proficiency check (IPC) flight in an aircraft, then received training at 2 and 4 months in (1) an aircraft, (2) an FTD, (3) a PCATD, or (4) none (control group). At the 6-month point, all groups then received another IPC in an aircraft. By comparing the performance of these four groups on the final IPC, they were able to demonstrate that the PCATD was effective for maintaining instrument currency. The pilots who trained on the PCATD during the 6-month period performed as well as those who trained on the FTD. Furthermore, both those groups performed at least as well as those who trained in the aircraft. An additional interesting finding from this study was that of the legally instrument-current pilots who entered this study, only 42.5% were able to pass the initial IPC in the aircraft.

While PCATDs have been shown to be useful in the training of instrument skills, they have been less successful in dealing with manual or psychomotor skills. Two studies have failed to find transfer of manual flying skills from the PCATD to either straight-and-level flight (Dennis and Harris 1998) or aerobatic flight (Roessingh 2005). However, the use of PC-based systems to teach teamwork skills has been successfully demonstrated in a study of U.S. Navy pilots (Brannick et al. 2005). In that study, pilots who received training in CRM on a PC later demonstrated better performance in a scenario executed in a high-fidelity flight simulator, compared to pilots who received only problem-solving exercises and video games such as have been used in commercial CRM training.

PC-based systems have also been used to teach decision-making and weather-recognition skills. A computer-based weather training program (WeatherWise), developed by Wiggins and O'Hare (2003) to improve GA pilot weather-related decision-making, has been shown to improve pilots' skill at recognizing deteriorating weather conditions. In a study by Kim (2011), a group of pilots who completed the WeatherWise training exhibited significantly higher weather assessment as measured by ceiling estimation ability, and decision accuracy as measured by flown distance into adverse weather condition than a control group. Although the risk assessments of the treatment and control groups were not significantly different between the two groups, pilots in the WeatherWise training group were more conservative toward flying into adverse weather condition than the control group.

6.7 SUMMARY

Training is a vast subject, since it draws upon many disciplines and scientific and technical traditions, from the learning theorists to the computer scientists and simulator engineers. For the most part, our current training programs produce graduates with the skills necessary to be good pilots. Research today is largely concerned with working at the edges to improve efficiency, reduce costs, and refine the training content. At the risk of doing a severe injustice to the extensive body of work that we have touched upon, sometimes only briefly in this chapter, let us offer the following summary:

- A well-designed pilot training system requires analysis and careful planning in order to produce a quality product.
- CRM has been a topic of debate for several years, with no clear resolution in sight. Whether it actually results in improved safety is still open to question.
- Simulators are unquestionably valuable tools in aviation training and have consistently been shown to have a positive TER, besides saving money and allowing us to train hazardous situations safely.
- PCs have made their way into aviation training. There seems to be little doubt that they can be used successfully for both initial and refresher instrument training. Whether they can also be used for contact training remains to be seen.

Finally, before we leave the subject of training, let us make a final observation about the current practice of aviation training. In particular, we are concerned with the pervasive practice of teaching subjects, such as meteorology, in a decontextualized manner. That is, in the typical aviation training school, there is a course on meteorology in which students learn the names of all the clouds, memorize the symbols that indicate wind speed and direction from the meteorological charts, and learn how to decipher the abbreviations contained in the METAR/TAF reports. Usually, all this takes place without any reference to the context in which such knowledge would be useful and applied. Hence, students memorize the content, without learning how to apply that knowledge when planning and conducting flights. Nor do they learn to appreciate the significance, from an operational or safety standpoint, of the information they are learning. The need for instruction to take place within the context of its application has been discussed cogently by Lintern (1995), who refers to this concept as situated instruction.

While this chapter has dealt at length with the rational processes of training system design exemplified by the SAT/ISD process, as Lintern (1995) notes, this process can have the effect of removing learning from the context in which it is to be applied. It is well to keep in mind that eventually, the pilot must integrate all that he or she has learned in order to successfully and safely conduct a flight. Over-compartmentalization and a rote-learning approach to instruction, even if the instruction includes all the separate skill elements, may not provide the goal of allowing the pilot to generalize from the classroom setting to the flight deck at the time at which the knowledge must be applied. Training must always be planned and conducted with this ultimate goal in mind.

6.8   OUTSIDE ACTIVITIES

Assuming you have read the preceding chapters, you will have noticed that some of them include this section at the end of the discussion. What do those sections have in common? If you answered something to the effect that, "they all got the reader to stop passively reading and get active," then you are correct. The next question is, why is that important? A little earlier in this chapter we mentioned the importance of situated and engaged learning. Could that be the answer?

So, what could you do to personally experience some of the learning and training concepts and activities discussed earlier? Here are some suggestions:

- Ebbinghaus investigated two key features associated with training—learning and forgetting—by learning sets of nonsense syllables (like ZOV) until he achieved perfect recall. He then recorded how many he was able to retain after various time intervals. You could measure how many repetitions it takes you to learn a small set of nonsense syllables and then how long you can retain them.
- Consider a typical task around the house (e.g., washing the car, putting up the Christmas tree, trimming the hedges) and develop a plan for training a new employee/spouse to perform that task. What does that person have to know? Can the task be broken down into subtasks? Does the person have to learn one skill before he or she can learn another skill? How will you measure successful completion of the tasks and subtasks?
- CRM is important both in crew situations and when flying single-pilot. How are your CRM skills? Check out http://www.crewresourcemanage-ment.net/ for fairly extensive training on improving CRM in both settings.

RECOMMENDED READINGS

Gagne, R.M., Briggs, L.J., and Wager, W.W. 1992. *Principles of Instructional Design.* New York, NY: Harcourt Brace Jovanovich.

Johnston, N., Fuller, R., and McDonald, N. 1995. *Aviation Psychology: Training and Selection.* Brookfield, VT: Ashgate.

O'Neil, H.F. and Andrews, D.H. 2000. *Aircrew Training and Assessment.* Mahwah, NJ: Erlbaum.

Telfer, R.A. and Moore, P.J. 1997. *Aviation Training: Learners, Instruction and Organization.* Brookfield, VT: Avebury.

REFERENCES

Amalberti, R. and Wibaux, F. 1995. Maintaining manual and cognitive skills. In Johnston, N., Fuller, R., and McDonald, N. (Eds.), *Aviation Psychology: Training and Selection* (pp. 339–353). Brookfield, VT: Ashgate.

Arthur, W., Bennett, W., Stanush, P.L., and McNelly, T.L. 1998. Factors that influence skill decay and retention: A quantitative review and analysis. *Human Performance* 11: 57–101.

Baubien, J.M. and Baker, D.P. 2002. *Airline Pilots' Perceptions of and Experiences in Crew Resource Management (CRM) Training.* Warrensdale, PA: SAE International.

Birnbach, R. and Longridge, T. 1993. The regulatory perspective. In Wiener, E., Kanki, B., and Helmreich, R. (Eds.), *Cockpit Resource Management* (pp. 263–282). San Diego, CA: Academic Press.

Brannick, M.T., Prince, C., and Salas, E. 2005. Can PC-based systems enhance teamwork in the cockpit? *International Journal of Aviation Psychology* 15: 173–187.

Carretta, T.R., Dunlap, R.D. 1998. *Transfer of Training Effectiveness in Flight Simulation: 1986 to 1997.* AFRL-HE-AZ-TR-1998–0078. Mesa, AZ: U.S. Air Force Research Laboratory, Human Effectiveness Directorate.

Casner, S.M., Heraldez, D., and Jones, K.M. 2006. Retention of aeronautical knowledge. *International Journal of Applied Aviation Studies* 6: 71–97.

Childs, J.M. and Spears, W.D. 1986. Flight-skill decay and recurrent training. *Perceptual and Motor Skills* 62: 235–242.

Childs, J.M., Spears, W.D., and Prophet, W.W. 1983. *Private Pilot Flight Skill Retention 8, 16, and 24 Months Following Certification.* DOT/FAA/CT-83/34. Washington, DC: Federal Aviation Administration.

Christian, D. and Morgan, A. 1987. Crew coordination concepts: Continental airlines CRM training. In Orlady, H.W., and Foushee, H.C. (Eds.), *Cockpit Resource Management Training* (NASA CP-2455) (pp. 68–74). Moffett Field, CA: NASA Ames Research Center.

Czarnecki, K.R. 2004. Respect the weather. *Flightfax* 32: 5–7.

Dennis, K.A. and Harris, D. 1998. Computer-based simulation as an adjunct to ab initio flight training. *International Journal of Aviation Psychology* 8: 277–292.

Diehl, A.E. 1991. Does cockpit management training reduce aircrew error? *22nd International Seminar, International Society of Air Safety Investigators.* Canberra, Australia, November, 4–7.

Ebbinghaus, H. 1913/1885. *Memory: A Contribution to Experimental Psychology.* Ruger, H.A., and Bussenius, C.A. (Trans.). New York, NY: Teachers College, Columbia University.

FAA. 2004. *Crew Resource Management Training.* Advisory circular 120–51E. Washington, DC: Federal Aviation Administration.

Fitts, P.M. and Posner, M.I. 1967. *Human Performance.* New York, NY: Prentice-Hall.

Flanagan, J.C. 1954. The critical incident technique. *Psychological Bulletin* 51: 327–358.

Fletcher, R., Flin, R., McGeorge, P., Glavin, R., Maran, N., and Patey, R. 2003. Anaesthetists' non-technical skills (ANTS): Evaluation of a behavioural marker system. *British Journal of Anaesthesia* 90: 580–588.

Foushee, H.C. 1984. Dyads and triads at 35,000 feet: Factors affecting group process and aircrew performance. *American Psychologist* 39: 885–893.

Gordon, J. and Zemke, R. 2000. The attack on ISD. *Training* April: 42–53.

Hays, R.T., Jacobs, J.W., Prince, C., and Salas, E. 1992. Flight simulator training effectiveness: A meta-analysis. *Military Psychology* 4: 63–74.

Helmreich, R.L., Merritt, A.C., and Wilhelm, J.A. 1999. The evolution of crew resource management training in commercial aviation. *International Journal of Aviation Psychology* 9: 19–32.

Henley, I.M.A. 2004. *Aviation Education and Training: Adult Learning Principles and Teaching Strategies.* Brookfield, VT: Ashgate.

Hergenhahn, B. and Olson, M. 2005. *An Introduction to the Theories of Learning*, 7th ed. New York, NY: Prentice-Hall.

ICAO. n.d. *Convention on International Civil Aviation—Annex 1: Personnel Licensing.* Montreal, Canada: Author.

Johnson, D.M. 2005. *Introduction to and Review of Simulator Sickness Research.* Research Report 1832. Ft. Rucker, AL: U.S. Army Research Institute for the Behavioral and Social Sciences.

Kim, C. 2011. The effects of weather recognition training on general aviation pilot situation assessment and tactical decision making when confronted with adverse weather conditions. All dissertations. Paper 754.

Kirkpatrick, D.L. 1976. Evaluation of training. In Craig, R.L. (Ed.), *Training and Development Handbook: A Guide to Human Resources Development.* New York, NY: McGraw-Hill.

Lintern, G. 1995. Flight instruction: The challenge from situated cognition. *International Journal of Aviation Psychology* 5: 327–350.

Lintern, G., Roscoe, S.N., Koonce, J.M., and Segal, L.D. 1990. Transfer of landing skills in beginning flight training. *Human Factors* 32: 319–327.

Macchiarella, N.D., Arban, P.K., and Doherty, S.M. 2006. Transfer of training from flight training devices to flight for ab initio pilots. *International Journal of Applied Aviation Studies* 6: 299–314.

Mangold, S. and Neumeister, D. 1995. CRM in the model AQP: A preview. In Jensen, R.S., and Rakovan, L.A. (Eds.), *Proceedings of the Eighth International Symposium on Aviation Psychology* (pp. 556–561). Columbus, OH: The Ohio State University.

Mazur, J.E. 2006. *Learning and Behavior,* 6th ed. New York, NY: Prentice-Hall.

Meister, D. 1985. *Behavioral Analysis and Measurement Methods.* New York, NY: John Wiley.

Mengelkoch, R.F., Adams, J.A., and Gainer, C.A. 1971. The forgetting of instrument flying skills. *Human Factors* 13: 397–405.

Moorman, R.W. 2002. The civilian looking military. *MS&T Magazine* 6: 18–20.

Norsk Luftfartsmuseum. 2005. *100 Years of Norwegian Aviation.* Bodø, Norway: Author.

O'Neil, H.F. and Andrews, D.H. 2000. *Aircrew Training and Assessment.* Mahway, NJ: Erlbaum.

Omrod, J.E. 2007. *Human Learning,* 5th ed. New York, NY: Prentice-Hall.

Ortiz, G.A. 1994. Effectiveness of PC-based flight simulation. *International Journal of Aviation Psychology* 4: 285–291.

Pfeiffer, M.G., Horey, J.D., and Butrimas, S.K. 1991. Transfer of simulated instrument training to instrument and contact flight. *The International Journal of Aviation Psychology* 1: 219–229.

Phillips, J. 1991. *Handbook of Training Evaluation and Measurement Methods,* 2nd ed. Houston, TX: Gulf Publishing Company.

Prophet, W.W. 1976. *Long-term Retention of Flying Skills: A Review of the Literature.* HumRRO Final Technical Report FR-ED(P) 76–35. Alexandria, VA: Human Resources Research Organization.

Reason, J. 1990. *Human Error.* New York, NY: Cambridge University Press.

Reason, J. 1997. *Managing the Risks of Organizational Accidents.* Aldershot, UK: Ashgate.

Roessingh, J.J.M. 2005. Transfer of manual flying skills from PC-based simulation to actual flight—Comparison of in-flight measured data and instructor ratings. *International Journal of Aviation Psychology* 5: 67–90.

Roscoe, S. 1980. *Aviation Psychology.* Ames, IA: Iowa State University Press.

Ruffner, J.W. and Bickley, W.R. 1985. *Validation of Aircrew Training Manual Practice Iteration Requirements.* Interim Report. ADA173441. Fort Rucker, AL: Anacapa Science Inc.

Salas, E., Bowers, C.A., and Edens, E. 2001. *Improving Teamwork in Organizations: Applications of Resource Management Training.* New York, NY: Erlbaum.

Salas, E., Burke, S., Bowers, C., and Wilson, K. 2001. Team training in the skies: Does crew resource management (CRM) training work? *Human Factors* 43: 641–674.

Salas, E., Wilson, K.A., Burke, C.S., and Wightman, D.C. 2006. Does crew resource management training work? An update, an extension, and some critical needs. *Human Factors* 48: 392–412.

Schendel, J.D., Shields, J.L., and Katz, M.S. 1978. *Retention of Motor Skills: Review.* Technical Paper 313. Alexandria, VA: U.S. Army Research Institute for the Behavioral and Social Sciences.

Stewart, J.E. and Dohme, J.A. 2005. Automated hover trainer: Simulator-based intelligent flight training system. *International Journal of Applied Aviation Studies* 5: 25–39.

Stewart, J.E., Dohme, J.A., and Nullmeyer, R.T. 2002. U.S. Army initial entry rotary-wing transfer of training research. *International Journal of Aviation Psychology* 12: 359–375.

Talleur, D.A., Taylor, H.L., Emanuel, T.W., Rantanen, E., and Bradshaw, G.L. 2003. Personal computer aviation training devices: Their effectiveness for maintaining instrument currency. *International Journal of Aviation Psychology* 13: 387–399.

Taylor, H.L., Lintern, G., Hulin, C., Talleur, D., Emanuel, T., and Phillips, A. 1999. Transfer of training effectiveness of a personal computer aviation training device. *International Journal of Aviation Psychology* 9: 319–335.

Taylor, H.L., Talleur, D.A., Emanuel, T.W., Rantanen, E.M., Bradshaw, G., and Phillips, S.I. 2001. Incremental training effectiveness of personal computers used for instrument training. *Proceedings of the 11th International Symposium on Aviation Psychology.* The Ohio State University, Columbus, OH.

Telfer, R.A. and Moore, P.J. 1997. *Aviation Training: Learners, Instruction and Organization.* Brookfield, VT: Avebury.

U.S. Air Force. 1993. *Instructional System Design.* AFMAN 36–2234. Washington, DC: Author.

U.S. Army. n.d. *Systems Approach to Training.* TRADOC- Pamphlet 350-70 (6 parts). Fort Monroe, VA: Author.

U.S. Department of Defense. 2001. *Instructional Systems Development/systems Approach to Training and Education (5 Parts).* MIL-HDBG-29612–2A. Washington, DC: Author.

U.S. Navy. 1997. *NAVEDTRA 130A Volume 1—Task Based Curriculum Development Manual (Developer's Guide).* Pensacola, FL: Naval Education and Training Command.

Vaden, E.A. and Hall, S. 2005. The effect of simulator platform motion on pilot training transfer: A meta-analysis. *International Journal of Aviation Psychology* 15: 375–393.

Wiegmann, D. and Shappell, S. 1999. Human error and crew resource management failures in Naval aviation mishaps: A review of U.S. Naval Safety Center data, 1990–96. *Aviation, Space, and Environmental Medicine* 70: 1147–1151.

Wiggins, M. and O'Hare, D. 2003. Weatherwise: Evaluation of a cue-based training approach for the recognition of deteriorating weather conditions during flight. *Human Factors* 45: 337–345.

Wilson-Donnelly, K.A. and Shappell, S.A. 2004. U.S. Navy/Marine Corps CRM training: Separating theory from reality. *Proceedings of the Human Factors and Ergonomics Society 48th Annual Meeting* (pp. 2070–2074). New Orleans, LA.

Wright, R.H. 1973. *Retention of Flying Skills and Refresher Training Requirements: Effects of Non-Flying and Proficiency Flying.* HumRRO Technical Report 73–32. Alexandria, VA: Human Resources Research Organization.

7 Human Factors and the Design of Aviation Systems

7.1 INTRODUCTION

> This, indeed, is the historical imperative of human factors—understanding why people do what they do so we can tweak, change the world in which they work and shape their assessments and actions accordingly.

Dekker 2003, p. 3

As noted in Chapter 1, aviation psychology is closely related to the field known as human factors. In recent years, the distinctions between aviation psychology, human factors, and the more hardware-oriented discipline of engineering psychology have become very blurred, with practitioners claiming allegiance to the disciplines performing very similar research and applying their knowledge in very similar ways. Traditionally, engineering psychology might be thought of as focusing more on the humans while human factors might focus somewhat more on the hardware and its interface with the human operator. For all practical purposes, however, the distinction between the two disciplines is irrelevant. It is mentioned here only to alert the reader to the terminology, since much of what we would label as aviation psychology is published in books and journals labeled as human factors.

Setting aside the differences in terminology, aviation psychology (or human factors, if you prefer) has a great deal to say about how aviation systems should be designed. To meet the goals of reducing errors, improving performance, and enhancing comfort, a system must accommodate the physical, sensory, cognitive, and psychological characteristics of the operator. A system must not demand that operators lift excessive weights nor press a control with an impossible amount of force. A system must not require that operators read information written in a tiny font or make fine distinctions of sound when operating in a noisy environment. A system must not demand complex mental arithmetic or the memorization and perfect recall of long lists of control settings, dial readings, and procedures. A system must not demand that operators remain immune to the social stresses placed on them by coworkers or to the demands of management to cut corners to accomplish the job. Moreover, in-so-far as possible, the design of the system should preclude the possibility of error or misuse.

Despite progress and many successes (for some examples, see Harris 1984), designing systems that preclude the potential for error remains an as yet unfulfilled goal—more so in general aviation aircraft and associated systems than in transport category aircraft. Wise et al. (1998, p. 107) noted that

> … the place where human factors could make it biggest impact in terms of safety and error prevention, general aviation (GA), is still basically a human factors waste land. If one looks at the current statistics of light aircraft accidents, it reads like a list of errors and design problems described.

7.2   SYSTEM DESIGN AND OPERATOR ERRORS

An earlier study of aircraft design–induced pilot errors conducted by the Civil Aeronautics Board (CAB 1967), predecessor to the National Transportation Safety Board (NTSB), compared accident records of 35 make and model airplanes to assess the influence of airplane design factors in GA accidents. That study found that certain types of accidents (involving retractable landing gear and fuel systems) were primarily related to detail design. The major design factors included improper sensing of controls, inadequate identification of controls, inadequate indication and/or warning to the pilot, and lack of standardization. For example, in one model of aircraft, a single fuel gauge was used to indicate the amount of fuel in two or more tanks. In this design, it is possible to have the gauge selected to one tank, but at the same time, fuel is being used from another tank.

As a further example of how a poor fuel control design can affect safety, consider the 1999 fatal crash involving the singer/songwriter John Denver. In that crash, the NTSB determined that Mr Denver fatally crashed his experimental aircraft into Monterey Bay because his attention during flight was diverted in an attempt to switch fuel tanks. The fuel selector valve on his amateur-built airplane was located behind the pilot's left shoulder, forcing him to turn in his seat to locate the handle. The NTSB concluded that this action likely caused him to inadvertently apply the right rudder, resulting in loss of aircraft control.

Failure to adequately guard controls against inadvertent activation can also lead to accidents. In December 1996, a flight crew noticed a minor fuel imbalance problem in their A-340 while enroute from Singapore to Sydney. The procedure to correct this imbalance required the crew to open the four fuel cross-feed valves located on the center overhead panel. This would then enable fuel transfer to occur. This procedure is conducted frequently in flight to maintain optimal aircraft weight and balance. Adjacent to those switches, and approximately 3 cm directly above them, are switches for the four engine-driven hydraulic pumps. If these are switched off, a drop in hydraulic pressure will occur. These switches are rarely, if ever, used in flight. The pilot monitoring the fuel system initially placed his finger on the correct switch, but was then distracted by a message on the engine condition and monitoring panel. While the pilot was observing that panel, his finger moved slightly over to the hydraulics switch. The pilot then pressed the incorrect switch, followed by the remaining three switches. This resulted in an immediate drop in hydraulic pressure and the nose of the aircraft pitched up. Fortunately, the flight crew noticed the problem before complete control was lost and used the side stick to keep the nose down, while they worked out what had happened and turned the

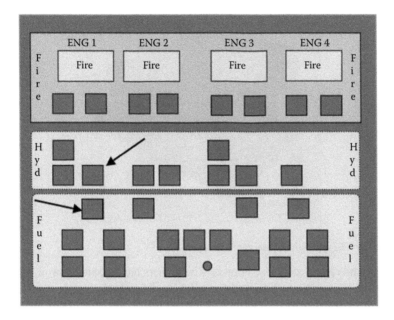

FIGURE 7.1 Layout of overhead panel from Airbus A340.

hydraulic switches back to their correct settings. The switch locations are shown in Figure 7.1.

A subsequent investigation of this incident by the Australian Transportation Safety Board (ATSB) found that

- The hydraulic switches were not guarded and were of very similar appearance to the fuel cross-feed switches.
- The switches were activated by the same push-button switching action and used the same while illumination to indicate activation.
- The hydraulic switches were located immediately above, and almost aligned with, the fuel cross-feed switches.

Placement of a simple guard over the rarely used hydraulic switches would have greatly reduced the likelihood of their inadvertent activation.* Figure 7.2 shows an example of a toggle switch with a simple guard in place, while Figure 7.3 shows the same switch with the guard raised.

To achieve the goals of error reduction and improved performance that we mentioned earlier requires knowledge of all the human factors that affect the interaction of humans and technological systems. Knowledge of human capabilities, strengths, and limitations informs the system design process, since this knowledge sets the bounds for the demands the system may make of the operator. An extensive body

---

* Even a switch guard will not deter the pilot who is determined to mess-up. One night a senior officer in the unit in which DH served in Vietnam managed to lift the switch guard and activate the switch that cut the external hoist cable on the helicopter. Fortunately, no one was on the hoist at the time.

FIGURE 7.2   Toggle switch with guard in place.

of research has addressed these bounds. Researchers have studied how much weight humans can lift to specified heights, the numbers of errors that occur when identical controls are placed side-by-side, how many numbers can be recalled from short-term memory, the font size of displays, legibility of displays under varying degrees of illumination, and the effects that the climate of an organization can have on the safety-related behavior of workers, to list but a few examples. The overall aim of this chapter is to demonstrate how psychological knowledge may be used when designing aviation systems, what principles should be applied, and common errors and problems that occur when humans interact with complex systems and equipment.

FIGURE 7.3   Toggle switch with guard raised.

7.3   TYPES OF HUMAN ERROR

The present status of aviation psychology and human factors owes much to the efforts of researchers during the Second World War. The sheer magnitude of the war effort led researchers on both sides of the conflict to conduct extensive studies with the aim of improving personnel performance and reducing losses due to accidents and combat. Perhaps, the most frequently cited study in the area of aviation psychology and human factors produced by that era was the work by Fitts and Jones (1947a, 1961a) on the causes of errors among pilots. They surveyed a large number of U.S. Army Air Force pilots regarding instances in which they committed or observed an error in the operation of a cockpit control (flight control, engine control, toggle switch, selector switch, etc.). They found that all errors could be classified into one of six categories:

- *Substitution errors*: Confusing one control with another or failing to identify a control when it was needed
- *Adjustment errors*: Operating a control too slowly or too rapidly, moving a switch to the wrong position, or following the wrong sequence when operating several controls
- *Forgetting errors*: Failing to check, unlock, or use a control at the proper time
- *Reversal errors*: Moving a control in the direction opposite to that necessary to achieve the desired result
- *Unintentional activation*: Operating a control inadvertently, without being aware of it
- *Unable to reach a control*: Inability to physically reach a needed control, or being required to divert their attention from external scan to a point that an accident or near-accident occurred

Substitution errors accounted for 50% of all the error descriptions reported, with the most common types of errors being confusion of throttle quadrant controls (19%), confusion of flap and wheel controls (16%), and selection of the wrong engine control or propeller feathering button (8%). Similar difficulties were encountered with the controls for the flaps and landing gear, which at that time were often located close to one another and used the same knob shape.

Fortunately, for today's pilots, many of the recommendations of Fitts and Jones and other researchers of that period have been implemented. The configuration of the six principal instruments, the order of controls on the throttle quadrant for propeller-driven aircraft, and the shapes of the controls themselves are all now fairly standardized. The shape of the knob for the landing gear resembles a wheel, the shape of the flaps knob resembles an airfoil, and the two controls are located as far apart as possible, while still remaining easily accessible to the pilot.

While these sorts of errors have been largely, though not entirely, eliminated, others remain. Forgetting errors, which in the Fitts and Jones study accounted for 18% of the total errors, remain a problem in today's aircraft. The shape of the landing gear control may have largely prevented its confusion with the flaps; however, the pilot must still remember to lower the gear prior to landing. Memory devices, paper checklists, and, in the case of more advanced aircraft, computer watchdogs all serve to prevent the pilot from making the all-too-human error of forgetting. Interestingly, one of the recommendations of Fitts and Jones (1961a, p. 333) was to make it "impossible to start the take-off run until all vital steps are completed." Clearly, this is a goal that still eludes us, since pilots still attempt takeoffs without first extending the leading-edge slats and flaps, and make landings without prior arming of the spoilers—typically, after defeating the warning systems put in place to prevent such events.

A different perspective on errors and error management was suggested by Reason (1992). He proposed that human error may be divided into either intentional or unintentional actions. Intentional actions are those that involve conscious choices and are largely due to judgment or motivational processes. In contrast, unintentional actions are those in which the right intention or plan is incorrectly executed. Each of these broad categories of error may be further divided, as shown below.

7.3.1 UNINTENTIONAL ACTIONS

These errors may result from slips, lapses, or mistakes. In each of the cases, the person intended to do one thing, but actually did something else.

Slips are typically errors of attention failure. For example, you might plan on driving to the store, but turn the way you usually do to go to work. Or, you might plan on lowering the landing gear as you cross abeam the end of the runway on downwind, but become distracted by something else, and omit the action.

Lapses occur when you fail to carry out an intended action. Lapses are characterized by memory failures. For example, you might fail to check the fuel levels in the tanks during your preflight inspection, even though you had intended to do so.

Mistakes occur when you plan to do something and carry out your plan successfully, but you do get the outcome you expected. This is often because your knowledge was inadequate.

7.3.2 INTENTIONAL ACTIONS

These actions involve a conscious choice to do something. In these cases, the person did what they intended to do, although the outcome may not be what they expected.

Mistakes can arise from intentional actions, just as they can arise from unintentional actions. In both cases, the mistake may be caused by a lack of knowledge, or the failure to appropriately apply some rule.

Violations involve deliberate departures from known rules and procedures. When a violation becomes the normal practice, it is considered a routine violation. Routine violations are often shortcuts taken to help get the job done more quickly or efficiently. For example, cutting back on reserve fuel in order to carry more cargo might be normal practice for all the pilots in an air-taxi operator. This sort of behavior may become pervasive in an organization, and will be reflected in the organizational climate and culture, discussed in a later chapter.

Situational violations occur when there is a disconnection between what the rules or procedures require and what you think is possible. For example, the maintenance procedures may require that you use a particular test tool. However, if it is not available, you might use an alternative tool, not expressly approved for that purpose.

Optimizing violations involve you doing something for personal gain, or simply for the thrill of doing it your way. Incentives, such as a bonus for saving fuel on flights, may encourage optimizing violations.

Exceptional violations are one-off actions taken to deal with an usual situation. For example, if someone were injured, you might speed to a hospital rather than waiting for an ambulance to arrive.

Clearly, human are quite adept at making errors. One of the keys to preventing errors, or at least to managing their consequences, is to understand how human characteristics interact with the physical and mental demands of a system. To do that, we must understand what human are capable of doing.

7.4 HUMAN CHARACTERISTICS AND DESIGN

At a more general level than the work by Fitts and Jones, Sinaiko and Buckley (1957, 1961, p. 4) list the following general characteristics of humans as a system component:

- Physical dimensions
- Capability for data sensing
- Capability for data processing
- Capability for motor activity
- Capability for learning
- Physical and psychological needs
- Sensitivities to physical environment
- Sensitivities to social environment
- Coordinated action
- Differences among individuals

All of these characteristics must be taken into account in the design of aviation systems. Some of the system requirements driven by these characteristics are reasonably well understood and have been addressed in system design for many years. For example, certainly since the work of Fitts and Jones following World War II, designers have been aware of the need to properly mark and separate controls, and to arrange displays in a consistent way. However, the implications of some of the characteristics are still being explored. The work over the past 20 years on crew resource management (see Helmreich et al. 1999 for an overview) is evidence of our growing understanding of the sensitivities of humans to their social environment and capabilities for coordinated action. Even more recently, researchers have begun to explore the influences of the organizational climate and culture on the performance of aircrew (Ciavarelli et al. 2001).

Of particular relevance to aviation psychology is the notion of differences among individuals. Although Sinaiko and Buckley (1957) list it as a separate characteristic, it is really inherent in all the other characteristics they list. Humans vary, often considerably, on every characteristic by which they may be measured. (Recall the discussion of this topic in Chapter 4.) The measurement of those individual differences and determination of how those differences contribute to other characteristics of interest, such as success in training, likelihood of an accident, skill at making instrument landings, or probability of being a good team member, is at the heart of aviation psychology.

In addition to examining the errors associated with controls, Fitts and Jones (1947b, 1961b) also examined errors in reading and interpreting aircraft instruments. As in their study of control errors, Fitts and Jones classified errors in reading or interpreting instruments into nine major categories. Errors in reading multi-revolution instrument indications accounted for the largest proportion of errors (18%). Misreading the altimeter by 1000 feet was the most common of these errors, by itself accounting for 13% of the total errors.

Among their several conclusions, Fitts and Jones (1961b, p. 360) note, "The nature of instrument-reading errors is such that it should be possible to eliminate most of the errors by proper design of instruments." Sixty years after the first publication of their work, current researchers could still arrive at the same conclusion. If most of the issues associated with the shape of controls have been resolved, problems with displays remain. However, they are not necessarily the same problems identified by Fitts and Jones. Multi-revolution instruments (most notably the altimeter) have been replaced with instruments that depict information differently—typically, along a vertical scale in the case of altitude. Yet, pilots still fly into the ground on occasion, because, even having read the instrument correctly, they have misprogramed the system that controls the vertical flight profile of their aircraft. Likewise, the radio navigation beacons that required pilots to aurally identify the Morse signal transmitted by the beacon, and that gave rise to signal interpretation errors, have given way to GPS navigation, with its own set of display problems and corresponding errors.

Each new generation of technology offers some solutions to the problems that existed in the older generation, while creating a whole new set of problems. This situation is succinctly described by Dekker (2002, p. 8) who notes, "... aerospace has seen the introduction of more technology as illusory antidote to the plague of human error. Instead of reducing human error, technology changed it, aggravated the consequences, and delayed opportunities for error detection and recovery."

7.5 PRINCIPLES OF DISPLAY DESIGN

One way to break this chain of technology and error is to step outside the specific technologies and look at overarching principles that should be applied to all new technology development. Thus, instead of looking for the best shape for the landing gear control, we might look for the general principles by which such controls should be designed. As an example, let us consider the design of aircraft displays. Wickens (2003), one of the preeminent researchers in the area of aviation displays, has enumerated seven critical principles of display design.

7.5.1 PRINCIPLE OF INFORMATION NEED

How much information does a pilot need? The short answer is just enough. Too little information (e.g., the absence of weather radar on days when thunderstorms are present) leaves the pilot flying, and making decisions, in the blind. Most pilots would agree that having more information is good, but the converse is also true. Having too much information can be as damaging as having too little. Too much information can lead to a cluttered flight deck (typified by the L-1011 and DC-10 era aircraft) with hundreds of dials and indicators. Searching for the needed information among all the extraneous information can lead to poor performance on critical, time-sensitive tasks. Current generation aircraft, in contrast, have combined many of the formerly separate information sources into combined displays that integrate information, such as engine health, into a single, easily interpretable instrument. When that information is needed, it is easily obtained. To determine how much information is enough, we turn to a family of techniques subsumed under the title task analysis[*] (cf. Meister 1985; Kirwan and Ainsworth 1992; Seamster et al. 1997; Annett and Stanton 2000; Shepherd 2001). Although several varieties of this technique exist and are used for sometimes differing purposes (e.g., for training development or for personnel selection, as mentioned in other chapters of this book), they share a general approach to the orderly specification of the tasks that a person must accomplish, the actions (both physical and cognitive) that the person must complete, and the information required to permit them to complete the actions. For example, we might specify the information required to complete a precision instrument approach, or the information required to identify which of several engines has failed. If the pilot is expected to complete these tasks (making the instrument approach and dealing with the failed engine), then they must have the required information. In addition, that information should not be hidden by or among other bits of information.

7.5.2 PRINCIPLE OF LEGIBILITY

In order to be useful, information presented on displays must be readable. Further, it must be readable under the conditions that exist in the aircraft flight deck. This means that the digits on the display must be large enough to be read by the pilot from his or her normal seated position. In some cases, they should also be readable by the other crewmember if, for example, there is only one such display on the flight deck, and both crewmembers must use it. Typically, designers solve this problem by locating common displays and controls midway between the two pilots on a central console.

Legibility also requires consideration of effects such as glare and vibration. Almost all pilots quickly learn to steady their hands when reaching to tune the radio, for example, since even mild turbulence can make such a task quite difficult to perform rapidly and accurately. This vibration also impacts the legibility of displays, and the usual solution is to incorporate a larger font size, such that the information can be read under the full range of operating conditions. The effects of the factors such as these on human performance have been extensively investigated and are

---

[*] This brief discussion cannot hope to do justice to a topic that is the subject of many volumes. The reader is encouraged to consult the general references to task analysis listed here for more information. However, even these are only a tiny sampling of the vast amount of information available. Since task analysis methods vary according to the intended use of the information, the survey of methods given in Annett and Stanton (2000) may prove most beneficial for the task analysis novice.

summarized by Boff et al. (1988). In addition, the Engineering Data Compendium is an extensive resource that is available online from the Human Systems Integration Information Analysis Center of the U.S. Air Force.* Readers may also find Sanders and McCormick (1993) and Wickens and Hollands (2000) as useful references on this topic.

7.5.3   Principle of Display Integration/Proximity Compatibility Principle

The novice pilot, particularly the novice instrument pilot, has no doubt that scanning the instruments to obtain the information required to control the aircraft and navigate requires effort. The level of effort required can be increased or decreased by the degree to which the instruments are physically separated. Thus, in all modern aircraft, the primary flight instruments are located directly in front of the pilot. This reduces the time required for the pilot to move his or her scan from one instrument to another. It also means that the instruments can be scanned without moving the head—thus reducing the potential for vestibular disorientation.

In addition, effort can be reduced if displays that contain information that must be integrated or compared are close together. This is seen most clearly in multiengine aircraft where two, three, or four sets of engine instruments are arrayed (in older aircraft) in columns, with each column corresponding to one engine, and each row one engine parameter (e.g., oil temperature or turbine speed). Given this arrangement, the pilot may quickly scan across all the engine temperature readings, for example, to identify an engine with an anomalous reading.

Further examples are evident in the navigation instruments. For example, the lights indicating passage of marker beacons during a precision instrument approach are typically located close to the primary flight control instruments and the instrument landing system (ILS) display. Having the lights in the direct field of view of the pilot, instead of somewhere in the radio stack, enhances the likelihood that they will be seen by the pilot. This is particularly important for these displays, since they usually are extinguished after passage, with no persistent indicator that an important event has transpired.

Integration of related information into a single instrument represents a means to further reduce pilot workload by eliminating the necessity to visually scan multiple instruments and, potentially, eliminating the necessity to cognitively combine separate bits of information. Perhaps, the best example of this integration is the display for the flight management system (FMS) on a modern transport category aircraft. This system brings together in one display (typically called the primary flight display [PFD]) virtually all the information required for control of the aircraft and for horizontal and vertical navigation. A typical PFD is shown in Figure 7.4. This is an amazingly dense display of virtually all the information needed to fly the aircraft. While it may look daunting, with a relatively small amount of training pilots can quickly learn to decipher all the display elements.

At a somewhat simpler level, the flight director built into the attitude displays of some general aviation aircraft illustrates the same principles of integration. The flight

---

* http://www.hsiiac.org/products/compendium.html

FIGURE 7.4   Primary flight display. (From National Aeronautics and Space Administration.)

director provides visual cues on the attitude indicator. In its simplest form, these cues can take the form of simple horizontal and vertical lines, depicting the localizer and glideslope for an ILS, for example. Essentially, this arrangement moves these indicators from the ILS display to the attitude indicator, thus eliminating the need for the pilot to move his or her scan between these two instruments. Another configuration makes use of a black inverted "V" that represents the visual cue from the flight director, as shown in Figure 7.5.

The triangle represents the aircraft on the attitude indicator. In this situation, the flight director cues indicate that the pilot needs to bank the aircraft to the left. If the pilot keeps the triangle tucked up into the black "V," they will satisfy the cues from the flight director and will follow the course (i.e., ILS localizer/glideslope, VOR radial, GPS course) desired.

7.5.4   PRINCIPLE OF PICTORIAL REALISM

This principle holds that the display should resemble or be a very similar pictorial representation of the information it represents. The moving tape that represents altitude by moving a tape vertically represents one application of this principle. The current generation of moving map displays that can show the location of the aircraft (often depicted with a small aircraft symbol) against a background of topographic imagery is arguably an even stronger example of this principle.

FIGURE 7.5   Typical general aviation flight director display.

7.5.5   Principle of the Moving Part

According to this principle, the element that moves on a display should correspond to the element that moves in a pilot's mental model of the aircraft. In addition, the direction of movement of the display element should correspond with the direction of movement in the mental representation. This principle is best illustrated by the instrument that most thoroughly violates the principle—the attitude indicator. In the attitude indicator, the horizon is depicted as a moving element, whereas the aircraft is shown as static. However, this is completely opposite to the pilot's mental model, in which the horizon is static, and it is the aircraft that banks, climbs, and descends. The sacrifice in human performance that is demanded by this arrangement is reflected in the finding that for novice pilots, the moving aircraft display is more effective than the moving horizon display. Furthermore, even for pilots who are experienced in flying with the traditional, moving horizon display, the moving aircraft display is no less effective (Previc and Ercoline 1999; Cohen et al. 2001).

7.5.6   Principle of Predictive Aiding

Predicting the future state of the aircraft (heading, altitude, rate of climb or descent, bearing to some beacon, etc.) is a complex and cognitively demanding task. In-so-far as possible, displays should assist the pilot in this task by showing what will happen in the future. This allows the pilot to take steps now, so that the desired state is achieved, or an undesirable state is avoided. Many of the current generation of FMS provide this service by showing predicted flight paths, based on current engine and control settings. However, valuable assistance may be obtained from far less sophisticated systems. Consider the example of the fuel gauge that we will discuss in more detail later in this chapter. Most current designs simply represent the current status of the fuel supply—somewhere between full and empty. However, a slightly more sophisticated gauge could show future states, such as when and/or where zero fuel remaining will be reached, based on the current fuel load and consumption rate. This simple predictive aiding might help prevent the 10% of all accidents due to fuel mismanagement.

7.5.7 PRINCIPLE OF DISCRIMINABILITY: STATUS VERSUS COMMAND

Preventing confusion among similar displays is a responsibility of designers. Unfortunately, engineering demands often lead to sacrifices in this area. One example is the use of identically sized displays for all the engine instruments, because commonality reduces cost. This arrangement, while saving money during manufacturing since only one size hole need be punched in the panel, can later lead to a pilot mistaking one instrument for another, with results that can range from humorous to disastrous.

Unambiguous information is essential for the safe operation of the aircraft. Particularly problematic are those instances in which similar information, with an entirely different meaning, is displayed in a common display. This is a condition that is not unknown in FMSs, and which is cited as the cause of at least one major crash (Air France Airbus A-320 that crashed in Mulhouse-Habsheim Airport, France).

7.6 ELECTRONIC DISPLAYS AND PRINTED CHECKLISTS

Besides Wickens, many other researchers have also evaluated display issues. For example, looking specifically at the symbols used in displays, Yeh and Chandra (2004) posed four questions to be addressed when evaluating the usability of a symbol:

- Is the symbol easy to find?
- Is the symbol distinctive from other symbols?
- Is the on-screen symbol size appropriate?
- Can all encoded attributes of the symbol be decoded quickly and accurately?

In addition to electronic displays, human factors design principles must also be applied to printed materials, such as the ubiquitous checklists and the maintenance procedures manuals. Ross (2004) notes the importance of checklist in aviation and cites Sumwalt (1991) who reported on 228 accidents in the NTSB records in which checklist misuse was a contributing factor in an accident. In addition, the Aviation Safety Reporting System (ASRS) contains numerous reports involving checklists. Perhaps, the most extensive work on the human factors of checklists was that conducted by Degani and Wiener (1990) under NASA sponsorship. They suggested that there are nine objectives of checklists:

1. Help the pilot accurately configure the aircraft for flight phase.
2. Provide a systematic method to verify configuration, even if the crew is fatigued.

3. Provide a systematic and convenient eye scan of cockpit panels.
4. Provide a sequential framework to meet cockpit operational requirements.
5. Provide a method of crewmember cross-checking.
6. Provide a systematic method of configuring the aircraft, keeping all crewmembers in the loop.
7. Provide a method of optimum crew coordination and distribution of cockpit workload.
8. Provide a quality control tool that can be used to evaluate pilots.
9. Promote a positive attitude about checklist use and safety.

In order to meet those objectives, checklists must be constructed so as to maximize their use by aircrew and minimize errors—particularly skipping items. To achieve those goals, a great deal of attention must be paid by aircraft manufacturers and regulatory agencies to both the content and the formatting of checklists. Degani (1992) lists several criteria for the optimum design of checklists, mainly dealing with issues such as the type of fonts to be used, the spacing of characters, and color use. In addition, regulatory agencies provide specific guidance on organization, content, and typography of checklists. (See *Human Performance Considerations in the Use and Design of Aircraft Checklists*, Federal Aviation Administration 1995, for examples.)

The principles espoused by Wickens and others in the design of aviation systems, along with the results of many empirical studies on the effects of system characteristics on human performance, are codified in government regulations pertaining to the design of aircraft control and display systems. Particularly detailed listings of design standards are also provided in the military standards and handbooks used to govern the design and development of new military aircraft and related systems. Indeed, much of the development of the knowledge relating to human capabilities and the corresponding standards for system design has been led by the military. One recent example of the military's efforts to improve the design process is the U.S. Army's MANPRINT program (Booher 1990, 2003).

Design, Guard, Warn, Train: This is the chain of activities, given in order of precedence, for building human considerations into the system development process. Early changes to the *design* of a system are more effective and less costly than later attempts to *guard* against operator error, to *warn* them of hazards, or to *train* them to use the system despite its inherent problems. Despite its popularity, *training* should be viewed as the solution of last resort.

7.7   AN EXAMPLE: DESIGN OF THE FUEL GAUGE

So far our discussion has been fairly abstract, to give you a general idea of how information gained from aviation psychology influences system design. Now, let us take a look at a concrete example, the ubiquitous fuel gage.

Since the fuel gage, at least in light aircraft, is possibly the simplest gage in the cockpit, you may wonder just what could be said about it, from the standpoint of aviation psychology. As it turns out, actually there is quite a lot.

Why worry about the fuel gage? There are a lot of fuel-related accidents and incidents. In the United States, approximately 10% of the accidents involving general aviation aircraft are attributed to fuel management, including fuel starvation (fuel left, but not being fed to the engine) or fuel exhaustion (no fuel left) (Aircraft Owners and Pilots Association 2006). And, about 20% of general aviation pilots report that they have been so low on fuel that they were worried about making it to an airport (Hunter 1995). One reason for these statistics may be the lowly fuel gage—unseen, unheeded, misunderstood.

Where should it be placed? There is a limited amount of space on the panel of an aircraft, so how does one decide what to put where? Previous studies have resulted in the classic "T" arrangement of the primary flight instruments. Beyond that arrangement, which is specified in the aircraft certification requirements by most civil aviation authorities, where should all the other dials, knobs, lights, and indicators be placed?

How big should it be? Since panel availability usually dictates the maximum size of the instrument, this comes down to the question of how large the indicator pointer and text should be.

How should it be labeled? Many fuel gages in light aircraft look much like their automotive counterparts, with markings for FULL, 3/4, 1/2, 1/4, and EMPTY. At first glance, these labels seem entirely satisfactory, but consider the mental effort required by the pilot to extract usable information from such a display. Let us pose the question, "Does the pilot care that the tank is 1/2 full?" We propose that the answer is no. In fact, what the pilot cares about is how much longer they can remain airborne without the engine quitting (i.e., remaining hours and minutes of available fuel) or how much further they can fly without becoming a glider (how many miles will the available fuel take me). The answer to either of those two questions will tell pilots if they can safely continue the flight or whether they must consider a diversion. Certainly, the answers can be derived from the current markings, but to do so the pilot must perform some intervening mental effort. First, they must convert the instrument reading, let us say 1/2, into gallons. Thus, the pilot looks at the gage, sees that it reads 1/2, and, remembering the total fuel capacity from the Pilots Operating Handbook (POH), calculates that there are now 10 gallons of fuel remaining (1/2 of the 20 gallons total usable fuel). Next, the pilot must compute the flight time that 10 gallons will afford. So, they must recall the fuel consumption rate of the engine at this particular pressure altitude and power setting (or find the POH and look up the data), and then compute the hours of remaining fuel, by doing a little mental division. All of this must be done, of course, without substantial error and while simultaneously flying the aircraft, navigating, and communicating. The frequency of fuel starvation and exhaustion accidents testifies to the difficulty of these seemingly trivial tasks.

What is the alternative? From the foregoing discussion, certain aspects of an alternative design for the fuel gage should be evident. First, the fuel gage needs to be located at a place on the instrument panel in which it will be noticed by the pilot.

Preferably, this should be very close to the normal instrument scan of the primary "T" instruments. Second, an alerting mechanism should be incorporated to draw the pilot's attention to certain pre-specified conditions (e.g., reaching a specific level of remaining fuel). Third, the fonts and symbols used on the display should be of sufficient size and illumination so as to be clearly visible under all operating conditions, without interpretation error. Finally, the scaling of the gage should be changed so that more relevant information is presented that does not require extra mental effort to process.

If a human-centered design is accomplished, then even a simple instrument such as a fuel gage can be substantially improved, so as to reduce operator error and improve performance. The key is to consider the display or control from the point of view of the operator and the underlying utility or purpose that the display or control serves. That is, what is the real need that is met by the control or display? In the case of the fuel gage, the real purpose is to inform the pilot of how much longer they can maintain powered flight. It is not to tell the pilot how many gallons of fuel remain unconsumed. That information, while easy for the aircraft designer and manufacturer to implement, represents but the first step in the process that provides the pilot with the information that is really needed. It is incumbent upon the pilot to insist that designers and manufacturers not take the easy path, but that they create systems and hardware that are optimal for the operator to use, not for the manufacturer to build.

7.8 INTERACTING WITH THE SYSTEM

The importance of crafting the interaction between the system and the human operator goes beyond the fairly simple issues of display markings. It also extends to the nature, sequencing, and amount of information provided to the pilot. Short-term memory is the term applied to human memory for information presented and retained for a fairly short time span—typically, on the order of a few seconds to a very few minutes. A common illustration from aviation would be the recall and read-back of a new frequency assigned by air traffic control. Typically, the sequence of events is as follows:

- ATC sends a voice radio message: "Aircraft 123, contact Center on 137.25."
- The Pilot of the aircraft responds by saying "Contact Center on 137.25, Aircraft 123."
- The pilot of the aircraft must then remember (hold in short-term memory) the values "137.25" while he reaches down and turns the radio frequency selector knobs to the appropriate setting.

Between the time that ATC says "137.25" and the time the pilot completes the action of switching the radio, a period of approximately 5–10 seconds may elapse. During that time, the pilot must keep the value "137.25" in his short-term memory. Usually, this is done without error, although on occasion pilots will make mistakes and enter the wrong frequency. One reason this happens only rarely is that both the span of information to be recalled and the length of time are short, relative to the capacity of humans. In this example, the span is five digits. Previous research has demonstrated that the short-term memory capacity of humans is around seven digits. The best known study of this phenomenon (Miller 1956) refers to this as the "magic number 7, plus or minus 2." As the number of digits to be recalled exceeds this "magic number," the rate of errors increases rapidly. For this reason, well-designed systems avoid requiring humans to hold more than seven digits (or other bits of information, such as words) in their short-term memory. Telephone numbers, for example, seldom exceed seven digits, and, in addition, take advantage of chunking to improve recall. Chunking refers to grouping of the digits so as to make them more memorable. For example, instead of listing a number as 1234567, the number is given as 123-4567, or 1 23 45 67. Both of the latter arrangements are much less susceptible to recall errors.

Two other psychological phenomena that influence the recall of information are serial position effect and confirmation bias. First, let us consider serial position effect. When learning a list of words or other information, it has been found that humans tend to recall the first and last items best. That is, they will recall the first word in the list and the last word in the list better than those that appeared in the middle. Consider how this might be important to a pilot when receiving a weather briefing. The research has shown that he or she is much more likely to recall the first and last things present than those in the middle. Might the weather service take this into account by placing the most important information (perhaps the information most critical to the safety of the flight) at the start and end of the briefing? This would maximize the likelihood of the pilot's recalling this critical information.

But, it is not just the position of information that affects the pilot's recall. The predisposition of the pilot to receive information also comes into play. Psychological research has shown that humans tend to look for information that confirms or supports their preexisting beliefs or views of the world. This tendency is called confirmation bias, and it, along with a large number of other biases, will be discussed in detail in Chapter 10. In the context of the weather briefing example given above, consider how this confirmation bias might influence the pilot in his recall or acceptance of information. If the pilot has already decided that the weather is adequate for his flight, then any information supporting that preconception will draw his notice and be recalled; however, any information not supporting that preconception will be ignored and forgotten.

Taken together, short-term memory limitations, serial position effect, and confirmation bias can be seen to have a significant impact on how information should be presented to pilots. First, it is clear that pilots should not be expected to hold large amounts of information in their short-term memory. Information presented early in a briefing may have been forgotten or displaced by information presented later. Thus, asking pilots to draw conclusions and make judgments based on comparisons or combinations of data presented over the course of an extended weather briefing is unrealistic. At a minimum, these data must be chunked or combined in meaningful ways so as to reduce the memory burden on the pilot. Second, information particularly germane to the safety of a flight should be placed at the beginning or end (or preferably, both) of the briefing to maximize recall. Finally, both the weather briefer and pilots need to be aware of the tendency to selectively attend to information that confirms the pre-existing concepts. Because the weather briefer usually adheres to a standard format, there is less likelihood that he will selectively brief the pilot based on the briefer's biases, but there has been no research that demonstrates that effect. However, the effect of confirmation bias on the receiver of information is well established, and only adherence to a disciplined approach to flight planning will allow the pilot to overcome this tendency.

7.9   CURRENT ISSUES

Many of the issues currently facing aviation psychology and human factors are an outgrowth of the adoption of the glass cockpit design for air transport aircraft over two decades ago, and the gradual infiltration of computers and computer-based technology into the flight decks and air traffic control systems during that period. The introduction of new flight control and management systems (FMS) has not been without its own set of difficulties. While the FMS takes over many of the tasks previously performed by crew members, it introduces new tasks of its own. These tasks, which might be referred to globally as "managing the management system" involve more planning and problem-solving, in place of the old psychomotor tasks that are now performed by the FMS. The design of the human interface to these systems has not been entirely satisfactory, and issues over mode confusion still arise. The design of a system in which the human is kept constantly aware of the present state and future state of the system has not yet been entirely achieved. This problem is likely to grow even more acute as FMS-like systems are installed in growing numbers of general aviation aircraft where they may be operated by pilots with very limited experience and training. A completely intuitive design for these systems will become a necessity, since the training required to operate the current systems will not be feasible.

7.9.1   Global Positioning System

The lack of an intuitive design is evident in the current generation of Global Positioning System (GPS) navigation systems for light aircraft. While GPS allows for highly accurate three-dimensional navigation at almost any point on the surface of the Earth, its implementation has been subject to a great deal of criticism. Almost without exception, the displays used for GPS in light aircraft are small and the controls crowded together. Further, the functions of the controls are mode dependent and the execution of tasks that in the traditional VOR navigation system required only a few tasks now require extensive scrolling through menus and multiple function selections.

Human factors issues associated with GPS displays and controls have been the subject of extensive research in recent years. Leading these efforts have been the research arms of the aviation regulatory agencies, particularly in the United States, Canada, and New Zealand. Researchers at the Civil Aerospace Medical Institute of the FAA have conducted several studies to identify problems in the usability of GPS receivers. These studies have ranged from evaluations of individual receivers to more wide-ranging global assessments and have identified many shortcomings of the GPS receiver interface.

Wreggit and Marsh (1998) examined one specific unit that was believed to be typical of a class of devices available at the time. They had nine general aviation pilots perform 37 GPS-related tasks requiring waypoint setting, GPS navigation, and GPS data entry and retrieval. Their results indicated that a number of the menu structures used by the device interfered with the pilots' successful entry of data, editing of stored data, and activation of functions. On the basis of their findings, Wreggit and Marsh provided recommendations for the redesign of the interface structure. Some of the specific recommendations included consistent assignment of a given function to one button; provision of consistent and meaning feedback; and provision for an "undo" or "back" function that would reduce the number of button presses.

Williams (1999a,b) conducted an extensive review of user interface problems with GPS receivers, using data collected from interviews with subject matter experts in the FAA, and from an inspection of the observation logs from an operational test of a GPS Wide Area Augmentation System. Although Williams notes several interface issues associated with the displays and controls, Williams (1999a, p. 1) notes, "Probably the most significant feature of GPS units, as far as the potential for user errors is concerned, is the sheer complexity involved in their operation." He points out that one measure of this complexity is the size of the instruction manual that accompanies each unit. Whereas the operation of the radio and display for a traditional VOR navigation system could be explained in, at most, 10 pages, manuals for GPS receivers typically contain 100–300 pages. Although there does not seem to be any published research on the subject, one can wonder just how many pilots have actually read all the instructions that accompany their GPS receiver. One might also speculate on how much of that material is actually retained.

In addition to the overriding issue of complexity, Williams (1999a,b) identifies a large number of specific human factors issues that detract from GPS receiver usability—many of which are hauntingly reminiscent of the problems identified by Fitts and Jones a half-century earlier. Some examples of the issues identified by Williams are as follows:

Button Placement: Inadvertent activation of GPS buttons, just like inadvertent activation of landing gear and flaps, is made more likely by the poorly considered placement of the buttons. In the example provided by Williams, a manufacturer has elected to place the *clear* button between the *direct-to* and the *enter* buttons. This is an unfortunate arrangement, since activation of the *direct-to* button is normally followed by the *enter* button. Placement of the *clear* button between these two buttons makes it much more likely that the pilot will activate the *clear* button, when the intention was to activate the *enter* button. Recovery from such an error may entail considerable reprograming of the GPS, perhaps at a time when the pilot is experiencing high workload from other activities, such as executing a missed approach.

Knob Issues: Many GPS receivers use a rotary knob to select and enter information. Often these knobs are used to select the alphanumeric characters of airports, VORs, and other navigation waypoints. Some of the knobs do not allow the user to back-track, so that if they overshoot the character they wanted, they must continue turning until they go through the entire list again. This can significantly increase the head-down time required to program the receiver—a problem that is particularly acute while in-flight. Furthermore, these knobs may function in more than one physical position, either pulled-out, or pushed-in, with the two positions providing entirely different functionality. Since there is no signal, other than a faint tactile sensation, to indicate which mode the knob is in, pilots can only determine what the knob is going to do by turning it, and observing what happens. Clearly, this is an arrangement that is ripe with potential for serious errors, particularly when the pilot's attention is directed elsewhere.

Button Labels: Williams (1999a, p. 4) notes "buttons that perform the same type of task on different units can have different labels." The lack of uniformity, coupled with the complexity mentioned earlier, makes it difficult for a pilot familiar with one GPS system to use another system.

Automatic versus Manual Waypoint Sequencing: Readers of pilot reports captured by the ASRS* soon come to recognize the familiar question posed by pilots of aircraft with modern FMSs. That question typically is, "What is it doing?" Alternatively, the question may be stated as, "Why is it doing that?" The "it" in both questions is the FMS and/or autopilot, and the questions are raised because the pilot is suffering from what is commonly termed mode confusion. The aircraft is behaving in a way that is not consistent with the pilot's mental model of what it should be doing. This discrepancy arises because the complexity of the FMS allows for it to operate in multiple modes. If the pilot thinks that the FMS is in one mode, but it is actually in another, then truly unexpected things can happen, occasionally resulting in accidents. One such example is the Air France Airbus A-320 that crashed in Mulhouse-Habsheim Airport, France, following a low altitude fly-by (Degani et al. 1996).

Regrettably, pilots of general aviation aircraft who are often envious of the equipment and capabilities of transport category aircraft now have the dubious honor of sharing the problem of mode confusion with their airline transport brethren. Williams (1999a, p. 4) reports that "One of the most often cited problems ... involved either placing the receiver in a mode where it automatically sequences from one waypoint to the next during the approach or in a non-sequencing mode." Winter and Jackson (1996) reported that pilots frequently forgot to take the GPS receiver out of the "hold" function after completing the procedure turn. Because of that error, they were unable to proceed to the next approach fix.

Many of these deficiencies were also noted by Adams et al. (2001) in their review of adverse events attributed to GPS usage. In addition to the usability issues, such as button placement and display size, identified by Williams (1999a,b), Adams et al. also highlighted problems that arose from pilot over reliance on GPS, programing errors, and lack of knowledge on the use of the GPS receivers. As a further illustration of the relative complexity of the GPS receivers, Adams et al. noted that while there were five steps to perform an approach using the traditional VOR system, there were 13 steps in an equivalent GPS approach.

Earlier we noted that the traditional approach to the development of highly usable systems was based on the sequence: *design, guard, warn, train*. Although GPS navigation arguably represents a remarkable step forward in the technology of air (and surface) transportation, GPS receivers (at least those marketed for general

---

* http://asrs.arc.nasa.gov/main_nf.htm

aviation aircraft) represent an equally remarkable failure to adhere to this philosophy. A failure to design usable receivers that prevent or mitigate errors leads to the necessity to warn users about their shortcomings and to attempt to remediate the problems by training users so that they do not fall victim to the interface idiosyncrasies. It is sad to note that 60 years after Fitts and Jones showed us how errors could be prevented by a focus on the user and simple design changes that many designers (and regulators) still have not taken their lessons to heart. It is a situation that is cogently described by Dekker (2001), in a report which he aptly titled, "Disinheriting Fitts & Jones '47."

This situation may also have contributed to the determination by the NTSB (2010) that, with regard to light aircraft, the introduction of glass cockpit PFDs has not yet resulted in the anticipated improvement in safety when compared to similar aircraft with conventional instruments. This echoes the findings of Sarter (2008) who reviewed the history and impact of research on mode errors in transport aircraft. She noted the hope that the introduction of the first highly automated glass cockpits in the late 1980s would reduce workload, errors, and training demands. However, "Workload was not reduced overall but rather redistributed over time and crew members ... and the potential for new kinds of errors was created" (p. 506).

7.9.2 ELECTRONIC FLIGHT BAGS

Clearly, there is a growing trend toward the digitalization of information. The once ubiquitous telephone directory is replaced by an app on your cell phone, or a Web site. Libraries are struggling to find ways to adapt to patrons' preferences for electronic over printed media. Newspapers are adapting or dying. In the flight deck, the reams of approach charts, company manuals, and checklists are giving way to digital representations either contained in the aircraft systems or brought aboard in the form of an electronic flight bag (EFB). There are obvious advantages to the EFB. Reduced weight and volume clearly favor the EFB, as does the ease of updates, which can be done almost instantly, vice the old procedure of swapping old pages for new or checking the dates of charts to ensure they were current. But, as with Sarter's (2008) comments on glass cockpits, new gadgets do not always live up to expectations and can produce new problems, even as they attenuate old ones.

Some studies (e.g., Shamo et al. 1998) have found that performance calculations and document retrieval were faster and more accurate with the EFB. However, Hamblin (2004) questioned those results, on the grounds that the device used a 10.8-inch diagonal display screen, which is much larger than most off-the-shelf EFBs, which use 6.8- to 8.2-inch diagonal screens. Using a commercially available EFB and software, Hamblin found a significant increase in information retrieval time when using the EFB, but only when the user had to manipulate the information depicted on the screen. He attributed this effect to the user interface, which was originally designed for use on a desktop computer with a mouse and keyboard and not optimized for a mobile device using multifunction buttons. He also found a significant effect on response times for pilots using EFB approach charts compared to conventional paper charts, as a function of workload. For easy approaches, there was no difference between the two conditions. However, as approaches became

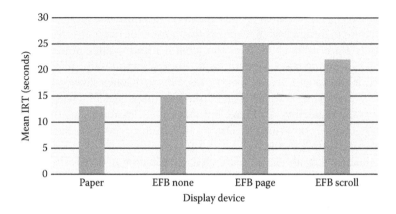

FIGURE 7.6 Mean information retrieval time for paper and electronic flight bag device. (Adapted with permission from Hamblin, C.J. 2004. Usability of mobile devices in the cockpit. *Usability News* [online]. Retrieved from: http://usabilitynews.org/ usability-of-mobile-devices-in-the-cockpit/.)

more challenging, pilots took longer to locate information using the EFB compared to the paper charts. These results are illustrated in Figures 7.6 and 7.7.

Regulatory agencies (see, e.g., Chandra et al. 2003; Federal Aviation Administration 2014) have provided guidance on the design and operational use of EFBs; however, it is clear that much additional work remains for these devices to achieve their promised impact of error and workload reduction. If you see a common theme emerging, then you are correct. New technologies bring new problems, and do not necessarily make things better—only different.

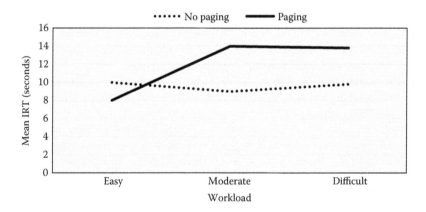

FIGURE 7.7 Mean information retrieval time for paper and electronic flight bag by workload. (Adapted with permission from Hamblin, C.J. 2004. Usability of mobile devices in the cockpit. *Usability News* [online]. Retrieved from: http://usabilitynews.org/ usability-of-mobile-devices-in-the-cockpit/.)

7.9.3 UNMANNED AERIAL VEHICLES

Unmanned aerial vehicles (UAVs), also known as remotely piloted vehicles (RPVs), and unmanned aerial systems (UASs) seem to be in the news daily, as some small UAV wanders into the vicinity of an airliner, crashes into the White House, or is basted from the sky over someone's garden by an irate homeowner with a shotgun and questionable judgment. Amusing or terrifying as these events may be, the small UAVs involved in these encounters have not drawn the interest of human factors researchers in the same way as their larger cousins—mainly operated by the military. In his speech at the Air War College at Maxwell AFB, Alabama, U.S. Secretary of Defense Robert M. Gates (2008) stated that, "Today, we now have more than 5,000 UAVs, a 25-fold increase since 2001." Given the increasing reliance of UAVs in intelligence-gathering and weapons delivery in the Middle-East and elsewhere, the number of UAVs in service as this is being written in 2016 is no doubt much larger.

The growth in UAVs over a 40-year period from their inception in the 1960s mimics the growth in numbers and sophistication of conventional aircraft from the first flights of the Wright brothers in 1903 to their large-scale production and utilization in World War II over a similar time period. Furthermore, just as conventional aircraft suffered from many human factors flaws (as noted earlier in the studies by Fitts and Jones), so to have UAVs experienced both conventional human factors issues of displays and control, and issues such as mission-handover procedures and external pilot control that are unique to UAVs.

It has been a bumpy ride since the early 1960s, when target drones (Ryan Firebees) were modified for reconnaissance missions. Derivatives of this UAV were subsequently used in reconnaissance missions over South-East Asia by the U.S. Air Force, and subsequent generations of UAVs have been adopted by military services throughout the world.[*] As with manned aircraft, UAVs have presented a variety of human factors issues, many of which have led to mishaps. There have been numerous studies of the human factors associated with UAV mishaps. A study of UAV reliability conducted by the U.S. Office of the Secretary of Defense (OSD 2003) found that human and ground control issues accounted for 17% of all UAV systems failures, compared to the generally accepted value of 85% for manned aircraft. The authors of that study suggested that the most likely explanation for the difference in human errors was that the element was simply overshadowed by the high unreliability of the other subsystems in the UAVs. They noted that this theory was supported by experiences with operational and developmental UAV systems, which indicated that "… the human-machine synergy is much more challenging when the human is on the ground" (p. 55). They attributed the increased challenge to the difficulty of maintaining situational awareness (e.g., of weather, targets, and obstacles) while looking at the remote world "through a soda straw." They also noted the difficulty in launch and recovery of UAVs and the associated value of automated takeoff and recovery.

---

[*] For a history of UAVs, see the Wikipedia article at https://en.wikipedia.org/wiki/Unmanned_aerial_vehicle or, for a more authoritative, but narrower account, see "Air Force UAVs: The Secret History" by Thomas Ehrhard, available from the Defense Technical Information Center. Look for document number: ADA525674.

Moreover, Thompson et al. (2005) questioned the low proportion of accidents attributed to human factors and noted that other studies (e.g., Manning et al. 2004) have reported prevalences of human factors mishaps two to three times that reported by the OSD report. They then undertook a quantitative analysis of 221 UAV mishaps using the Human Factors Analysis and Classification System (HFACS). They found that 60% of the mishaps involved human causal factors. Human factors were solely involved in 24% of the mishaps, and a combination of human factors and mechanical factors was involved in 36%.

As shown in Figure 7.8, decision-making errors accounted for the almost half of the root-cause errors for all the services. Skill-based errors were substantial factors for both the Air Force and Navy/Marines, while violations accounted for a significant number of the errors for the Army. However, as Thompson et al. note, comparisons among the services is problematic, because of differing policies regarding the investigation of UAV mishaps (prior to 2003 the U.S. Army treated them as ground mishaps), and differences in the manner in which the UAVs are operated. The Air Force operators fly from a vehicle-centric prospective (i.e., using a nose camera image), while the Army and Navy/Marine pilots fly from an exocentric perspective (i.e., they observe the UAV from a position beside the runway).

Manning et al. (2004) analyzed U.S. Army UAV accidents for the period 1995–2003 and found human error present in approximately one-third of accidents. No single human causal factor was found to be responsible for all accidents; however, analyses using both HFACS and the standard Army procedures (U.S. Army, DA PAM 385-40) identified individual unsafe acts or failures as the most common human-related causal factor category. This was present in approximately 61% of the 18 human error-related accidents, and in 20% of all 56 accidents. Decision errors were listed as the single largest (11%) of the unsafe acts.

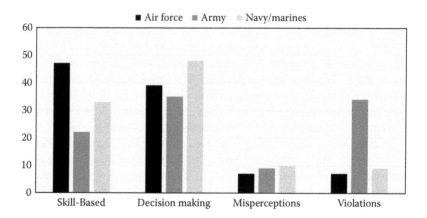

FIGURE 7.8 Military UAV error types for each service. (Adapted from Thompson, W., Tvaryanas, A., and Constable, S. 2005. *U.S. Military Unmanned Aerial Vehicle Mishaps: Assessment of the Role of Human Factors Using Human Factors Analysis and Classification System (HFACS)*. Technical Report HSW-PE-BR-TR-2005-0001. Brooks City-Base, TX: Human Systems Wing (311th), U.S. Air Force. Figure 3, p. 13.)

In an analysis of military UAV accidents conducted by the FAA, human factors issues varied across UAV type from 21% to 68% (Williams 2004). Williams reported that many of the accidents could have been anticipated through an analysis of the user interfaces employed and the implementation of procedures for their use. By far, the largest human factors issue was the difficulty experienced by external pilots. These pilots operate the UAV, at least during the landing phase, by directly observing the UAV in the same way as operators of radio-controlled model aircraft. For the RQ-5 Hunter UAV, landings accounted for 47% of the human factors–related mishaps. In contrast, the Predator (MQ-1 and MW-9) operated by the U.S. Air Force has in internal point-of-view control configuration. For this, UAV landing errors account for only 13% of the human factors issues for Predator landings. However, even for the Predator human factors causal factors still accounted for 67% of all accidents—mainly caused by procedural errors on the part of the flight crew. However, they had some help from the designers. In one accident, the crew erased the internal RAM aboard the aircraft during a flight—something that a good design should have made impossible. (Remember the Design-Guard-Warn-Train rule!)

In one final example, Merlin (2013) provides a series of case studies of mishaps involving UAVs, dating back to the 1960s. Although the primary focus is on the engineering aspects of the mishaps, human factors are identified in some instances. In particular, he provides an analysis of human factors in the crash in southern Arizona on April 25, 2006 of a Predator-B operated by the U.S. Customs and Border Protection Agency. This crash, which occurred outside a military reservation, was investigated by the NTSB who found that mode-confusion error by the two-person crew, coupled with failures to adhere to checklists and confusing control configurations all contributed to the crash.

The similarity of the human factors issues identified in these studies of UAV crashes to those discussed earlier for manned aircraft should be evident. Confusing displays, systems that allow operators to make catastrophic actions, and failures on the part of crews to adhere to checklists and established procedures all contribute to accidents among military UAVs, just as they do in manned aircraft. In addition, UAV operators experience some conditions not found in manned aircraft. These include the following:

- Extended missions, lasting 14 or more hours, producing fatigue, boredom, and decreased vigilance.
- Psychosocial impact on crews who may operate UAVs thousands of miles distant from the battle area. The impact of spending the day flying surveillance and combat missions, and then walking out of the control building to go home to a family is as yet an unexplored area.
- Multiple crew-changes during a single mission. One crew may handle the launch, another crew the mission activities, and yet another the landing operation.
- Multi-ship control. In theory, a UAV pilot might control multiple UAVs. This presents some interesting issues with regard to task prioritization and sharing.

- Response latencies. If a UAV is being remotely controlled via terrestrial or satellite-based radio link, as opposed to a pilot in the cockpit, latencies may exist between pilot input and aircraft response. Zingale and Taylor (2015) examined the effects of control latency and found that latencies greater than about 500 m had significant effects on pilot performance. (Manned aircraft latencies are typically around 150 m.)

It should now be clear that not having a pilot in the UAV does not mean that there are no human factors issues. Until those Terminator robots from the future arrive, there will always be humans involved somewhere in a system, and wherever there are humans, there are human factors. Further, although all the studies to date have involved military UAVs, civil UAVs cannot be far off. Consider recent advances in driver-less cars and experiments by Amazon™ among others to use small UAVs to deliver packages. Clearly, the technology required for autonomous UAV operations at a commercial level is approaching maturity, with the major impediments at this point being regulatory and procedural.

The potential benefits of autonomous air vehicles moving goods from major air cargo facilities are surely not lost on FedEx, UPS, or other air cargo carriers. But, before that happens, UAV system reliability, including human factors issues, must be substantially improved. Having a 2 kg UAV crash into the side of your house is an annoyance. Having a 20,000 kg air freighter crash into your house is something entirely different.

Finally, if you doubt that commercial UAVs are in your future, ask yourself when you last rode in an elevator that had an operator.

7.10   SUMMARY

The central message that the reader should take away from this chapter is that systems—mechanical systems, social systems, training systems, display systems— must be designed so that they conform to the characteristics of their users and the tasks that they must perform. The design of systems is an engineering process that is marked by a series of trade-off decisions. The designer may trade weight for speed, increased power for increased reliability, and the size and legibility of displays for the presentation of additional information. The list is almost endless. In each of these design decisions, the engineer is striving to meet some design criteria, without being able to simultaneously meet all criteria equally well. In our everyday world, we often wish to satisfy competing criteria. For example, we might wish to have a very large house, and simultaneously wish to have a very small monthly house payment. Unless a rich uncle dies and leaves us a pot of money, we are forced to compromise with a house that is big enough and a mortgage payment that is not too big.

Usually, the engineers produce a workable design that does not sacrifice the elements critical to successful operation of the system for the sake of competing criteria. Sometimes, however, they produce controls with the same knobs (it saves production costs to have all the knobs identical) leading to confusion during moments of high workload. They may also produce instrument panels in which essential, if rarely used, information is hidden either physically, on a dial that cannot be seen without a great deal of effort, or logically, as part of a multifunction display system in which the needed information lurks beneath two or three levels of menus. However, the reasons that systems are poorly designed from the standpoint of the human user do not serve as excuses for those designs.

The reader should now be aware of some of the features and considerations that go into the production of usable aviation systems, both manned and unmanned. We hope that you will use that knowledge at the least to be an informed consumer of those systems, and even more to become an active advocate for improved aviation systems.

7.11 CONTROLLERS AND MAINTAINERS ARE IMPORTANT TOO!

Although we have not mentioned air traffic control or maintenance human factors issues in the preceding discussions, have no doubt that they are equally relevant for aviation maintenance technicians (AMTs) and air traffic controllers (ATCs). Extensive human factors programs directed at ATC issues are carried out by the FAA, usually at the William J. Hughes Technical Center in New Jersey, and by Eurocontrol at their Experimental Centre at Brétigny-sur-Orge, near Paris, France. You may obtain further information on Eurocontrol[*] from their Web site.

For many years beginning in the 1980s, the FAA conducted an extensive research program to identify human factors issues associated with AMTs. This resulted in the production of a number of guides that are available from the FAA.[†] In addition, excellent sources for AMT human factors information are

- FAA (2014) Operator's Manual: Human Factors in Aviation Maintenance
- FAA AMT Handbook (8083-30)
- AMT Handbook Addendum: Human Factors (an addendum to 8083-30)

7.12 OUTSIDE ACTIVITIES

You are surrounded by devices and systems with designs that range from delightful to infuriating. Take a look around and see if the displays on your television, computer, cellphone, and myriad other appliances embody the principles enumerated earlier. There are Web sites that provide examples of really bad designs, but not so many that illustrate really good designs. Perhaps, that is because a really good interface design is one that you do not notice; it simply does its job and is intuitive to the point of invisibility. We suggest that the display shown in Figure 7.9 might be one such design.

This display seems to provide all the information that someone watching a baseball game needs, in a very succinct format, needing only a brief explanation. In this case, the pitcher (Lester) has thrown 68 pitches in the game, and he is currently pitching against Connoly (the batter). There are zero balls and one strike. The two teams are Saint Louis (STL) and Chicago Cubs (CHC), and the score is 4 to 2 (STL

---

[*] Eurocontrol: http://www.eurocontrol.int/articles/human-performance-atm
[†] FAA: https://www.faa.gov/about/initiatives/maintenance_hf/

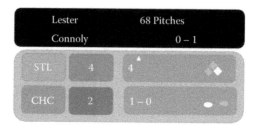

FIGURE 7.9   Baseball game status display.

is winning). The game is in the top of the fourth inning, with one runner at first base, and there is one out. This little display, or something very much like it, is tucked into the corner of the screen so that the view of the action on the field is unobstructed, and it tells the viewer everything they need to know about the status of the game. Pretty impressive, for such a small box of information.

On the other hand, an elevator button that provides no feedback when pressed, so you do not know whether it worked when you pushed it or if it is simply broken, is a pretty poor idea. This is a bad design that we recently encountered. Look around and see what you can find.

Here is a hint—start with your TV/cable/satellite remote control. Have you ever used all those little buttons, and do you have any idea what they do? For an interesting exercise, keep a count of how often you use each of the buttons. You might be surprised just how few functions you actually use, compared to all the functions that are available. Look at the errors you make. Are some controls frequently activated in error? Why? How many steps does it take to complete tasks? Are some buttons multifunction, so that in one mode (e.g., TV) they do one thing, but in another mode (perhaps satellite) they do something else entirely? How do you know what mode is active?

Finally (especially for those who drive rental cars often), when you move from one car to another, do you have trouble locating the controls? After driving a car with a console-mounted gear selector, do you find yourself reaching down toward a non-existent control when driving a car with the gear selector mounted on the steering column? How often have you turned on the windshield wipers when trying to turn on the lights? (Remember the discussion of negative transfer from Chapter 6?) Without consulting the owners' manual, can you reset the clock in the car? If you were designing cars, what would you do differently? Which way do the little rotary switches on the steering wheel stalks operate in cars? Do all cars have the same orientation? Look around and think about how all the controls and displays in your world work and how they might be better designed.

RECOMMENDED READINGS

Barnhart, R.K., Hottman, S.B., Marshall, D.M., and Shapee, E. (Eds.). 2010. *Introduction to Unmanned Aircraft Systems.* Boca Raton, FL: CRC Press.
Diaper, D. and Stanton, N. 2004. *The Handbook of Task Analysis for Human-Computer Interaction.* Mahwah, NJ: Lawrence Erlbaum.

Endsley, M.R. 2003. *Designing for Situation Awareness: An Approach to User-Centered Design*. New York, NY: Taylor and Francis.

Federal Aviation Administration. 2008. *Aviation Maintenance Technician Handbook—General*. FAA-H-8083-30. Washington, DC: Author.

Federal Aviation Administration. 2014. *Operator's Manual: Human Factors in Aviation Maintenance*. Washington, DC: Author.

Federal Aviation Administration. n.d. AMT handbook addendum: Human factors (Chapter 14) published separately from *Aviation Maintenance Technician Handbook—General*. FAA-H-8083-30. Washington, DC: Author.

Green, R.G., Muir, H., James, M., Gradwell, D., and Green, R.L. 1996. *Human Factors for Pilots*, 2nd ed. Burlington, VT: Ashgate.

Lidwell, W., Holden, K., and Butler, J. 2003. *Universal Principles of Design: 100 Ways to Enhance Usability, Influence Perception, Increase Appeal, Make Better Design Decisions, and Teach Through Design*. Gloucester, MA: Rockport Publishers.

Norman, D.A. 2013. *The Design of Everyday Things*. New York, NY: Basic Books.

Noyes, J. 1999. *User-Centered Design of Systems*. New York, NY: Springer-Verlag.

Proctor, R.W. and Van Zandt, T. 2008. *Human Factors in Simple and Complex Systems*. Boca Raton, FL: Taylor and Francis.

Salas, E. and Maurino, D. 2010. *Human Factors in Aviation*, 2nd ed. Burlington, MA: Academic Press.

Salvendy, G. 1997. *Handbook of Human Factors and Ergonomics*, 2nd ed. New York, NY: Wiley.

Stanton, N. 2005. *Handbook of Human Factors and Ergonomics Methods*. Boca Raton, FL: CRC Press.

Stanton, N.A., Salmon, P.M., Walker, G.H., Barber, C., and Jenkins, D.P. (Eds.). 2005. *Human Factors Methods: A Practical Guide for Engineering and Design*. Aldershot, UK: Ashgate.

Vicente, K. 2004. *The Human Factor*. New York, NY: Routledge.

Woodson, W.E. 1992. *Human Factors Design Handbook*. New York, NY: McGraw-Hill.

REFERENCES

Adams, C.A., Hwoschinsky, P.V., and Adams, R.J. 2001. Analysis of adverse events in identifying GPS human factors issues. In *Proceedings of the 11th International Symposium on Aviation Psychology*. Columbus, OH: The Ohio State University.

Aircraft Owners and Pilots Association. 2006. *Accident Trends and Factors for 2005*. 2006 Nall Report. Frederick, MD: Author.

Annett, J. and Stanton, N. 2000. *Task Analysis*. New York, NY: Taylor and Francis.

Boff, K.R., Kaufman, L., and Thomas, J.P. (Eds.). 1988. *Handbook of perception and human performance*. New York, NY: John Wiley and Sons.

Booher, H.R. 1990. *Manprint*. New York, NY: Springer.

Booher, H.R. 2003. *Handbook of Human Systems Integration*. New York, NY: Wiley.

Chandra, D.C., Yeh, M., and Riley, V. 2003. *Human Factors Considerations in the Design and Evaluation of Electronic Flight Bags (EFBs) Version 2*. Report No. DOT-VNTSC-FAA-03-07. Cambridge, MA: USDOT Volpe Center.

Chandra, D.C., Yeh, M., Riley, V., and Mangold, S.J. 2003. Human Factors Considerations in the Design and Evaluation of Electronic Flight Bags (EFBs), Version 2. DOT-VNTSC-FAA-03-07. Volpe Center, Cambridge, MA: Federal Aviation Administration.

Ciavarelli, A., Figlock, R., Sengupta, K., and Roberts, K. 2001. Assessing organizational safety risk using questionnaire survey methods. In *Proceedings of the 11th International Symposium on Aviation Psychology*. Columbus, OH: The Ohio State University.

Civil Aeronautics Board. 1967. *Aircraft Design-Induced Pilot Error.* Washington, DC: Author.

Cohen, D., Otankeno, S., Previc, F.H., and Ercoline, W.R. 2001. Effect of "inside-out" and "outside-in" attitude displays on off-axis tracking in pilots and nonpilots. *Aviation, Space, and Environmental Medicine* 72: 170–176.

Degani, A. 1992. *On the Typography of Flight-Deck Documentation.* NASA Contractor Report 177605. Moffett Field, CA: NASA-Ames Research Center.

Degani, A., Shafto, M., and Kirlk, A. 1996. Modes in automated cockpits: Problems, data analysis, and a modeling framework. *Proceedings of the 36th Israel Annual Conference on Aerospace Sciences*, Haifa, Israel.

Degani, A. and Wiener, E.L. 1990. *Human Factors of Flight Deck Checklists: The Normal Checklist.* NASA Contractor Report 177549. Moffett Field, CA: NASA-Ames Research Center.

Dekker, S.W.A. 2001. Disinheriting Fitts and Jones '47. *International Journal of Aviation Research and Development* 1: 7–18.

Dekker, S.W.A. 2002. *The Re-invention of Human Error.* Technical Report 2002-01. Ljungbyhed, Sweden: Lund University School of Aviation.

Dekker, S.W.A. 2003. *Punishing People or Learning From Failure? The Choice is Ours.* Ljungbyhed, Sweden: Lund University School of Aviation.

Ehrhard, T.P. 2010. *Air Force UAVs: The Secret History.* Arlington, VA: The Mitchell Institute for Airpower Studies.

Federal Aviation Administration. 1995. *Human Performance Considerations in the Use and Design of Aircraft Checklists.* Washington, DC: Author.

Federal Aviation Administration. 2014. *Guidelines for the Certification, Airworthiness, and Operational Approval of Electronic Flight Bag Computing Devices.* A Electronic Flight Bag (EFB) Job Aid. DOT-FAA-AC120-76C. Washington, DC: Author.

Fitts, P.M. and Jones, R.E. 1947a. *Analysis of Factors Contributing to 460 "Pilot Error" Experiences in Operating Aircraft Controls.* Memorandum Report TSEAA-694-12. Wright-Patterson Air Force Base, OH: Aero Medical Laboratory, Air Materiel Command.

Fitts, P.M. and Jones, R.E. 1947b. *Psychological Aspects of Instrument Display. I: Analysis of 270 "Pilot-Error" Experiences in Reading and Interpreting Aircraft Instruments.* Memorandum Report TSEAA-694-12A. Wright-Patterson Air Force Base, OH: Aero Medical Laboratory, Air Materiel Command.

Fitts, P.M. and Jones, R.E. 1961a. Analysis of factors contributing to 460 "pilot error" experiences in operating aircraft controls. In Sinaiko, E.W. (Ed.), *Selected Papers on Human Factors in the Design and Use of Control Systems* (pp. 332–358). New York, NY: Dover Publications.

Fitts, P.M. and Jones, R.E. 1961b. Psychological aspects of instrument display. I: Analysis of 270 "pilot-error" experiences in reading and interpreting aircraft instruments. In Sinaiko, E.W. (Ed.), *Selected Papers on Human Factors in the Design and Use of Control Systems* (pp. 359–396). New York, NY: Dover Publications.

Gates, R.M. 2008. War College in Maxwell, Alabama on April 21, 2008. Retrieved from: http://www.cfr.org/world/secretary-defense-gates-speech-air-war-college/p16085

Hamblin, C.J. 2004. Usability of mobile devices in the cockpit. *Usability News* [online]. Retrieved from: http://usabilitynews.org/usability-of-mobile-devices-in-the-cockpit/

Harris, D.H. 1984. Human factors success stories. In *Proceedings of the 28th Annual Meeting of the Human Factors Society* (pp. 529–533). Santa Monica, CA: The Human Factors Society.

Helmreich, R.L., Merritt, A.C., and Wilhelm, J.A. 1999. The evolution of crew resource management training in commercial aviation. *International Journal of Aviation Psychology* 9: 19–32.

Hunter, D.R. 1995. *Airman Research Questionnaire: Methodology and Overall Results.* DOT/FAA/AAM-95/27. Washington, DC: Federal Aviation Administration.

Kirwan, B. and Ainsworth, L.K. 1992. *A guide to task analysis*. London, UK: Taylor and Francis.

Manning, S.D., Rash, C.E., LeDuc, P.A., Noback, R.K., and McKeon, J. 2004. *The Role of Causal Factors in U.S. Army Unmanned Aerial Vehicle Accidents*. USAARL Report No. 2004-11. Fort Rucker, AL: U.S. Army Aeromedical Research Laboratory.

Meister, D. 1985. *Behavioral Analysis and Measurement Methods*. New York, NY: John Wiley.

Merlin, P.W. 2013. *Crash Course: Lessons Learned from Accidents Involving Remotely Piloted and Autonomous Aircraft*. Edwards, CA: NASA Dryden Flight Research Center, National Aeronautics and Space Administration.

Miller, G.A. 1956. The magical number seven, plus or minus two: Some limits on our capacity for processing information. *The Psychological Review* 63: 81–97.

National Transportation Safety Board. 2010. *Introduction of Glass Cockpit Avionics into Light Aircraft*. Safety Study NTSB/SS-01/19. Washington, DC: Author.

Office of the Secretary of Defense. 2003. *Unmanned Aerial Vehicle Reliability Study*. Washington, DC: Author.

Previc, F.H. and Ercoline, W.R. 1999. The "outside-in" attitude display concept revisited. *International Journal of Aviation Psychology* 9: 377–401.

Reason, J. 1992. *Human Error*. Cambridge, UK: Cambridge University Press.

Ross, P. 2004. Human factors issues of the aircraft checklist. *Journal of Aviation/Aerospace Education and Research* 13: 9–14.

Sanders, M.S. and McCormick, E.J. 1993. *Human Factors in Engineering and Design*, 7th ed. New York, NY: McGraw-Hill.

Sarter, N. 2008. Investigating mode errors on automated flight decks: Illustrating the problem-driven, cumulative, and interdisciplinary nature of human factors research. *Human Factors* 50: 506–510.

Seamster, T.L., Redding, R.E., and Kaempf, G.L. 1997. *Applied Cognitive Task Analysis in Aviation*. Aldershot, UK: Ashgate.

Shamo, M.K., Dror, R., and Degani, A. 1998. Evaluation of a new cockpit device: The integrated electronic information system. In *Proceedings of the Human Factors and Ergonomics Society Meeting 42nd Annual Meeting* (pp. 138–142). Chicago, IL: Human Factors and Ergonomics Society.

Shepherd, A. 2001. *Hierarchical Task Analysis*. New York, NY: Taylor and Francis.

Sinaiko, H.W. and Buckley, E.P. 1957. *Human Factors in the Design of Systems*. NRL Report 4996. Washington, DC: Naval Research Laboratory.

Sinaiko, H.W. and Buckley, E.P. 1961. Human factors in the design of systems. In Sinaiko, E.W. (Ed.), *Selected Papers on Human Factors in the Design and Use of Control Systems* (pp. 1–41). New York, NY: Dover Publications.

Sumwalt, R.L. 1991. Checking the Checklist. *Professional Pilot* March: 62–64.

Thompson, W., Tvaryanas, A., and Constable, S. 2005. *U.S. Military Unmanned Aerial Vehicle Mishaps: Assessment of the Role of Human Factors Using Human Factors Analysis and Classification System (HFACS)*. Technical Report HSW-PE-BR-TR-2005-0001. Brooks City-Base, TX: Human Systems Wing (311th), U.S. Air Force.

Wickens, C.D. 2003. Aviation displays. In Tsang, P.S. and Vidulich, M.A. (Eds.), *Principles and Practice of Aviation Psychology* (pp. 147–200). Mahway, NJ: Erlbaum.

Wickens, C.D. and Hollands, J.G. 2000. *Engineering Psychology and Human Performance*, 3rd ed. Upper Saddle River, NJ: Prentice-Hall.

Williams, K.W. 1999a. *GPS User-Interface Design Problems*. DOT/FAA/AM-99/13. Washington, DC: Federal Aviation Administration.

Williams, K.W. 1999b. *GPS User-Interface Design Problems: II*. DOT/FAA/AM-99/26. Washington, DC: Federal Aviation Administration.

Williams, K.W. 2004. *A Summary of Unmanned Aircraft Accident/incident Data: Human Factors Implications*. DOT/FAA/AM-04/24. Washington, DC: Federal Aviation Administration.

Winter, S. and Jackson, S. 1996. *GPS Issues.* DOT/FAA/AFS-450. Oklahoma City, OK: Federal Aviation Administration, Standards Development Branch.

Wise, J.A., Abbott, D.W., Beringer, D.B., Koonce, J.M., Kite, K., and Stokes, A.F. 1998. Human factors in light general aviation aircraft: A failure for our profession? In *Proceedings of the Human Factors and Ergonomics Society Annual Meeting* (pp. 107–111). Chicago, IL: Human Factors and Ergonomics Society.

Wreggit, S.S. and Marsh, D.K. 1998. *Cockpit Integration of GPS: Initial Assessment—Menu Formats and Procedures.* DOT/FAA/AM-98/9. Washington, DC: Federal aviation Administration.

Yeh, M. and Chandra, D. 2004. Issues in symbol design for electronic displays of navigation information. *Proceedings of the 23rd DASC Conference* October 24–28, 2003, Salt Lake City, UT.

Zingale, C.M. and Taylor, E.G. 2015. Effect of control latency on unmanned aircraft systems during critical phases of flight. In *Proceedings of the 18th International Symposium on Aviation Psychology* (pp. 183–188), Dayton, OH.

8 Stress and Human Reactions

An important part of psychology is the study of variations in how we think, feel, and react. Although it is important to be aware of such variations, there are a number of commonly shared patterns in terms of reactions, for example, to dramatic and stressful events. Hence, this chapter discusses both individual differences in personality and mental health and reactions to everyday stress and more significant incidents. Finally, this chapter investigates common psychological reactions in passengers.

8.1 PERSONALITY AND INDIVIDUAL DIFFERENCES

Personality is a sweeping construct. It may be defined broadly as every internal factor that contributes to consistent behavior in different situations, or, narrowly, as encompassing only emotions and motivation. For a long time, the psychology community has been engaged in discussions on how many personality traits or dimensions are necessary to describe someone, as outlined in Chapter 4. The most widely used model today is the Five-Factor Model (FFM) of personality, which includes *extraversion, agreeableness, conscientiousness, neuroticism,* and *openness to experience* (Costa and McCrae 1997). Some measures use *emotional stability* instead of *neuroticism.* In other words, the positive end of the scale is applied.

Most techniques for personality characteristic measurements use statements combined with a point scale ranging from one to five (or, in some cases, seven), to which subjects note their level of agreement. Combinations of positively and negatively phrased statements are often used for the different dimensions. For example, "I am often anxious" may be used instead of "I am never anxious."

Studies have shown that this five-factor solution may be replicated across language and cultural barriers, and a satisfactory correspondence between the subjects' description of themselves and how others perceive them has been established, particularly when described by persons who know them well (see, e.g., Digman 1990). However, not all researchers agree that the FFM represents a comprehensive description of personality. Some think it contains too few (or too many) traits. Others find the model simplistic or that it fails to explain "how we have developed into being who we are" (refer to Block 1995, for a critical analysis). Despite these criticisms, the model has been widely used in research involving personality and appears to be widely accepted as a good starting point for personality assessments (see, e.g., Digman 1990; Goldberg 1993). An example of items may be found online in an open-access database with over 3000 items where researchers are free to sample items on a number of FFM and other traits (Goldberg et al. 2006).*

Studies have demonstrated a considerable inheritable component in personality characteristics and that personality traits continue to develop even after young adulthood and into old age, but that the largest changes are seen before the age of 30 (Roberts et al. 2006; Terracciano et al. 2006). Many studies have documented gender differences in the FFM traits, and a review of findings from 55 nations indicated that women reported higher levels of neuroticism, extraversion, agreeableness, and conscientiousness than did men across most nations (Schmitt et al. 2008).

8.1.1 Other Personality Traits

Besides the FFM and its associated empirical systems, specific traits are often used to describe personalities or aspects thereof, which may be of importance in some situations. These traits are typically tied to certain theories, or are particularly suited to explain reactions (or predict behavior) in certain situations. The following are examples of such traits: *Type A behavior, locus of control (LOC), psychological resilience, hardiness*, and *social intelligence*. Type A behavior and LOC are discussed in more detail in Section 8.3.4.

Psychological resilience has been studied, in particular in relation to people who thrive despite challenges and misfortune. Important factors here are personal attributes such as social skills and leading a structured life; however, external support from family and friends is also important (Friborg et al. 2005). Hardiness is a related construct to resilience and mostly studied in military samples. It may be seen as a set of personal characteristics, which may help people turn stressful circumstances from potential disasters into opportunities for enhanced performance, leadership, and conduct (Bartone 2006). In several studies, hardiness has been linked to favorable outcomes such as military skills and competence (Johansen et al. 2014), and it may be relevant also to other safety sensitive and high-risk occupations. Social intelligence usually refers to social skills and the ability to understand one's own and others' reactions. These skills are potentially useful in many occupations, as most jobs require some interaction and collaboration with other people (Silvera et al. 2001).

These traits are more or less related to the personality traits contained in the FFM. For example, LOC correlates with *neuroticism*, such that those with internal LOC are considered more emotionally stable. In addition to traits mentioned in scientific literature, a number of poorly documented theories on personality can be found in popular science magazines and the like, often accompanied by different tests that reportedly measure these theories' accompanying traits. However, documentation to support the reliability and validity of such tests is usually few and far between.

While the measurement techniques assessing the FFM traits and other personality traits were designed to measure aspects of an individual's established personality, other methods or diagnostics systems are used to document problems such as high levels of anxiety and depression, or to establish whether someone is suffering from mental health disorder.

---

* http://ipip.ori.org

8.2   MENTAL HEALTH

The FFM traits measure normal variations in important personality traits where people differ in terms of how extroverted or conscientious they are. Personality traits are related to many important outcomes including training and work performance as outlined in Chapter 5. Personality traits are also linked to mental health problems such as depression, anxiety, and substance use disorders (Kotov et al. 2010). This applies especially to *neuroticism and conscientiousness* where the largest differences between groups diagnosed with a mental health disorder and control groups were detected (Kotov et al. 2010). Scoring high on *neuroticism* and low on *conscientiousness* may be seen as risk factors associated with many mental health disorders (Kotov et al. 2010). Meta-analyses of longitudinal studies (Jeronimus et al. 2016) have indicated that *neuroticism* represents a risk that exists prior to the development of common mental health disorders. Certain constellations of personality traits may therefore be seen as constituting a vulnerability factor for developing mental health problems rather than stemming from the same underlying cause.

Mental health has been defined by WHO (2013, p. 7) as "...a state of well-being in which every individual realizes his or her own potential, can cope with the normal stresses of life, can work productively and fruitfully, and is able to make a contribution to her or his community."

This means that everyone has a mental health, and that it is more than the absence of mental disorders or problems. For an individual, it may vary over time, and it is a vital part of a person's health in general. There are many different types of mental health problems and disorders. They differ in terms of severity, how common they are, and also in terms of causes. Around 20% of the world's population have some form of mental health problem or disorder, and only a small percentage receive professional help from mental health services for their problems (WHO 2013). Mental disorders are characterized by abnormal behavior, thoughts, and feelings, which may result in problems at work and in relation to other people. In most cases, mental health problems are caused by many contributing factors including genetic, biological, and environmental influences and stressors. Some of these influences or factors may have a negative impact on mental health and may be labeled risk factors whereas others have the opposite impact and are called protective factors. Risk and protective factors may be both individual and environmental, and may interact in different ways. Individual factors could include personality traits and intelligence, lifestyle, and the use of alcohol, and environmental factors could include family- and work-related factors. Having a family may be protective as social support is in most cases a protective factor, but family life can also be a cause for worry and conflicts and thus constitute a risk factor. Correspondingly, having a meaningful job may contribute to an individual's self-esteem and coping, but also sometimes be a source of stress and burden. Environmental influences may together with an individual vulnerability cause mental health problems, and there are also some environmental influences, for example, exposure to trauma, that may cause mental health problems without any individual vulnerability. In most cases, mental health disorders and problems result from a complex interplay between individual and environmental influences.

8.2.1 PREVENTION AND TREATMENT

Different types of treatment for mental health problems exist depending on the nature of the problem. It may include medications as well as more psychosocial treatments such as cognitive therapy or behavioral therapy. The choice of therapy should rely on the best available research evidence of what actually works. Ideally, there should be studies documenting that a certain type of treatment is effective in reducing symptoms in groups of patients compared to control groups; for example, that cognitive therapy is effective in reducing depression among patients suffering from major depression compared to a control group or to other types of treatment. If there are many studies supporting the effectiveness of a certain type of therapy, then these can be summarized either through systematic reviews or meta-analyses. The Cochrane Collaboration (www.cochranelibrary.com) is an international organization that conducts systematic reviews that may be used as the basis for selecting the best available therapy. In many countries, these types of reviews are used as the basis for forming guidelines for what type of treatment should be offered for both medical and mental health problems. For some types of mental health problems, there is solid evidence, whereas for other types of illnesses there is less convincing evidence. The term evidence-based practice is frequently used by both psychiatrists and clinical psychologists and means that the treatment offered should be based on research evidence, clinical expertise, and the clients or patients' wishes, values, and needs (Sackett et al. 1996). In addition to different types of treatment for mental health problems, there is also an increased focus on prevention and health promotion. Mental health promotion refers to activities or interventions that aim at strengthening protective factors such as resilience and coping skills but also creating supportive environments (Barry and Jenkins 2007). Different types of prevention exist, and may be directed at everyone; for example, everyone working in the aviation industry where the purpose is to prevent a specific problem (e.g., alcohol abuse). This strategy is labeled universal prevention, and instead of targeting a specific group, the intervention is for everyone. One universal preventive measure related to alcohol would be to restrict access to alcohol. There are other types of prevention, labeled selective and indicated where the intervention is targeted either toward people at risk (selective prevention) or people who have symptoms or early signs of a problem (indicated prevention). Ideally, there should be a system that covers health promotion, prevention, and treatment, as indicated in Figure 8.1.

8.2.2 DIAGNOSING MENTAL HEALTH PROBLEMS

There are several systems for diagnosing and classifying mental disorders such as the DSM-5 (American Psychiatric Association 2013), which is probably the most widely used system in addition to the ICD-10 (International Statistical Classification of Diseases and Related Health Problems) developed by the World Health Organization (2016). The DSM-5 system includes in Section II a list of diagnostic categories: depressive disorders, schizophrenia and other psychotic disorders, trauma- and stressor-related disorders, personality disorders, and substance-related and addictive disorders. Many of these diagnostic categories have several symptoms that need to

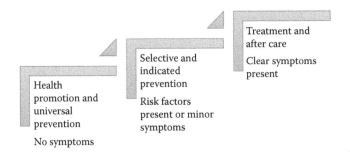

FIGURE 8.1   How to promote good mental health.

present over a certain time period and result in a lowered level of functioning before the diagnosis can be determined. In addition, significant psychosocial and contextual features also need to be considered when diagnosing a person. This is usually done by conducting a clinical structured interview, and it may sometimes be supplemented with specific tests for assessing, for example, depressive symptoms or neuropsychological tests to examine cognitive impairment. A precise diagnosis requires cooperation from the person being interviewed, and unless the person is willing to discuss symptoms and report problems, assigning a correct diagnosis becomes very difficult for the clinician.

When determining if a person suffers from a mental health disorder, it is important to rule out alternative explanations such as the symptoms being caused by a medical condition or the use of substances/medications. A person may, after losing a loved or going through a difficult breakup, display many different symptoms including depressive symptoms, anger, sleeping problems, and loss of appetite, without this constituting a disorder. Pilots, like most people, are not immune to life stressors and hardship and may experience reactions to life events and also experience mental health problems and disorders.

The DSM-5 system (APA 2013) includes a large number of diagnostic categories— too many according to critics—and a comprehensive overview is beyond the scope of this book. Some of the more relevant diagnoses are outlined briefly in Table 8.1.

Another way of classifying mental health disorders is between severe mental health disorders versus minor mental health problems. Psychotic disorders such as schizophrenia or bipolar disorders are more severe and are associated with a loss of contact with reality, lack of insight in the disorder, and many other symptoms including reduced functioning in major areas such as work and family life. These types of disorders are relatively rare, and the estimated lifetime prevalence for schizophrenia is between 0.30% and 0.70% (APA 2013) and for any type of psychotic disorder is 3.5% (Perälä et al. 2007). For major depression, the prevalence is much more common, and in a year, almost 7% of the population may experience a major depressive disorder.

A person may suffer simultaneously from several different disorders, for example, both anxiety and depression or having an eating disorder in addition to a personality disorder. This phenomenon is referred to as comorbidity and may make the diagnosis and treatment more difficult. The advantage of such classification system like DSM-5

TABLE 8.1

Overview of Some Diagnostic Categories in DSM-5

Category	Key Features	Explanation and Examples
Schizophrenia	Defined by abnormalities in one or more domains: delusions, hallucinations, disorganized thinking or abnormal behavior, and negative symptoms	Delusions are fixed beliefs which are clearly implausible and could be that the person has grandiose ideas about being a famous person or being under surveillance by the police/government when this is clearly not the case. Hallucinations could include hearing voices. Negative symptoms could include social withdrawal and little expression of emotions
Bipolar disorder	Involves both manic and depressive episodes	The manic episodes may involve an abnormally elevated, expansive, and irritable mood, inflated self-esteem, decreased need for sleep and often activities that may have painful consequences (e.g., foolish investments). Depressive episodes are characterized by feelings of sadness, hopelessness, insomnia, inability to concentrate, and fatigue
Major depressive disorder	Depressed mood and loss of interest or pleasure	Other symptoms may be weight loss, insomnia, loss of energy, restlessness, concentration problems, and thoughts of death
Anxiety disorders	Excessive anxiety and worry difficult to control for the person	Other symptoms may be restlessness, easily fatigued, muscle tension, sleep disturbances, or irritability
Specific phobia	Fear of anxiety for a specific object or situation	The anxiety is out of proportion to the actual danger and causes impairment or distress, e.g., socially or at work. It could be related to objects (e.g., spiders) or situations (fear of flying or elevators)
Panic disorder	Intense fear or intense discomfort	Accompanied by symptoms such as pounding hart, sweating, nausea, dizziness, and fear of losing control or going crazy
PTSD	Exposure to actual or threatened death, serious injury, or violence and presence of distressing memories or dreams	Also often avoidance of the stimuli that may remind of the situation, negative mood, and cognitions. Irritable behavior, problems with concentration and sleep
Alcohol use disorder	Problematic pattern of alcohol use and significant impairment and distress	Other symptoms may include recurrent alcohol use despite social problems, work problems caused by alcohol use, use in situation where it may be dangerous, and tolerance and withdrawal symptoms
Personality disorder	Includes 10 specific disorders characterized with an enduring pattern of inner experience and behavior that depart from what is considered appropriate in the culture, is inflexible, and results in distress or impairment	Examples are antisocial personality disorders (disregard for and violation of the rights of others) and obsessive–compulsive disorder (preoccupied with orderliness, perfectionism, and control)

or other similar systems is that a correct diagnosis is a necessary requirement for choosing the best treatment. One disadvantage is that people may feel stigmatized by being assigned to a diagnostic category as mental health problems are still associated with a lack of knowledge and misconceptions about the cause and treatment options.

8.2.3 MENTAL HEALTH PROBLEMS AMONG AIRCREW

Mental health problems and disorders among pilots, ATCOs, and other types of personnel in aviation may impair performance and therefore be a threat to flight safety. Following the Germanwings Flight 925 accident (BEA 2016) where a pilot deliberately flew a commercial aircraft into the ground, the topic has been discussed by many including the European Cockpit Association (ECA), the European Association for Aviation Psychologists, and also the European Aeromedical Association. These three organizations have collaborated and issued a joint statement in order to promote mental health and openness and to support pilots who need help to deal with mental health issues (see, e.g., eaap.net). The Aerospace Medical Association (AsMA) has twice issued recommendations related to mental health among pilots following accidents attributed to severe mental health problems and with updated recommendations after the Germanwings accident in 2015 (AsMA 2012, 2016). The expert group stated that serious mental health disorders (e.g., psychosis) are relatively rare and their onset is difficult to predict, and that preventive efforts should be aimed at more common mental health problems such as depression, anxiety, and substance misuse (AsMA 2012, 2016). They have also stated that barriers toward discussions about mental health problems between the aeromedical examiner and the pilot should be recognized, and the awareness should be raised about the topic among aircrew, their families and flight organizations. They have also suggested that mental health should be assessed as part of the initial pilot selection and recurrent for pilots who have a history of mental health problems (AsMA 2016), but that routinely screening for serious mental health disorders is probably not effective.

There may be many reasons why a pilot may be reluctant to discuss mental health problems with the examining physician during the annual medical assessment, including fear of losing his or her license with both personal and financial costs as a result. This may prevent the pilot from receiving adequate and timely help, and this could potentially make the problems worse and prolong the time for recovery. More could probably be done to increase knowledge about mental health problems and reduce stigma so that more pilots and other professionals working in aviation report mental health problems, get treatment, and return to work. This would probably increase individual well-being, but also promote safety. Stigma has been seen as composed of three aspects: knowledge (ignorance), attitudes (prejudice), and behavior (discrimination) (Evans-Lacko et al. 2010). Perceived stigma may prevent help-seeking and also put an additional burden on the person experiencing mental health problems. As a preventive measure, peer support programs (PSPs) have been suggested. These programs may include a safe zone where pilots can receive confidential counseling and support from peers, and if needed be referred to treatment. Many of these programs have so far focused on alcohol abuse and help to deal with personal and family problems, but have lately also been extended to include mental health problems. Different types of PSPs are described by the AsMA expert working group (AsMA 2016). In early 2016, the European Aviation Safety Agency (EASA 2016) suggested to make such programs mandatory across Europe to ensure they are available to all commercial pilots. This is why ESAM, ECA, EAAP, and the Mayday Foundation set up the European Pilot Peer Support Initiative (EPPSI) to exchange best practices and to facilitate communication between stakeholders engaged in or planning to engage in PSPs (eppsi.eu).

8.3 WHAT IS STRESS?

We are continually bombarded with influences, expectations, and demands placed on us by our surroundings. Work commitments or the lack of time and resources to complete tasks are typical examples. Both paid work and unpaid work (e.g., caring for family members) are applicable factors in this regard. To meet social demands or solve work-related tasks, the individual relies on different sets of resources, including knowledge, experience, and personal attributes. Some theories describe stress as the result of factors or elements that have a negative impact on the individual; for example, distracting noise or pressure at work (stimulus-based theories), while other theories are concerned with the consequences of stress, such as various emotional and physical reactions (response-based theories). The latter tradition is exemplified by Selye (1976). He describes a general stress response that is valid for everyone and consists of three phases: the alarm phase, the resistance phase, and the exhaustion phase.

A more modern understanding requires stress to be regarded as the interaction between demands and the resources available to the individual. When demands placed on an individual exceed his or her resources, stress develops. In these interaction models, an important point is that the person must evaluate the demands and consider whether or not these demands exceed his or her resources. Due to this cognitive evaluation, what one individual considers a stressor is not necessarily considered a stressor by someone else (noted in, e.g., Lazarus, 1976). Balance between external demands and personal attributes is perceived as challenging and satisfying to the individual (Frankenhaeuser 1991), whereas imbalance is a precursor to emotional, physical, and behavioral consequences. Frankenhaeuser's (1991) *biopsychosocial model* (depicted in Figure 8.2) delineates the relationship between stress and health. In that model, the person is subjected to various demands, such as intense workloads, time constraints, shift work, problems, or conflicts. The person relates this to his or her resources, including experience, physical and mental health, personal abilities, and, potentially, external support. If demands surpasses the person's resources, stress ensues, accompanied by both psychological and physiological reactions. Immediately, various stress hormones are released into the body (adrenaline, noradrenaline, and cortisol). These hormones produce a number of advantageous effects in precarious situations; however, problems may arise if the individual is exposed to these effects for an extended period of time. If a person is continually stressed, or if there is not enough time to rest, the body is unable to normalize the physiological reactions in time for the next work session. Stress is also an unpleasant experience, with short-term and long-term consequences for the affected person's productivity. More on this is discussed later.

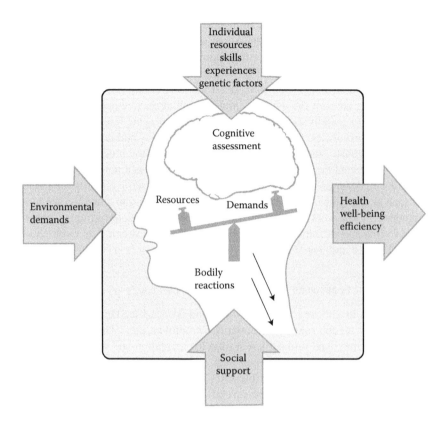

FIGURE 8.2 The biopsychosocial stress model. (With kind permission from Springer Science+Business Media: *Women, Work, and Health. Stress and Opportunities*, The psychophysiology of sex differences as related to occupational status, 1991, pp. 39–61, Frankenhaeuser, M., New York, NY: Plenum Press.)

There are other models that describe work-related stress, such as Karasek's demand–control model (Karasek 1979; Karasek and Theorell 1990), which describes how stress relates to various consequences such as health risks and behavior within the organization. In this model, work-related demands are described as "high" or "low," and, similarly, the individual's ability to affect or control the situation is deemed "high" or "low." Combining high demands with low levels of control increases the risk of psychological impacts and physical illness, such as cardiovascular diseases (Yoshimasu 2001). On the other hand, combining high demands and a high level of control encourages learning and has a motivational effect. Later expansions on this model have pointed out that social support, such as assistance and encouragement by colleagues, may reduce stress and minimize risks associated with negative consequences of stress. There are several forms of social support, such as care and empathy, as well as assistance of a more practical nature, and being applauded for doing a good job.

Keeping in mind that stress results from an appraisal process, and that the same situation may result in stress for one person but not for another, there are some stressors that may be perceived as problematic by many professionals working in aviation. A comprehensive review by Albuquerque and Fonseca (2017) lists a number of stressors that may be a factor for pilots but also for other types of personnel in aviation. These include physical/physiological stressors, as outlined in Chapter 3, and job-related stressors such as difficult working conditions including pressure toward reducing costs in the aviation industry and atypical employment. The third group of stressors is individual stressors related to managing family life, shift work, and other responsibilities. Different types of stressors may add up, especially if they occur simultaneously, and the combined impact may be too much to handle for the individual. Different coping strategies for managing stress among pilots have been outlined by Eriksen and Bor (2017) and include individual strategies for reducing stress such as living healthy, sleep hygiene, exercise, relaxation techniques, and having interests outside work. In addition, they describe work-related strategies that may be used to manage workload and establish boundaries between paid work and private life (Eriksen and Bor 2017).

8.3.1 Conflicts between Work and Private Life

Today, many of us choose to combine work and private life. This means that many must be adept at several roles (parent, partner, employee, etc.). The total workload is substantial and may lead to insufficient time for recreation and rest. Thus, conflicts may arise from the interaction between work and private life. At the same time, there are positive aspects of having multiple roles, such as increased self-confidence and greater financial freedom. There are several approaches to the competing demands between paid work and family life, frequently referred to as work-to-home conflicts. One is that time management becomes difficult, and it seems like "there are not enough hours in the day." Another is that work causes stress and exhaustion, leading to the inability to engage in quality family time as much as one would like to. Several studies have described a connection between work-to-home conflicts and burnout (Martinussen and Richardsen 2006; Martinussen et al. 2007) and between work-to-home conflicts and reduced satisfaction with one's partnership, as well as reduced job satisfaction (Allen et al. 2000). Some studies have pointed to a so-called "crossover effect" between partners: stress and tension experienced at work by one person is transferred to his or her partner, who subsequently has to deal with the stress by serving as a buffer (Westman and Etzion 1995). This transfer probably occurs because the person empathizes with his or her partner; however, a more direct effect is plausible as exhausted and frustrated persons have "less to give" when they come home from work. A study of couples with young children revealed that men were more likely to become passive and withdrawn upon returning home after a difficult day at work, while women were more likely to become aggressive (Schultz et al. 2004). In short, the study indicated that having a difficult day at work might have consequences for your partner, and that there are gender-related differences in how we react to such situations. These findings have since been supported by a survey of male flight controllers, which revealed that they often reacted with withdrawal after a stressful day at work. The study also revealed that satisfaction was greater when their partner accepted such behavior.

Although fewer studies have investigated how family or private matters negatively affect job performance, we can safely assume that such effects would be undesirable. Some examples of demanding tasks at home include dealing with disease, partnership breakdowns, and caring for many young children. However, negative emotions are not the only emotions transferable between home and work. Positive experiences at work may transfer to family life as one arrives home contented and uplifted, and, conversely, positive events at home may lead to a better day at work. Arguably, people with family commitments may find it easier to set boundaries for their work commitments, which, in the absence of a family, might have absorbed a greater part of the day. Thus, family commitments become a legitimate excuse, both to the employer, and, not least, to oneself. In particular, young, single professionals presumably experience greater pressure to perform and are more likely to work longer hours, indicating that individuals with family commitments are not the only ones struggling to find the balance between work and leisure. Further, modern communications (such as e-mail and cell phones) may enable the person to continue working even after official work hours.

Several studies have indicated the continuation of traditional labor-sharing practices in households, in which women account for cooking, cleaning, and caring for children, while men are mainly responsible for tasks such as maintenance and car repairs (Lundberg et al. 1994; Lundberg and Frankenhaeuser 1999; Østlyngen et al. 2003). A Norwegian study involving parents with young children (0–6 years) demonstrated that females did about 70% of the domestic work; however, this study included a relatively high percentage of mothers who worked part-time (Kitterød 2005). Nonetheless, the study indicates a larger total workload for women in comparison to men, leaving them with a reduced amount of time (after finishing the day's paid and domestic work) available for relaxation and recreation. A study of junior managers employed at the car manufacturer Volvo in Sweden revealed that stress hormone levels were equal in female and male managers during work hours, but a difference was noticeable after work hours. Rising levels were recorded in females between 6:00 and 8:00 p.m., while in males the corresponding values decreased during the same period (Frankenhaeuser 1991). The physiological data were consistent with the self-reporting of weariness. Thus, male junior managers started relaxing immediately after work. This was not the case for females until much later in the evening. Therefore, females had a shorter time available for relaxation than did males, possibly incurring negative health consequences in the long term (Lundberg 2005).

8.3.2 Working Shift

Shift work is commonplace for many people in aviation, as is night shifts for some. Crewmembers who travel across time zones also experience problems due to jet lag. The notion of shift work usually applies to work taking place outside of regular day time hours (6:00 a.m. to 6:00 p.m.); however, there are different types of shift work arrangements, many of which apply some form of rotating shifts. Shift work has several consequences in relation to health issues, sleep, work achievements, the risk of accidents, increased work-to-home conflicts, and participation in social activities taking place on weekday evenings and weekends. Working shifts may also influence one's relationship with the employer, for example, in the form of reduced work satisfaction (Demerouti et al. 2004).

8.3.2.1 Sleep

Sleep difficulties are one of the most common problems associated with shift work in general and night shifts in particular. In human beings, body temperature and the production of hormones, stomach acids, and urine follows a cycle of approximately 24 hours. External factors such as light exposure influences the internal clock (or "body clock") and its adjustment. Hence, at night, the body is expecting to do something completely different from working. Most adults usually sleep between 6 and 9 hours each night, averaging from 7 to 7.5 hours (Ursin 1996). Physiological measurements make it possible to map the various phases of sleep, including the *rapid eye movement* (REM) phase, in which dreams occur. Throughout the night, the different phases are repeated. Toward the end of the night, deep sleep subsides and it is common to wake up a couple of times. Sleep varies according to body temperature, which is at its lowest point in the morning (between 4:00 a.m. and 6:00 a.m.) and this is when it is most difficult to stay awake (Pallesen 2006). There are several theories on the function of sleep, that is, why we sleep. Some are based on the theory of evolution and postulate that it is safer to be inactive in darkness, as we cannot see where we are going. A second group of theories argue that sleep has an important restorative function on the body, and that certain types of hormones (which boost the growth of body tissues) are produced during sleep (Pallesen 2006). In addition, it appears that sleep has a restorative function relating to brain cells and the protection of these from cell degeneration processes (Pallesen 2006).

Sleep is normally regulated by how long we have been awake as well as our daily routines and habits (Waage et al. 2006). Thus, it is more difficult to sleep during the day than the night, and commonly people who go to bed after a night shift experience less total sleep, more frequent sleep interruptions, and they may have to get up to go to the toilet even though this normally is not necessary when sleeping through the night. There are, however, individual differences in tolerance to night and shift work. Some studies have shown that mature individuals (over the age of 45) have greater problems sleeping or resting after working a night shift, and that problems increase with age (Costa 2003). Some people, however, find it easier to work night shifts as they get older. Increased experience in this type of work and the acquisition of adaptive techniques are possible interpretations of the result in these cases. Perhaps, the worker's children have grown up, making the family situation more accepting of sleeping during the day. Typically, however, studies into the consequences of shift and night work are likely to be influenced by a "selection effect." It is reasonable to assume that those who are greatly discomforted by such work hours would quit the job after a period of time, resulting in a selection process in which those who experience less discomfort continue working. Estimates show that as many as 20% of shift workers quit after a relatively short period of time (Costa 1996).

8.3.2.2   Health Implications

Several studies have found adverse health implications in shift workers, including increased exposure to cardiovascular diseases, problems with digestion, and cancer (Costa 1996). A longitudinal Danish study that monitored a vast number of subjects over a period of 12 years demonstrated that shift workers were more likely to develop cardiovascular disease compared to daytime workers (Tüchsen et al. 2007). Females working shifts more frequently report problems linked to menstruation; some studies have found a connection between shift work and miscarriages, low birth weight, and premature birth (Knutsson 2003). A meta-analysis of 13 studies on the link between breast cancer in women and night shift work suggested an increased breast cancer risk. Approximately half of these studies were based on cabin crew, while the remaining studies were based on females in other types of night shift work. The reasons for the elevated cancer risk are uncertain, but a possible explanation is that working nights reduces the production of melatonin, which is considered to have a cancer-preventing effect (Megdal et al. 2005). Presumably, the negative health effects are direct effects of disruptions to the biological 24-hour rhythm, as well as behavioral changes due to shift work. For example, sleep deprivation can lead to the use of alcohol to induce sleep, or excessive smoking to stay awake at night. It is also possible that shift work contributes to work-to-home conflicts, which heighten stress levels and further exacerbate the adverse health implications of shift work.

8.3.2.3   Accident Risk

A number of studies have examined how sleep deprivation affects performance and how it relates to accidents. Laboratory studies have looked at the connection between reduced sleep and cognitive and psychomotor tasks, revealing that tasks requiring constant attention are more affected by sleep deprivation, while more advanced tasks, such as reasoning, were less affected (Åkerstedt 2007 provides a summary). One study, in which subjects were asked to operate a flight simulator at night, demonstrated that their reduction in performance was equivalent to a blood alcohol level of 0.05% (Klein et al. 1970).

The consequences of sleep deprivation generally increase during an extended period without sleep. However, it also depends on the person's day-to-day routines, such that performance improves during the day relative to the night (Åkerstedt 2007). Even after a prolonged period of being awake, performance will improve somewhat during the time period in which he or she is normally awake (the "day time" according to the person's body clock).

Working shifts, and working night shifts in particular, is associated with elevated risk of accidents (a summary is provided in Folkard and Tucker 2003). Several studies, for example, from the field of medicine, show that doctors make more mistakes if they are sleep deprived (during, e.g., 24-hour shifts) and need longer time to perform basic tasks, such as intubating a patient (Åkerstedt 2007). A number of studies into motor vehicle accidents point to drowsiness, and particularly driving after night shifts, as an important factor in many accidents. In a survey of pilots asked to describe how drowsiness typically affected them, the most common symptoms were reduced attention and lack of concentration (Bourgeois-Bougrine et al. 2003). Accordingly, the remainder of the crew reported evidence of tiredness primarily in the form of longer response times, greater error frequency, and poor communication (Bourgeois-Bougrine et al. 2003).

8.3.2.4 Private Life

There are individual differences in the ability to deal with shift work. These differences are usually attributed to biological, social, and health issues, although the organization of the work and shift schedule does play a part. Employees who are privileged enough to have a certain level of flexibility and influence on the shift work roster are generally more content and experience fewer problems associated with shift work (Costa et al. 2006). For most people, however, shift work is problematic and has significant consequences for one's private life. There are issues with meeting family commitments and participating in social activities, which typically take place in the afternoon. Having a day off on a weekday is not the same as having a day off on the weekend. Family commitments may also make it more difficult to sleep during the day to recuperate after a night shift or having been awake for a long period of time. Mood volatility after night shifts undeniably places additional demands on the individual and the family. A study of police officers in the Netherlands concluded that the timing of shift work is a decisive factor as to the level of work-to-home conflicts and recommended avoiding shifts that involve regular weekend work (Demerouti et al. 2004).

Some studies have described problems with combining shift work and family life as higher for females than males, and women with young children in particular report shorter and more interrupted sleep after night shifts, as well as accumulated tiredness (Costa 1996).

8.3.3 BURNOUT AND ENGAGEMENT

Burnout can be regarded as a stress reaction occurring after long-term, work-related demands and pressure. Maslach and Jackson (1981, 1986) have defined burnout as a three-dimensional psychological syndrome consisting of *emotional exhaustion* (a condition including overwhelming emotional and physical exhaustion), *depersonalization* (characterized by negative emotions and cynical attitudes toward the recipients of one's service or care), and reduced *personal accomplishment* (a tendency to evaluate negatively one's own work). Initial studies of burnout were based on workers in care professions such as nursing. Then, burnout was considered to be triggered by high interpersonal demands. More recently, however, burnout has been found in professions that do not necessarily involve caring for patients, clients, or pupils. The three dimensions have subsequently been generalized into the dimensions *exhaustion*, *cynicism*, and a lack of *professional efficacy* (Richardsen and Martinussen 2006).

A number of work environment factors have proven to be associated with burnout. Leiter and Maslach (2005) have described six categories of such factors. One of these is workload. There may be either too much to do (or not enough time available to do it) or insufficient resources to solve given tasks. Insufficient control or autonomy in the workplace is also associated with burnout. If a person feels powerless to control resources required to complete tasks, or unable to influence how the job is done, reduced personal accomplishment may result. Some work-related factors have a preventive effect on burnout or serve as a "buffer." These factors include social support or assistance provided by management or colleagues. Being rewarded, being acknowledged, and feeling fairly treated (in terms of promotions and other perks) are positive resources. Sometimes, an employee may find that the organization has different values to his or her own, through, for example, being told to withhold information or deceive someone. At present, however, what happens when values held by employees differ from those of employers is insufficiently researched.

Although early research into burnout was directed at particular jobs (such as the above-mentioned nurses), not only those in demanding care professions are at risk. There are few studies aimed at burnout in aviation professions, and most work-related stress studies focus on short-term effects, such as measuring blood pressure changes in flight controllers when exposed to elevated air traffic density levels.

A study of Norwegian air traffic controllers concluded that the burnout rate was not significantly higher than for other professions included in the study. Both the experienced levels of conflict and work-to-home-related conflicts were associated with exhaustion in this group (Martinussen and Richardsen 2006). Most people would consider flight control to be a highly stressful profession; thus, it is surprising that this group did not have elevated burnout rates. On the other hand, flight controllers go through a process of strict selection, education, and training to enable them to perform extremely demanding tasks. Hence, there appears to be a balance between the tasks to be solved and the skills and abilities of the employees. This does not mean that the individuals are immune to the demands and requirements of the organization, or that access to resources would not have a positive effect. Similar results have been found for the police profession, which considers organizational issues to be more frustrating and demanding than the job itself (Martinussen et al. 2007).

Traditionally, studies into work environments and burnout have focused greatly on negative aspects and attempted to establish the illness-inducing sides of the work environment (Maslach et al. 2001). Recently, however, researchers have turned their eyes on studying the opposite of burnout—that is, engagement—to find out what causes this outcome. Schaufeli and Bakker (2004) present a model that describes how resources and workplace demands relate to both engagement and burnout (Figure 8.3). This model tells us that burnout is first and foremost associated with demands, and secondly, with a lack of resources, while engagement is predominantly associated with access to resources such as rewards, recognition, and support. Burnout and engagement have consequences for the organization. Burnout implies negative consequences whereas engagement has a positive impact. Examples of organizational consequences are intention to quit, work satisfaction, work performance, and feeling commitment to the organization. Burnout also has negative consequences for the affected individual's health and quality of life.

8.3.4 Individual Differences and Stress

There is little doubt that some working environments or factors are generally considered stressful. Yet, people with certain personality characteristics experience stress

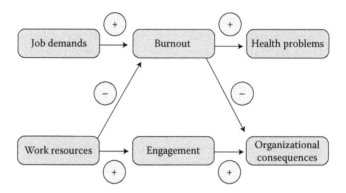

FIGURE 8.3 Job demands–resources model for burnout and engagement.

more often and more intensely than others. It is therefore of interest to study these differences in detail. Studies have shown that *neuroticism* is associated with burnout. Although some of the other FFM personality characteristics also have been found to be associated with burnout, findings vary greatly between studies.

Two physicians (Rosenman and Friedman 1974) working with individuals suffering from cardiovascular disease claimed to have observed certain recurring traits in their patients. They labeled some of their patients' behavior *Type A*—characterized by irritability, time constraints, competitive mentality, aggression, hostility, and ambitiousness. Patients who did not display these properties were labeled *Type B*. Several methods of measuring and mapping Type A personalities have since been developed, of which the most well-known and widely used is the Jenkins Activity Survey. This method condenses the mentioned characteristics into two dimensions: *impatience–irritability* and *achievement strivings*. The latter represents a positive side, namely, that the person sets goals and works hard to achieve them. The former dimension represents the less positive side and is characterized by impatience and aggression. *Impatience–irritability* is related to health issues, while *achievement strivings* is associated with enhanced work achievements and better student grades. Researchers have established the existence of a significant inheritable component in Type A behavior; Type A has also been found to be a risk factor in the development of cardiovascular diseases (e.g., Yoshimasu 2001). The link is thought to occur as Type A, in particular due to the *impatience–irritability* aspect, is associated with greater physiological activation including elevated blood pressure levels and heart rate. However, lifestyle choices, such as alcohol and smoking, may also contribute to this pattern.

What are the consequences of Type A behavior in the workforce? In fact, many organizations are likely to reward Type A personalities, at least those aspects relating to *achievement strivings*; however, *impatience–irritability* may cause problems for the individual and his or her surroundings. Perhaps, Type A behavior directly influences work-related satisfaction and the experience of stress and burnout. The combination of aspects of the work environment and, for example, *impatience–irritability* may cause particularly unfortunate outcomes for certain individuals. Type A personalities may even intuitively choose professions that are more challenging or involve a greater pace and work load. It may be the case that Type A personalities affect their work environment in certain ways and therefore contribute to creating a more stressed environment.

Another personal attribute under investigation is LOC—the extent to which the person feels that he or she can influence or control events and situations. Internal LOC has been shown to be associated with several work-related variables, including improved motivation and commitment (Ng et al. 2006). People with active coping techniques (that is, the person acts strategically to handle difficult situations) generally score lower on burnout than people who use more emotion-focused coping techniques (e.g., the person attempts to deal with emotions by seeking comfort in other people).

People also differ according to gender, age, and other circumstantial factors. Generally, low correlations exist between burnout and factors such as age and gender. Sometimes, younger professionals have been found to be more exposed to burnout, while in other studies (e.g., flight controllers and the police) the "age effect" is reversed (Martinussen and Richardsen 2006; Martinussen et al. 2007). However, such correlations are found to be weak. This also applies to differences due to gender. Some studies find that females report a greater degree of *exhaustion* than males, and that males have higher *cynicism* scores; others find no gender differences.

8.3.5 Consequences of Stress

Stress has both short-term and long-term consequences that may affect an individual in relation to job performance. A critical stress situation may arise when something unusual takes place during a flight. Examples of stress situations may be indications of technical difficulties or a rapid deterioration of weather conditions. It is important to know typical reactions in such situations, be aware of how the crew responds to stress, and understand how it affects decisions made during the flight.

It is difficult to measure how stress affects, for example, various cognitive functions. There are ethical considerations involved in exposing subjects to stressful situations in experiments to study how they react. A possible solution to this problem is to use a simulator to study how people handle various abnormal situations. This provides a controlled environment in which emergency situations can be manufactured, workloads and time constraints can be increased, and reactions can be recorded. Although many simulators are highly realistic, they will never be identical to real-world experiences; thus, the possibility that findings are not transferrable to real-world situations must not be ignored. A second option is to study incidents that have already taken place, reconstruct the decisions made, and observe how stress contributed to the event. The drawback of this method is that it is based on the human recollection and perception of the event and what happened. Another issue is that situations may appear quite differently in hindsight, compared to how the situation actually occurred was experienced by the people involved. No matter which design is chosen, there are challenges and shortcomings; however, there are some consistent findings on the immediate effect of stress on cognitive functions and decision-making capacity. According to a review provided by Orasanu (1997), stress may have the following effects:

- People make more errors.
- Attention is reduced, causing tunnel vision or selective hearing.
- Scanning (vision) becomes more chaotic.
- Short-term memory is reduced.
- Change of strategy: speed gains preference to accuracy. People act as though time limits apply. Strategies are simplified.

Thus, cognitive functions are subject to a number of stress-related consequences in terms of how we perceive our surroundings, process information, and make decisions. An important aspect regarding aviation is the need to constantly take in and monitor information. In a high-stress situation, the capacity to do so diminishes, reducing the ability to understand what is being said over the radio, or what another person says to you. Similarly, the information you supply to someone stressed may be poorly understood, or not understood at all.

By short-term memory, we refer to the processes or structures that contribute to the temporary storage and processing of information. It enables us to read a couple of sentences while storing and processing information about, say, the last word in each sentence, and to repeat those words in the correct order. Some argue that there are clear limitations on short-term memory, and early studies revealed a short-term memory capacity in adults of seven numbers (± 2). However, later studies have pointed out more of a complexity in this matter. For instance, grouping a set of numbers and remembering them as one (e.g., "2," "4," and "5" as "245") makes it possible to recall even more numbers. On the other hand, more complex elements (words, for example) are more difficult to remember, reducing the number of retainable elements to less than seven. In stressful situations, this capacity will be further reduced, with consequences for the ability to perform basic mental arithmetic, such as calculating the remaining flight time when the fuel tank is half full.

In connection with incidents and accidents, there has been much focus on decision-making: how was the situation perceived, and what was the chosen course of action? Klein (1995) has studied decision-making in real-life situations, in aviation and in general, for many years, and developed a model called *recognition-primed decision* (RPD). His model involves experts using their knowledge to recognize or identify the problem and choosing a solution that has been proven successful in previous, similar situations. If the solution to the current situation is suitable, it is applied, and only one solution is considered at a time. This model has since been expanded by Orasanu (1997), who describes a model that can be used even in unfamiliar situations. The first thing the person does is to evaluate the situation: What is the problem? Are the warning signs clear and unambiguous, or are they changing? Often, experts in such situations also consider how much time is available to take the necessary steps, and evaluate the level of risk involved. Then, the person must evaluate whether any existing procedure is available to remedy the situation. Perhaps, there is more than one solution? One possibility is, of course, that there are no known solutions, which triggers the need to create a new and untested course of action.

In general, cognitive processes that involve retrieval of information from long-term memory are resilient to stress, while processes that require the use of short-term memory are more vulnerable. In other words, if the warning signs are well known and clear, and a standard solution is applicable, the situation will not be significantly prone to stress. On the other hand, if the signs are obscure, or keep changing, and multiple courses of action must be considered, the situation is prone to stress. Perhaps, it is not surprising that experienced pilots do not make as many mistakes under pressure as less experienced pilots; they have a greater number of experiences stored in their long-term memory and are more likely to use a rule-based approach rather than having to consider several options or even improvise new solutions. It is therefore important to have knowledge of both stress and how we are affected by acute stress; for example, a common mistake is to assume that time is more precious than necessary. Another consequence of stress is the simplification of strategies, such as preferring speed over accuracy. It is important to be trained in managing stressful situations to familiarize oneself with critical situations and learn how they can be resolved. It is also important to be aware of strategies to reduce workloads in stressful situations; for example, how to distribute tasks between members of the crew in the best possible way.

8.3.6 EXTREME STRESS

Persons affected by accidents in aviation, both directly and indirectly (e.g., close colleagues perishing in a plane crash), are exposed to stress in a different sense to everyday stress. Extreme stress reactions vary from a strong feeling of surreality immediately after the event to an apparent absence of a reaction. However, the long-term effects must also be considered; although an individual may seem to handle the situation well initially, it may take time for a reaction to manifest itself.

Persons exposed to trauma are at risk of developing posttraumatic stress disorder (PTSD), characterized by discomforting thoughts or dreams in which the trauma is relived. PTSD is in the DSM-5 system part of the category *trauma- and stressor-related disorders*. Affected individuals feel numb and avoid situations that remind them of the accident. Restlessness, nervousness, and sleep problems are also common. PTSD can lead to a reduction in the affected individual's ability to perform his or her duties to the same level as before the accident. In some cases, the condition is characterized by fear, helplessness, aggression, and/or a hostile attitude. Why the condition is characterized by negative emotions has not yet been made clear; however, a possible explanation is that people who have been exposed to a traumatic event have a reduced threshold for perceiving a situation as threatening. This leads to anxiety and avoidance, but also aggression and more easily finding oneself in an attack position. The link between the severity of PTSD symptoms and aggression is stronger in individuals traumatized by acts of war than in individuals experiencing other traumatic events (Orth and Wieland 2006). In most cases, these symptoms will subside in the weeks and months following the experience, although a few develop a chronic condition associated with depression, substance abuse, anxiety, and inability to work. Even though most people regain their ability to work after a traumatic incident, it is important to be able to identify individuals who are at risk of developing PTSD. It is safe to assume that social interventions, such as care and support from colleagues and management, will be of use to many of those affected. Population studies from the United States have shown that 50%–60% of the population has experienced a traumatic event at least once in their lifetime, while only a small proportion (5%–10%) developed PTSD (Ozer et al. 2003). Therefore, it is of interest to explore the factors or conditions that help us understand why some people develop PTSD and others do not. A meta-analysis of a number of studies examining these factors found that individual factors, such as a record of previous mental health problems and prior exposure to trauma, were associated with more severe PTSD symptoms. Other factors, such as previous involvement in life-threatening situations, social support networks, and emotions that were experienced during the event itself, were also associated with PTSD symptoms (Ozer et al. 2003).

When it comes to vulnerability factors, those who were directly involved in the accident are considered more vulnerable than those who are not directly exposed to the event. Persons not appropriately trained, for example, in relation to the necessary rescue efforts, are more likely to have stronger and longer-lasting reactions. In addition, the severity of the situation (e.g., as measured by the number of dead and injured or intense and overwhelming sensory impressions) is likely to increase the probability of developing PTSD (Ozer et al. 2003). Many people do not develop PTSD despite experiencing traumatic events. They respond in a resilient way, and the lack of negative outcomes has been explained by Stress Inoculation Theory (Seery et al. 2010). According to this theory, moderate exposure to stressful incidents may increase self-confidence for handling stress and make the person more resilient for future adversities. A longitudinal study indicated that moderate exposure to adverse events resulted in better life satisfaction and lower distress compared to groups with no or high adversity (Seery et al. 2010).

All organizations should have routines for how accidents are dealt with and how those involved are to be cared for after the accident. The most common approach is to review the event with those involved within 48–72 hours after the event. This requires getting together in groups under the leadership of someone trained in such exercises. Typically, this entails restating exactly what has happened as well as sharing thoughts and emotions. Those involved are informed about common reactions to accidents or dramatic events. These measures are intended to minimize acute symptoms and make those involved more capable of dealing with their reactions in the time to come. One specific program is called Critical Incident Stress Management (CISM), where the purpose is to mitigate reactions after a critical incident so that people can return to work as soon as possible (Leonhardt and Vogt 2006). The program includes information, training, and support, and it has been used for different professionals in aviation including air traffic controllers and pilots (Leonhardt and Vogt 2006). Another benefit of conducting such group interventions is the identification of people in need of extra counseling and care. For those who need more support, there are a number of different types of individual therapy, such as cognitive behavioral therapy. This form of therapy contains an exposure part and provides a structured framework to deal with thoughts and emotions. Other cognitive behavioral methods emphasize assisting the person in dealing with anxiety. A different form of therapy consists of what is called "eye movement desensitization," which consists of having the patient visualizing the traumatic event while watching a moving stimulus.

Meta-analyses have found that therapy represents an efficient treatment of PTSD, and that up to 67% of those who complete the treatment no longer satisfy the criteria to be re-diagnosed with PTSD (Bradley et al. 2005). It is important to encourage affected individuals to keep working and maintain frequent exposure to the situation by, for example, returning to aviation. Studies have revealed that those who return to work are better off in the long term than those who choose to change professions, even for individuals who initially had similar symptoms.

8.4   PASSENGER REACTIONS

Most of the intended readers of this book love to fly, but some passengers may consider air travel stressful and best avoided. They may become argumentative or quarrelsome, risking a fine or imprisonment for their behavior, and pilots and cabin crew may be called upon to deal with them. The final part of this chapter will therefore address distressed and disorderly passengers.

8.4.1   Fear of Flying

Extreme fear of flying, or flight phobia, implies an exaggerated fear of flying compared to the real risk involved. Affected individuals travel by air in great discomfort or avoid it altogether. Some have to travel by air as a work requirement, in which case fear of flying can be particularly inconvenient. Fear of flying can also be a significant impediment to holiday arrangements. In a survey of a group of randomly selected Norwegian nationals, about one in two said they were never afraid of flying, while the remainder indicating varying degrees of discomfort (Ekeberg et al. 1989). A similar study conducted in 2002 after the terror act of September 11th resulted in almost identical prevalence numbers for fear of flying (Ekeberg et al. 2014). The participants were also asked about the situations that gave most reasons for concern when flying, and the most frequently mentioned situations were turbulence, unusual noises, and terrorism and hijacking (Ekeberg et al. 2014). The fact that the prevalence numbers did not increase could indicate that September 11th did not increase fear of flying, but that fearful passengers were more likely to attribute their fear to terrorism.

International studies indicate that between 10% and 40% of passengers are affected by fear of flying (the significant variation in this figure is probably due to phrasing of questions and the composition of the group surveyed). A Norwegian survey (Martinussen et al. 2011) asked participants: "To which degree are you afraid of flying?" The results are outlined in Table 8.2.

The group surveyed consisted of students as well as passengers surveyed at an airport in Northern Norway. The survey found no correlation between age and fear of flying; however, females were more likely to report fear of flying than males. Participants disclosing any form of discomfort during flight were asked about which factors caused the greatest amount of fear; commonly these were cabin movement, vibrations, noises, or turbulence announcements. Participants were also asked how

TABLE 8.2
Extent to Which the Survey's Participants Are
Afraid of Flying

	Total $N = 268$
Not afraid at all	56%
Sometimes a little afraid	29%
Always a little afraid	8%
Sometimes very afraid	4%
Always very afraid[a]	4%

[a] Combined category based on three alternatives, all involving very afraid.

they reacted to such situations. Typical reactions were palpitations and believing something was going to go wrong. In addition, many reported great attentiveness to aircraft noises and closely watching the behavior of cabin crew.

Even aviation personnel can develop a flight phobia. Although the prevalence of this problem is uncertain, one study examined a group of aviation personnel who were seeking support for various psychological problems. Fourteen percent reported fear of flying, a quarter of which said they had experienced an accident or known someone who had been involved in one. In addition to fear of flying, about half of the individuals in the group had been diagnosed with a mental illness such as depression (Medialdea and Tejada 2005). This would apply accordingly to passengers suffering from flight phobia; that is, secondary issues such as claustrophobia (fear of confined spaces) or other psychiatric disorders may be involved as well.

8.4.1.1   Symptoms

Symptoms of fear of flying are the same as other forms of anxiety, and may include palpitations, dizziness, chest pressure, paleness, cold sweat, and a strong need to use the bathroom. Physical symptoms are often accompanied by feelings of surreality, feeling faint, or thinking that one is about to go insane. Characteristics of phobias normally include high levels of anxiety in everyday situations, an absence of rational explanations to the response, a loss of control over the response, and insufficient coping strategies to deal with the response.

There are a number of methods created to measure fear of flying. Examples are the *Flight Anxiety Modality Questionnaire* (FAM) and the *Flight Anxiety Situations Questionnaire* (FAS) (Van Gerwen et al. 1999). In both questionnaires, the responders are asked to rate each item on a five-point Likert scale. Some questions (from FAM) relate to physical symptoms (1–3) and the second category is concerned with thought processes (4–6), as follows:

1. I am short of breath.
2. I feel dizzy, or I have the feeling that I'm going to faint.
3. I have the feeling that I'm going to choke.

4. I think the particular plane I am on will crash.
5. I attend to every sound or movement of the plane, and wonder if everything is fine.
6. I continuously pay attention to the faces and behavior of the cabin crew.

Such measuring instruments can be used to establish the extent to which someone is afraid of flying, and may also be used in research to study the effectiveness of treatments. It is also possible to employ physiological measurements (of, e.g., the subjects' heart rate) to complement the self-report.

8.4.1.2   What Is There to Be Afraid Of?

You may ask, what does someone suffering from flight phobia worry about? Normally, affected individuals are concerned about conditions outside their control, such as poor weather conditions, technical failures, terrorism, and human error (in pilots or flight controllers). In other cases, the source of worry is self-consciousness about one's own reactions and unusual behavior, such as fainting in the aircraft. Some find the whole experience leading up to a flight to be worse than the flight itself, including issues relating to check-in, queues, delays, and time-consuming security checks. On the other hand, air travel may enable positive experiences; however, this aspect has been studied to a lesser extent than the negative implications of air travel. The previously mentioned study of Norwegian students and passengers also assessed the joys of flying in addition to fear of flying (Martinussen et al. 2011). Positive emotions toward flying was negatively related to fear of flying as could be expected but it was also related to experienced stress at the airport and satisfaction with check-in and the security controls (Martinussen et al. 2011).

8.4.2   Treatment

The chosen course of treatment depends on whether fear of flying is the only problem, or if the person has other phobias, depression, or other mental illness. Studies show that people suffering from personality disorders benefit from standard treatments of flight anxiety (Van Gerwen et al. 2003). Thus, those suffering from mental illnesses should not avoid treatment for aviophobia; however, these individuals are unlikely to receive the full treatment required for separate disorders. A summary of treatment types revealed that most involved some form of mapping the individual's problem (Van Gerwen et al. 2004). Typically, treatment is of relatively short duration (1–3 days) and takes place in a group setting; the content usually consists of relaxation exercises, as well as some form of cognitive behavioral therapy. In most cases, therapy concludes with exposure to flying in flight simulators or real-world aircraft. Recently, a number of studies have emerged that use personal computers as a medium for exposure to flying (see, e.g., Rothbaum et al. 2006). These studies involve simulating a flight using visual, auditory, and physical stimuli (vibrations) combined with relaxation techniques, provisioning of a framework to structuring emotions and stopping undesired trains of thought.

When asked about which methods passengers use to help them relax, about 37% of passengers respond that they sometimes or often use alcohol to reduce anxiety related to flying. A total of 47% seek distractions and just below 10% use some form of medication. A recent longitudinal study of the long-term effects of cognitive behavioral therapy indicated that an increase in the use of adaptive coping strategies and a reduction of maladaptive coping strategies were associated with improvements 3 years after treatment (Busscher and Spinhoven 2016). Examples of adaptive coping mechanisms are putting things in perspective or attaching a positive meaning to the event. Maladaptive coping mechanisms involve catastrophizing, self-blame, or trying to avoid the event. Booklets and information have been developed to advise passengers suffering from fear of flying how to cope and prepare for a flight. These points are based on advice produced at a conference (Airborne et al. 2000) at which a number of flight phobia experts convened to discuss the topic (quoted in Van Gerwen et al. 2004). There are also a number of organizations that promote the study and treatment of flight anxiety (such as the Valk Foundation, accessible at http://www.valk.org), and both online treatments and apps are now available to people who suffer from fear of flying.

Advice to sufferers of fear of flying from Van Gerwen et al. (2004, p. 33) includes the following:

- Avoid caffeine, sugar, nicotine, and self-medication.
- Practice relaxation.
- Drink plenty of water and avoid alcohol. Alcohol does not decrease fear but increases it and contributes to dehydration.
- Pay attention to your breathing and regularly carry out your breathing exercises.
- Turbulence is uncomfortable, but safe when your seatbelt is fastened.
- Stop the "what ifs" and focus on "what is."
- Keep flying. Do not avoid it.
- Motivation is the key to change.
- Planes are designed and built to fly.
- Write on cards reminders of personal coping instructions that work for you.

8.4.3 THE PAINS AND PLEASURES OF AIR TRAVEL

After the September 11, 2001, attacks on the United States, many people avoided air travel for a while, causing passenger figures to plummet. The number of travelers had more or less rebounded by 2003; however, the number of Americans traveling abroad was still in decline (Swanson and McIntosh 2006). In a British survey, a large majority of respondents (85%) said the September 11 events did not influence their future travel plans (Gauld et al. 2003). Such terrorist attacks are probably regarded as isolated events, causing the majority of the population to think it will not happen to them. For some, however, this will be a source of concern, especially when combined with media attention on other health risks such as deep vein thrombosis and cardiovascular and infectious diseases, such as the recent emergence of Severe Acute Respiratory Syndrome (SARS). The flight-related increase in the occurrence of blood clots, for example, is extremely low except for individuals belonging to a particularly susceptible group (Owe 1998; Bendz 2002); however, there is often a difference between the real, objective risk that something bad will happen and the subjectively observed risk. There are also significant differences between people in terms of risk aversion. Typically, people are willing to take greater risks when in a position of control or influence, which is rarely the case in air travel unless the person in question is piloting the aircraft.

In addition, everyday events or factors may act as stressors; for example, the purpose of the trip itself, such as doing something one does not look forward to or leaving one's family for a long period of time. Other aspects include the trip to the airport, check-in, and security controls, of which the conditions are constantly changing and becoming more stringent. It may be difficult to estimate the amount of time the boarding process will take, and to decide whether delays will ensue. Sometimes, many different things will go wrong at the same time, causing the accumulation of various stressors. People also differ in relation to personality and coping techniques, and will therefore react in different ways to identical events, much in the same way that people react differently to work-related stress. In a British study, travelers were asked which factors led to anxiety, and the most common responses were delays (mentioned by 50% of respondents) and boarding the plane (mentioned by 42% of respondents) (McIntosh et al. 1998). In a more recent study, Norwegian passengers were asked about both the positives and the negatives of air travel (Martinussen et al. 2011). A total of 268 individuals participated in the survey, consisting in part of travelers and in part of individuals recruited at the University of Tromsø. Participants were asked how they usually experienced check-in and security controls. Twenty-four percent said they experienced check-in as either moderately or very stressful. In total, 11% of respondents reported dissatisfaction with the way check-in was conducted. When it came to security controls, 24% were dissatisfied with the way they were conducted and a total of 40% reported experiencing this aspect of air travel as moderately or very stressful. Those who felt unable to influence events and felt that information was lacking at the airport were likely to be more stressed during check-in and when going through security; these respondents also experienced lesser degrees of pleasure in relation to air travel, as well as greater degrees of anxiousness (Martinussen et al. 2011).

Participants were asked about the positive sides of air travel; 72% said they looked forward to it, and 56% reported excitement about being in an airport. In other words, most people see positive sides of air travel, although there are negative aspects as well.

Swanson and McIntosh (2006) have launched a model for stress related to air travel. The model describes various factors that may be considered demands or stressors passengers are exposed to. These factors involve check-in, security controls, the flight itself, and conditions in the cabin (i.e., poor air quality and limited space). The moderating variables are described as personality traits, coping mechanisms, and demographic variables such as gender. These variables may enhance or reduce the effects of stressors. The model also describes possible aftereffects of flight-related stress, such as physiological reactions, health complaints and aviophobia, and even anger and frustration. This model is similar to general stress models with the notable exception that it is not yet supported by much research, although the model itself is highly persuasive. The model can be extended to include resources that are thought to alleviate stress, examples of which may be access to information and influence (or control) over the situation.

8.4.4 UNRULY PASSENGER BEHAVIOR

At 10,000 feet, a female passenger attempts to open the rear exit door of an aircraft traveling from Zurich, Switzerland to Copenhagen, Denmark. Presumably, the woman is mentally ill and wants to take her own life. The cabin crew manages to overpower her, and she is handed over to the Copenhagen police force upon landing (*Dagbladet*, November 23, 2006). Another episode reported in the media involved a Norwegian male on a flight from Bangkok to Copenhagen who started to act in a rowdy manner (*Dagbladet*, November 13, 2003). The man was under the influence of alcohol and wanted to leave the aircraft. He was particularly loud, aggressive, and uncooperative. Several passengers got involved in the struggle to calm the man down, and a doctor on board gave him a sedative injection, which seemed to have little effect. The unruly passenger was finally brought under control and was strapped to his chair for the remainder of the flight, after which the Copenhagen police dealt with the ordeal. These are but a few examples of situations in which aircraft passengers display behavior that violates the rules and regulations of air travel. Presumably, the media only covers more serious events, leaving minor incidents unreported. Examples of the latter typically include verbal abuse such as insulting, harassing, or sexually charged statements to cabin crewmembers or fellow passengers.

Why did the woman want to leave the aircraft? Was she trying to take her own life, or was she simply unaware of her surroundings? Similarly, one may wonder what provoked the episode involving the heavily intoxicated male on the flight from Bangkok, and how alcohol affected the situation. In these types of scenarios, the consequences for the cabin crew and other passengers getting involved in or observing the incident must be considered. We will return to these questions after taking a closer look at the term "air rage."

8.4.4.1 What Is Air Rage?

Aggressive passengers or customers are not unique to aviation; they may be regarded generally as work-related violence, which occurs in many professions, including health-care services, education, and service industries. In education, students may threaten their teachers, send or pass on e-mails with inappropriate content, and, in a small number of cases, engage in physical violence. This chapter will only investigate work-related violence that is initiated by passengers (not by coworkers). The motivating factors to such incidents are often real or imaginary inadequacies in the service provided or failure to meet demands, such as issues with seat reservations or the provision of additional alcohol. In some cases, the passenger may object to given instructions, or refuse to accept current regulations pertaining to, for example, smoking or seat belts. The unique attribute of aviation is that a disorderly passenger cannot simply be "set off at the next stop" and that it is rather difficult to obtain additional assistance: As soon as the passengers have boarded and the aircraft taken off, the crew is left to handle problems on its own.

Generally, a distinction is made between the terms *air rage* and *unruly behavior or misconduct*. An unruly passenger normally refuses to accept regulations that apply aboard the aircraft. He or she may engage in threats, abusive language, and/or noisy and inappropriate behavior, and refuse to follow instructions given by crewmembers. However, a disorderly passenger remains nonviolent. The notion of air rage applies to cases that involve physical violence. Disorderly passengers and air rage is a problem worldwide, which, in the worst-case scenario, may be considered a safety threat. NASA investigations revealed that errors occurred in 15 of 152 cases in which one of the pilots had to get involved to subdue a disorderly passenger or was sought by cabin crew to help. Such errors included flying at the wrong altitude or choosing the wrong runway, all potentially dangerous situations. In addition to being a safety threat, air rage and unruly passengers often cause discomfort for the other passengers, cabin crew, and, potentially, the pilots. It may also necessitate additional landings and delays. In some cases, the situation may escalate from dealing with a disorderly passenger to dealing with air rage (i.e., the person ends up resorting to violence). In other cases, there can be few indications that there is something wrong, and a seemingly unprovoked attack on the crew may occur. An example of the latter was the case of a Norwegian Kato Air flight in 2004 from Narvik to Bodø (two cities in Northern Norway) in which a passenger attacked the pilots with an axe, and a full-blown disaster was only marginally avoided. The passenger was later sentenced to 15 years imprisonment. Such events may appear similar to terrorism; however, disorderly passengers and air rage are not considered to be politically or ideologically motivated.

8.4.4.2   How Frequently Does Air Rage Occur?

It is difficult to judge the extent of the problem, and whether or not it is on the rise, mainly because its registration has been insufficient in many countries. The phenomenon first gained widespread attention in the middle of the 1990s. There is great complexity in determining whether people started taking notice of the problem because occurrence rates were rising or because changes in the aviation industry were causing dissatisfaction in customers leading to a greater number of disorderly passengers. Currently, there is little empirical evidence available in this particular field. A possible explanation for this vacuum may be that it is difficult to define what constitutes unruly behavior (or air rage) and that the registration methods used by various airlines have not gone through the necessary standardization processes. An analysis of the available statistics revealed disparities between different airlines, although several reported an increase in air rage and disorderly behavior (Bor 1999). British Airways reported 266 occurrences during 1 year (1997–1998) in which a total of 41 million passengers were transported. The probability of witnessing or experiencing air rage thus seems quite small. However, there may be inadequacies in the reporting of these events; for example, it is fair to assume that only more serious events were reported. The International Air Transport Association (IATA) reported an increase in reported incidents in 2015 compared to 2014 where the numbers were one incident per 1205 flights and one per 9136 a year earlier (IATA 2016). The majority of incidents involved verbal abuse and failure to follow instructions, and 11% involved physical aggression toward other people or damage to the aircraft (IATA 2016).

8.4.4.3 What Causes Air Rage and Unruly Behavior?

There are a number of factors said to contribute to, or be associated with, disorderliness in passengers; however, a lack of data to support these claims is apparent, and conclusions are often based on information from secondary sources (such as the media). A study based on several hundred media reports on the issue found that essentially, there were three factors associated with disorderly or violent passengers: alcohol, nicotine deprivation, and mental illness (Anglin et al. 2003). These are all factors that can be amplified by environmental stressors, such as confined spaces, poor air quality, delays, and, perhaps, poor service. A typical example of air rage involves a male passenger with a history of violent behavior who chain smokes and consumes a large amount of alcohol daily. He continues drinking on board and is infuriated when refused the opportunity to smoke. The study estimated that alcohol was a contributing factor in 40% of cases (Anglin et al. 2003). Other studies based on reports from companies in the United States and Britain have found that alcohol was a contributing factor in, respectively, 43% and 50% of the reported cases (Connell et al. 1999). In nearly every other incident, the violent passenger had started drinking before boarding the flight. Although we have limited knowledge about how alcohol interacts with other factors, we can assume that it is unlikely to be the only factor. It is more likely that alcohol reduces the person's inhibitions and sense of judgment, which in a high-stress situation leads him or her to use aggressive behavior as a solution to problems.

Generally, there are little data available to describe typical characteristics of disorderly passengers: they may be traveling alone, a couple or a group traveling together. Sometimes, socioeconomically well-placed individuals, such as artists or lawyers, have been involved in incidents using verbal and physical abuse. Perhaps, such personality types are unaccustomed to taking orders or guidance from other people; they may not accept instructions from someone they perceive as of a lower rank than themselves. The cabin crew, on the other hand, has to alternate between servicing passengers and being responsible for onboard safety. To some passengers, this duality may be difficult to accept, as they only expect service and not instructions or commands.

The phenomenon of air rage and disorderly passengers may be better understood in light of general stress theory, with the addition of a number of contributing factors. The cause of disorderliness, then, lies in the exposure to a sequence of events, each of which acts as a source of frustration (delays, queuing, and security checks). In addition, this is combined with alcohol and a triggering event such as being refused to take carry-on luggage. Moreover, many people are anxious about flying to some extent, which may be a factor as well. In some cases, the cabin crew's behavior and communication with the disorderly individual can contribute to the incident developing in a negative direction. For example, raising one's voice to the individual may be necessary to make oneself heard in the cabin as there is usually considerable background noise; however, the upset individual may perceive the behavior as reproving and impolite.

8.4.4.4 What Can Be Done to Prevent Air Rage?

Airlines provide cabin crew with training in dealing with disorderly passengers, including worst-case scenarios that involve physically strapping passengers to their seats. Some companies practice zero-tolerance policies in the event of air rage, resulting in police prosecution and being denied future flights with the company. Another important factor is training cabin crew in how to manage frustrated and upset passengers in general. Naturally, crewmembers are required to respond to complaints and expressions of inconvenience in a polite and respectful manner. Providing information about delays and other irregularities is also important. Recognizing and preempting problems caused by passengers suffering from mental illness, or under the influence of alcohol, is part of the training. Crucial preventive measures include refusing intoxicated persons permission to board and limiting access to alcohol in airports and, not least, onboard. Training may also consist of learning how to calm a person down in a polite manner without causing the situation to escalate.

8.5   SUMMARY

This chapter has discussed individual differences in personality and mental health, and common ways in how people react to different stressors in life. We have established that when the experienced level of stress exceeds the amount the person is able to cope with, various emotional, cognitive, and physiological reactions emerge. These reactions are of significance to one's general health condition, work achievements, performance, and job satisfaction. Stress has both short-term and long-term effects on the individual, and it is important to be familiar with these effects for one's own sake and because most aviation professions demand significant cooperation with colleagues and others. The chapter has mostly related to persons working in aviation; however, passenger issues have been described to a certain extent.

8.6   OUTSIDE ACTIVITIES

- Take a look at the job demands–resources model (Figure 8.3). Try to outline what constitutes job demands for you in your current job and similarly job resources. What can be done to reduce job demands (both things that you can do and what can the organization do)? Are there possibilities for increasing or adding new job resources?
- Learn more about mental health. In most countries, the health authorities have information available on their Web pages, and sometimes also the local associations for medical doctors and psychologists. You can typically find information about different mental health disorders and types of treatment. See, for example, the U.S. Department of Health & Human Services: mentalhealth.gov

RECOMMENDED READINGS

Bor, R., Eriksen, C., Oakes, M., and Scragg, P. (Eds.). 2017. *Pilot Mental Health Assessment and Support. A Practitioner's Guide.* New York, NY: Routledge.

Bor, R. and Hubbard, T. (Eds.). 2006. *Aviation Mental Health: Psychological Implications for Air Transportation.* Aldershot, UK: Ashgate.

Bor, R. and Van Gerwen, L. (Eds.). 2003. *Psychological Perspectives on Fear of Flying.* Aldershot, UK: Ashgate.

REFERENCES

Aerospace Medical Association (AsMA). 2012. Pilot mental health: Expert working group recommendations. *Aviation, Space and Environmental Medicine* 83:1184–1185.

Aerospace Medical Association (AsMA). 2016. Pilot mental health: Expert working group recommendations—Revised 2015. *Aerospace Medicine and Human Performance* 87: 505–507.

Åkerstedt, T. 2007. Altered sleep/wake patterns and mental performance. *Physiology and Behavior* 90: 209–218.

Albuquerque, C. and Fonseca, M. 2017. Psychosocial stressors associated with being a pilot. In Bor, R., Eriksen, C., Oakes, M., and Scragg, P. (Eds.), *Pilot Mental Health Assessment and Support* (pp. 287–308). New York, NY: Routledge.

Allen, T.D., Herst, D.E.L., Bruck, C.S., and Sutton, M. 2000. Consequences associated with work-to-family conflict: A review and agenda for future research. *Journal of Occupational Health Psychology* 5: 278–308.

American Psychiatric Association (APA). 2013. *Diagnostics and Statistical Manual of Mental Disorders*, 5th ed. Arlington, VA: American Psychiatric Publishing.

Anglin, L., Neves, P., Giesbrecht, N., and Kobus-Matthews, M. 2003. Alcohol-related air rage: From damage control to primary prevention. *The Journal of Primary Prevention* 23: 283–297.

Barry, M. and Jenkins, R. 2007. *Implementing Mental Health Promotion.* New York, NY: Churchill Livingstone.

Bartone, P.T. 2006. Resilience under military operational stress: Can leaders influence hardiness? *Military Psychology* 18 (Suppl): 131–148.

BEA (Bureau d'Enquetes et d'Analyses pour la securite l'aviation civile). 2016. *Final Report of the March 2015 Accident of Airbus A320, D-AIPX.* Retrieved from: https://www.bea. aero/uploads/tx_elydbrapports/BEA2015-0125.en-LR.pdf

Bendz, B. 2002. Flyreiser og venøs trombose [Air travel and deep vein thrombosis]. *Journal of Norwegian Medical Association* 122: 1579–1581.

Block, J. 1995. A contrarian view of the five-factor approach to personality description. *Psychological Bulletin* 117: 187–215.

Bor, R. 1999. Unruly passenger behaviour and in-flight violence. A psychological perspective. In Jensen, R., Cox, B., Callister, J., and Lavis, R. (Eds.), *Proceedings of the Tenth International Symposium on Aviation Psychology.* Columbus, OH: Ohio State University.

Bourgeois-Bougrine, S., Carbon, P., Gounelle, C., Mollard, R., and Coblentz, A. 2003. Perceived fatigue for short and long-haul flights: A survey of 739 airline pilots. *Aviation, Space, and Environmental Medicine* 74: 1072–1077.

Bradley, R., Greene, J., Russ, E., Dutra, L., and Westen, D. 2005. A multidimensional meta-analysis for psychotherapy for PTSD. *American Journal of Psychiatry* 162: 214–227.

Busscher, B. and Spinhoven, P. 2016. Cognitive coping as a mechanism of change in cognitive–behavioral therapy for fear of flying: A longitudinal study with 3-year follow-up. *Journal of Clinical Psychology* 72: 1–12.

Connell, L., Mellone, V.J., and Morrison, R.M. 1999. Cabin crew safety information article. In Jensen, R., Cox, B., Callister, J., and Lavis, R. (Eds.), *Proceedings of the Tenth International Symposium on Aviation Psychology.* Columbus, OH: Ohio State University.

Costa, G. 1996. The impact of shift and night work on health. *Applied Ergonomics* 27: 9–16.

Costa, G. 2003. Factors influencing health of workers and tolerance to shift work. *Theoretical Issues in Ergonomics Science* 4: 263–288.

Costa, G., Sartori, S., and Åkerstedt, T. 2006. Influence of flexibility and variability of working hours on health and well-being. *Chronobiology International* 23: 1125–1137.

Costa, P.T. and McCrae, R.R. 1997. Personality trait structure as a human universal. *American Psychologist* 52: 509–516.

Demerouti, E., Geurts, S.A., Bakker, A., and Euwema, M. 2004. The impact of shiftwork on work-home conflict, job attitudes and health. *Ergonomics* 47: 987–1002.

Digman, J.M. 1990. Personality structure: Emergence of the five-factor model. *Annual Review of Psychology* 41: 417–440.

EASA. 2016. *Follow-up of Germanwings Flight 9525 Accident*. Retrieved on November 7, 2016 from: https://www.easa.europa.eu/easa-and-you/aircrew-and-medical/follow-up -germanwings-flight-9525-accident#0

Ekeberg, O. I., Fauske, B., and Berg-Hansen, B. 2014. Norwegian airline passengers are not more afraid of flying after the terror act of September 11. The flight anxiety, however, is significantly attributed to acts of terrorism. *Scandinavian Journal of Psychology* 55:464–468.

Ekeberg, Ø., Seeberg, I., and Ellertsen, B.B. 1989. The prevalence of flight anxiety in Norway. *Nordic Journal of Psychiatry* 43: 443–448.

Eriksen, C. and Bor, R. 2017. Promoting good psychological health amongst pilots: Coping strategies for identifying and managing stress to reduce risk of mental health problems and improve performance at work. In Bor, R., Eriksen, C., Oakes, M., and Scragg, P. (Eds.), *Pilot Mental Health Assessment and Support* (pp. 309–324). New York, NY: Routledge.

Evans-Lacko, S., Little K., Meltzer H., Rose, D., Rhydderch, D., Henderson, C., and Thornicroft, G. 2010. Development and psychometric properties of the Mental Health Knowledge Schedule. *Canadian Journal of Psychiatry* 55: 440–448.

Folkard, S. and Tucker, P. 2003. Shift work, safety, and productivity. *Occupational Medicine* 53: 95–101.

Frankenhaeuser, M. 1991. The psychophysiology of sex differences as related to occupational status. In Frankenaeuser, M., Lundberg, U., and Chesney, M. (Eds.), *Women, Work, and Health. Stress and Opportunities* (pp. 39–61). New York, NY: Plenum Press.

Friborg, O., Barlaug, D., Martinussen, M., Rosenvinge, J.H., and Hjemdal, O. 2005. Resilience in relation to personality and intelligence. *International Journal of Methods in Psychiatric Research* 14: 29–42.

Gauld, J., Hirst, M., McIntosh, I.B., Swanson, V. 2003. Attitudes to air travel after terrorist events. *British Travel Health Association Journal* 3: 62–67.

Goldberg, L.R. 1993. The structure of phenotypic personality traits. *American Psychologist* 48: 26–34.

Goldberg, L.R., Johnson, J.A., Eber, H.W., Hogan, R., Ashton, M.C., Cloninger, C.R., and Gough, H.C. 2006. The International Personality Item Pool and the future of public-domain personality measures. *Journal of Research in Personality* 40: 84–96.

International Air Transport Association (IATA). 2016. Collaboration needed to stem unruly passenger incidents. Press release no 53. Retrieved on November 28, 2016 from: http://www.iata.org/pressroom/pr/Pages/2016-09-28-01.aspx

Jeronimus, B.F., Kotov, R., Riese, H., and Ormel, J. 2016. Neuroticism's prospective association with mental disorders halves after adjustment for baseline symptoms and psychiatric history, but the adjusted association hardly decays with time: A meta-analysis on 59 longitudinal/prospective studies with 443 313 participants. *Psychological Medicine* 46: 2883–2906.

Johansen, R.B., Laberg, J.C., and Martinussen, M. 2014. Military identity as predictor of perceived military competence and skills. *Armed Forces and Society* 40: 521–543.

Karasek, R.A. 1979. Job demands, job decision latitude, and mental strain: Implications for job redesign. *Administrative Science Quarterly* 24: 285–308.

Karasek, R.A. and Theorell, T. 1990. *Healthy Work: Stress, Productivity, and the Reconstruction of Working Life*. New York, NY: Basic Books.

Kitterød, R.H. 2005. *Han jobber, hun jobber, de jobber. Arbeidstid blant par av småbarnsforeldre [He works, she works, they work. Work hours among couples with small children]*. Oslo, Norway: Statistics Norway.

Klein, D.E., Brüner, H., and Holtman, H. 1970. Circadian rhythm of pilot's efficiency, and effects of multiple time zone travel. *Aerospace Medicine* 41: 125–132.

Klein, G.A. 1995. A recognition-primed decision making (RPD) model of rapid decision making. In Klein, G.A., Orasanu, J., Calderwook, R., and Zsambok, C.E. (Eds.), *Desicion Models in Action: Models and Methods* (pp. 138–147). Norwood, NJ: Ablex Publishing Corporation.

Knutsson, A. 2003. Health disorders of shift workers. *Occupational Medicine* 53: 103–108.

Kotov, R., Gamez, W., Schmidt, F., and Watson, D. 2010. Linking "big" personality traits to anxiety, depressive, and substance use disorders: A meta-analysis. *Psychological Bulletin* 136: 768–821.

Lazarus, R. 1976. *Pattern of Adjustment*. McGraw-Hill: New York.

Leiter, M. and Maslach, C. 2005. *Banishing Burnout. Six Strategies for Improving Your Relationship with Work*. San Francisco, CA: Jossey-Bass.

Leonhardt, J. and Vogt, J. 2006. *Critical Incident Stress Management in Aviation*. Aldershot, UK: Ashgate Publishing.

Lundberg, U. 2005. Stress hormones in health and illness: The roles of work and gender. *Psychoneuroendocrinology* 30: 1017–1021.

Lundberg, U. and Frankenhaeuser, M. 1999. Stress and workload of men and women in high ranking positions. *Journal of Occupational Health Psychology* 4: 142–151.

Lundberg, U., Mårdberg, B., and Frankenhaeuser, M. 1994. The total workload of male and female white collar workers as related to age, occupational level, and number of children. *Scandinavian Journal of Psychology* 35: 315–327.

Martinussen, M., Gundersen, E., and Pedersen, R. 2011. Predicting fear of flying and positive emotions towards air travel. *Aviation Psychology and Applied Human Factors* 1: 70–74.

Martinussen, M. and Richardsen, A.M. 2006. Job demands, job resources, and burnout among air traffic controller. *Aviation, Space, and Environmental Medicine* 77: 422–428.

Martinussen, M, Richardsen, A.M., and Burke, R.J. 2007. Job demands, job resources and burnout among police officers. *Journal of Criminal Justice* 35: 239–249.

Maslach, C. and Jackson, S.E. 1981. The measurement of experienced burnout. *Journal of Occupational Behavior* 2: 99–113.

Maslach, C. and Jackson, S.E. 1986. *Maslach Burnout Inventory Manual*, 2nd ed. Palo Alto, CA: Consulting Psychologists Press, Inc.

Maslach, C., Schaufeli, W., and Leiter, M.P. 2001. Job burnout. *Annual Review of Psychology* 52: 397–422.

McIntosh, I.B., Swanson, V., Power, K.G., Raeside, F., and Dempster, C. 1998. Anxiety and health problems related to air travel. *Journal of Travel Medicine* 5: 198–204.

Medialdea, J. and Tejada, F.R. 2005. Phobic fear of flying in aircrews: Epidemiological aspects and comorbidity. *Aviation, Space, and Environmental Medicine* 76: 566–568.

Megdal, S.P., Kroenke, C.H., Laden, F., Pukkala, E., and Schernhammer, E.S. 2005. Night work and breast cancer risk: A systematic review and meta-analysis. *European Journal of Cancer* 41: 2023–2032.

Ng, T.W.H., Sorensen, K.L., and Eby, L.T. 2006. Locus of control at work: A meta-analysis. *Journal of Organizational Behavior* 27: 1057–1087.

Orth, U. and Wieland, E. 2006. Anger, hostility, and posttraumatic stress disorder in trauma-exposed adults: A meta-analysis. *Journal of Consulting and Clinical Psychology* 74: 698–706.

Orasanu, J. 1997. Stress and naturalistic decision making: Strengthening the weak links. In Flin, R., Salas, E., Strub, M., and Martin, L. (Eds.), *Decision Making Under Stress. Emerging Themes and Applications* (pp. 43–66). Aldershot, UK: Ashgate.

Østlyngen, A., Storjord, T., Stellander, B., and Martinussen, M. 2003. En undersøkelse av total arbeidsbelastning og tilfredshet for psykologer i Norge [A survey of total workload and work satisfaction among psychologists in Norway]. *Journal of the Norwegian Psychological Association* 40: 570–581.

Owe, J. O. 1998. Helsemessige problemer hos flypassasjerer [Health problems in airline passengers]. *The Journal of the Norwegian Medical Association* 118:3623–3627.

Ozer, E.J., Best, S.R., Lipsey, T.L., Weiss, D.S. 2003. Predictors of posttraumatic stress disorder and symptoms in adults: A meta-analysis. *Psychological Bulletin* 129: 52–73.

Pallesen, S. 2006. Søvn [Sleep]. In Eid, J. and Johnsen, B.J. (Eds.), *Operativ Psykologi [Operational Psychology]* (pp. 196–215). Bergen, Norway: Fagbokforlaget.

Perälä, J., Suvisaari, J., Saarni, S.I., Kuoppasalmi, K., Isometsä, E., Pirkola, S., Partonen T., et al. 2007. Lifetime prevalence of psychotic and bipolar I disorders in a general population. *Archives of General Psychiatry* 64: 19–28.

Richardsen, A.M. and Martinussen, M. 2006. Måling av utbrenthet: Maslach Burnout Inventory [Measuring burnout: The Maslach Burnout Inventory]. *Journal of the Norwegian Psychological Association* 43: 1179–1181.

Roberts, B.W., Walton, K., and Viechtbauer, W. 2006. Patterns of mean-level change in personality traits across the life course: A meta-analysis of longitudinal studies. *Psychological Bulletin* 132: 1–25.

Rosenman, R.H. and Friedman, M. 1974. Neurogenic factors in pathogenesis of coronary heart disease. *Medical Clinics of North-America* 58: 269–279.

Rothbaum, B.O., Anderson, P., Zimand, E., Hodges, L., Lang, D., and Wilson, J. 2006. Virtual reality exposure therapy and standard (in-vivo) exposure therapy in the treatment for the fear of flying. *Behavior Therapy* 37: 80–90.

Sackett, D.L., Rosenberg, W.M., Gray, J.A., Haynes, R.B., and Richardson, W.S. 1996. Evidence based medicine: What it is and what it isn't. *British Medical Journal* 312(7023): 71–72.

Schaufeli, W.B. and Bakker, A. 2004. Job demands, job resources, and their relationship with burnout and engagement: A multi-sample study. *Journal of Organizational Psychology* 25: 293–315.

Schmitt, D.P., Realo, A., Voracek, M., and Allik, J. 2008. Why can't a man be more like a woman? Sex differences in Big Five personality traits across 55 cultures. *Journal of Personality and Social Psychology* 94: 168–182.

Schultz, M.S., Cowan, P.A., Pape Cowan, C., and Brennan, R.T. 2004. Coming home upset: Gender, marital satisfaction, and the daily spillover of workplace experience into couple interactions. *Journal of Family Psychology* 18: 250–263.

Seery, M.D., Holman, E.A., and Silver, R.C. 2010. Whatever does not kill us: Cumulative lifetime adversity, vulnerability, and resilience. *Journal of Personality and Social Psychology* 99: 1025–1041.

Selye, H. 1976. *The Stress of Life*. New York, NY: McGraw Hill.

Silvera, D., Martinussen, M., and Dahl, T.I. 2001. The Tromsø Social Intelligence Scale, a self-report measure of social intelligence. *Scandinavian Journal of Psychology* 42: 313–319.

Swanson, V. and McIntosh, I.B. 2006. Psychological stress and air travel: An overview of psychological stress affecting airline passengers. In Bor, R. and Hubbard, T. (Eds.), *Aviation Mental Health: Psychological Implications for Air Transportation* (pp. 13–26). Aldershot, UK: Ashgate.

Terracciano, A., Costa, P.T., and McCrae, R.R. 2006. Personality plasticity after age 30. *Personality and Psychology Bulletin* 32: 999–1009.

Tüchsen, F., Hannerz, H., and Burr, H. 2007. A 12 year prospective study of circulatory disease among Danish shift workers. *Occupational Environmental Medicine* 63: 451–455.

Ursin, R. 1996. *Søvn: En lærebok om søvnfysiologi og søvnsykdommer [Sleep: A Textbook on Sleep Physiology and Sleep pathology].* Oslo, Norway: Cappelen Akademisk Forlag.

Van Gerwen, L.J., Delorme, C., Van Dyck, R., and Spinhoven, P. 2003. Personality pathology and cognitive-behavioral treatment of fear of flying. *Journal of Behavior Therapy and Experimental Psychiatry* 34: 171–189.

Van Gerwen, L.J., Diekstra, R.F.W., Arondeus, J.M., and Wolfger, R. 2004. Fear of flying treatment programs for passengers: An international update. *Travel Medicine and Infectious Disease* 2: 27–35.

Van Gerwen, L.J., Spinhoven, P., Van Dyck, R., and Diekstra, R.F.W. 1999. Construction and psychometric characteristics of two self-report questionnaires for the assessment of fear of flying. *Psychological Assessment* 11: 146–158.

Waage, S., Pallesen, S., and Bjorvatn, B. 2006. Skiftarbeid og søvn [Shift work and sleep]. *Journal of the Norwegian Psychological Association* 44: 428–433.

Westmann, M. and Etzion, D. 1995. Crossover of stress, strain and resources from one spouse to another. *Journal of Organizational Behavior* 16: 169–181.

World Health Organization (WHO). 2013. *Mental Health Action Plan 2013-2020.* Geneva, Switzerland: Author. Retrieved from: http://apps.who.int/iris/bitstream/10665/89966/1/9789241506021_eng.pdf?ua=1

World Health Organization (WHO). 2016. *ICD-10: International Statistical Classification of Diseases and Related Health Problems.* Geneva, Switzerland: Author. Retrieved from: http://apps.who.int/classifications/icd10/browse/2016/en#/V

Yoshimasu, K. 2001. Relation of type A behavior pattern and job-related psychosocial factors to non-fatal myocardial infarction: A case-control study of Japanese male workers and women. *Psychosomatic Medicine* 63: 797–804.

9 Culture, Organizations, and Leadership

9.1 INTRODUCTION

This chapter discusses organizational and cultural factors and how these factors influence people working in aviation. The aviation industry is an international business in which individuals with different cultural backgrounds must work together to make sure that aircraft arrive at their destination in a safe and timely manner. Communication problems can lead to irritation and disagreement and may even have serious safety repercussions. Communication and coordination are always demanding, especially when people have different cultural backgrounds, genders, and languages. Toward the end of this chapter, we discuss organizational changes and leadership and how these influence employees and the jobs that need to be done.

9.2 DO ORGANIZATIONAL ISSUES PLAY A ROLE IN ACCIDENTS?

In the past decades, a number of significant accidents have occurred, such as the 1986 meltdown at the nuclear power station in Chernobyl, the explosion at the North Sea Piper Alpha oil rig in 1988, and, more recently, the space shuttle *Columbia* disaster (2003). These accidents have in common that organizational factors were mentioned as contributing causes (Pidgeon and O'Leary 2000). The constructs of culture or safety culture are often mentioned as part of an explanation of what causes accidents or problems within the organization.

In several preceding chapters, we have focused on individuals and individual differences. This has included selection and training as well as their importance to a person's performance. In this chapter, we will look at organizational issues and aspects of the system that may be significant for how a person acts and, not least, the consequences of these actions for safety.

Major accidents, whether they are plane crashes or nuclear disasters, have tremendous human, economic, and environmental consequences. Thus, attempting to unveil the causes of accidents is not something new. Wiegmann et al. (2004) describe various historical stages in how attempts have been made to explain such accidents. The first stage (technical period) was distinguished by rapid technological development, during which investigators looked for inadequacies and outright flaws in technical systems. In the next phase, focus shifted toward human error (period of human error), and investigators sought to find errors in the human operator. This was followed by the sociotechnical stage, where the interface between human operators and technology was examined. In the final phase, which the authors labeled the organizational culture period, individuals are no longer regarded as operators of machinery isolated from the world at large, but rather as workers in a team within a given cultural context.

9.3   WHAT IS CULTURE?

The term "culture" has been associated with organizations since the early 1980s. There are about as many definitions of culture as there are publications about it. By "organizational culture," one normally means, somewhat inaccurately, "the way things are done around here." A more formal definition can be found in the book on organizational culture by Bang (1995, p. 23): "Organizational culture is the set of commonly shared norms, values, and perceived realities which evolve in an organization as its members interact with each other and their surroundings." Schein (1996, p. 236) defines the term as the "set of shared, taken for granted implicit assumptions that a group holds, and that determines how it perceives, thinks about, and reacts to various environments." These definitions differ in the sense that the former describes how the culture takes shape (i.e., through interaction), whereas the latter describes its effect on the members of the group.

There are also a number of other related terms, such as *climate*. Many articles and empirical studies use these terms interchangeably—that is, without clarifying their differences. Thus, scientists studying these phenomena are mapping approximately the same thing, although they appear to use different constructs for what these things are (Mearns and Flin 1999 provide a summary).

Schein (1990) considers climate to be a manifestation and measurable aspect of culture. Thus, culture is a deeper phenomenon that is not easily charted or categorized. Others say that although culture is what is shared, or common, for members, climate is a kind of "average" of the group members' experience—preferably the interpersonal relationships within the organization. The last word has hardly been spoken on this matter. In part, it is likely that the constructs have different histories and associated measurement techniques; however, the subjects of these studies are presumably overlapping phenomena. Climate is usually measured using standardized scales—an approach critics label as insufficient to get hold of the culture (see, e.g., Schein 1990). These critics suggest that methodologies such as interviews and observations are the preferred alternatives. Most empirical studies of culture, however, have used questionnaires to measure the construct.

As it relates to definitions of culture, the term "organization" applies to both businesses (e.g., airlines) and groups composed in different ways, such as pilots (a profession) or subgroups within a business (e.g., women or technicians). It is common to study national cultures—that is, the extent to which differences exist between nations. In aviation, therefore, we may assume that individuals are affected by several cultures: national, professional, and company (the airline for which the person works) cultures. Cultures may develop in many different social systems as people interact over time. According to Schein (1990), the conditions necessary for cultural development include that the individuals must have worked together for a long enough time to have experienced and shared important problems. They must have had the opportunity to solve these problems and observe the effect of implemented solutions. Last, but not least, the group or organization must have taken in new members who have been socialized into the way the group thinks, feels, and solves problems. The advantage of having a culture is that it makes events more predictable and gives things meaning, which may reduce anxiety in group members (Schein 1990).

Subcultures, which may be in conflict or support each other, can also form within an organization. They may be based on profession, workplace (sea vs. land), gender, or age. In the wake of corporate mergers, subcultures can form based on the formerly separate companies. In conflicts between subgroups, each side will typically view the other from a polarized, black-and-white perspective: "They are bad. We are good—we have the correct values." One explanation for the rise of such conflicts may be that groups have a need to preserve their social identity and will defend themselves against those who want to destroy or threaten their culture (Bang 1995). However, when such conflicts are allowed to thrive, they can sometimes be devastating for an organization, with harmful consequences for the well-being and health of individuals in the worst-case scenario. Subcultures arise in most organizations, and it is probably naïve to think that conflicts will never arise between them. Presumably, how the organization and its leadership manage such conflicts would be more important than preventing their rise.

9.4 NATIONAL CULTURE

Aviation is, in almost every respect, an international industry. This forces companies and individuals to interact with people from other cultures, who often have a language other than English as their first language. National culture affects the way people communicate and act. The most popular model and method for studying these national differences are based on Geert Hofstede's questionnaire for work-related values (Hofstede 1980, 2001). Hofstede developed the measurement instrument in connection with an extensive study of IBM employees in 66 countries conducted from 1967 to 1973. Participants noted the importance or significance of given values—that is, the extent to which they agreed or disagreed with the statements. The questions were placed in four scales (power-distance [PD], uncertainty-avoidance [UAV], individualism-collectivism [IND], and masculinity-femininity [MAS]). Descriptions of these with corresponding sample statements are given in Table 9.1. Hofstede later added two dimensions to the original four which included *long-term orientation* versus *short-term normative orientation* (preference for tradition vs. change) and *indulgence* versus *restraint* (enjoying life vs. strict social norms) (Hofstede et al. 2010).

Other scientists have used this measurement instrument in corresponding cross-cultural studies, and a reasonable amount of support for these four dimensions has been established. However, the instrument has been criticized, notably for its low internal consistency as to the different scales (Hofstede 2002; Spector and Cooper 2002). Additional studies using other types of measurement instruments have discovered other dimensions important to multicultural research such as cultural values, saving face, and how cultures express emotions and deal with conflicts (see Strauch 2010 for an overview). Hofstede's study is nonetheless both impressive and important because of the great number of countries and individuals that participated and because it facilitates comparisons between his data and other findings.

TABLE 9.1

Hofstede's Scales for Measuring National Culture

	What Does It Measure?	Sample Question
Power-distance (PD)	Denotes the degree to which power is unequally distributed between managers and subordinates and the extent to which this is accepted. Low PD values have been recorded in Austria, Israel, and the Scandinavian countries; high PD levels have been found in the Philippines and Mexico.	How often are employees afraid to express disagreement with their managers?
Uncertainty-avoidance (UAV)	Denotes the extent to which members of a culture feel threatened or anxious due to uncertainty and unpredictable situations. Countries including Greece, Portugal, and several Latin American countries report high levels of UAV; the United States, Singapore, Sweden, and Denmark report low UAVs.	How often do you feel nervous and tense at work?
Individualism-collectivism (IND)	The extent to which focus is on the individual (i.e., the individual's rights and responsibilities vs. the group's). High levels of individualism are found in Western nations such as the United States; several countries in Asia have low scores.	How important is it that you fully use your skills and abilities on the job?
Masculinity-femininity (MAS)	Measures the extent to which the culture emphasizes efficiency and competition versus more social (feminine) values. Countries with high femininity scores include the Scandinavian countries; Japan and some nations in Southern Europe and Latin America have low scores.	How important is it to have security of employment?

Source: Based on Hofstede, G. 1980. *Culture's Consequences: International Differences in Work-Related Values.* Beverly Hills, CA: Sage.

A study by Merritt (2000) that included almost 10,000 pilots from 19 countries revealed that two of the four dimensions (IND and PD) were replicable, whereas there were issues with some of the original questions for masculinity and UAV. However, a clear correspondence was present between Hofstede's ranking of countries according to cultural dimensions and the scores of pilots from the various countries. In addition, there were some differences between pilots as a group and the IBM employees used as a reference by Hofstede. For example, pilots had higher PD than Hofstede's group, underlining aspects of the piloting profession in which a clear-cut hierarchy (i.e., between captains and first officers) exists and is generally accepted.

A study by Sherman et al. (1997) found differences between countries in terms of how pilots regard rules and procedures, the usefulness of automation, and the extent to which they accepted a definitive hierarchy (chain of command) between captains and first officers.

In another study of military pilots from 14 NATO countries, the values on Hofstede's scales were compared to accident statistics for those countries (Soeters and Boer 2000). Data were collected over a 5-year period (1988–1992), and the number of lost planes per 10,000 flight hours was used to describe the accident ratio. This number was then correlated with the national values for the four cultural dimensions. Three out of the four dimensions were significantly correlated with results for IND ($r = -0.55$), PD ($r = 0.48$), and UAV ($r = 0.54$) (Soeters and Boer 2000). There was no significant correlation between the masculinity index and accident ratio. Correlations increased when accidents due to mechanical failure were removed. The numbers thus indicate greater accident rates in countries that have low individualism scores and high PD and UAV scores.

The results are interesting; however, it is important to keep in mind that the number of countries involved was only $N = 14$ because the nations (not the pilots) were the subjects of the study. In other words, the correlations are based on a fairly small sample. In addition, a correlation is not the same as causality. Many other factors vary among countries, and these factors may cause the observed variations in the number of accidents. In addition, culture was not measured in the military pilots, but the results from Hofstede's study were used. Therefore, it is possible that figures are slightly different from what they would have been if culture had been measured in military pilots for the same time frame in which the accident statistics were collected. However, the study indicates that cultural factors and how they relate to accidents may be worth further investigation.

A third study (Li et al. 2007) compared accident statistics and accident causes from India, Taiwan, and the United States. A total of 523 accidents, including a combined 1762 cases of human error, were investigated. The study summarized results from former accident surveys that used the HFACS system (Wiegmann and Shappell 2003) to classify errors. This system is based on Reason's model, which is discussed in greater detail in Chapter 11. The study found significant differences among countries in what were reported as causes. Organizational causes were reported more frequently in Taiwan and India (countries with high PD and low individualism scores) than in the United States (Li et al. 2007). This suggests a hierarchy in which employees expect to be told what to do (to a greater extent than in Western nations) and collective decisions are preferred to individual decisions. The authors see this aspect as a possible explanation for more frequent reporting of organizational errors. There is less spontaneous feedback in the system by the means of open discussion, and subordinates have less authority and autonomy in decision-making and, perhaps, in correcting errors and flaws. The same authors have later suggested that the design of modern flight decks has a Western bias (low PD) where the design and procedures are not congruent with Asian mental models. This may contribute to or worsen failures in crew resource management (CRM) (Harris and Li 2008).

A review by Strauch (2010) of cultural factors as causal factors in transportation accidents indicated that cultural factors may explain team errors, especially in high workload and high stress operations based on both studies from aviation and marine operations. Many of the included studies did, however, suffer from methodological shortcomings including failure to control for other differences between countries besides cultural factors (Strauch 2010).

9.4.1 PROBLEMS RELATING TO THE STUDY OF CULTURAL DIFFERENCES

Studying national differences in culture or, for that matter, other aspects is a complicated job. Completing the study or survey in approximately the same way in vastly different countries represents one of the challenges. For example, is it possible to sample participants in a similar way, and is the same procedure used in all the countries included in the study? The nature of the matter is that the more different the countries are, the more difficult it becomes to complete such a task. There may be different regulations as to the available registries of the target group and whether permission will be granted to extract information from these groups. For example, comparing nurses from the Netherlands to Malaysian pilots would hardly make a good basis for attributing potential findings to cultural differences alone. Ideally, the groups in question should be as similar as possible, even though researchers typically have to admit that, in practice, it is impossible to complete a survey in exactly the same way in all countries. Greater similarity between groups (in terms of other variables) generates a greater degree of certainty to conclusions that differences are due to cultural factors.

Another issue is represented by the challenge of translating questionnaires between different languages. Even though a substantial amount of effort is put into translations, a statement may convey a different meaning in another language, or certain words and expressions may not exist in the target language or correspond to the original one. Often, a translation is made from the original language to the target language (e.g., English to Norwegian). Then, someone else who is also proficient in both languages translates the text back into the original language (in this case, English). Finally, the two English versions are compared, and at this point, ambiguities in the translators' efforts and what needs to be adjusted become clear. The most important point here is that a perfect, word-for-word translation is not necessarily desirable; the important thing is to preserve meaning. Finally, issues may arise in cross-cultural studies because people from different cultures have different response styles. This means that some cultures may have a greater tendency to agree to a specific statement; in other cultures, opinion is expressed more freely and the extreme ends of the scale are used to a greater extent.

9.5 PROFESSIONAL CULTURE

Many occupations or professions have strong cultural identities. This applies to psychologists, air traffic controllers, and pilots, to mention but a few examples. Often, there is fierce competition to be selected and successfully complete the required (and often extensive) education. Upon completion of training, many people within the profession join powerful unions, which act to preserve the rights and interests of members. Some unions offer members sponsored education to maintain or build additional skills; they also typically provide guidelines for ethical behavior within the profession. Thus, unions help to socialize new members into the group (profession) by exercising control over the members to some extent. Professionals, including pilots, psychologists, and physicians, are often highly enthusiastic and proud workers. They will make every effort to be successful, and few people quit the profession after having entered the work force. On the other hand, a strong professional culture can give individuals a false sense of invulnerability and disregard for their own limitations, according to Helmreich and Merritt (1998). Some people may be aware of various human limitations in general, but unaware of this applying to them (a form of unrealistic optimism).

A study by Helmreich and Merritt (1998, p. 35) revealed that a large proportion of pilots and physicians strongly believed that they were able to do their job just as well in below-average conditions—that is, that equally sound judgments were made in an emergency compared to under normal conditions or that personal issues were put on hold while working. There were also some differences between the groups; 60% of doctors declared that they still worked efficiently when tired, compared to only 30% of pilots. Together, the doctors' perceptions were somewhat less realistic than the pilots'. What caused this distinction is not yet clear. However, the long-term focus on human factors in aviation may have made its impact. For example, pilots must complete mandatory CRM courses, whereas this is relatively new to medical professions.

Within a profession, there may be subgroups with which an individual feels more or less associated. Subgroups may be based on specialization, workplace, and/or gender. Examples include military versus civilian pilots or clinical psychologists versus psychology professors.

One study examined cultural changes in a major Norwegian airline, with a sample of 190 pilots (Mjøs 2002). Significant differences were found between the scores for this group and national norms based on Hofstede's figures. The greatest difference was found for the masculinity index, where pilots scored much higher than expected.

An international study of flight controllers from Singapore, New Zealand, and Canada investigated how they perceived their work environment (Shouksmith and Taylor 1997). The idea was that there would be greater differences between flight controllers from an Eastern culture compared to the two Western countries. The flight controllers were asked about what they considered stressful in their work environment, and many similarities were found. For example, flight controllers from all three countries mentioned technical limitations, periods of high traffic, and fear of causing accidents among the top five most important sources of stress.

On the other hand, Singaporean flight controllers also mentioned problems with local management in the top five, whereas the two remaining groups mentioned the general working environment as a top-five stressor. The authors attribute this difference partly to cultural factors such as higher PD in Asia compared to Western nations, causing more severe implications when disagreements arise between subordinates and management. Even external environmental factors may explain some of the differences; for example, more frequently occurring bad weather in Canada could have led flight controllers to mention this factor as one of the most significant work-related stressors.

9.6   ORGANIZATIONAL CULTURE

As in national and professional cultures, there may be cultural variations between airlines operating in a country. In a Norwegian study including three airlines (Mjøs 2004), significant differences were found in three of the four Hofstede dimensions

(PD, MAS, and UAV). The participating pilots ($N = 440$) were also asked to report any errors made during the past year as part of the survey. A total of 10 indicators, such as forgetting important checklist points or choosing the wrong taxiway, were included. For each pilot, a total error score was calculated and correlated with the stated cultural dimensions (PD, UAV, IND, and MAS). A strong association ($r = 0.54$) was found between PD and the number of operational errors (i.e., the occurrence of errors increased with perceived PD). As mentioned earlier, correlations are not necessarily evidence of cause and effect; however, the result is interesting. We may only speculate as to mechanisms behind such correlations. Kjell Mjøs (2004) suggests a model where cultural variables have consequences for the social environment in a cockpit, which has consequences for communication between pilots that, in turn, can lead to operational errors.

Ten years after the first data were collected, a follow-up survey was conducted with a smaller selection of pilots from the largest airline from the previous study (Mjøs 2002). The purpose of this study was to investigate potential changes in the airline's culture over time. Mjøs found a significant change in the scores for dimensions PD, IND, and UAV. The social climate had also improved in this period. Some pilots were evaluated while performing an exercise in a simulator. A lower number of operational errors were recorded in the follow-up study compared to 10 years earlier. One of the study's weaknesses was that it did not survey exactly the same persons both times; however, this would obviously be difficult to accomplish due to the gap in time between the two surveys. Additionally, because the surveys were anonymous, it would have been impossible to record individual scores over time. It is also important to be aware that the study explains neither the cause of the cultural changes nor whether the recorded performance improvements can be attributed to these changes.

9.7 SAFETY CULTURE

Safety culture is a term that has been widely used in aviation and also, to some extent, in other industries where consequences of error are significant—for example, in high-tech factories and nuclear power plants, in surgery rooms, and in various modes of transport. Such systems often involve close interaction between technology and human operators, and errors may have disastrous consequences. There are a number of definitions of safety culture (for a summary, see Wiegmann et al. 2004). A relatively simple definition is that safety culture refers to the fundamental values, norms, presumptions, and expectations that a group shares concerning risk and safety (based on Mearns and Flin 1999).

Like organizational culture and organizational climate, boundaries between what is meant by safety culture and safety climate are unclear. Some people are of the opinion that they are different but related terms. That is, safety climate is measured using a questionnaire and provides a snapshot of how the employees perceive safety (often in relation to a specific issue), whereas safety culture refers to more lasting and fundamental values and norms that partially overlap the national culture of which the organization is a part (Mearns and Flin 1999). In practice, however, the notions are used interchangeably, and quantitative questionnaires often overlap in terms of content. Zohar (2010) has argued that the measurement of safety climate should involve the employees' shared perceptions of the priority of safety compared to other competing priorities such as reducing costs. Wiegmann et al. (2004) have described a number of traits or presumptions that are shared in the different definitions of safety culture. These commonalities are that safety culture is something a group of people have in common, it is stable over time, and it is reflected in the organization's will to learn from mistakes, events, and accidents. Two large-scale meta-analyses based on many industrial sectors have found small to medium large mean corrected correlations between safety climate and different aspects of safety performance including accidents (Clarke 2006; Christian et al. 2009). These correlations do not explain how safety culture influences group members' behavior, and it may be either directly or through affecting the employees' attitudes and motivation to behave in a way that enhances safety. On the basis of the meta-analysis results, Christian et al. (2009) developed and tested a model for how safety climate was related to accident and injuries. The model suggested that safety climate influenced employees' motivation and knowledge, which in turn influenced safety performance, and finally safety performance was directly linked to accidents and injuries.

9.7.1 What Characterizes a Sound Safety Culture?

An important aspect in a sound safety culture is management commitment and involvement in the promotion of safety. To achieve this, it is crucial that the highest levels of management make the necessary resources available and support the work involved. It must be reflected in all aspects of the organization, and routine evaluation and system improvements must take place. However, not only the higher levels of management but also lower level administrators, who should participate in activities related to improving safety, are important. Little is gained by sending employees to safety classes if those who are monitoring the implementation of routines do not participate.

Another indicator of safety culture is that those who are performing the specific jobs are given the responsibility and authority to be the last resort in case of errors. In other words, they feel enabled, and they regard their role as an important part in securing safety. This involves playing an active role and being heard in the work to improve safety. The organization's reward system is another aspect. Are reward systems in place to promote safety, or are employees punished or neglected when taking on an issue? A final concern is the extent to which the organization is willing to learn from previous mistakes and that employees are given feedback through the reporting system. Encouraging employees to report errors and mistakes but doing nothing to correct them would be very demotivating for those who do so.

9.7.2 How Does a Safety Culture Develop?

Safety cultures can be categorized in several ways, and they are often based on elements mentioned in the previous section. Hudson (2003) has developed a model for

TABLE 9.2

Development of a Safety Culture

	Type	Statement Typical of Culture
High-level information flow and trust	Generative	Safety is the way we do business around here.
	Proactive	We work on the problems that we still find.
	Calculative	We have systems in place to manage all hazards.
	Reactive	Safety is important. We do a lot every time we have an accident.
Low degree of flow of information and trust	Pathological	Who cares as long as we are not caught?

Source: Based on Hudson, P. 2003. *Quality and Safety in Health Care* 12: 7–12.

various safety cultures—from pathological to mature, or developed, cultures. The different categories are presented in Table 9.2 with sample statements for typical ways of regarding safety. This model expands on Westrum's model (Westrum and Adamski 1999), which contained three stages or organization types: *pathological, bureaucratic,* and *generative.*

The five stages in Hudson's model provide a framework for classifying safety cultures and describing various levels of cultural maturity. In *pathological* cultures, safety is seen as a problem caused by operators. Making money and avoiding being caught by authorities are dominant motivations. In *reactive* organizations, safety is beginning to be taken seriously, but only after an accident has already occurred. In *calculating* cultures, safety is maintained by various administrative systems and is primarily an issue imposed on employees. Some extent of labor force involvement in the safety work characterizes *proactive* cultures; in the most advanced type of safety culture (*generative*), safety is everyone's responsibility. The focus on safety is an important part of how business is conducted, and, even though there are few accidents or incidents, people do not relax (and rest on their laurels), but remain alert to dangers.

An advanced safety culture may also be described, according to Hudson (2003), by the four elements shown in Figure 9.1:

- *Information* means that all employees are informed and that information is shared within the organization. Importantly, bearers of bad news are not blamed. Instead, employees are encouraged to report problems.
- *Trust* is developed through treating employees in a fair way and not punishing those who report errors and mistakes.
- *Change* describes such organizations. This means the organization is adaptable and learns from the times when something goes wrong and the times when something works well.
- *Concern or worries* imply a type of constant apprehensiveness and understanding of the fact that even though all precautions are made, something may go wrong.

FIGURE 9.1 Elements that characterize a sound safety culture.

9.7.3 STUDIES OF SAFETY CULTURE IN AVIATION

Several questionnaires have been developed to map safety culture in aviation; most are multidimensional and consider many of the aspects mentioned in the previous section. A study of ground personnel in a Swedish airline surveyed nine aspects, including communication, learning, reporting, and risk perception (Ek and Akselsson 2007). In the survey, managers were asked to reflect on what they thought the employees' responses would be. Managers were more positive about safety culture than operators. Meanwhile, significant consistencies were found for their evaluations of the various aspects of the company's safety culture. The lowest scores were given for the "justness" and "flexibility" dimensions; this applied to both management and employees. The former dimension assessed the extent to which making occasional mistakes was accepted, while the latter measured the extent to which employees were encouraged to provide suggestions for improvements. The highest scores were given for the dimensions "communication" and "risk perception" (Ek and Akselsson 2007).

Schwarz and colleagues have conducted several studies of safety culture among air traffic controllers and developed scales that may be used to assess safety culture in the ATM (air traffic management) environment (Schwarz and Kallus 2015; Schwarz et al. 2016). The measurement instrument (Safety Culture Development Questionnaire [SCDQ]) included scales assessing five dimensions: *informed culture, reporting and learning culture, just culture, flexible culture*, and *management's safety attitudes* (Schwarz and Kallus 2015). The SCDQ was used in a study of the relationship between safety culture and experienced stress and organizational resilience among ATM staff. The model tested indicated that stress had a negative impact on safety culture development and a positive impact on resilient behavior (Schwarz et al. 2016). In an organizational context, resilience means the ability of the organization to cope with and recover from difficult situations similar to individual resilience as described in Chapter 8 as a personality trait.

Safety culture in aviation has also been linked to more objective outcomes, and a small-scale meta-analysis based on four studies (Goodhearth and Smith 2014) estimated the correlation between safety culture and the outcome variable to be mean $r = 0.48$. The outcome variable included pilot performance, errors, or incident rates. Unfortunately, the number of studies was rather small and mostly based on military samples.

9.8 WOMEN AND AVIATION

Estimates indicate that about 6% of today's pilot population are women (Mitchell et al. 2010). There is reason to believe that this could change in the future job market, but the rate at which it would happen is uncertain. Naturally, it is difficult to predict how the industry will change over time and what the need for various professions will be in the years to come. The International Civil Aviation Organization (ICAO) predicts a worldwide shortfall of approximately 25,000 pilots per year between 2010 and 2030 (ICAO 2011). Other agencies have also predicted a shortfall of pilots in the years to come making it even more important to recruit female pilots (for an overview, see Bridges et al. 2014, p. 4).

Thus, it is reasonable to believe that airlines will recruit pilots and personnel outside national borders and in other groups than those who have chosen the piloting profession traditionally. It is difficult to know exactly what motivates young people in their choice of profession. A study by Gibbon (2014) based on interviews with women and girls indicated a number of obstacles involved when asked about being a pilot. Very few thought that they might like to pursue a flying career for a number of reasons, including perceptions that flying is not a job for girls, and that they lack typical pilot traits or that it would be too difficult or dangerous. Probably, a number of factors are involved when choosing a profession, such as subjective considerations of abilities and interests as well as external factors such as available opportunities, financial situation, and what they are familiar with through family and friends. Sometimes, even personal experiences may play a part in staking out a career path, as was the case with one of the first Norwegian female aviators, Gidsken Jacobsen (Gynnild 2008, p. 30):

> A day in June 1928, a big, three-engine seaplane roared through Ofotfjorden and landed outside Narvik. Somewhere in the sea of spectators was Gidsken Jakobsen. The visit from above became a turning point in her life. "From the day I saw Nilsson's [flying] machine at the docks, there was nothing I'd rather do than fly," she said years later. "Imagine flying around in the air like Nilsson and his crew, from place to place, to get to know the country from the air and awaking the interest in thousands of people for what they loved more than anything else: To fly!"

Gidsken Jakobsen was raised in Narvik in the Northern part of Norway in the 1920s. She was not quite like other girls; she learned how to drive cars and motorbikes at an early age. At the age of 21, she left for Stockholm to take her pilot's license at the Aero-Materiell flight school. Subsequently, she learned to fly seaplanes and, with the help of her father, bought a seaplane that was given the name *Måsen* (*The Seagull*) (Gynnild 2008). There is no doubt that Gidsken Jakobsen lived an untraditional and exciting life, with great firmness of action and lust for life. Other examples of female pioneers can be found in Norway and in other countries, such as Dagny Berger and Elise Deroche, who got their pilot's licenses in 1927 and 1910, respectively. Harriet Quimby crossed the English Channel in 1912 and Amelia Earhart crossed the Atlantic in 1932 (Wilson 2004).

Despite the fact that women were at the center of early aviation and that there were many female pioneers, the piloting profession of today is distinctly male dominated. It is difficult to say why more women are not fascinated by the act of flying. Probably, there are individual reasons and reasons based on the nature of aviation. Perhaps, the profession is seen as particularly masculine because history is full of heroic achievements performed by men—"the right stuff." Thus, young females would rather choose other education paths and career opportunities. Perhaps, the thought of entering a trade where one risks being isolated and perhaps lives with negative and sexist comments from colleagues and others is less than appealing. A study based on interviews among both male and female commercial pilots in the United Kingdom indicated a number of obstacles to greater female participation in the aviation industry including negative comments and remarks from colleagues and passengers (McCarthy et al. 2015). Research into interactions between pilots has long been concerned with communication and cultural differences and their impact on aviation safety. Still, research into gender issues in aviation, both in terms of attitudes toward female pilots and consequences for interactions between pilots, is insufficient.

9.8.1 Attitudes toward Female Pilots

To provide information about attitudes toward female pilots, a study was initiated in South Africa, the United States, Australia, and Norway; female and male pilots were asked about how they regarded female pilots (Kristovics et al. 2006). The subjects were asked to express their opinions on a number of statements about female pilots. In addition, the survey presented an open question to which participants could express in their own words what they thought about the issues raised by the survey and the survey itself. The survey contained four sections of questions (examples are presented in Table 9.3). The participants responded by expressing their agreement or disagreement on a five-point scale. Results were then summarized for each dimension so that a high score represented a positive attitude and a low score indicated a negative attitude. Some of the questions thus needed to be reversed to combine the scores into a unified index.

A total of 2009 pilots (312 females and 1697 males) with an average age of 36 participated in the survey. There were different proportions of participants from the four different countries, with 53% from Australia, 28% from South Africa, 9% from the United States, and 10% from Norway. Results revealed gender-related differences for all four dimensions; that is, male pilots regarded female pilots in a more negative light than female pilots did. Differences were greatest for the statements in the categories "decision/leadership" and "affirmative action." A more recent study of U.S. pilots using the same questionnaire confirmed that there were still significant gender differences on all of the four scales (Walton and Politano 2014).

There were also differences between countries, as presented in Figure 9.2.

TABLE 9.3

Examples of Questions from the Survey on Attitudes toward Female Pilots

Category	Sample Statements
Decision/leadership	Female pilots often have difficulty making decisions in urgent situations. Female pilots' decision-making ability is as good in an emergency situation as it is in routine flights.
Assertiveness	Male pilots tend to "take charge' in flying situations more than female pilots. Male flight students tend to be less fearful of learning stall procedures than female students.
Hazardous behavior	Male pilots are more likely to run out of fuel than female pilots. Male pilots tend to take greater risks than female pilots.
Affirmative action	Professional female pilots are only in the positions they are in because airlines want to fulfill affirmative action quotas. Flight training standards have been relaxed so that it is easier for women to get their wings.

The following results are based on male pilots only because the numbers of female pilots were very low in some participating countries. For three of the four dimensions, the Norwegian pilots were more positive than pilots from other countries, whereas for the dimension labeled "hazardous behavior" the situation was reversed. Statements in the latter category were of the type: "Male pilots tend to take greater risks than female pilots," and Norwegian pilots, to a lesser extent, agreed with these

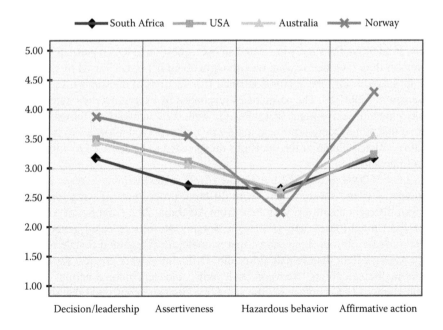

FIGURE 9.2 Differences in attitude between four countries based on male pilots' responses.

statements. This probably reflects the equality-mindedness of Norwegians, in which female pilots would not be viewed as being more careful or apprehensive than male colleagues. In summary, the results of the survey revealed that male Norwegian pilots were more positive about female pilots than their U.S., Australian, and South African counterparts. Perhaps, this expresses stronger ideals of equality in Norway compared to the other countries involved in the investigation, which is in line with Hofstede's (1980) findings for Scandinavian countries.

The group contained 158 pilot instructors. As a subgroup, instructors were found to be more positive toward female pilots compared to the group at large. Additionally, those who had had the opportunity to fly with a female copilot were more positive toward female pilots than those who had not.

Participants had the opportunity to provide supplemental comments to the survey, and there were several similarities in negative commentary from different countries (Mitchell et al. 2005). Some were about the aviation industry not being suited for women, exemplified in statements such as "A female pilot = an empty kitchen" and "If women were meant to fly, the sky would be pink." The least amount of negative commentary was from the Norwegian group. Positive comments were often about how female pilots were just as good as male pilots, or better, and that it was unreasonable to judge people solely based on gender. Many Norwegian respondents (most of whom were military pilots) commented that because both males and females went through the same selection process, they were equally capable of performing the given tasks.

9.9 REORGANIZATION AND ADAPTING TO NEW WORKING CONDITIONS

Many industries are subject to restructuring and reorganization. Such changes are often attributed to a need or desire to improve the company's efficiency and profitability. Sometimes, economic conditions or strategic decisions lead to downsizing. However, one problem with downsizing is that the tasks to be performed do not disappear with the sacked staff; consequently, a greater workload rests on those who remain employed in the company. In addition, new technologies are often introduced, so employees must be willing to learn new skills and perform new tasks. Industries that were previously regarded as firmly established and able to offer attractive working conditions are no longer plentiful, leading to more short-term planning by employers and employees.

Restructuring is regarded as a common and correct strategy that, according to McKinley and Scherer (2000), provides managers with a feeling of cognitive order—a positive emotion that increases the probability of further restructuring. Although organizational changes are usually carried out with the best intentions, studies point to negative consequences in the form of stress and reduced work satisfaction among employees, as well as lower than expected financial gains for the company (for a review, consult Mentzer 2005). One interpretation of such outcomes involves insufficient and inappropriate management of human factors—in other words, underestimating the impact that expansive restructuring processes have on employees.

9.9.1 REACTIONS TO ORGANIZATIONAL CHANGES

For employees, consequences of corporate reorganization may be considerable. Work is a very important part of most people's lives, and significant changes in a company can be perceived as a critical life event. What individuals are most concerned about will vary, but may include questions such as

- How will this influence my day-to-day work routine and my career?
- Will my skills and experience be adequate in the future?
- Will I be in demand in the new organization?
- Will I be treated fairly in the reorganization process?

Restructuring may be seen in light of general stress theories—for example, Frankenhaeuser's biopsychosocial model, which was mentioned in Chapter 8. In such models, restructuring would be regarded as a stressor to which individuals compare their resources. If demands surpass resources, stress arises and, in turn, this has negative health implications. What makes such a comparison or evaluation difficult is the scarcity of information about what will happen (and when). In the case of mergers and acquisitions, employees are usually not informed until relevant decisions have been made. Decision-making processes are typically secret on the grounds of protecting the company's interests. Internal rumors about what is about to happen often circulate, and this only makes it more difficult for employees to determine what will be required of them in the future and which tasks will be faced in the new organization. It is common not to know whether one has a job in the "new" company. That said, not everyone would react in a negative way to the message of an imminent restructuring or reorganization. Some people may consider such changes natural and appropriate, with opportunities for them to "climb the ladder."

In addition to individual reactions, what are the consequences of restructuring and downsizing to the organization? Initially, a more productive and dynamic organization is desired, but this outcome cannot be taken for granted. Potential savings must be weighed against possible negative consequences, such as increases in absences due to illness, higher turnover rates, and organizational unrest. Restructuring—in particular, downsizing—leads to reduced trust in management and lower work satisfaction among employees. How strong employees' reactions will be depends on a number of circumstances. An important factor is the extent of the changes. The merger of two large organizations and the fusion of two smaller departments within an organization are different, for example. A decisive factor, though, is how the changes are communicated—notably, that the necessity of change is emphasized. Good communication contributes to reductions in anxiety and negative reactions, as well as improved work satisfaction in employees.

A study of Canadian hospital employees ($N = 321$) compared reactions to various forms of organizational changes including structural changes, workplace changes, and introduction of new technology (Bareil et al. 2007). Direct comparisons in how subjects reacted were possible because the subjects went through the same changes. About a quarter of the subjects reacted with the same degree of discomfort to all the different types of changes, while the majority (about three quarters) experienced varying degrees of discomfort according to the type of change. Thus, it appears the type of change (situational factors), rather than personal characteristics (dispositional factors), is more important in terms of the level of discomfort associated with the changes.

In a Norwegian study into the restructuring and downsizing of a large oil company operating off the coast of Norway, employees' ($N = 467$) attitudes were investigated using a questionnaire (Svensen et al. 2007). The survey was conducted after the announcement (but before the implementation) of restructuring plans. About a third responded positively to the changes. The most important factors predicting a positive attitude were feelings of responsibility to the organization, involvement, participation, team leadership, and efficiency.

9.9.2 DOWNSIZING

Downsizing has a number of negative implications for both those who lose their jobs and those who remain with the organization. Further, several studies show business earnings rarely improve as a consequence of downsizing (Mentzer 1996). Those who remain in the organization may suffer from so-called "survivor sickness"—a condition characterized by job security issues and negative or cynical attitudes toward the company. Even managers charged with executing reorganization and downsizing processes may experience stress, feelings of guilt, and, occasionally, aggression toward employees.

A study of employees in different sectors (including banking, insurance, and technology) investigated reactions in the wake of downsizing (Kets de Vries and Balazs 1997). The study was based on qualitative interviews of employees who lost their jobs ($N = 60$) and employees who remained with the company, so-called "survivors" ($N = 60$). Subjects in the former group were categorized according to their reactions: (a) the adapting (43%), (b) the depressed (30%), (c) those who see new opportunities (17%), and (d) the hostile (10%). In addition, combinations of reaction patterns were observed. Managers who had had to fire people were also subject to the study, and most of them said it was a difficult process. Great variations in the way managers reacted, ranging from distancing themselves from the problem to depression and feelings of guilt, were reported.

A survey conducted by Mari Rege at the University of Stavanger (in collaboration with Statistics Norway) tracked a large group of employees over 5 years (Rege et al. 2009). Employees in stable and secure companies were analyzed and compared to employees in companies exposed to downsizing. Downsizing was found to have a number of health-related consequences for the individual, particularly males. In males, results revealed higher mortality rates (14%), inability to work (24%), and risk of divorce (11%). The researchers attributed the gender-related differences to males taking job loss more seriously because male identities are more closely tied to their paid work. The study also revealed that the negative effects on someone who had lost his or her job depended on the sector in which he or she worked. The most severe consequences were observed in manufacturing industries.

9.9.3 Psychological Contracts

When seen as isolated or separate incidents, the reactions that managers and employees display in the previously described situations may seem strange, irrational, and even surprising. However, reactions become more predictable when viewed as reactions to intense stress. Both sides have been through a very difficult process that included losing one or more colleagues and, perhaps, friends. Moreover, they have been forced to change their perception of having worked in a financially solid company.

Downsizing may be regarded as a serious breach of the psychological contract that exists between employees and employers. Psychological contracts are individual expectations shaped by the organization about how exchanges should take place between the employee and the organization (see, e.g., Rousseau 1995). Contracts are expectations about the future that are based on trust, acceptance, and reciprocity; they make it easier for people to plan and anticipate future events. Often these contracts contain the contributions expected of the employee as well as the compensation offered by the organization in return. For example, the employee promises to work hard, be loyal, and contribute to fulfilling the company's mission statement. The employer, on the other hand, promises ongoing employment, payment, and opportunities for personal development and career advancement. Such contracts are not necessarily synonymous with written contracts, and there may be certain disagreements about what the contract involves.

Psychological contracts are formed in many ways—for instance, through verbal expression, written documents, observation of how others are treated within the organization, and company policy or culture. They may be expressed in writing or by stories and myths about how things have been done before. Because contracts are formed by the person perceiving and integrating information, there is an obvious chance that misinterpretations can occur. Breach of contract arises when an employee feels that the organization has not fulfilled its duties. However, the organization or local management may have a different view.

Studies of people starting out in a new job show that contracts are often breached. One study revealed that 54% experienced a breach of contract during the first 2 years (Robinson and Rousseau 1994). Thus, breaches of psychological contracts are not unusual in an organization. The severity of the breach will affect the severity of reactions and consequences. Breaches may occur knowingly and intentionally or because the business does not have the necessary resources to meet contractual requirements. Often, severe breaches of contract can be devastating and lead to negative reactions in employees, such as mistrust, anger, and wanting to quit the job. Generally, repeated offenses may degrade the relationship between the employee and the organization (Robinson and Rousseau 1994).

A number of factors influence the severity and nature of the consequences of breach of contract. One aspect is whether the breach occurred on purpose and whether similar breaches have occurred previously (a "string" of breaches). If an employer is unable to keep his or her promise to provide sponsored education because of a budget deficit, the employee may find it more acceptable than if the manager simply thinks such training is a bad investment. Events in the aftermath of a contractual breach may help to repair the relationship or, conversely, enforce its negative consequences.

9.10 LEADERSHIP

Sound management is important in many aspects of the working environment, particularly in relation to the development of a safety culture and in terms of processes of organizational change. A number of theories describe various leaders or leadership types. Leadership, naturally, does not exist in a vacuum but in a historical and cultural context; what works in one situation may not automatically transfer to a different organization or to a different point in time. In a time when many organizations are constantly changing and reinventing themselves, enormous demands are placed on managers to motivate and inspire employees. Many studies have shown a correlation between stress (burnout) and various forms of support or, perhaps, lack of support from managers (Lee and Ashforth 1996). Thus, it is crucial for an organization to be able to select and develop good leaders who earn and maintain employees' trust.

9.10.1 THREE LEADERSHIP TYPES

Many theories and research traditions describe what makes a good leader. Some emphasize a leader's personality characteristics and others focus on what he or she actually does. A number of studies on leadership were conducted at Ohio State University in the postwar era. Two dimensions were identified as characteristic of effective leaders: that they were considerate and that they took initiative in generating structure (see, e.g., Judge et al. 2004). Other research groups have identified similar dimensions, but with different denotations, such as "relation-oriented leadership" and "task-oriented leadership."

Many new publications and books have been written recently on transactional leadership and transformational leadership (Burns 1978; Bass 2007). These leadership theories involve aspects concerning managers, subordinates, and the interactions between these two sides:

In *transactional leadership*, the exchange of rewards for results and completion of tasks is emphasized. Alternatively, the employees are allowed to do their jobs as long as production targets are achieved; that is, error correction is considered sufficient. This may involve a passive, apprehensive style (the manager avoids action until something goes wrong) or an active style (the manager reacts to errors made by employees).

In *transformational leadership*, emphasis is not only on transactions between employees and management (work for payment and other benefits), but also on the leader's ability to inspire, motivate, and devise original ideas. The person must be charismatic, set a good example, and be able to communicate his or her vision, thus elevating employees toward the organization's common goal. This leadership type is also described according to its impact on employees. Transformational leadership is associated with increased work satisfaction and motivates employees to perform better.

These two leadership styles are not mutually exclusive. Rather, they complement each other. A manager–employee relationship often starts as a transactional relation—that is, a process of clarifying the expectations that both sides have. However, transformational leadership is necessary if employees are to be motivated to put in additional effort (Bass 2007). Transformational leaders motivate employees to work not only for immediate rewards in self-interest, but also for the benefit of the group, the company, or, indeed, the country. Work becomes an activity greater than something done just to get paid, and this recognition contributes to an increase in employees' self-esteem and devotion to their tasks.

Evidence tells us that this categorization of leadership is not tied to a particular type of organization or culture, and the dimensions have been established in a number of organization types, such as the armed forces and the private and public sectors of many countries (Bass 2007). However, the ways in which the different forms of leadership are revealed may vary between cultures. For example, the way a leader rewards or shows appreciation for employees will vary between countries such as Norway and Japan.

The two forms of leadership are often contrasted to laissez-faire leadership, or a lack of leadership. Managers who exhibit such leadership do not recognize their responsibility as leaders and do not provide assistance or communicate their opinions on important issues regarding the organization. This form of leadership is the least effective and also represents the type of management under which employees are the least content with the status quo.

The different forms of leadership are often quantified using the measurement instrument called MLQ (multifactor leadership questionnaire) (Bass 1985). The instrument has subsequently been revised and consists, in short, of various statements on leadership to which employees respond on a scale from zero (*the behavior is never observed*) to four (*the behavior is often, if not always, observed*). Three scales map *transformational leadership* and, accordingly, three measure *transactional leadership*. However, only one scale measures *laissez-faire leadership*. A number of studies have used this instrument or variants of it in which the different scales are correlated with work performance measures (subjective and objective). Summaries show that positive correlations are strongest for transformational scales and some of the transactional scales, whereas correlations between laissez-faire leadership and work results are negative (see, e.g., Bass 2007). These findings are generally based on North American studies; however, a clear connection between transformational leadership and variables such as work satisfaction and efficiency has been supported in Norwegian surveys as well (Hetland and Sandal 2003).

Gender issues and leadership have been subject to plenty of discussion. For example, is it true that females have different leadership styles from those of males? In most industries, women are underrepresented in leadership positions, particularly at the highest levels. Do female leadership styles constitute a barrier to clinching those top jobs? A meta-analysis of 45 studies that investigated gender differences found generally minor differences in male and female leadership (Eagly et al. 2003). Women had somewhat higher scores for transformational leadership, and men scored higher on the scales measuring laissez-faire leadership and the two forms of transactional leadership—that is, intervening only when something goes wrong. These results are positive for the case of female leadership. In other words, no evidence supports claims that female leaders use less effective leadership styles—quite the contrary.

With regard to the correlation between personality and leadership styles, several studies have been executed on the topic. A meta-analysis of over 20 studies conducted by Bono and Judge (2004) revealed low correlations between personality traits (the "Five-factor" model) and the various scales presented in MLQ. The greatest and most stable correlations were found for the scales for transformational leadership and the personality traits extroversion (mean $r = 0.24$) and neuroticism (mean $r = -0.17$).

A more recent addition to the research on leadership has been the study of destructive leaders. The term has been used to describe both active destructive leadership behavior such as bullying or abusive supervision, and passive forms such as failure to lead at all. Einarsen Aasland, and Skogstad (2007) proposed the following definition:

> The systematic and repeated behaviour by a leader, supervisor or manager that violates the legitimate interest of the organisation by undermining and/or sabotaging the organisation's goals, tasks, resources, and effectiveness and/or the motivation, well-being or job satisfaction of subordinates (p. 208).

This means that destructive leadership is more than the absence of positive leadership and may impact both the organization and employees. According to their model for leadership (see Figure 9.3), leadership behavior can be evaluated along two dimensions: subordinate- and organization-oriented behaviors. The subordinate dimension may range from bullying and harassment to behaviors that promote engagement and the well-being of employees. The organization dimension ranges from behavior that includes working against the goals of the organization to constructive behavior such as setting clear goals, promoting a safety culture, and implementing changes.

The model results in four categories of leadership labeled *tyrannical leadership behavior, derailed leadership behavior, supportive-disloyal leadership*, and *constructive leadership* where the first three may be categorized as different forms of destructive leadership and only *constructive leadership behavior* may be seen as

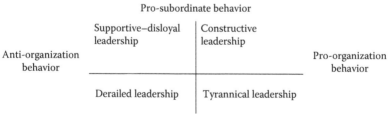

FIGURE 9.3 Model for constructive and destructive leadership. (Based on Einarsen, S., Aasland, M.S., and Skogstad, A. 2007. *The Leadership Quarterly* 18: 207–216.)

effective where the leader is able to balance the needs of the organization with the needs of the employees. Destructive leadership has in meta-analyses been linked to negative outcomes such as turnover and reduced efficiency in addition to lowered job satisfaction and increased levels of burnout (Tepper 2007; Schyns and Schilling 2013; Mackey et al. 2015). Why some leaders display destructive behavior and have a negative impact on their followers is still unclear. Some of the explanations have been related to leadership characteristics such as having narcissistic personality traits whereas others have focused on cultural factors or aspects of the working environment. There may also be some combinations of leaders and subordinates that simply constitute a very poor match.

9.10.2 LEADERSHIP AND SAFETY

Few studies on leadership in aviation have been conducted. However, a number of studies in other sectors may shed light on the relationship between leadership and safety. Several studies have investigated the connection of management, safety climate, and work-related accidents. A model for the relationship among these elements was developed by Barling et al. (2002). In this model, transformational leadership affects the security climate, which, in turn, affects the occurrence of accidents. The model also contained the important notion of safety awareness. Enforcement of this notion implies that employees are aware of the dangers associated with the various operations and know what needs to be done when accidents and dangerous situations arise. The model was tested on a group of young employees, mainly in the service sector. Results indicate that the most important effect of transformational leadership was its influence on safety awareness in individual employees; in turn, this affected the safety climate and, ultimately, the number of accidents (Barling et al. 2002).

Others have researched corresponding models for different sectors—for example, factory workers in Israel, where safety climate was found to be a mediating variable between leadership styles and the number of accidents (Zohar 2002). In this study, both transformational and transactional leadership predicted accidents; however, the effects were mediated through a certain aspect of the safety climate that was labeled "preventive action." This dimension contained questions that mapped the extent to which immediate superiors discussed safety issues with employees and whether they accepted safety advice from employees. The study concluded that leadership dimensions associated with concern for the welfare of employees and personal relations promoted improved supervision and thus improved the safety climate and reduced the number of accidents (Zohar 2002).

9.11 SUMMARY

For better or worse, people are influenced by the cultural context of groups or communities to which they belong. In this chapter, we have looked at how national, professional, and organizational cultures influence people working in aviation. Culture affects not only the behavior of a person, but also the way he or she communicates and perceives other people and the world (worldview).

Aviation is an inherently international industry that, similarly to many other industries, faces challenges in the form of tough competition, market instability, and increased focus on security and terrorism. Restructuring and downsizing are of great importance to the welfare of employees and, in turn, their performance and duties in relation to the organization. Sound leadership is of decisive importance to development of a safety culture and to reducing unintended consequences of restructuring and reorganization.

9.12 OUTSIDE ACTIVITIES

- Try to picture two leaders that you have had in the past, one excellent that you really liked and one that you did not like at all. Take a look at the model of leadership behaviors (Figure 9.3), and use the two dimensions to describe the type of behaviors your leaders displayed. On the basis of this, in which of the four categories would you place your leaders?
- Narcissism has been seen as an ingredient in destructive leadership, but is also one of the traits displayed by many leaders today. If you are interested in learning more about narcissism in an organizational contexts you can read more in Campbell et al. (2011). There is also an online interactive version of the Narcissistic Personality Inventory that may be used for educational purposes (Raskin and Terry 1988): http://personality-testing.info/tests/NPI/

RECOMMENDED READINGS

Bridges, D., Neal-Smith, J., and Mills, A.J. (Eds.). 2014. *Absent Aviators: Gender Issues in Aviation*. Aldershot, UK: Ashgate.

Helmreich, R.L. and Merritt, A.C. 1998. *Culture at Work in Aviation and Medicine*. Aldershot, UK: Ashgate.

Hollnagel, E., Woods, D.D., and Leveson, N. (Eds.). 2006. *Resilience Engineering. Concepts and Precepts*. Aldershot, UK: Ashgate.

REFERENCES

Bang, H. 1995. *Organisasjonskultur (3.utgave) [Organizational Culture]*. Oslo, Norway: Tano AS.

Bareil, C., Savoie, A., and Meunier, S. 2007. Patterns of discomfort with organizational change. *Journal of Change Management* 7: 13–24.

Barling, J., Loughlin, C., and Kelloway, E.K. 2002. Development and test of a model linking safety-specific transformational leadership and occupational safety. *Journal of Applied Psychology* 87: 488–496.

Bass, B.M. 1985. *Leadership and Performance Beyond Expectations*. New York, NY: Free Press.

Bass, B.M. 2007. Does the transactional–transformational leadership paradigm transcend organizational and national boundaries? *American Psychologist* 52: 130–139.

Bono, J.E. and Judge, T.A. 2004. Personality and transformational and transactional leadership: A meta-analysis. *Journal of Applied Psychology* 89: 901–910.

Bridges, D., Neal-Smith, J., and Mills, A.J. (Eds.). 2014. *Absent Aviators: Gender Issues in Aviation*. Aldershot, UK: Ashgate.

Burns, J.M. 1978. *Leadership*. New York, NY: Harper & Row.

Campbell, W.K., Hoffman, B.J., Campbell, S.M., and Marchisio, G. 2011. Narcissism in organizational contexts. *Human Resource Management Review* 21: 268–284.

Christian, M.S., Bradley, J.C., Wallace, J.C., and Burke, M.J. 2009. Workplace safety: A meta-analysis of the roles of person and situation factors. *Journal of Applied Psychology* 94: 1103–1127.

Clarke, S. 2006. The relationship between safety climate and safety performance: A meta-analytic review. *Journal of Occupational Health Psychology* 11: 315–327.

Eagly, A.H., Johannsesen-Schmidt, M.C., and van Engen, M.L. 2003. Transformational, transactional, and lassez-faire leadership styles: A meta-analysis comparing women and men. *Psychological Bulletin* 129: 569–591.

Einarsen, S., Aasland, M.S., and Skogstad, A. 2007. Destructive leadership behaviour: A definition and conceptual model. *The Leadership Quarterly* 18: 207–216.

Ek, Å. and Akselsson, R. 2007. Aviation on the ground: Safety culture in a ground handling company. *International Journal of Aviation Psychology* 17: 59–76.

Gibbon, D. 2014. Difficult dangerous, not a job for girls. In Bridges, D., Neal-Smith, J., and Mills, A.J. (Eds.), *Absent Aviators: Gender Issues in Aviation* (pp. 43–72). Aldershot, UK: Ashgate.

Goodheart, B.J. and Smith, M.O. 2014. Measurable outcomes of safety culture in aviation—A meta-analytic review. *International Journal of Aviation, Aeronautics, and Aerospace* 1(4). Retrieved from: http://commons.erau.edu/ijaaa/vol1/iss4/1

Gynnild, O. 2008. *Seilas i storm. Et portrett av flypioneren Gidsken Jakobsen [Sailing in Storm: A Portrait of the Aviation Pioneer Gidsken Jacobsen].* Stamsund, Norway: Orkana Forlag and the Norwegian Aviation Museum.

Harris, D. and Li, W.-C. 2008. Cockpit design and cross-cultural issues underlying failures in crew resource management. *Aviation, Space, and Environmental Medicine* 79: 537–538.

Helmreich, R.L. and Merritt, A.C. 1998. *Culture at Work in Aviation and Medicine.* Aldershot, UK: Ashgate.

Hetland, H. and Sandal, G.M. 2003. Transformational leadership in Norway: Outcomes and personality correlates. *European Journal of Work and Organizational Psychology* 12: 147–170.

Hofstede, G. 1980. *Culture's Consequences: International Differences in Work-related Values.* Beverly Hills, CA: Sage.

Hofstede, G. 2001. *Culture's Consequences: Comparing Values, Behaviors, Institutions and Organizations Across Nations*, 2nd ed. Thousand Oaks, CA: Sage.

Hofstede, G. 2002. Commentary on "An international study of the psychometric properties of the Hofstede values survey module 1994: A comparison of individual and country/province level results." *Applied Psychology: An International Review* 51: 170–178.

Hofstede, G., Hofstede, G.J., and Minkov, M. 2010. *Cultures and Organizations. Software of the Mind*, 3rd ed. New York, NY: The McGraw-Hill.

Hudson, P. 2003. Applying the lessons of high-risk industries to health care. *Quality and Safety in Health Care* 12: 7–12.

International Civil Aviation Organization. 2011. *Global and Regional 20-year Forecasts.* Montreal, Canada: Author.

Judge, T.A., Piccolo, R.F., and Ilies, R. 2004. The forgotten one? The validity of consideration and initiating structure in leadership research. *Journal of Applied Psychology* 89: 36–51.

Kets de Vries, M.F.R., and Balazs, K. 1997. The downside of downsizing. *Human Relations* 50: 11–50.

Kristovics, A., Mitchell, J., Vermeulen, L., Wilson, J., and Martinussen, M. 2006. Gender issues on the flight-deck: An exploratory analysis. *International Journal of Applied Aviation Studies* 6: 99–119.

Lee, R.T. and Ashforth, B.E. 1996. A meta-analytic examination of the correlates of the three dimensions of job burnout. *Journal of Applied Psychology* 81: 123–133.

Li, W.C., Harris, D., and Chen, A. 2007. Eastern minds in Western cockpits: Meta-analysis of human factors in mishaps from three nations. *Aviation, Space, and Environmental Medicine* 78: 420–425.

Mackey, J.D., Frieder, R.E., Brees, J.R., and Martinko, M.J. 2015. Abusive supervision: A meta-analysis and empirical review. *Journal of Management*. doi: 10.1177/0149206315573997

McCarthy, F., Budd, L., and Ison, S. 2015. Gender on the flight deck: Experiences of women commercial airline pilots in the UK. *Journal of Air Transport Management* 47: 32–38.

McKinley, W. and Scherer, A.G. 2000. Some unanticipated consequences of organizational restructuring. *Academy of Management Review* 25: 735–752.

Mearns, K.J. and Flin, R. 1999. Assessing the state of organizational safety—Culture or climate? *Current Psychology* 18: 5–17.

Mentzer, M.S. 1996. Corporate downsizing and profitability in Canada. *Canadian Journal of Administrative Sciences* 13: 237–250.

Mentzer, M.S. 2005. Toward a psychological and cultural model of downsizing. *Journal of Organizational Behavior* 26: 993–997.

Merritt, A. 2000. Culture in the cockpit. Do Hofstede's dimensions replicate? *Journal of Cross-Cultural Psychology* 31: 283–301.

Mitchell, J., Kristovics, A., and Bishop, R. 2010. Glass cockpits in general aviation: A comparison of men and women pilots' perceptions. *International Journal of Applied Aviation Studies* 10: 11–29.

Mitchell, J., Kristovics, A., Vermeulen, L., Wilson, J., and Martinussen, M. 2005. How pink is the sky? A cross-national study of the gendered occupation of pilot. *Employment Relations Record* 5: 43–60.

Mjøs, K. 2002. Cultural changes (1986–96) in a Norwegian airline company. *Scandinavian Journal of Psychology* 43: 9–18.

Mjøs, K. 2004. Basic cultural elements affecting the team function on the flight deck. *International Journal of Aviation Psychology* 14: 151–169.

Pidgeon, N. and O'Leary, M. 2000. Man-made disasters: Why technology and organizations (sometimes) fail. *Safety Science* 34: 15–30.

Raskin, R. and Terry, H. 1988. A principal-components analysis of the Narcissistic Personality Inventory and further evidence of its construct validity. *Journal of Personality and Social Psychology* 54: 890–902.

Rege, M., Telle, K., and Votruba, M. 2009. The effect of plant downsizing on disability pension utilization. *Journal of the European Economic Association* 7: 754–785.

Robinson, S.L. and Rousseau, D.M. 1994. Violating the psychological contract: Not the exception but the norm. *Journal of Organizational Behavior* 15: 245–259.

Rousseau, D.M. 1995. *Psychological Contracts in Organizations*. London, UK: Sage Publications.

Schein, E.H. 1990. Organizational culture. *American Psychologist* 45: 109–119.

Schein, E.H. 1996. Culture: The missing concept in organization studies. *Administrative Science Quarterly* 41: 229–240.

Schwarz, M., Kallus, K.W., and Gaisbachgrabner, K. 2016. Safety culture, resilient behavior, and stress in air traffic management. *Aviation Psychology and Applied Human Factors* 6: 12–23.

Schwarz, M. and Kallus, W. 2015. Safety culture and safety-relevant behavior in air traffic management validation of the CANSO safety culture development concept. *Aviation Psychology and Applied Human Factors* 5: 3–17.

Schyns, B. and Schilling, J. 2013. How bad are the effects of bad leaders? A meta-analysis of destructive leadership and its outcomes. *The Leadership Quarterly* 24: 138–158.

Sherman, P.J., Helmreich, R.L., and Merritt, A.C. 1997. National culture and flight deck automation: Results of a multination survey. *International Journal of Aviation Psychology* 7: 311–329.

Shouksmith, G. and Taylor, J.E. 1997. The interaction of culture with general job stressors in air traffic controllers. *International Journal of Aviation Psychology* 7: 343–352.

Soeters, J.L. and Boer, P.C. 2000. Culture and flight safety in military aviation. *International Journal of Aviation Psychology* 10: 111–113.

Spector, P.E. and Cooper, C.L. 2002. The pitfalls of poor psychometric properties: A rejoinder to Hofstede's reply to us. *Applied Psychology: An International Review* 51: 174–178.

Strauch, B. 2010. Can cultural differences lead to accidents? Team cultural differences and sociotechnical system operations. *Human Factors* 52: 246–263.

Svensen, E., Neset, G., and Eriksen, H.R. 2007. Factors associated with a positive attitude towards change among employees during early phase of a downsizing process. *Scandinavian Journal of Psychology* 48: 153–159.

Tepper, B.J. 2007. Abusive supervision in work organizations: Review, synthesis, and research agenda. *Journal of Management* 33, 261–289.

Walton, R.O. and Politano, P.M. 2014. Gender-related perceptions and stress, anxiety and depression on the flight deck. *Aviation Psychology and Applied Human Factors* 4: 67–73.

Westrum, R. and Adamski, A.J. 1999. Organizational factors associated with safety and mission success in aviation environments. In Garland, D.J., Wise, J.A., and Hopkin, V.D. (Eds.), *Handbook of Aviation Human Factors* (pp. 67–104). Mahwah, NJ: Lawrence Erlbaum Associates.

Wiegmann, D.A. and Shappell, S.A. 2003. *A Human Error Approach to Aviation Accident Analysis: The Human Factors Analysis and Classification System*. Burlington, VT: Ashgate.

Wiegmann, D.A., Zang, H., Von Thaden, T.L., Sharma, G., and Gibbons, A.M. 2004. Safety culture: An integrative review. *International Journal of Aviation Psychology* 14: 117–134.

Wilson, J. 2004. *Gender-based Issues in Aviation, Attitudes Towards Female Pilots: A Cross-cultural Analysis*. Unpublished doctoral dissertation. Faculty of Economic and Management Sciences, University of Pretoria, Pretoria, South Africa.

Zohar, D. 2002. The effects of leadership dimensions, safety climate, and assigned priorities on minor injuries in work groups. *Journal of Organizational Behavior* 23: 75–92.

Zohar, D. 2010. Thirty years of safety climate research: Reflections and future directions. *Accident Analysis* 42: 1517–1522.

10 Aeronautical Decision-Making

10.1 INTRODUCTION

> You got to know when to hold 'em, know when to fold 'em, know when to walk away, know when to run.

Schlitz 1977

That bit of lyrics from *The Gambler* pretty much sums up what pilot judgment or aeronautical decision-making (ADM) is all about. You may know how to play the game, but you also need to know when to play and when to fold—when to fly and when to walk. This is not a new idea. In a study conducted in 1940, flight instructors rated civilian pilot trainees on pilot competency, including judgment. The factors that were rated as important in assessing judgment were as follows:

- How good is his judgment with regard to taking flying risks (weather, stunting, etc.)?
- Does he show respect for an aircraft and its motor?
- How well is he satisfied with his flying ability?
- Is he inclined to show off while flying a plane?
- How carefully does he check his plane and engine before taking off? (Guilford and Lacey 1947, p. 124)

Although the title of this chapter is Aeronautical Decision-Making, it could just as well be driver decision-making, medical decision-making, decision-making for golfers, or any of the countless other situations in which people make decisions. Regardless of the setting, the processes and the factors that influence the quality of those processes are essentially the same. Of course, the consequences of the decisions in aviation can often be more serious than in other settings. Deciding to press on into deteriorating weather may lead to a more interesting experience than deciding to have a pizza for lunch.

The goal of this chapter is to help you understand how decisions are made, what shapes those decisions, and how you can improve your personal decision-making. Decision-making is a very complex subject that can be looked at from a variety of perspectives, and each has something to contribute to our understanding of decision-making, both in the cockpit and elsewhere. We will start by defining decisions and decision-making. Next, we will look at what is involved in decision-making in general and some of the many factors that can have an impact on this process. Finally, we will look specifically at ADM, why it is such an important concept, and some of the many efforts to understand and improve decision-making in the cockpit. Let us start with a discussion of just what we mean by ADM, and decisions in general.

10.2   DEFINING ADM

The Federal Aviation Administration (FAA) defines ADM as a systematic approach to the mental process used by pilots to determine the best course of action in response to a given set of circumstance. The trouble with that definition is that it is prescriptive, rather than descriptive. That is, it defines what the FAA would *like* ADM to be—a *systematic* approach and a *best course* of action. That is an idealized situation, as opposed to what really happens. Further, systematic approaches and best courses of action may not be the best overall approach to making decisions. For inexperienced pilots, a systematized approach (using, e.g, the DECIDE or similar models to be discussed later) may well be the best way to approach decision-making. However, expert pilots tend to rely upon a process called recognition-primed decision-making, in which they almost instantly arrive at a decision, based upon the similarity of the current situation to those they have experienced before.

In addition, a decision that satisfies certain basic criteria (safety, efficiency, availability of alternatives, etc.) may not be the optimal course of action, but may be entirely satisfactory under the circumstances. In fact, there may be no single "best" course of action. Flying, and most of life's decisions, is not like picking an investment to give the best rate of return. In that case, arguably, there is a single criterion that can be satisfied—making the most money in a given period of time—and, the problem is to pick the investment, or set of investments, which maximizes that criterion. However, in most situations, there are multiple criteria that need to be considered. For example, when flying, we want to arrive at our destination intact, but we also want to arrive on time, with minimal discomfort due to turbulence, and at a minimum cost. Even with this relatively limited set of criteria, selecting a course of action that optimizes each separate criterion is effectively impossible. Rather, we pick a course of action that generally keeps each criterion within acceptable bounds, and recognizes that some criteria (such as arriving intact) are more important than others.

For our purposes, let us define decision-making as a cognitive process by which we acquire and use information to makes choices from among alternatives. We can then look at how that process works, and why it may produce good or not so good choices.

10.3   TYPES OF DECISIONS

There are many different ways of looking at decisions. Some might be called discrete decisions, such as deciding to buy a pizza or burger for lunch, deciding to press on into weather, or to take off over gross weight. But, there are other ways you can describe decisions, as shown in Figure 10.1.

Besides the discrete choice, you can also look at decisions as continuing over a long period of time. For example, after you decide to take off, you must then keep making the decision to continue or divert. This sort of decision is not as obvious as the discrete decision, but is more like a background activity, akin to the *problem vigil* phase of decision-making in Jensen's (1995) decision-making model that we will examine later.

```
┌─────────────────────────────────────────────┐
│              Decision taxonomy                │
│  ─────────────────────────────────────────   │
│                                               │
│  • Duration                                   │
│     • Discrete—Do I go or not?                │
│     • Continual—Do I keep going or not?       │
│  • Purpose                                    │
│     • Strategic—Where do I want to go?        │
│     • Tactical—How do I get there?            │
│  • Cognitive workload                         │
│     • Low—Simple, well-learned tasks          │
│     • High—Complex, ill-defined problems      │
│                                               │
└─────────────────────────────────────────────┘
```

FIGURE 10.1   Decision taxonomy.

You might also look at the purpose of decisions. For example, you could decide that you want to go to some destination on the opposite side of a large body of water. You then have to make a series of tactical decisions about just how to get there. Do you fly over the water to get there, or do you divert along an overland route? Do you try to fly between the thunderstorms, do you make a lengthy diversion around them, or do you land and wait for them to pass over?

Cognitive workload is also an important consideration. Some decisions are fairly well defined and involve situations that you have faced many times in the past. Decisions of this sort do not usually require a lot of cognitive effort. You simply repeat whatever worked last time. However, occasionally, you will run into complex situations that you have not previously encountered, and in those cases you will need to invest a lot of cognitive effort into deciding on a course of action.

10.4   DECISION MODELS AND PROCESSES

Let us think about what you need in order to make a decision. First, you need some information about the world around you and how it is put together. For example, you need to know that flying into a cloud will result in your not being able to see the horizon, and that if that happens, then there is a strong probability that you will have trouble maintaining control of the aircraft.

You also need a process or system for combining that information to arrive at a decision. For example, you should know where to go for information about the weather, and how to put together the various bits of information about frontal systems, wind speeds, dew points, and visibility to make an informed decision about the suitability of the weather for flight. When you combine knowledge with a process, you can arrive at a decision, as shown in Figure 10.2.

You can think of knowledge as being two types: technical knowledge, for example, what you learned in flight training, and knowledge about what you personally can and will do. Most pilots have good technical knowledge, but are often lacking in knowledge about their personal capabilities and the things that can negatively impact their performance. We will talk more about this problem later.

Knowledge + Process = Decision

- Knowledge
  - Environment
    - What's happening out there
    - What's happening in here
  - Relationships
    - If I see this, then there is probably some of that
    - If I do this, then that will happen
- Process
  - Where do I look for information
  - How do I combine data

FIGURE 10.2   What is required for a decision?

Besides knowledge, you also need a process. Many different processes have been proposed, and they range from very simple to very complex. For example, the process currently being advocated by the FAA involves just three elements: perceive, process, and perform. This is a fairly simple model, in which perception leads to a processing of information, which then leads to performance. You might re-write this model as looking, thinking, and acting.

10.4.1   THE DECIDE MODEL

The DECIDE model (Benner 1975), originally based on hazardous materials emergencies, is a six-element decision-making process that can help to organize a person's thoughts and prevent them from overlooking potentially important facts. The DECIDE model includes the elements shown in Figure 10.3.

10.4.2   JENSEN'S PILOT JUDGMENT MODEL

Jensen (1995) proposed a somewhat more detailed Judgment Model with stages that consisted of

- *Problem vigil*: The pilot maintains a constant state of vigil so that changes in the environment (e.g., appearance of dark clouds) can be detected.

D – Detect the fact that a choice must be made
E – Estimate the significance of the choice
C – Choose a safe outcome
I – Identify plausible actions
D – Do the best option
E – Evaluate the effect of the action

FIGURE 10.3   DECIDE model.

- *Recognition*: The pilot realizes the changes in the environment could affect the safety of the flight (e.g., development of dark clouds could lead to a severe thunderstorm).
- *Diagnosis*: The pilot attempts to understand the nature of the problem (e.g., assess the possibility that cloud development could lead to a potentially dangerous storm and its implications for flight).
- *Alternative identification*: The pilot identifies various alternatives (i.e., the choice of an alternative flight path).
- *Risk assessment*: The pilot tries to determine the risks associated with the alternatives (gains vs. losses).
- *Background factors*: The pilot's decisions are influenced by personal and social pressures.
- *Decision-making*: The pilot chooses the final course of action (e.g., whether to continue visual flight rules [VFR] flight into instrument meteorological conditions (IMC) or to divert).
- *Action*: The pilot applies the decision by moving flight controls, interacting with passengers, air traffic control (ATC), and other crewmembers.

10.4.3   A DETAILED DECISION MODEL

Figure 10.4 depicts an even more detailed model that tries to capture both the decision-making process and the various factors that influence decisions. The center column shows the stages in the decision-making process. The left column is a plain language description of that stage, and the right column lists some of the factors that impact each of the stages. All of these decision-making models share the same general chronology of events, beginning with the recognition that the need for a decision exists, and ending with the execution of the decision and continued monitoring of the situation. We will use the model in Figure 10.4 as a guide for our discussion of the decision-making process.

10.4.3.1   Perception

Similar to the FAA model, we start with perception—taking information from all the senses either directly or through electronic means. But, in this model, we try to list some of the factors that act upon perception and the subsequent processing stages. At the perceptual stage, one factor is attention control. Basically, this means whether we are paying attention to the external stimuli. Think of attention control as the beam of a flashlight that we can shine around the cockpit, illuminating different dials and displays. This is also sometimes called division of attention, and that is an interesting title, since it highlights the notion that you have only a limited amount of attention, which must be divided among the various inputs. Applying too much of your attention resource to one display while neglecting another can produce unfortunate consequences.

10.4.3.2   Recognition

Once you have acquired some sensory information, you must determine what it is. Recognition of external stimuli is accomplished by comparing the stimuli to the store of information contained in your memories. It is theorized that this takes place

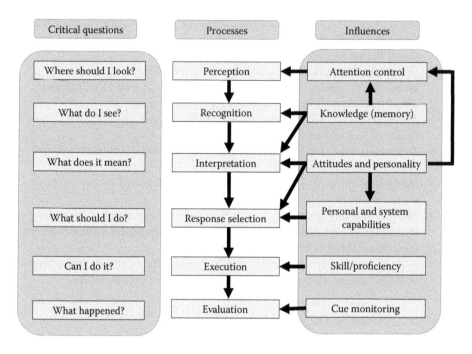

FIGURE 10.4 Decision process and influence model.

primarily by a pattern-matching process, in which your brain compares the new stimulus to the vast number of stored patterns to see if it can find a match. If it does, then you are said to recognize the stimulus.

For a simple example, if you look out the windshield and see some clouds, then that perceptual stimulus is compared to your memories of clouds to see if you have encountered this stimulus before. Is this a little fair-weather cumulus cloud, or is this an anvil-headed thunderstorm? Your brain is really quite good at performing these comparisons and will arrive at an answer amazingly quickly.

Experts, pilots with a large and varied store of experiences gained over many years and thousands of hours of flight, will have a very large repertoire of experiences and can therefore match almost all incoming stimuli to the memory of a similar experience. Technically, this is known as recognition-primed decision-making and is a characteristic of decision-making among experts in all domains. Unfortunately, those with relatively little experience do not have that vast storehouse of experience to draw from. Therefore, their recognition and decision-making processes are constrained, and we will discuss some of the ways to help novices later in the chapter.

10.4.3.3   Interpretation

Once you have perceived and recognized a situation, you must determine what it means with respect to you. That is, what are the implications of an anvil-shaped thunderstorm for you on this particular flight? Does it present a hazard? How severe is the hazard? Am I willing to expose myself to this hazard by continuing the flight, or do I need to take some action?

These sorts of questions, and the answers that you generate, are based primarily on your knowledge of this and similar situations, but also on your personality and your personal level of risk tolerance. This is where attitudes, such as denial and impulsivity, come into play, as they will shape how you interpret the situation.

This and the preceding two stages constitute what is termed situation awareness (SA). SA is the perception of the elements in the environment within a volume of time and space, the comprehension of their meaning, and the projection of their status in the near future. Most problems in SA arise from a failure to perceive the relevant elements in the environment. That is, pilots either do not know where to look or do not recognize what they see, which leads to an accident.

10.4.3.4   Response Selection

Some psychologists like to describe the decision-making process as consisting of a problem recognition phase and a response selection phase. The problem recognition phase would correspond to the first three stages in this model. We perceive the external stimuli, recognize them, and determine that a problem exists that requires us to make some decision.

Picking an appropriate response is the next stage in our decision-making process. Picking a response depends on what both you and the aircraft are capable of doing. If you find yourself flying into an area of rising terrain, you might want to climb, but the aircraft might not be capable of climbing at that altitude. Or, you might be flying into deteriorating weather conditions in a fully IFR capable aircraft, but lack the personal skills needed to maintain safe instrument flight.

Unfortunately, cognitive biases, personality, and risk tolerance get involved in the response selection, such that we tend to overestimate our personal capabilities and underestimate the risks we have encountered. These will be discussed in greater detail later.

10.4.3.5   Execution

Having identified a problem and determined a response, we must now execute that response. Your current skill levels are the critical components here. To borrow an example from a different domain, consider the golfer who knows the exact distance to the hole from his or her current position and has a club that he or she used during the warm-up session to hit the ball that distance. The question is whether he or she is sufficiently skilled to execute the shot under the current conditions. Even golf pros do not hit the ball perfectly every time, and for amateurs, the likelihood of a miss-hit shot landing in the water or the woods is fairly high. Hence, he or she needs to watch the ball carefully to see where it goes.

10.4.3.6   Evaluation

Watching where the golf ball goes leads us to the final stage of evaluation. Did we get the ball on the green, or do we need to hit it again? Setting our golf clubs aside and getting back in the cockpit, imagine that in response to IFR conditions at our destination airport we decided to execute a nonprecision VOR approach—under the circumstances, that may be an appropriate and reasonable decision. However, in reading a lot of accident reports, almost all the decisions leading up to the accident seemed appropriate and reasonable at the time. So, we must be continually vigilant to ensure that our decision is being executed properly and is leading to the outcome we expected. On an instrument approach, the boundary conditions that necessitate a change of plan, such a drifting too far off course, are fairly well defined. In other situations, such as a cross-country flight through mountainous terrain, we may need to set our own boundary conditions and take immediate action if a condition is exceeded. To put it more simply, if you find that you cannot climb and there is a big mountain ahead of you, it is definitely time to do something else, and you really need to have determined that something else much earlier.

10.5   DECISION STRATEGIES

We have talked about knowledge and processes, but we also need to be aware of the overall strategies used in decision-making. Some of the more common strategies that people use when making decisions are shown in Figure 10.5.

10.5.1   OPTIMIZING

Optimizing means that we try to select the course of action with the best payoff. However, while it is theoretically attractive, from a practical standpoint this is a very difficult strategy to follow, since it requires that we have access to reliable, relevant information that covers all the factors influencing the decision. And, we need time in which to carefully consider each and every alternative. While this may be a good approach for a company considering the acquisition of another company, it is really not too practical for pilots, or anyone else involved in a fast-paced dynamic process with limited access to information and limited time to arrive at a decision. Note, however, that this is essentially what the FAA definition of ADM would require.

- Goal: Select the course of action with the highest payoff
  - Estimation of costs and benefits of every viable course of action.
  - Simultaneous or joint comparison of costs and benefits of all alternatives.
- Problems
  - High information-processing load on humans.
  - High cost in time, effort, and money.

Decision strategies

- Optimizing
- Satisficing
- Quasi-satisficing
- Sole decision rule
- Selection by elimination
- Incrementalism and muddling through

FIGURE 10.5   Decision-making strategies.

- Decisions are made under severe time pressure.
- Optimization on stated objectives may result in suboptimization on unstated, less tangible objectives.
- Therefore, people often
  - Do not consider all alternatives.
  - Do not evaluate all alternatives thoroughly and rigorously.
  - Do not consider all objectives and criteria.
  - Place more weight on intangible objectives and criteria.

10.5.2 SATISFICING

Rather than trying to achieve the absolute best solution with the optimizing strategy, most people tend to use a strategy in which they find a good-enough solution and go with that. If a decision generally achieves the goal of getting the plane where you want it to go, while preserving a reasonable level of safety and comfort, then it is probably not a bad solution. This is generally the strategy used by most people in most situations. For example, few people find the perfect house of their dreams that satisfies absolutely all their wishes. Instead, they pick a house that fits their budget and has more or less the floor plan they want in a location that is not too far from work. It is not perfect, but it is good enough.

- Decision-makers satisfice rather than maximize.
- They choose courses of action that are "good enough"—that meet a certain minimal set of requirements.
- Human beings have limited information-processing capabilities.
- Optimization may not be practical, particularly in a multi-objective problem, yet knowing the optimal solution for each objective and under various scenarios can provide insight to make a good satisficing choice.

10.5.3 SOLE DECISION RULE

It could be argued that a lot of what we do in aviation is based on this rule. For example, we generally do what the regulatory authorities tell us to. Think of vertical and horizontal separation, minimum descent altitudes, and similar sorts of rules. We also use some fairly hard and fast decisions rules in situations such as rejected takeoff speeds. Taken to an extreme, of course, this can lead to impulsive, poorly considered decisions. Sometimes, situations are such that the old rule just will not work, and a good decision-maker must recognize when that occurs and be ready to broaden his or her search for a solution. The catastrophic failure of the hydraulic system on the DC-10 at Sioux City might be an example of such a situation in which there are no established procedures for handling the situation.

- Tell a qualified expert about your problem and do whatever he or she says—that will be good enough.
- Rely upon a single formula as the sole decision rule.

- Use only one criterion for a suitable choice, for example, do nothing that will take you toward rising terrain.
- Impulsive decision-making usually falls under this category.

10.5.4 SELECTION BY ELIMINATION

If you can determine what the most important criterion is, then selection by eliminating those alternatives that do not meet that criterion may be an effective strategy. For example, if you are running low on fuel over the ocean, then an alternative that does not allow you to reach dry land may be eliminated immediately. Once you have found a solution that gets you to dry land, then you can apply another criterion, such as reaching an airport capable of handling your aircraft.

Obviously, this strategy is not without its drawbacks. For example, you may not be able to find a solution that meets the criterion of reaching dry land, and you will have wasted a lot of time that could have been devoted to finding a nice place to ditch—hopefully next to a coast guard cutter. Also, like the optimization strategy, this process can become mentally demanding and does not guarantee that you will find a solution to the prime criterion.

- Eliminate alternatives that do not meet the most important criterion.
- Repeat process for the next important criterion, and so on.
- Decision-making becomes a sequential narrowing-down process.
- "Better" alternatives might be eliminated early on—improper weights assigned to criteria.
- Decision-maker might run out of alternatives.
- For complex problems, this process might still leave decision-maker with large number of alternatives.

10.5.5 INCREMENTALISM

Later, we will look at a study conducted at the Ohio State University that tried to characterize the behavior of expert pilots. One thing they found was that the top-performing pilots used what they termed progressive decision-making. In some ways, this is similar to incrementalism, in that these expert pilots made initial decisions when dealing with an in-flight problem, and then continued to refine their solution incrementally. This is in contrast to the poorer-performing pilots who made quick decisions and then failed to refine their solution or further investigate the nature of the problem. The incremental approach recognizes that initial solutions may not be optimal, but that in most cases, the solution can be refined to better suit the situation.

- Often, decision-makers have no real awareness of arriving at a new policy or decision—decision-making is an ongoing process—and the satisficing criteria themselves might change over time.
- Make incremental improvements over current situation and aim to reach an optimal situation over time.
- Useful for "fire-fighting" situations.

10.6 WHERE DECISIONS GO ASTRAY

We have examined many different ways of looking at decision-making. Now, let us examine some of the factors that can influence decisions—not usually for the better. As we saw in Chapter 3, many physiological factors can influence decision-making. In addition, there are a number of psychological and social factors that can also influence your decisions. These are termed cognitive biases. A cognitive bias, such as those listed in Table 10.1, is a pattern of deviation in decision-making that occurs in particular situations. As the term implies, cognitive biases are deviations from the norm or from rationality in decision-making. Some of the more common biases are listed and discussed below. However, psychologists have identified many more factors and the reader who would like a more extensive list should consult Jenicek (2001), or Kahneman et al. (1982). An excellent and very readable account is also available in the book, *Thinking, Fast and Slow*, by Kahneman (2011).

A recent study (Walsmsley and Gilbey 2016) demonstrated the effects that three of these biases can have on pilot performance. In that study, the researchers evaluated the effects of the anchoring and adjustment bias, confirmation bias, and outcome bias on the decisions of pilots in three separate studies. In each case, the cognitive bias negatively influenced the pilots' decisions. In the study of anchoring and adjustment bias, pilots placed too much importance on the initial weather reports they received and failed to adjust their perceptions in the face of new, contrary evidence. In the study of confirmation bias, pilots failed to favor disconfirmatory evidence over confirmatory evidence when deciding which environmental cues were more useful

TABLE 10.1
Psychological Biases That Influence Decisions

Bias	Description
Self-serving bias	Overestimating personal capabilities and underestimating situational demands (it won't happen to me; I'm better than average)
Confirmation bias	The tendency to search for or interpret information in a way that confirms one's preconceptions
Serial position effect	Information presented early is remembered better than information presented later
Loss-aversion bias	The strong tendency for people to prefer avoiding losses rather than acquiring gains
Valence effect of prediction bias	The tendency to overestimate the likelihood of good things happening and to underestimate the chance of bad things happening
False consensus effect bias	The tendency for people to overestimate the degree to which others agree with them
Anchoring bias	The tendency to rely too heavily, or "anchor," on one trait or piece of information
Outcome bias	The tendency to judge the quality of a decision by its eventual outcome, instead of judging it based on the quality of the decision at the time it was made

in deciding to continue a flight. Rather, they used evidence (weather information) that was consistent with their hypothesis. Finally, in a demonstration of the effects of outcome bias, pilots interpreted the decisions of pilots who flew into deteriorating weather conditions more favorably when the outcome was positive than when it was negative.

10.6.1 SELF-SERVING BIAS

Whenever pilots are surveyed and asked to rate themselves on their piloting skills, they generally rate themselves as better than average. This is a widespread observation, and not limited just to pilots. There have been many studies that have reported that people generally feel themselves to be above average. While they tend to overestimate their personal capabilities, they also tend to underestimate the demands of situations and the likelihood that something bad, for instance an accident, will happen to them. This is termed "self-serving bias."

In our model of decision-making, we noted that response selection was affected by our estimation of our personal capabilities. If you seriously overestimate your capabilities and underestimate the demands of a situation, bad things are likely to follow.

10.6.2 CONFIRMATION BIAS

People have a strong tendency to look for information that confirms their own preconceptions. Imagine you want to make a cross-country trip to visit your brother, and when you talk with him he tells you that the weather is great. If you then get a weather briefing, you are more likely to pay attention to and remember the parts of the briefing that support your planned flight than those that would cause you to reconsider. Good decision-makers always look for disconfirming information—information that contradicts their initial decision.

10.6.3 SERIAL POSITION EFFECT

Even the order in which you receive information is important. Information is weighted more strongly when it appears early in a series, even when the order is unimportant. For example, people form a more positive impression of someone described as "intelligent, industrious, impulsive, critical, stubborn, envious" than when they are given the same words in reverse order (Kahneman 2011).

10.6.4 LOSS-AVERSION BIAS

Some research has shown that pilots are more likely to press on into deteriorating weather late in a trip compared to early. This is an example of loss-aversion bias. Diverting late in the trip means the loss of all the time, fuel, and money spent to get to that point. However, if the weather is encountered shortly after taking off, then the loss is not very great, and pilots are more likely to turn around. O'Hare and Smitheram (1995) demonstrated that the way in which a decision is framed—as a potential gain or a sure loss—affects the decisions pilots make in these situations.

10.6.5   Valence Effect

The valence effect of prediction bias is similar to the self-serving bias mentioned earlier. In general, people have trouble estimating the likelihood of events—both good and bad. So, they tend to overestimate the likelihood of a sudden break in the weather that will allow them to take off, while they underestimate the likelihood of a sudden deterioration in the weather that will force them to make a diversion.

10.6.6   False Consensus Effect

People assume that their beliefs and opinions are shared by those around them. This bias can be very strong, such that when shown that a consensus does not exist, people will assume those who disagree with them are defective. In the cockpit, such a mistaken belief in shared viewpoints could obviously lead to disastrous consequences. Thus, one of the major thrusts of the crew resource management (CRM) initiative is to encourage a better understanding among the crewmembers of their differing viewpoints.

10.6.7   Anchoring Bias

Often the first piece of information offered serves as an anchor, or a reference point for subsequent information. Once this anchor is set, subsequent judgments are made by adjusting away from that anchor. For example, an initial report of severe weather in an area may serve as an anchor for following reports. By comparison, the subsequent weather seems favorable, even if it is, by an objective standard, still dangerous for flight.

10.6.8   Outcome Bias

It is common to judge the quality of a decision by the outcome. Thus, someone might make a risky stock purchase, but if the stock price rises and the person makes a profit, then the decision is judged to have been good—even if the preponderance of evidence available at the time of the decision argued strongly against the purchase.

10.7   WHEN DECISIONS TAKE FLIGHT: ADM

If you made it to here, then you now know a lot (perhaps more than you wanted) about decision-making. Now, let us look at decision-making specifically in aviation. Everyone agrees that decision-making is important, and that poor decisions contribute to accidents, both in the cockpit and elsewhere. A study by Jensen and Benel (1977) marks the beginning of the modern interest in ADM. They found that approximately 80% of accidents were associated with some sort of human factors, and that poor decision-making was involved in 50% of fatal accidents. More recent studies by the National Transportation Safety Board (NTSB 2003) and by Wiegmann et al. (2005) have reported that about 30% of fatal general aviation accidents involve poor decision-making.

A search of the NTSB database for Part 91 (general aviation) accidents during the period 2000–2015 produced 159 reports in which decision-making was mentioned as part of the probable cause. About two-thirds of those accidents involved a fatality. The accidents run the gamut of aviation, including a commercial rated pilot repositioning the airplane from Texas to Wisconsin, with an intermediate stop in Missouri, where he refueled, but did not visually check the tanks. At about 20 minutes from his destination, the engine ran out of gas and the pilot made a forced landing to a snow-covered field (NTSB, CEN14CA124). There were no injuries in this case, but other pilots were not so fortunate.

In an accident that occurred near Aurora, Colorado, a pilot was showing off his newly purchased twin aircraft. The pilot's friends and several other witnesses reported observing the pilot performing low-level, high-speed aerobatic maneuvers before the airplane collided with trees and then terrain. A 1.75-L bottle of whiskey was found in the airplane wreckage. A review of the pilot's FAA medical records revealed that he had a history of alcohol dependence but had reportedly been sober for almost 4 years. Toxicological testing revealed that the pilot had a blood alcohol content of 0.252 mg of alcohol per deciliter of blood, which was over six times the limit (0.04) Federal Aviation Regulations allowed for pilots operating an aircraft (NTSB, CEN14FA163).

A large proportion of the accidents (almost all fatal) in which poor decision-making is a causal factor involve flight into IMC. Typical of these accidents is one that occurred on a moon-less night near Vaughn, Minnesota. In this case, a noninstrument-rated pilot departed on a cross-country flight. About 3 hours later, the airplane stopped at an airport and was refueled. The airplane subsequently departed again and flew toward the destination airport. Radar data showed that the airplane then climbed to 10,500 feet mean sea level but that it subsequently began to descend; the last radar return showed the airplane at 7100 feet mean sea level. The airplane was reported missing when it did not arrive at the destination. Multiple weather sources showed that IMC existed along the route of flight and that these were reported before the accident airplane departed. Additionally, the freezing level was at the surface, and moderate turbulence was expected from the surface through 24,000 feet. Pilots flying in the area around the time of the accident confirmed the presence of turbulence and/or mountain-wave conditions, and they indicated the presence of icing in the clouds with cloud tops near 9000 feet. No record could be found of the pilot receiving a weather briefing prior to the flight (NTSB, CEN15FA092).

10.7.1 The Origins of Modern ADM

We are pretty safe in saying that about a third to a half of fatal accidents are more-or-less directly attributable to a poor decision or decisions. However, do not assume we blame the pilot for the decision. As you will see in Chapter 11, it is a great deal more complex than that. Nevertheless, it is understandable that the report by Jensen and Benel (1977) generated a great deal of interest among regulatory authorities and researchers. The study by Jensen and Benel was a seminal work in that it specifically identified decision-making as contributing to a large proportion of fatal general aviation accidents. That study sparked a great deal of interest in how pilots make decisions that put them at risk of being in an accident, and how decision-making may be improved. Indeed, one of the first outcomes from this focus on decision-making was a report by Berlin and his associates (Berlin and Holmes 1981; Berlin et al. 1982a,b,c) in which they described a training program aimed specifically at addressing the decision-making shortcomings identified in the Jensen and Benel study. Working at Embry-Riddle Aeronautical University under the sponsorship of the U.S. FAA, Berlin et al. developed a training program and student manual that included the following:

- Three subject areas
  - Pilot: Including the pilot's state of health, competency in a given situation, level of fatigue, and other factors effecting performance.
  - Aircraft: Considerations of the airworthiness, powerplant, and performance criteria such as weight and balance.
  - Environment: Including the weather, airfield altitude and temperature, and outside inputs such as weather briefings, or ATC instructions.
- Six action ways
  - Do–No Do
    - Do: The pilot did something he should not have done.
    - No Do: The pilot did not do something he should have done.
  - Under Do–Over Do
    - Under Do: The pilot did not do enough, when he should have done more.
    - Over Do: The pilot did too much, when he should have done less.
  - Early Do–Late Do
    - Early Do: The pilot acted too early, when he should have delayed acting.
    - Late Do: The pilot acted too late, when he should have acted earlier.
- Poor judgment behavior chain
  - One poor judgment increases the probability that another poor judgment will follow.
  - The more poor judgments made in sequence, the more probable that others will continue to follow.
  - As the poor judgment chain grows, the alternatives for safe flight decrease.
  - The longer the poor judgment chain becomes, the more probably it is than an accident will occur.
- Three mental processes of safe flight
  - Automatic reaction: The mode of thinking that allows the pilot to maintain control of the aircraft while simultaneously engaging in other activities. This is a challenge for student pilots who are too busy trying to keep the wings level; but, with practice, pilots quickly learn to do several things more-or-less simultaneously.

- Problem resolving: The mode of thinking that helps a pilot overcome undesirable situations by means of a systematic process. In this mode, the pilot must work through a problem, as contrasted with the automatic reaction mode.
- Repeated reviewing: In this mode of thinking, the pilot is continuously aware of all the factors (pilot/aircraft/environment) that affect safe flight. By repeated reviewing, the pilot keeps an awareness of all conditions that contribute to safe flight or have the potential to impact the flight.
- Five hazardous thought patterns: Having one or more of these hazardous thought patterns predisposed pilots to act in ways that placed them at greater risk for accident involvement.
  - Anti-authority: No one can tell me what to do.
  - Impulsivity: Do something quickly.
  - Invulnerability: It won't happen to me.
  - Macho: I can do it.
  - External control (resignation): What's the use.

The second volume of this report (Berlin et al. 1982b) contained detailed descriptions and exercises corresponding to the elements listed above. This included an instrument that pilots could use to do a self-assessment of their hazardous thought patterns. An initial, small-scale evaluation of the training manual was conducted using three groups of students at Embry-Riddle Aeronautical University. One of the three groups received the new training program, and the other two groups served as controls. In this evaluation, the experimental group had significantly better performance on written tests and on an observation flight than the two control groups. On the basis of these findings, the authors concluded that the training manual had a positive effect on the decision-making of the test subjects.

On the basis of the positive initial results, a series of publications using material taken from the Berlin et al. training manual were produced by the FAA. Each publication was tailored to fit the needs and experiences of a particular segment of the pilot population. The publications included:

- *ADM for Helicopter Pilots* (Adams and Thompson 1987)
- *ADM for Instructor Pilots* (Buch et al. 1987)
- *ADM for Student and Private Pilots* (Diehl et al. 1987)
- *ADM for Instrument Pilots* (Jensen et al. 1987)
- *ADM for Commercial Pilots* (Jenson and Adrion 1988)
- *Risk Management for Air Ambulance Helicopter Operators* (Adams 1989)

In addition to these publications that are rather narrowly aimed at training specific skills in defined groups of pilots, Jensen (1995) has produced a text that covers the common elements across all these publications in greater depth. This book also incorporates considerations of CRM, a concept that developed more-or-less in parallel with the work on pilot decision-making. However, while the decision-making work was typically oriented toward general aviation pilots, the work on CRM grew out of reviews of accidents in the air carrier community.

10.7.2 EVALUATING ADM

Following the release of the ADM training manual by Berlin et al. (1982a,b) and the initial evaluation of the effectiveness of this training in the United States, similar studies were conducted elsewhere. In Canada, a study that evaluated air cadets was conducted in which the judgment of the cadets was tested during a flight by asking them to perform an unsafe maneuver. Pilots who received the ADM training made correct decisions in 83% of the test situations, compared to 43% of the pilots who did not receive such training (Buch and Diehl 1983, 1984). A further study (Lester, et al. 1986) of pilots attending flight schools in Canada also showed a significant impact for the ADM training. In that study, 70% of the group that received ADM training chose the correct responses on an observation flight, compared to 60% of the pilots in the control group.

Similar results were noted in a study conducted in Australia (Telfer and Ashman 1986; Telfer 1987, 1989) using students from five flying schools in New South Wales. Even though the samples used were quite small (only 20 total subjects divided among three groups), significant differences were found among the groups in favor of the ADM training.

The results from these evaluations of ADM training and others (Connolly and Blackwell 1987; Diehl and Lester 1987) were reviewed by Diehl (1990), who provided a summary of the results in terms of reductions in pilot error. Those results are reproduced in Table 10.2.

Given the consistently significant results demonstrated by the ADM training in reducing error among pilots in these studies, it seems clear that the training does have an impact on pilot behavior. However, there are significant issues that were not addressed by these studies. For example, how long does the effect last following training? Since all the evaluations were conducted either immediately following the completion of pilot training or shortly thereafter, the rate at which the training effect

TABLE 10.2
Results of ADM Training Evaluation Studies

Researchers	Environment	Experiment n	Control n	Error Reduction (%)
Berlin et al. (1982a)	Aeronautical university	26	24	17
Buch and Diehl (1983)	Flying schools	15	25	40
Buch and Diehl (1983)	College	17	62	9
Telfer and Ashman (1986)	Aero clubs	8	6	8
Diehl and Lester (1987)	Fixed-base operators	20	25	10
Connolly and Blackwell (1987)	Aeronautical university	16	16	46

Source: Adapted from Diehl, A.E. 1990. *Proceedings of the 34th Meeting of the Human Factors Society* (pp. 1367–1371). Santa Monica, CA: Human Factors Society.

Note: All results significant, $p < 0.05$.

decays cannot be determined. This is important because if the effect only lasts a short time, then the training must be repeated frequently to maintain the effect.

Additionally, what parts of the training are having an impact? Recall from the list of contents presented earlier that ADM training covers a fairly broad spectrum of topics, ranging from decision heuristics (DECIDE model) to personality traits (five hazardous attitudes). Since these were all covered at the same time during the ADM training, it is not possible from the existing data to determine if they are all needed, or if only one or two of the individual components are responsible for the improvements in behavior.

Finally, an inspection of the data in Table 10.2 suggests that the venue in which the training is administered may influence the magnitude of the effect. Specifically, it is interesting to note that the smallest effects were noted in the least rigorous training environments (The Aero Clubs and Fixed-Base Operators), while much larger effects were found in the Aeronautical University and Flight School environments.

All of these would be important issues to consider and investigate more fully. Indeed, this approach to developing an intervention without an underlying theoretical rationale and without a firm empirical basis has exposed ADM training to some criticism (cf. O'Hare and Roscoe 1990; Wiggins and O'Hare 1993). These criticisms are reflected in studies of one major component of ADM training, the five hazardous thoughts, or as they are sometimes called, "hazardous attitudes."

10.7.3 Hazardous Attitudes

All of the ADM training manuals, including the FAA publications listed earlier, have included an instrument for the self-assessment of hazardous attitudes. Although the content varies with the specific group of pilots for whom the training was designed, all the instruments consist of some number (typically 10) of scenarios in which an aviation situation is described. Five alternative explanations for the course of action taken by the pilot in the scenario are then provided and the pilot completing the instrument is asked to choose the one that he or she thinks best applies. The following example is taken from the FAA publication aimed at student and private pilots (Diehl et al. 1987):

- You have just completed your base leg for a landing on runway 14 at an uncontrolled airport. As you turn to final, you see that the wind has changed, blowing from about 90°. You make two sharp turns and land on runway 8. What was your reasoning?
  - You believe you are a really good pilot who can safely make sudden maneuvers.
  - You believe your flight instructor was overly cautious when insisting that a pilot must go around rather than make sudden course changes while on final approach.
  - You know there would be no danger in making the sudden turns because you do things like this all the time.
  - You know landing into the wind is best, so you act as soon as you can to avoid a crosswind landing.
  - The unexpected wind change is a bad break, but you figure if the wind can change, so can you.

Each of the five alternatives is keyed to one of the five hazardous attitudes. In the previous example, the keyed attitudes are: (a) macho; (b) anti-Authority; (c) invulnerability; (d) impulsivity; and (e) resignation. Thus, the person who selected alternative *a* as being the best explanation for the behavior of the pilot in the scenario would be espousing a macho attitude. Using the scoring key provided in the training manuals, pilots can compute their scores for each of the five hazardous attitudes and can create a profile of their hazardous attitudes. From that profile, they may identify which, if any, of the attitudes is dominant. The text of the training manuals then provides some guidance on dealing with each of the hazardous attitudes, and proposes some short, easily remembered "antidotes" for each attitude. For example, the "antidote" for having a macho attitude is, "Taking chances is foolish" (Diehl et al. 1987, p. 63).

10.7.4 MEASURING HAZARDOUS ATTITUDES

Three studies (Lester and Bombachi 1984; Lester and Connolly 1987; Lubner and Markowitz 1991) have compared the hazardous attitudes scales with other personality measures. These have included the Rotter Locus of Control scale, and several scales from the Cattell 16 PF. In all of these studies, the scores for the individual hazardous attitudes were found to be highly correlated with each other. Moderate to low correlations were also observed with the other personality measures, and with external criteria such as involvement in near-accidents. However, the interpretation of the results from these studies is problematic.

Hunter (2004) has criticized the use of the self-assessment instrument used in the various FAA publications because it utilized an ipsative format. As Anastasia (1968, p. 453) notes, an ipsative scale is one in which, "the strength of each need is expressed, not in absolute terms, but in relation to the strength of the individual's other needs ... an individual responds by expressing a preference for one item against another." In this type of scale, having a high score on one subscale forces the scores on the other subscales to be low. Because of this restriction, ipsative scales are subject to significant psychometric limitations. These limitations make the use of traditional statistical analysis methods (such as correlation) inappropriate in many instances. Hence, the studies that have tried to correlate hazardous attitude scores taken from the self-assessment instrument with other criteria (such as scores on other psychological instruments) are seriously flawed and cannot, for the most part, provide useful and reliable information. (For a discussion of the difficulties associated with ipsative scoring methods, see Saville and Wilson 1991; Bartram 1996.)

To address this problem, Hunter (2004) recommended that researchers use scales based on Likert scale items. This type of item, widely used in psychological research, typically consists of a statement (e.g., "I like candy") to which the respondent expresses his or her degree of agreement by selecting one of several alternatives (e.g., "Strongly Agree," "Agree," "Disagree," "Strongly Disagree").

Hunter and other researchers (Holt et al. 1991) have developed instruments for the assessment of hazardous attitudes using Likert scale items. In a comparison of the traditional instrument contained in the FAA training materials and the Likert-style instruments (Hunter 2004), the superiority of the Likert instruments both in terms of reliability and correlations with external criteria (involvement in hazardous events) was clearly demonstrated. Using these measurement instruments, it is possible to empirically demonstrate that pilots' attitudes can affect the likelihood of their involvement in an accident.

Hazardous attitudes are but one of several psychological constructs that have been investigated as possible factors that affect decision-making and impact the likelihood of accident involvement. These constructs include locus of control (LOC), risk perception, risk tolerance, and situational awareness.

10.8   LOCUS OF CONTROL

LOC refers to the degree to which persons believe that what happens to them is under their personal control (internal LOC) or whether what happens to them is a result of external factors (e.g., luck, of the actions of others) over which they have no control (external LOC). This construct was first proposed by Rotter (1966), and since that time, it has been used in a variety of settings (see Stewart 2006, for a review). Wichman and Ball (1983) administered the LOC to a sample of 200 general aviation pilots and found that the pilots were significantly more internal than Rotter's original sample. They also found that the pilots who were higher on LOC internality were more likely to attend safety clinics, possibly indicating a greater safety orientation among this group, compared to the pilots with a greater LOC externality.

Several variations on the Rotter LOC scale have been constructed that assess LOC perceptions in a particular domain. These include LOC scales that are specific to driving (Montag and Comrey 1987) and medical issues (Wallston et al. 1976). These development efforts were spurred by the belief, noted by Montag and Comrey (1987, p. 339) that "Attempts to relate internality-externality to outside criteria have been more successful when the measures of this construct were tailored more specifically to the target behavior (e.g., drinking, health, affiliation), rather than using the more general I-E scale itself."

Continuing in this same vein, Jones and Wuebker (1985) developed and validated a safety LOC scale to predict employees' accidents and injuries in industrial settings. They found that participants in the lower accident risk groups were significantly more internal on the safety LOC than participants in the high-risk groups. In a subsequent study of safety among hospital workers, Jones and Wubker (1993) found that workers who held more internal safety attitudes were significantly less likely to have an occupational accident compared to employees with more external attitudes.

On the basis of these results, Hunter (2002) developed an Aviation Safety Locus of Control (AS-LOC) scale by modifying the Jones and Wuebker (1985) scale so as to put all the scale items into an aviation context. Two example items from the AS-LOC, measuring internality and externality, respectively, are

- Accidents and injuries occur because pilots do not take enough interest in safety.
- Avoiding accidents is a matter of luck.

In an evaluation study conducted using 176 pilots who completed the AS-LOC over the Internet, Hunter (2002) found a significant correlation ($r = -0.205$; $p < 0.007$) between internality and involvement in hazardous events. In contrast, a nonsignificant correlation ($r = 0.077$) was found between externality and the hazardous event scale score. Consistent with the previous research, pilots exhibited a substantially higher internal orientation than external orientation on the new scale. Similar findings were also reported by Joseph and Ganesh (2006) who administered the AS-LOC to a sample of 101 Indian pilots. As in the previous research, the Indian pilots also had significantly higher internal than external LOC scores. An interesting finding of this study is that the civil pilots had higher internal LOC scores than the military pilots. Additionally, the transport pilots had the highest internal scores of any of the pilot groups, followed by fighter pilots and helicopter pilots. Given the differences in accident rates among these groups, it would be interesting to investigate the degree to which these differences in AS-LOC scores are attributable to training, formal selection processes, or some sort of self-selection process.

10.9   RISK PERCEPTION AND RISK TOLERANCE

Risk assessment and management is one component of the broader process of pilot decision-making. As noted earlier, poor pilot decision-making has been implicated as a leading factor in fatal general aviation accidents (Jensen and Benel 1977), and poor risk assessment can contribute significantly to poor decision-making. To address the question of risk perception among pilots, O'Hare (1990) developed an Aeronautical Risk Judgment Questionnaire to assess pilots' perceptions of the risks and hazards of general aviation. Hazard awareness was assessed by (a) having pilots estimate the percentage of accidents attributable to six broad categories, (b) ranking the phases of flight by hazard level, and (c) ranking detailed causes of fatal accidents (e.g., spatial disorientation, misuse of flaps). O'Hare found that pilots substantially underestimated the risk of general aviation flying relative to other activities, and similarly underestimated their likelihood of being in an accident. On the basis of these results, he concluded that, "… an unrealistic assessment of the risks involved may be a factor in leading pilots to 'press on' into deteriorating weather" (O'Hare 1990, p. 599).

This conclusion was supported by research (O'Hare and Smitheram 1995; Goh and Wiegmann 2001) that shows that pilots who continue flight into adverse weather conditions have a poor perception of the risks. Interestingly, similar results are found in studies of youthful drivers (Trankle et al. 1990) who have significantly poorer perceptions of the hazards involved in driving compared to older, safer drivers.

Risk perception and risk tolerance are related and often confounded constructs. Hunter (2002, p. 3) defined risk perception as "the recognition of the risk inherent in a situation," and suggested that risk perception may be mediated both by the characteristics of the situation and the characteristics of the pilot experiencing the situation. Therefore, situations that present a high level of risk for one person may present only low risk for another. For example, the presence of clouds and low visibility may present a very high risk for a pilot qualified to fly only under visual meteorological conditions (VMC), but the same conditions would present very little risk for an experienced pilot qualified to fly in IMC in an appropriately equipped aircraft. The pilot must therefore perceive accurately not only the external situation, but also their personal capacities. Underestimation of the external situation and overestimation of personal capacity lead to a misperception of the risk and is frequently seen as a factor in aircraft accidents. Risk perception may therefore be conceived as primarily a cognitive activity, involving the accurate appraisal of external and internal states.

By contrast, Hunter (2002, p. 3) defined risk tolerance as "the amount of risk that an individual is willing to accept in the pursuit of some goal." Risk tolerance may be affected both by the person's general tendency to risk aversion and the personal value attached to the goal of a particular situation. In flying, just as in everyday life, some goals are more important than others, and the more important the goal, the more risk a person may be willing to accept.

Noting that previous studies had assessed pilots' estimates of global risk levels for broad categories (e.g., pilot, weather) and drawing upon the extensive driver research, Hunter (2002, 2006) proposed that more specific measures of risk perception and risk tolerance were needed. These new measures would operate at a tactical level, involving specific aviation situations, as opposed to the strategic level measures used previously. Using this approach, he developed two measures of risk perception and three measures of risk tolerance.

The risk perception measures included one measure (Risk Perception—Self) that asked pilots about the risk they personally would experience in a set of situations and another measure (Risk Perception—Other) that asked pilots about the risk that some other pilot would experience in another set of situations. Examples of both types of measures are given below:

- Risk Perception—Other
  - Low ceilings obscure the tops of the mountains, but pilots think that they can see through the pass to clear sky on the other side of the mountain ridges. They start up the wide valley that gradually gets narrower. As they approach the pass, they notice that they occasionally lose sight of the blue sky on the other side. They drop down closer to the road leading through the pass and presses on. As they go through the pass, the ceiling continues to drop and they find themselves suddenly in the clouds. They hold their heading and altitude and hope for the best.
  - Pilots are in a hurry to get going and do not carefully check their seat, seat belt, and shoulder harness. When they rotate, the seat moves backward on its tracks. As it slides backward, pilots pull back on the control yoke, sending the nose of the aircraft upward. As the airspeed begins to decay, they strain forward to push the yoke back to a neutral position.
  - Just after takeoff, pilots hear a banging noise on the passenger side of the aircraft. They look over at the passenger seat and find that they cannot locate one end of the seatbelt. They trim the aircraft for level flight, release the controls, and try to open the door to retrieve the seatbelt.
- Risk Perception—Self

- At night, fly from your local airport to another airport about 150 miles away, in a well-maintained aircraft, when the weather is marginal VFR (3 miles visibility and 2000 feet overcast).
- Fly in clear air at 6500 feet between two thunderstorms about 25 miles apart.
- Make a traffic pattern so that you end up turning for final with about a 45° bank.

In the case of the Risk Perception—Other scale, pilots were asked to rate the risk for a third-party, low-time general aviation pilot, using a scale from 1 (very low risk) to 100 (very high risk). For the Risk Perception—Self scale, pilots were asked to rate the risk if they personally were to perform this tomorrow, also using the 1–100 rating scale.

To measure risk tolerance, Hunter (2002, 2006) created three variants of a risky gamble scenario, each in an aviation setting. One variant involved making repeated flights in aircraft with a known likelihood of mechanical failure, while the other two involved flights between thunderstorms of varying distance and through mountainous areas with deteriorating weather. All three variants were structured such that the participants could gain points (and potential prizes) by accepting the risk and taking a flight; however, should they fail to complete a flight (i.e., crash), they would lose points. This manipulation was intended to provide a motivation to complete flights, while at the same time encouraging some degree of caution, since crashes could result in the loss of real prizes.

These measures and several others were administered to a large sample of pilots over the Internet. In general, support was found for the risk perception scales, in terms of their correlations with pilot involvement in hazardous aviation events. Pilots who experienced more hazardous events tended not to have rated the scenarios as risky, compared to pilots with fewer hazardous events. However, the measures of risk tolerance were not significantly correlated with hazardous aviation events. This led Hunter to conclude that poor perception of risks was a more important predictor of hazardous aviation events, and by extension of aviation accidents, than was risk tolerance.

Risk perception has been studied in a variety of setting and populations. Joseph and Reddy (2013) examined risk perception and safety attitudes among Indian army helicopter pilots. They found that higher risk-taking tendency was associated with low scores on measures of risk perception. In addition, higher risk-taking was also associated with higher risk attitudes scores. In Australia, researchers presented pilots with a risky flight scenario in a simulator and examined their attitudes, risk perception, and personal characteristics (e.g., age and flight time) (Drinkwater and Molesworth 2010). They found that there was a clear distinction in terms of risk perception between the pilots who elected to undertake the risky flight and the pilots who did not. In addition, there were differences in attitudes and demographic characteristics between the two groups.

Note that for a pilot to be effective at risk perception they must simultaneously make two very important calculations. First, they must evaluate the situation to determine exactly what is required for a successful conclusion. Second, they must evaluate their own capabilities to determine if they have what is demanded by the situation. Imagine the following situation. A pilot is flying in IMC and must make an instrument approach to near minimums at the destination airport. The pilot must then decide (1) what level of performance is needed to successfully execute the approach and (2) whether his or her level of proficiency is adequate for the task. For some conditions (e.g., blowing snow, high crosswinds, turbulence, rising terrain around the airfield), the approach may require a fairly high level of precision on the approach. Does this pilot possess that level of skill at that particular time? Remember self-serving bias? This can be a very tricky mental calculation. To underestimate the situational requirements or to overestimate your personal capabilities can lead to a tragic conclusion. This two-faceted calculation is the essence of risk perception.

Finally, there are many studies of risk perception and risk tolerance outside aviation. There is an extensive literature on the effects of risk perception on drivers (e.g., see Deery 1999; Hayakawa et al. 2000; Simsekoglu et al. 2013), which consistently find that poor risk perception and risk tolerance are associated with accidents. Interestingly, some jurisdictions (e.g., Victoria, Australia) use a hazard perception test as part of the driver licensing process. The importance of risk perception in maintaining safety in an industrial setting is also recognized. For example, Exxon-Mobil (Fennell 2012) has an extensive program to train employees to recognize hazards and to improve risk tolerance and perception, and risk perception has also been investigated as a factor in safety of off-shore petroleum operations (Rundmo 1997).

Having now looked at both LOC and risk perception and tolerance, you might wonder just how those constructs are related, and how they might interact to affect behavior. Well, you are in luck, because You et al. (2013) conducted just such a study to examine the relationships between LOC, risk perception, flight time, and safety operation behaviors among Chinese airline pilots. They surveyed 193 pilots using measures of LOC, risk perception, and safety-oriented behaviors (SB). They then used a technique called structural equation modeling to examine the interrelationships among the variables. The results are depicted in Figure 10.6. In this diagram, rectangles are measured or observed variables, ovals are latent constructs (i.e., they are not directly measured), and the arrows indicate relationships. The numbers shown in the figure reflect the strength of the effects and the orientation.

What the figure shows is that the latent variable risk perception is reflected by scores on five measures of risk perception: general flight risk, high flight risk, altitude risk, driving risk, and everyday risk. So you can see that risk perception is most heavily related to items in the test that measured risk associated with altitude. Similarly, the latent variable SB is defined by items that assess understanding of the automation system, leadership, communications, and SA. The numbers indicate the relative contribution of each of the observed variables to the latent trait.

Notice that both internal and external LOC impact risk perception; however, the effect of external LOC is negative, while the effect of internal LOC is positive. So, external LOC decreases risk perception, while internal LOC increases risk perception. However, only internal LOC had a direct effect on SB. The direct effect of risk

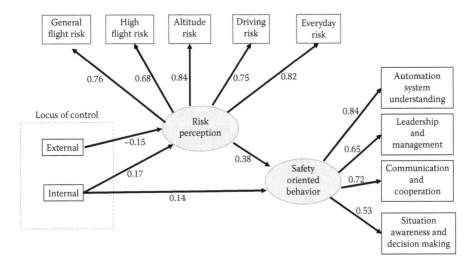

FIGURE 10.6 Path diagram showing relationships among LOC, risk perception, and safety behaviors. (Reprinted from *Accident Analysis and Prevention*, 57, You, W. et al., The effects of risk perception and flight experience on airline pilots' locus of control with regard to safety operation behaviors, 131–139, Copyright 2013, with permission from Elsevier.)

perception on SB was also positive. Therefore, high levels of risk perception and internal LOC increase the likelihood that a pilot will engage in safety behaviors.

10.10 SITUATION AWARENESS

In common terms, SA means knowing what is going on around you. For a pilot, this means knowing where their aircraft is with respect to other aircraft in the vicinity, important objects on the ground (e.g., runways, mountains, tall radio towers), and weather elements such as clouds, rain, and areas of turbulence. In addition, SA means knowing what the aircraft is doing at all times, both externally (i.e., turning, descending) and internally (i.e., fuel status, oil pressure). (Students of Eastern philosophy may recognize this Zen-like state as mindfulness, or being one with the moment.) Moreover, SA has both a present and a future component. Thus, having good SA means that a pilot knows all the things going on right now and can reliably estimate what will be happening a few minutes or a few hours from now. This distinction is reflected in the definition of SA proposed by Endsley (1988, p. 87) who describes SA as "the perception of the elements in the environment within a volume of time and space, the comprehension of their meaning, and the projection of their status in the near future."

SA is particularly important in the framework of Klein's recognition-primed decision (RPD) model that emphasizes the importance of SA (Kaempf et al. 1996). Klein's RPD model suggests that pilots actually perform little real problem-solving. Rather, the major activity is recognizing a situation, and then selecting one of the limited numbers of solutions that have worked in the past. Clearly, in such a model, awareness of surroundings is very important for the detection of changes in the environment that may be used as part of the recognition process.

Within the RPD theoretical framework experience is critical, as it builds the repertoire by which one may accurately identify the salient cues and correctly diagnose the situation. According to Klein (2000, p. 174),

> The most common reason for poor decisions is a lack of experience. It takes a high degree of experience to recognize situations as typical. It takes a high degree of experience to build stories to diagnose problems and to mentally simulate a course of action. It takes a high degree of experience to prioritize cues, so workload won't get too high. It takes a high degree of experience to develop expectancies and to identify plausible goals in a situation.

Although SA is an intriguing construct, it could be argued that it is simply a meta-construct, incorporating some or all of the other, more basic constructs previously discussed. For example, from Endsley's (1988) definition, SA would subsume the risk perception elements discussed earlier, since proper detection and evaluation of the cues associated with, for example, deteriorating weather conditions would fall within the definition of SA. The same argument could be made regarding self-knowledge of internal states such as attitudes. The question, therefore, is whether SA is something more than the sum of the constituent parts? Or is it simply another category to which behavior and accidents may be consigned, without delving into an understanding of why they occur? As noted earlier, describing is not the same thing as explaining. The present authors suggest that the latter description is more accurate, but the interested reader may wish to consult the literature (the book by Endsley and Garland 2000, a good source) and make up their own mind.

10.11 OTHER PERSPECTIVES ON ADM

10.11.1 How Do You Combine Information to Make a Decision?

In a study conducted using pilots from the United States, Norway, and Australia, Hunter et al. (2003) used a mathematical modeling technique to examine the manner in which pilots combined information about visibility, cloud ceiling, precipitation, and terrain to make judgments about the safety of a flight. In this study, pilots were given three maps depicting flights in their respective countries. One map depicted a flight over level terrain, while another showed a flight over mountainous terrain. The final map depicted a flight over a large body of water. A total of 326 American, 104 Norwegian, and 51 Australian pilots then completed a scenario-based judgment task in which they provided a safety rating to each of 27 weather scenarios for each of the three routes. The 27 weather scenarios were based on combinations of varying level of visibility, ceiling, and precipitation. These safety ratings were then used to develop individual regression equations for each pilot. The regression equation for a pilot then described the information combination process he or she used to assign the safety ratings. Two interesting results were observed. First, the safety ratings for the 27 scenarios were very similar for the three diverse groups of pilots. Second, two methods for combining the information

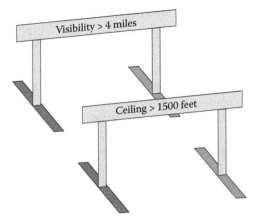

FIGURE 10.7   Multiple-hurdle decision strategy.

to arrive at an assessment of the safety of the flight were used: (1) a multiple-hurdle model (shown in Figure 10.7) and (2) a compensatory model (shown in Figure 10.8). For each of the three groups, the compensatory model of information use was favored over the noncompensatory (multiple-hurdle) model. The use of a compensatory weather model means that a pilot might decide that conditions are suitable for flight when the ceiling is high (a safe situation), but the visibility is low (an unsafe situation), since the high ceiling compensates for the low visibility in the overall evaluation of the situation. In contrast, in a noncompensatory multiple-hurdle model, each aspect of the situation is individually examined and compared to a criterion. A decision to initiate a flight is only made if all the factors individually meet their respective criteria. In this model, a high value on one variable cannot compensate for a low value on another variable. Hunter et al. argue that for inexperienced pilots using a compensatory decision model puts them at greater risk of being in an accident.

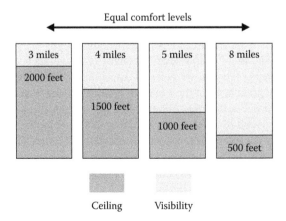

FIGURE 10.8   Compensatory decision strategy.

10.11.2   How Do Great Pilots Make Decisions?

Researchers at the Ohio State University (Kochan et al. 1997) used structured interviews to identify the characteristics of expert general aviation pilots. The found that such a pilot was, "highly motivated, confident (but not overconfident), has superior learning and performance skills, applies those skills in a changing environment, and possesses a type of judgment described by many as 'magic' or 'natural' " (p. 14). On the basis of the interview, and using actual accidents taken from the NTSB accident reports, Kochan et al. developed an experimental flight scenario designed to test pilot expertise. Experienced pilots were presented with the flight scenario in a table-top simulation. The results of this simulation suggested that "... when compared to competent pilots, expert pilots tend to (1) seek more quality information in a more timely manner; (2) make more progressive decisions to solve problems; and, (3) communicate more readily with all available resources" (p. i).

In a subsequent study of pilots flying a demanding scenario in a simulator, it was found that some pilots tended to make a decision fairly rapidly in response to a problem, such as partial loss of power, and then to take no further action to diagnose the problem or refine their responses (Barber 1999). These were called knee-jerk responses, because they were quick, but there was no further effort put forth to validate the original decision. In contrast, some pilots, generally those who were more experienced in general aviation flights, exhibited a very different sort of response to a problem. The initial response of these pilots may have been very similar to that of the knee-jerk pilots, but this group continued to investigate other solutions and to validate their original decision. The second type of pilots, who used what was termed progressive decision-making, generally exhibited superior performance in the flight scenarios.

10.11.3   How Do Social Relationships Influence Decisions?

We often fail to take into account that humans are very social animals. That is, we generally like being around other people, and we like them to like us. In order to maintain that social relationship, we have evolved a very keen sense that enables us to detect what others expect of us. People who are unable to figure out what everyone wants of them tend to go live in cabins in the woods.

Psychologists say that "people tend to behave in accordance with the perceived expectation of others." That is, we behave like we think others expect us to behave. That works really great most of the time, but it can also lead to some problems.

For example, a new pilot may observe that the old pilot that most of the other pilots look up to is a bit of a risk-taker, is kind of sloppy at preflight planning, and is not above bending the rules when needed to complete a mission. He comes to the not unreasonable belief that this is the sort of behavior that is expected of pilots in this organization, and modifies his own behavior to fit that model. This is not a good thing.

So, we need to realize that our behavior and decisions are being constantly shaped by the people around us, while at the same time we are shaping them. Picking a good role model, and being a good role model, is important, and if you notice that the heroes in your organization seem to be skating on thin ice rather frequently, perhaps it is time to look for a job elsewhere, or to have a serious talk with your flying club's safety pilot. Strong role models, passenger demands, and peer pressure can all influence ADM for better or worse.

10.12   IMPROVING YOUR ADM

So, how do we improve decision quality? That is, how do we do better ADM? Well, there are three basic ways in which we can improve. We can expand our knowledge, we can sharpen our decision-making processes, and we can acquire new skills so that we have more options open to us.

Probably, the best way to improve your decisions is to improve your knowledge. Recall that earlier we noted that poor risk perception was a major cause of accidents. Mostly, this is simply because pilots lack the knowledge to recognize the risks they are running in various situations. Knowing more means you can better assess the risks and can avoid or mitigate those situations that carry high risk.

Besides technical knowledge about, for example, weather or your aircraft, you also need to improve your knowledge about yourself. Recall those psychological factors that can influence your decision-making, and our model that shows that attitudes, and other factors such as LOC and risk perception play an active part in shaping our assessment of situations and our selection of an appropriate response.

Finally, you need to examine your own history. One of the strongest predictors of future behavior is past behavior. So, if you did risky things in the past, you are probably going to do risky things in the future. If you have a tendency toward close calls, then you should be aware of that and consider modifying your practices to curb that tendency. Perhaps, all you need is a bit of training with a good instructor.

Just as there are tests of weather knowledge, there are also tests that measure your attitudes, personality traits, and behavioral history. Links to those tests are given at the end of this chapter.

Besides expanding your knowledge, you can also improve the process you use to make decisions. There are two broad methods for doing that. First, you could consider adopting one of the algorithms for decision-making. These are primarily designed for relatively inexperienced pilots, perhaps someone with less than 2000 hours, and help you by setting up a standardized method for processing information. There are many guides to these methods, and a few links to those resources are provided at the end of the chapter.

You can also take a more generalized approach. For example, the research at the Ohio State University that produced the knee-jerk and progressive decision-making pilot types also resulted in the production of a short training course to help set personal minimums as a means of controlling risk by making some important decisions long before the flight is undertaken. Personal minimums training is offered by civil aviation authorities in several countries, and through the FAA Web site.

Another generalized approach would be to create packages of predetermined decisions for various situations that you might face. For example, you might make a fairly detailed set of plans for dealing with low visibility in the area of your home airport. This would include specific triggers for action based upon the weather conditions, and a variety of alternatives that could be put into action. By reducing the problem to a set of if–then questions, you can reduce the need for in-flight decision-making. In this way, you can mimic the recognition-primed decision-making of experts by having created a set of virtual memories and responses beforehand.

If you improve your skills, then you will increase the range of options open to you and increase the probability of successfully executing a decision. Additional training beyond that required for a certificate is available from a variety of sources. These include flight training with a qualified flight instructor and Internet-based training.

Finally, you should also check your decision-making skills. A good flight review should not just assess whether you can take off and land the aircraft, but should also assess whether you can make good decisions regarding when and where to fly. Be sure that your instructor covers this aspect when assessing our proficiency as a pilot, since poor decision-making is much more likely to result in a fatal accident than poor crosswind landing skills. You might also try an online Pilot Situational Judgment Test that research has shown is a predictor of accident involvement (Hunter 2003). A link to that test is also provided at the end of this chapter.

Decision-making is a complex process that can be viewed in a variety of ways, and which is subject to a large number of influences. To improve your ADM, you need to improve your knowledge and skills, understand the factors that influence decisions, and understand just how your own tendencies and skills are impacting your decisions. Once you understand your own capabilities, the capabilities of your aircraft, and the demands of the situation, you can take steps, such as setting personal minimums, to manage your decision-making and the risks of aviation.

10.13　SUMMARY

As have seen in this chapter, decision-making is a complex process that has often been implicated in aviation accidents. Although, as we will argue in the next chapter, poor decisions by themselves should not be described as a cause of accidents, ineffective decision-making certainly plays a part in increasing the likelihood of an accident occurring. To make effective decisions, pilots need both knowledge and a process to use that knowledge effectively. Several decision-making models have been suggested over the years, including the DECIDE model, Professor Richard Jensen's model of pilot expertise, and the model we have proposed that focuses on understanding the psychological factors that influence each step of the decision process.

We noted that there are several strategies that pilots may use when making decisions. Probably, the most frequently used strategy is that of satisficing—that is, picking a solution that generally satisfies our needs, even if it is not the optimal solution. This approach of picking a "good-enough" solution works amazing well both in aviation and elsewhere.

We also drew attention to the numerous psychological biases that can influence decisions. Two of the most important biases are the self-serving bias and the confirmation bias. These two biases act to make us overestimate our capabilities while underestimating the risks presented by situations. They also act to limit our effective use of information, by blinding us to information that does not conform to what we expect or believe. These are very powerful influences on pilot decisions making and behavior, and should not be underestimated.

For at least the previous three decades, the importance of ADM has been recognized by researchers and regulators. As a result, several programs aimed at improving ADM have been developed, and are available to pilots today. Further, research has shown the importance of several factors, such as LOC and risk perception, in addition to hazardous attitudes, in ADM. Links to Web sites that provide self-assessment tools for those psychological factors and to ADM training are provided at the end of this chapter.

10.14   OUTSIDE ACTIVITIES*

Now that you have learned about the decision-making process, and some of the ways in which it can be disrupted, take a look at some of the resources available to you to improve your decision-making.

10.14.1   TRAINING

One of the best sources for free training is the FAA.

- Start with their safety home page: https://www.faasafety.gov/
- Look at the activities in your area: https://www.faasafety.gov/WINGS/pub/accreditedactivities/activitySearch.aspx
- Search for an online training course: https://www.faasafety.gov/gslac/ALC/course_catalog.aspx

Free training is also available from several other sources:

- A quick checklist lets you assign a score to the risk associated with a particular flight: http://www.avhf.com/html/Training/RiskAssessment.htm
- Develop your own Personal Minimums Checklist to identify and control the risk factors associated with flights: http://www.avhf.com/html/Training/PCL/PCL_Home.asp
- This program teaches pilots the skills needed to recognize, diagnose, and solve in-flight problems based on the research on knee-jerk versus progressive decision-making: http://www.avhf.com/html/Training/SDM/SDM_Home.asp
- This program includes actual in-flight videos of light aircraft penetrating marginal VFR and IMC weather and shows you the critical indicators of deteriorating weather. Learn how to select a diversion airport, and practice on several real-world flights: http://www.avhf.com/html/Training/WW/ww_home.htm
- Videos produced by the Civil Aviation Authority of New Zealand give a unique perspective on the same problems faced by pilots around the world: http://www.avhf.com/html/Training/NZ/NZ_Intro.asp
- For a really nice discussion about human factors for pilots (but with a disappointingly short section on ADM), check out this booklet from the Civil

---

* These Web links were valid at the time this chapter was written in mid-2016.

Aviation Safety Authority of Australia: http://www.skybrary.aero/solutions/casa/resource_guide.pdf
- Read about DECIDE, FOR-DEC, and about 24 other decision models: http://www.flight.org/decision-making-models-in-aviation
- For a general discussion of ADM: http://www.free-online-private-pilot-ground-school.com/Aeronautical_decision_making.html
- Finally, if you are a member of the Aircraft Owners and Pilots Association (AOPA), try some of their training: http://www.aopa.org/Education/Online-Courses?page=1

10.14.2 SELF-ASSESSMENT

- Evaluate your attitudes with the classic scale from the FAA or with one of the newer, improved scales: http://www.avhf.com/html/evaluation/HazardAttitude/Hazard_Attitude_Intro.htm
- Measure your AS-LOC: http://www.avhf.com/html/evaluation/SafetyLOC/Safety_LOC.asp
- Assess your level of risk perception: http://www.avhf.com/html/evaluation/RP/RP_home.htm
- Look at how your pilot judgment compares to experts: http://www.avhf.com/html/Evaluation/SJT/SJT_Intro.asp
- Count the number of times you have been involved in a hazardous aviation event: http://www.avhf.com/html/evaluation/HunterCriticalEvents/hes.asp
- See how well you can spot the hazards in some simulated flights: http://www.avhf.com/html/Research/Haz_Percep/Haz_Percep_Intro.asp

RECOMMENDED READINGS

Botterill, L. and Mazur, N. 2004. *Risk and Risk Perception: A Literature Review*. RIRDC Publication No. 04/03. Kingston, Australia: Rural Industries Research and Development Corporation.

Chaiken, S. and Stangor, C. 1987. Attitudes and attitude change. *Annual Review of Psychology* 38: 575–630.

Cooper, J. and Croyle, R.T. 1984. Attitudes and attitude change. *Annual Review of Psychology* 35: 395–426.

Federal Aviation Administration. 1991. *Aeronautical Decision Making*. AC 60-22. Washington, DC: Author.

Hastie, R. 2001. Problems for judgment and decision making. *Annual Review of Psychology* 52: 653–658.

Kahneman, D. 2011. *Thinking, Fast and Slow*. New York, NY: Farrar, Straus and Giroux.

Kahneman, D., Slovic, P., and Tversky, A. 1982. *Judgment Under Uncertainty: Heuristics and Biases*. New York, NY: Cambridge University Press.

Koelher, D.J. and Harvey, N. (Eds.). 2004. *Blackwell Handbook of Judgment and Decision Making*. Carlton, Australia: Blackwell Publishing.

Pickens, J. 2005. Attitudes and perceptions. In Borkowski, N. (Ed.), *Organizational Behavior In Health Care*. Sudbury, MA: Jones and Bartlett.

Simpson, P.A. 2001. *Naturalistic Decision Making in Aviation Environments*. DSTO-GD-0279. Fishermans Bend, Australia: Defense Science and Technology Organization.

Wood, W. 2000. Attitude change: Persuasion and social influence. *Annual Review of Psychology* 51: 539–570.
Zsambok, C.E. and Klein, G. 1997. *Naturalistic Decision Making.* Mahwah, NJ: Erlbaum.

REFERENCES

Adams, R.J. 1989. *Risk Management for Air Ambulance Helicopter Operators.* Technical Report DOT/FAA/DS-88/7. Washington, DC: Federal Aviation Administration.
Adams, R.J., and Thompson, J.L. 1987. *Aeronautical Decision Making for Helicopter Pilots.* DOT/FAA/PM-86/45. Washington, DC: Federal Aviation Administration.
Anastasia, A. 1968. *Psychological Testing.* New York, NY: Macmillan.
Barber, S. 1999. Teaching judgment and en-route dynamic problem solving techniques to general aviation pilots. In Jensen, R.S. (Ed.), *Proceedings of the 10th International Symposium on Aviation Psychology* (pp. 1021–1026). Columbus, OH: The Ohio State University.
Bartram, D. 1996. The relationship between ipsatized and normative measures of personality. *Journal of Occupational and Organizational Psychology* 69: 25–39.
Benner, L. 1975. DECIDE in hazardous materials emergencies. *Fire Journal* 69: 13–18.
Berlin, J.I., Gruber, E.V., Holmes, C.W., Jensen, R.K., Lau, J.R., and Mills, J.W. 1982a. *Pilot Judgment Training and Evaluation—Vol I.* Technical report DOT/FAA/CT-81/56-I. Washington, DC: Federal Aviation Administration.
Berlin, J.I., Gruber, E.V., Holmes, C.W., Jensen, R.K., Lau, J.R., and Mills, J.W. 1982b. *Pilot Judgment Training and Evaluation—Vol 2.* Technical report DOT/FAA/CT-81/56-II. Washington, DC: Federal Aviation Administration.
Berlin, J.I., Gruber, E.V., Holmes, C.W., Jensen, R.K., Lau, J.R., and Mills, J.W. 1982c. *Pilot Judgment Training and Evaluation—Vol 3.* Technical report DOT/FAA/CT-81/56-III. Washington, DC: Federal Aviation Administration.
Berlin, J. and Holmes, C. 1981. Developing a civil aviation pilot judgment training and evaluation manual. In Jensen, R.S. (Ed.), *First Symposium on Aviation Psychology*, April 21–22, 1981 (pp. 166–170). Columbus, OH: Ohio State University.
Buch, G.D. and Diehl, A.E. 1983. *Pilot Judgment Training Manual Validation.* Unpublished report. Ontario, Canada: Transport Canada.
Buch, G.D. and Diehl, A.E. 1984. An investigation of the effectiveness of pilot judgment training. *Human Factors* 26: 557–564.
Buch, G., Lawton, R.S., and Livack, G.S. 1987. *Aeronautical Decision Making for Instructor Pilots.* DOT/FAA/PM-86/44. Washington, DC: Federal Aviation Administration.
Connolly, T.J. and Blackwell, B.B. 1987. A simulator-based approach to training in aeronautical decision making. In Jensen, R.S. (Ed.), *Proceedings of the Fourth International Symposium of Aviation Psychology* (pp. 251–257). Columbus, OH: Ohio State University.
Deery, H.A. 1999. Hazard and risk perception among young novice drivers. *Journal of Safety Research* 30: 225–236.
Diehl, A.E. 1990. The effectiveness of aeronautical decision making training. In *Proceedings of the 34Th Meeting of the Human Factors Society* (pp. 1367–1371). Santa Monica, CA: Human Factors Society.
Diehl, A.E., Hwoschinsky, P.V., Lawton, R.S., and Livack, G.S. 1987. *Aeronautical Decision Making for Student and Private Pilots.* DOT/FAA/PM-86/41. Washington, DC: Federal Aviation Administration.
Diehl, A.E. and Lester, L.F. 1987. *Private Pilot Judgment Training in Flight School Settings.* DOT/FAA/AM-87/6. Washington, DC: Federal Aviation Administration.
Drinkwater, J.L. and Molesworth, B.R.C. 2010. Pilot see, pilot do: Examining the predictors of pilots' risk management behavior. *Safety Science* 48: 1445–1451.

Endsley, M.R. 1988. Design and evaluation for situation awareness enhancement. In *Proceedings of the Human Factors Society 32nd Annual Meeting I* (pp. 97–101). Santa Monica, CA: Human Factors Society.

Endsley, M.R., and Garland, D.J. 2000. *Situation Awareness Analysis and Measurement.* Mahway, NJ: Erlbaum.

Fennell, D. 2012. Strategies for understanding and addressing risk tolerance. Paper presented at the *Petroleum Safety Conference*, Banff, Canada: Enform.

Goh, J. and Wiegmann, D.A. 2001. Visual flight rules flight into instrument meteorological conditions: An empirical investigation of the possible causes. *International Journal of Aviation Psychology* 11: 359–379.

Guilford, J.P. and Lacey, J.I. 1947. *Printed Classification Tests.* Army Air Forces Aviation Psychology Program Research Reports Report No. 5. (AD 651781). Washington, DC: Department of Defense.

Hayakawa, H., Fischbech, P.S., and Fischhoff, B. 2000. Traffic accident statistics and risk perceptions in Japan and the United States. *Accident Analysis and Prevention* 32: 827–835.

Holt, R.W., Boehm-Davis, D.A., Fitzgerald, K.A., Matyuf, M.M., Baughman, W.A., and Littman, D.C. 1991. Behavioral validation of a hazardous thought pattern instrument. In *Proceedings of the Human Factors Society 35th Annual Meeting* (pp. 77–81). Santa Monica, CA: Human Factors Society.

Hunter, D.R. 2002. Development of an aviation safety locus of control scale. *Aviation, Space, and Environmental Medicine* 73: 1184–1188.

Hunter, D.R. 2003. Measuring general aviation pilot judgment using a situational judgment technique. *The International Journal of Aviation Psychology* 13: 373–386.

Hunter, D.R. 2004. Measurement of hazardous attitudes among pilots. *International Journal of Aviation Psychology* 15: 23–43.

Hunter, D.R. 2006. Risk perception among general aviation pilots. *International Journal of Aviation Psychology* 16: 135–144.

Hunter, D.R., Martinussen, M., and Wiggins, M. 2003. Understanding how pilots make weather-related decisions. *The International Journal of Aviation Psychology* 13: 73–87.

Jenicek, M. 2001. *Medical Error and Harm: Understanding, Prevention, and Control.* Boca Raton, FL: Taylor and Francis.

Jensen, R.S. 1995. *Pilot Judgment and Crew Resource Management.* Brookfield, VT: Ashgate.

Jensen, R.S. and Adrion, J. 1988. *Aeronautical Decision Making for Commercial Pilots.* DOT/FAA/PM-86/42. Washington, DC: Federal Aviation Administration.

Jensen, R.S., Adrion, J., and Lawton, R.S. 1987. *Aeronautical Decision Making for Instrument Pilots.* DOT/FAA/PM-86/43. Washington, DC: Federal Aviation Administration.

Jensen, R.S. and Benel, R.A. 1977. *Judgment Evaluation and Instruction in Civil Pilot Training.* FAA-RD-78-24. Washington, DC: Federal Aviation Administration.

Jones, J.W. and Wuebker, L. 1985. Development and validation of the safety locus of control scale. *Perceptual and Motor Skills* 61: 151–161.

Jones, J.W. and Wuebker, L.J. 1993. Safety locus of control and employees' accidents. *Journal of Business and Psychology* 7: 449–457.

Joseph, C. and Ganesh, A. 2006. Aviation safety locus of control in Indian aviators. *Indian Journal of Aerospace Medicine* 50: 14–21.

Joseph, C. and Reddy, S. 2013. Risk perception and safety attitudes in Indian Army aviators. *The International Journal of Aviation Psychology* 23: 49–62.

Kaempf, G., Klein, G., Thordsen, M., and Wolf, S. 1996. Decision making in complex naval command-and-control environments. *Human Factors* 38: 220–231.

Kahneman, D. 2011. *Thinking, Fast and Slow.* New York, NY: Farrar, Straus and Giroux.

Kahneman, D., Slovic, P., and Tversky, A. 1982. *Judgment Under Uncertainty: Heuristics and Biases.* New York, NY: Cambridge University Press.

Klein, G. 2000. *Sources of Power: How People Make Decisions*. Cambridge, MA: MIT Press.

Kochan, J.A., Jensen, R.S., Chubb, G.P., and Hunter, D.R. 1997. *A New Approach to Aeronautical Decision-Making: The Expertise Method*. DOT/FAA/AM-97/6. Washington, DC: Federal Aviation Administration.

Lester, L.F. and Bombachi, D.H. 1984. The relationship between personality and irrational judgment in civil pilots. *Human Factors* 26: 565–572.

Lester, L.F. and Connolly, T.J. 1987. The measurement of hazardous thought patterns and their relationship to pilot personality. In Jensen, R.S. (Ed.), *Proceedings of the Fourth International Symposium on Aviation Psychology* (pp. 286–292). Columbus, OH: Ohio State University.

Lester, L.F., Diehl, A., Harvey, D.P., Buch, G., and Lawton, R.S. 1986. Improving risk assessment and decision making in general aviation pilots. *The 57th Annual Meeting of the Eastern Psychological Association*. Atlantic City, NJ.

Lubner, M.E. and Markowitz, J.S. 1991. Rates and risk factors for accidents and incidents versus violations for U.S. airmen. *International Journal of Aviation Psychology* 1: 231–243.

Montag, I. and Comrey, A.L. 1987. Internality and externality as correlates of involvement in fatal driving accidents. *Journal of Applied Psychology* 72: 339–343.

National Transportation Safety Board. 2003. *Annual Review of Aircraft Accident Data U.S. General Aviation, Calendar Year 2003*. NTSB/ARG-07/1. Washington, DC: Author.

O'Hare, D. 1990. Pilots' perception of risks and hazards in general aviation. *Aviation, Space, and Environmental Medicine* 61: 599–603.

O'Hare, D. and Roscoe, S. 1990. *Flightdeck Performance: The Human Factor*. Ames, IA: Iowa State University Press.

O'Hare, D. and Smitheram, T. 1995. "Pressing on" into deteriorating conditions: An application of behavioral decision theory to pilot decision making. *International Journal of Aviation Psychology* 5: 351–370.

Rotter, J.B. 1966. Generalized expectancies for internal versus external control of reinforcement. *Psychological Monographs* 80: Whole No. 609.

Rundmo, T. 1997. Associations between risk perception and safety. *Safety Science* 24: 197–209.

Saville, P. and Wilson, E. 1991. The reliability and validity of normative and ipsative approaches in the measurement of personality. *Journal of Occupational Psychology* 64: 219–238.

Schlitz, D. 1977. *The Gambler* [Recorded by K. Rogers]. On *The Gambler* (CD). Nashville, TN: Sony/ATV Music Publishing.

Simsekoglu, O., Nordfjaern, T., Zavareh, M.F., Hezaveh, A.M., Mamdoohi, A.R., and Rundmo, T. 2013. Risk perceptions, fatalism and driver behaviors in Turkey and Iran. *Safety Science* 59: 187–192.

Stewart, J.E. 2006. *Locus of Control, Attribution Theory, and the "Five Deadly Sins" of Aviation*. Technical Report 1182. Fort Rucker, AL: U.S. Army Research Institute for the Behavioral and Social Sciences.

Telfer, R. 1987. Pilot judgment training: The Australian study. In Jensen, R.S. (Ed.), *Proceedings of the Fourth International Symposium on Aviation Psychology* (pp. 265–273). Columbus, OH: Ohio State University.

Telfer, R. 1989. Pilot decision making and judgement. In Jensen, R.S. (Ed.), *Aviation Psychology* (pp. 154–175). Bookfield, VT: Gower Technical.

Telfer, R. and Ashman, A.F. 1986. *Pilot judgment training: An Australian Validation Study*. Unpublished manuscript. Callaghan, Australia: University of Newcastle.

Trankle, U., Gelau, C., and Metker, T. 1990. Risk perception and age-specific accidents of young drivers. *Accident Analysis and Prevention* 22, 119–125.

Wallston, B.S., Wallston, K.A., Kaplan, G.D., and Maides, S.A. 1976. Development and validation of the health locus of control (HLC) scale. *Journal of Consulting and Clinical Psychology* 44: 580–585.

Walsmsley, S. and Gilbey, A. 2016. Cognitive biases in visual pilots' weather-related decision making. *Applied Cognitive Psychology* 30: 532–543.

Wichman H. and Ball, J. 1983. Locus of control, self-serving biases, and attitudes towards safety in general aviation pilots. *Aviation Space and Environmental Medicine* 54: 507–510.

Wiegmann, D., Faaborg, T., Boquet, A., Detwiler, C., Holcomb, K., and Shappell, S. 2005. *Human Error and General Aviation Accidents: A Comprehensive, Fine-Grained Analysis Using HfACS*. DOT/FAA/AM-05/24. Washington, DC: Federal Aviation Administration.

Wiggins, M. and O'Hare, D. 1993. A skills-based approach to training aeronautical decision-making. In Telfer, R.A. (Ed.), *Aviation Instruction and Training* (pp. 430–475). Brookfield, VT: Ashgate.

You, W., Ji, M., and Han, H. 2013. The effects of risk perception and flight experience on airline pilots' locus of control with regard to safety operation behaviors. *Accident Analysis and Prevention* 57: 131–139.

11 Aviation Safety

11.1 INTRODUCTION

There is an American cowboy rodeo saying that states, "There's never been a horse that can't be rode, there's never been a rider that can't be throw'd." That adage applies equally well to aviation. There has never been a pilot so skilled that he or she cannot have an accident. Clearly, there are some pilots who are exceptionally skilled and cautious. However, given the right set of circumstances, even they can make an error of judgment or find that the demands of the situation exceed their capacity or the capabilities of their aircraft. What sets these particular pilots apart is that these combinations of events and circumstances occur very rarely; their attributes, including attitudes, personality, psychomotor coordination, aeronautical knowledge, skills, experiences, and a host of other individual characteristics, make them less likely to experience hazardous situations and more likely to survive the situations if they occur. In contrast, for pilots at the low end of the skill continuum, every flight is a risky undertaking. In this chapter, we will explore some of the research that has attempted to explain, from the perspective of human psychology, how these groups of pilots differ, why accidents occur, and what might be done to reduce their likelihood.

11.2 ACCIDENT INCIDENCE

To begin, let us examine the incidence of aviation accidents, so that we may understand the extent of the problem. Table 11.1 shows the numbers of accidents and corresponding accident rates (number of accidents per 100,000 flight hours) for two recent years in the United States. From this table, the differences in accident rates between the large air carriers (very low rates), the smaller carriers, and general aviation are evident. Over that span of operation, the accident rate increases about 30-fold. To put these statistics in a slightly different light, on a per mile basis, flying in an air carrier is about 50 times safer than driving. However, flying in general aviation is about seven times riskier than driving.

These accident rates are typical of the rates found among Western Europe, New Zealand, and Australia. For example, data from the Australian Transport Safety Bureau (ATSB 2007) show fixed-wing, single-engine general aviation accident rates (accidents/100,000 hours) of 10.26 and 7.42, for 2004 and 2005, respectively. Note that these rates are somewhat inflated, relative to the United States, since they do not include multiengine operations normally used in corporate aviation, traditionally one of the safest aviation settings.

11.2.1 INTERPRETING SAFETY STATISTICS

This brings up an important point that must be made regarding safety statistics. It is very important to note the basis on which the statistics are calculated. For example,

TABLE 11.1

Incidence of Accidents in the United States

	2009		2010	
	Number	**Rate[a]**	**Number**	**Rate[a]**
Large air carriers	30	0.17	30	0.16
Commuter	2	0.69	6	1.90
Air taxi	47	1.60	32	1.05
General aviation	1480	7.20	1436	6.87

Source: Federal Aviation Administration (FAA). 2012. *Administrator's Handbook.* Washington, DC: Author.

[a] Rate is given as accidents per 100,000 flight hours.

in Table 11.1, the rates are given in terms of numbers of accidents per 100,000 flight hours. This is a commonly used denominator, but by no means the only one that is reported. Our comparison of accident risk in driving and aviation cited above used accidents per mile traveled. Some statistics are in terms of numbers of departures (typically, accidents per one million departures). It is important for the reader to make note of these denominators so that comparisons are always made between statistics using the same denominator. In addition, as in our comparison between the statistics from the United States and Australia, it is important to know exactly what has been included in the calculations. In this case, exclusion of the very safe, multiengine corporate operations could lead to the conclusion that general aviation is safer in the United States than in Australia—a conclusion that is not warranted by the data provided.

Accident statistics can also be misleading, or at least confusing, when they fail to account for differences in the population from which samples (the people involved in accidents) are drawn. For example, in a recent edition of the Nall Report produced by the Aircraft Owners and Pilots Association (AOPA 2015), it is reported that holders of a private pilot certificate were involved in 43% of noncommercial fixed-wing general aviation accidents during 2012, while commercial pilots were involved in 29% of the accidents. One might conclude from those data that commercial pilots were considerably safer than private pilots. However, an examination of the data from the FAA (2012) shows that private pilots constitute 43% of the pilot population, and commercial pilots make up 26%—approximately the same proportions as were reported to be involved in accidents. If there were no difference in accident propensity between private and commercial pilots, then we would expect to see exactly the results reported in the Nall Report. So, encouraging private pilots to obtain a commercial certificate would not, in all likelihood, prove to be an effective way to improve general aviation safety.

11.3 CAUSES OF ACCIDENTS

For every complex question, there is a simple answer—and it's wrong. (Attributed to H.L. Mencken)

Before we begin to talk about the causes of accidents, we need to make clear what we mean by a cause. Step away from the flight line for a moment and into the chemistry laboratory. If we were to put a few drops of a solution containing silver nitrate (AgCl) into another solution that contains sodium chloride (NaCl), common table salt, we would observe the formation of some white particles (silver chloride, AgCl) that would sink to the bottom of our test tube. This simple test for the presence of chlorine in water by the addition of aqueous silver nitrate is, in fact, one of the most famous reactions in chemistry and is among the first learned by all budding chemists. The point to be made here is that this reaction, and the formation of the precipitate, will happen every single time that we mix solutions of silver nitrate and sodium chloride. Nor will the precipitate form, unless we add the silver nitrate. The addition of the silver nitrate to the sodium chloride solution is a necessary and sufficient condition for the formation of the precipitate. We may truly say that one causes the other.

Now step back outside the laboratory and consider what happens in the real world. For example, let us imagine that you are driving to work one morning and the traffic is very heavy, so that you are following closely behind the vehicle ahead of you. Occasionally, the vehicle you are following will brake sharply, so that you have to react quickly and apply your brakes to keep from hitting it. This happens dozens, perhaps hundreds, of times during your trip and you are always successful in avoiding an accident. During the same trip, you listen to music on the radio and occasionally change the station by glancing at the radio and pressing the buttons to make your selection. You may do this several times during the course of the trip, also without incident. There may even be occasions when, as you are changing stations on the radio, the vehicle ahead of you brakes, and you glance up just in time to notice their brakes and slow down. Fortunately, you are a careful driver and usually maintain an adequate spacing between you and the vehicle you are following, so that you are always able to react in time, even if you were temporarily distracted by the radio. You may do this every day for years, without incident. However, on one particular morning you are delayed leaving the house, so that you did not get your usual cup of coffee, and are feeling a little sleepy. You are also feeling a bit rushed, since you need to be at the office at your usual time, and you have gotten a late start. Perhaps, this has led you to follow the vehicle ahead of you a little more closely than usual, and now, as you are reaching over to change the radio, the driver ahead of you brakes more sharply than usual, you do not notice the vehicle's brake lights quite soon enough, or react quickly enough, to slow your vehicle. An accident occurs. But, what was the cause of the accident?

From the official standpoint (the one that will go on the police report), you were the cause, and this is yet another example of human error. However, that is not a very satisfying explanation. It is not satisfying because it describes as an error, actions you have taken on almost every trip for many years. Surely, there have been many days on which you left the house late and hurried to make up time. Surely, there have been days when you felt a little sleepy when driving to work. Likewise, you have handled heavy traffic and changing radio stations innumerable times previously. All of these actions and conditions have existed previously and we have not called them errors and the causes of an accident, because until this particular day no accident had occurred. None of these conditions and events is necessary and sufficient for an accident to occur. However, each of them, in their own small way, increased the likelihood of an accident.

Therefore, we suggest that the best way to understand the causes of accidents is to view them as events and conditions that increase the likelihood of an adverse event (an accident) occurring. None of the usual list of causes—following too close, inattention, sleepy driver, distraction—will cause an accident to occur each and every time they are present. However, they will each independently increase the likelihood of an accident. Moreover, their joint presence may increase the likelihood far more than the simple sum of their independent effects. For example, following too closely in traffic and driving while drowsy both increase the risk of an accident, let us say by 10% each. However, following too closely in traffic *while* drowsy might increase the risk of an accident by 40%, not the 20% obtained by simply summing their independent contributions. So, the combination of these two conditions is far more dangerous than either by itself.

Causes are best understood not as being determinants of accidents, but as being facilitators of accidents. They increase the probability that an accident occurs, but they do not demand that it occurs. This argument implies that accidents generally have multiple facilitating components (causes).

Most authors, at least in recent years, acknowledge in the introduction to their research that there is no single cause for accidents, and then proceed to ignore that statement in the conduct and interpretation of their research. Arguably, the present authors could be included in that indictment. However, to atone for those past literary indiscretions, let us now reiterate that point. *There are no single causes for accidents.*

Usually, the "cause" is simply the last thing that happened before the crash. Only a few years ago, an Airbus landed in the Hudson River after both engines failed at 3200 feet while taking-off from LaGuardia Airport. The newspapers report that the *cause* of the crash was the ingestion of a flock of geese. However, they also report that the captain of the flight was an experienced glider pilot, with an exceptional interest in safety. Clearly, multiple *causes* are at work here—the flock of geese may have *caused* the engines to quit, but the experience and skill of the captain may have been the *cause* of the relatively benign water landing resulting in no fatalities. In exploring causes and effect relationships, we may move away from the final cause to whatever extent results in a comprehensive understanding of the event. For example, we might ask what caused the geese to be in the flight path of the aircraft. Did placing a major airport along a river in the flyway for migratory waterfowl play some part? We might also ask what part the pilot's gliding experiences played in the outcome. Did they "cause" a catastrophic event to become an exciting, but injury-free event? When we take a more situated view, we recognize that there are no "isolated" events. Everything happens in a context. The need to view accidents in context is best articulated by Dekker (2001, p. 41), who noted that "Human actions and assessments can be described meaningfully only in reference to the world in which they are made." In a subsequent paper (Dekker 2002), he argued cogently for the abandonment of the construction of causes as the explanations for accidents, but rather for the deepening of our insights into the patterns of failure and the mechanisms by which failure occurs. To borrow yet another quote from Dekker (2002, p. 7), "The point in learning about human error is not to find out where people went wrong. It is to find out why their assessments and actions made sense to them at the time, given how their situation looked from the inside."[*]

This general world view of accident causes is also evident in the work of Leveson (2004) and Dismukes et al. (2006). Leveson criticizes the event chain analysis model of accidents and argues for a more systems approach. He cites Rasmussen (1997), who argued that "an explanation of the accident in terms of events, acts, and errors is not very useful for design of improved systems." Dismukes et al. also advocate a view of accidents in terms of multicausality and the need to understand the deep structure underlying accidents. Dismukes et al. (2006, p. 11) note two fallacies about human error that pervade accident analysis:

- *Myth*: Experts who make errors performing a familiar task reveal lack of skill, vigilance, or conscientiousness.
  - *Fact*: Skill, vigilance, and conscientiousness are essential but not sufficient to prevent error.
- *Myth*: If experts can normally perform a task without difficulty, they should always be able to perform that task correctly.
  - *Fact*: Experts periodically make errors as a consequence of subtle variations in task demands, information available, and cognitive processing.

Each accident occurs because of a complex web of interacting circumstances, including environmental conditions, pilot attributes, aircraft capabilities, and support system (e.g., air traffic control, weather briefer) weaknesses. A complete explanation of how those elements interact to produce an accident is far beyond our current science. Science does not, at this time, allow us to predict with anything approaching certainty that under a well-specified set of circumstances an accident will occur; this is definitely not the chemistry laboratory.

To begin with, we do not know the set of circumstances that should be specified. Nor do we know the values to assign to the various elements so that they combine properly. Despite this abundant ignorance, we are able to make some statements regarding probabilities. That is, we are able to say with some confidence that accidents are more likely to occur under some circumstances than under other circumstances. The identification of these circumstances, and the establishment of the degree of confidence with which we may assert our beliefs, is the topic to be considered next.

Many efforts have been conducted to identify the causes for aircraft accidents over the years. Although they suffer from the implicit assumption of single causes, which we have dismissed as naive, they nevertheless can make a contribution to our understanding of accident causality by identifying some of the circumstances and attributes associated with accidents.

---

[*] Readers with an interest in accident causality are strongly encouraged to read Dekker's publications on the subject—particularly *The Field Guide to Understanding Human Error and The Re-Invention of Human Error*. See the Additional Readings list for publication details.

TO LOOK AT ACCIDENT CAUSALITY IN A SLIGHTLY DIFFERENT WAY, CONSIDER THIS PARABLE

Imagine you are standing in a calm pool of water. You reach into your pocket and grasp a handful of pebbles and toss them into the pool. Each of the pebbles disturbs the surface of the pool, creating an exceptionally complex set of interacting waves. Since some of the pebbles are larger than others, their waves are higher than those of the smaller pebbles. Where the waves intersect, they combine algebraically, depending on the phase and magnitude of each individual wave. At some points, they combine to produce a wave that reaches high above the surface. At other points, they cancel each other out. Occasionally, several of the individual waves will intersect at just the right moment to produce a freak wave of exceptional height that will cause the water to lap over the tops of your boots—an adverse event. For all intents and purposes, the occurrence of this freak wave is random and largely unpredictable. Its production depends on the number of pebbles plucked from your pocket, the size of the pebbles, the height of their toss into the pool, and the amount of dispersion of the pebbles as they fell down into the water. It will also depend upon who else is standing in or around the pool tossing pebbles into the water.

Observation of many tosses of pebbles into the pool and the use of statistics will allow us to predict that a freak wave will occur every so often—let us say once in every 100 tosses. However, we cannot reliably say whether any particular toss will produce the freak wave, nor can we say where on the surface of the pool this wave will occur. Even so, we are not powerless to prevent its occurrence. We might, for instance, reduce the number of pebbles we throw. We might reduce the size of the pebbles. We might change the vigor with which we throw them into the air. We might throw them less vertically and more laterally so as to increase their dispersion. We might also make rules about how often the people on the shore can throw pebbles into the pond.

Freak waves might still occur, but now we might only see them once in every 1000 tosses. Further reductions might be achieved by, for example, coating the pebbles with some substance that reduces their friction as they pass through the surface of the water, hence producing individual waves of still lower magnitude. However, even with all these procedural and technological advances, as long as we toss pebbles into the pool, there is some nonzero chance that a freak wave will occur. Completely eliminating freak waves (and the attendant adverse event—wet feet) requires that we and our companions abandon our practice of tossing pebbles into the pool or that we take a radically different approach. For example, we might wait for winter when the pool freezes.

11.4   CLASSIFICATION OF AIRCRAFT ACCIDENTS

According to the AOPA (2006), causes of accidents may be broken down into three categories:

- *Pilot-Related*: Accidents that arise from the improper action or inaction of the pilot
- *Mechanical/Maintenance*: Accidents that arise from failure of a mechanical component or errors in maintenance
- *Other/Unknown*: Accidents that include causes such as pilot incapacitation, as well as accidents for which a cause could not be determined

Table 11.2 shows the distribution of accidents among those three categories of cause for general aviation accidents in 2005. Clearly, the predominant major cause for both levels of severity was the pilot. Taking only those accidents in which the pilot was the major cause, the AOPA further divided the accidents among the categories shown in Table 11.3. Interpretation of the data presented in Table 11.3 is made difficult by the mixture of stage of flight categories (i.e., preflight/taxi, takeoff/climb, and landing) with two categories (fuel management, weather) that are conceptually unrelated to the other stage of flight categories. This admixture of taxonomic elements muddies the interpretation of an analysis of only dubious initial value. At most, one might inspect these data and conclude that maneuvering flight is a dangerous phase. However, these data say nothing about why maneuvering flight is dangerous, nor do they demonstrate that it is relatively more dangerous than other stages of flight, since there is no control for exposure—the amount of time spent in that flight stage. We belabor this point to reinforce the notion that categories are not causes. Categories do not explain why accidents occur. They simply point to times, conditions, and circumstances under which accidents are more likely. To illustrate this point one last time, an accident does not occur simply because the pilot is in maneuvering flight. It occurs while the pilot is in maneuvering flight, *and* decided to buzz his friend's house, *and* was distracted, *and* flew too slowly, *and* stalled the aircraft, *and* encountered a downdraft, *and* was flying an underpowered aircraft, *and* had too much load on board; *and* the list could go on for a very long ways. The reader should

TABLE 11.2
Causes of General Aviation Accidents in 2005

Major Cause	All Accidents		Fatal Accidents	
Pilot	1076	74.9%	242	82.9%
Mechanical/maintenance	232	16.2%	22	7.5%
Other/unknown	128	8.9%	28	9.6%
Total	1436		292	

Source: AOPA (Aircraft Owners and Pilots Association). 2006. *The Nall Report*. Frederick, MD: Author.

TABLE 11.3

Accident Categories for Pilot-Related Accidents

Category	Total		Fatal	
Preflight/taxi	38	3.5%	1	0.4%
Takeoff/climb	165	10.5%	33	13.6%
Fuel management	113	10.5%	20	8.3%
Weather	49	4.6%	33	13.6%
Other cruise	21	2%	14	5.8%
Descent/approach	49	4.6%	25	10.3%
Go-around	43	4.0%	15	6.2%
Maneuvering	122	11.3%	80	33.1%
Landing	446	41.4%	8	3.3%
Other	30	2.8%	13	5.4%

Source: AOPA (Aircraft Owners and Pilots Association). 2006. *The Nall Report.* Frederick, MD: Author.

recall our earlier discussion about how each of these "causes" increases the likelihood of an accident, while not guaranteeing its occurrence.

In a seminal and frequently cited study, Jensen and Benel (1977) noted all aircrew errors could be classified into one of three major categories based on behavioral activities: *procedural, perceptual motor,* and *decisional tasks.* This conclusion was based on an extensive review of all U.S. general aviation accidents occurring from 1970 to 1974 using data from the National Transportation Safety Board (NTSB). Of the fatal accidents involving pilot error during that period, they found that 264 were attributable to procedural errors, 2496 had perceptual-motor errors, and 2940 were characterized as having decisional errors. Examples of procedural tasks include management of vehicle subsystems and configuration, while related errors would include retracting the landing gear instead of flaps or overlooking checklist items. Perceptual-motor tasks include manipulating flight controls and throttles, while errors would include over shooting a glide-slope indication or stalling the aircraft. Decisional tasks include flight planning and in-flight hazard evaluation, while errors would include failing to delegate tasks in an emergency situation or continuing flight into adverse weather.

Diehl (1991) analyzed U.S. Air Force and U.S. civil air carrier accident data for accidents that occurred during 1987, 1988, and 1989. His analysis of the air carrier data indicated that 24 of the 28 major accidents (those resulting in destroyed aircraft and/or fatalities) involved aircrew error. Of these accidents, there were 16 procedural, 21 perceptual-motor, and 48 decisional errors cited (the errors sum to more than 24 because some accidents involved multiple errors). During the same time period, there were 169 major mishaps reported for the U.S. Air Force involving destruction of the aircraft, over one million dollars in damages, or fatalities. Of the 169 major mishaps, 113 involved some type of aircrew error. These included 32 procedural, 110 perceptual-motor, and 157 decisional errors. These types of errors were labeled "slips," "bungles," and "mistakes," respectively (Diehl 1989).

TABLE 11.4
Types of Aircrew Errors in Major Accidents

| | Category of Error | | |
Kind of Operation	Procedural "Slips" (%)	Perceptual-Motor "Bungles" (%)	Decisional "Mistakes" (%)
General aviation	5	44	52
Airlines	19	25	56
Military	11	37	53

Source: Adapted from Diehl, A.E. 1991. Does cockpit management training reduce aircrew error? *The 22nd International Seminar of the International Society of Air Safety Investigators.* Canberra, Australia, November 1991.

The comparison of the incidence of these three types of errors among the three aviation sectors is depicted in Table 11.4. It is interesting to note that even though these three sectors differ vastly with regard to many aspects (e.g., training, composition of aircrew, type of aircraft, and type of mission), the relative incidence of the errors is remarkably similar for all three groups.

11.4.1 THE SWISS-CHEESE MODEL OF ACCIDENT CAUSALITY

The analyses discussed so far were largely conducted on an *ad hoc* basis. That is, they were not conducted on the basis of a specific, well-defined theory of why accidents occur. However, the work of Perrow (1984) on the nature of accidents in closely coupled systems and the work by Reason (1990, 1997) have led to one theoretical conceptualization of why accidents occur. This theory, most widely articulated by Reason, is commonly referred to as the Swiss-cheese model. This theory suggests that governments, organizations, and people create barriers to the occurrence of accidents. Examples of barriers include regulations that prescribe certain rest periods between flights; checklists that must be followed during the planning and conduct of a flight; procedures for the execution of an approach to landing; and standard operating procedures for resolving normal and abnormal situations. Each of these barriers is created to prevent or require behavior that results in safe operations. As long as the barrier is in place and intact, no errors associated with that barrier can occur. The barrier acts as a shield to prevent them from occurring or to prevent the effects of failures of other barriers from resulting in an accident. One might envision these barriers as stacked one against the other. However, no barrier is perfect. Each might be described as having "holes"—areas in which the defenses associated with a particular barrier are weak or missing, hence, the Swiss-cheese description, as depicted in Figure 11.1.

The "Swiss-cheese" model of accident causation was operationalized by Wiegmann and Shappell (1997, 2001, 2003) who developed a system for categorizing accidents according to the sequential theory proposed by Reason. Wiegmann and Shappell termed this approach the Human Factors Analysis and Classification System (HFACS). HFACS is a taxonomy that describes the human factors that

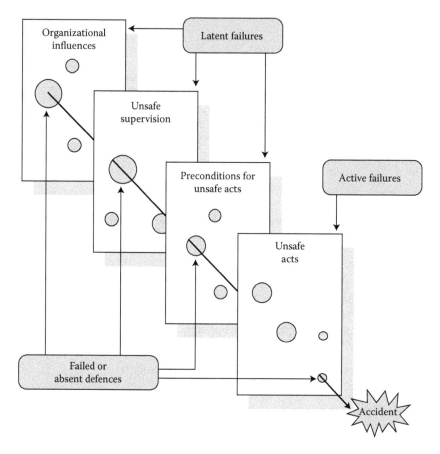

FIGURE 11.1 Swiss-cheese model of accident causation. (Adapted from Shappell, S.A. and Wiegmann, D.A. 2000. *The Human Factors Analysis and Classification System-HFACS.* DOT/FAA/AM-00/7. Washington, DC: Federal Aviation Administration.)

contribute to an accident. The classification system has four levels, arranged hierarchically. At the highest level are the organizational influences. Next are aspects of unsafe supervision, followed by the preconditions for unsafe acts. Finally, at the lowest level, are the unsafe acts of operators. These levels correspond with the barriers to accidents shown in Figure 11.1. These major components may be further broken down into the elements shown below (Shappell and Wiegmann 2000):

- Organizational influences
  - Resource management
  - Organizational climate
  - Organizational process
- Unsafe supervision
  - Inadequate supervision
  - Planned inappropriate operations

- • Failed to correct a problem
  - • Supervisory violations
- • Preconditions for unsafe acts
  - • Substandard conditions of operators
    - – Adverse mental states
    - – Adverse physiological states
    - – Physical and mental limitations
  - • Substandard practices of operators
    - – Crew resource management
    - – Personal readiness
- • Unsafe acts of operators
  - • Errors
    - – Skill-based
    - – Perceptual
    - – Decision
  - • Violations
    - – Routine—Habitual departures from rules sanctioned by management
    - – Exceptional—Departures from rules, not sanctioned by management

HFACS has been used in a variety of settings, including analyses of accidents in the U.S. military services, and analyses of accidents among air carriers and general aviation in the United States (e.g., see Shappell and Wiegmann 2002, 2003; Shappell et al. 2006). It has also been used in settings outside the United States (e.g., see Gaur 2005; Li and Harris 2005; Markou et al. 2006).

In a study conducted by the ATSB, Inglis et al. (2007) compared of U.S. and Australian accident causes using HFACS. The results of their analyses are shown in Table 11.5. The authors concluded that

… the proportion of accidents that involved an unsafe act was similar: of the 2,025 accidents in Australia, 1,404 (69%) were identified as involving an unsafe act while 13,700 accidents (72%) in the US involved an unsafe act. Moreover, the pattern of

TABLE 11.5
Accidents Associated with Each HFACS Unsafe Act

Unsafe Act	Australia		United States	
	Frequency	%	Frequency	%
Skill-based error	1180	84	10,589	77.3
Decision error	464	33	3996	29.2
Perceptual error	85	6.1	899	6.6
Violation	108	7.7	1767	12.9
Total	1404		13,700	

Source: Inglis et al. 2007. *Human Factors Analysis of Australian Aviation Accidents and Comparison with the United States.* Aviation Research and Analysis Report—B2004/0321. Canberra, Australia: Australia Transport Safety Bureau.

results between US and Australian accidents was remarkably similar. The rank order of unsafe act categories was the same in the accident sets for both countries. Skill-based errors were by far the most common type of aircrew error followed by decision errors, violations and perceptual errors, in that order. (Inglis et al. 2007, p. 39)

Although HFACS has achieved widespread use, it is not without its limitations, critics, and alternatives. For example, it is important to note that HFACS is a secondary analysis process. That is, HFACS does not deal with primary data. Rather, it deals with data generated by accident investigators, and it is in that sense removed from the reality of the accident. In contrast, consider a botanist classifying a new leaf. The botanist examines the leaf itself—the shape, arrangement of veins, coloration, and perhaps even the chemical composition of the leaf. The botanist does not examine a narrative description of someone else's impressions of a leaf. Yet, this is precisely the case with HFACS. The analysts using HFACS use as their data the narrative report of an accident prepared by an accident investigator. While studies (Wiegmann and Shappell 2001; Shappell et al. 2006) have shown that these analysts exhibit good reliability in their judgments, the results are still subject to the validity, or lack thereof, of the original accident investigator. Further, the analysts are largely confined to examining only those data that the original investigator considered relevant and/or those data required by the regulatory body responsible for the investigation.

At a more basic level, the use of "disembodied data," to use Dekker's (2001) phrase, to explain a complex event after-the-fact, is arguably a futile endeavor. It is only with hindsight that we are able to label decisions as poor judgment or actions as mistakes. Taken within the context of the situation, these decisions and actions may well have seemed entirely appropriate and correct to the individuals at the time, and given the knowledge they possessed. Further, the utility of assigning accidents to categories is not entirely clear. Knowing that an accident belongs to a specified category does not imply that we know why the accident occurred. To know that an accident occurred because of a "skill-based pilot error" does not tell us why what we have labeled as an error after the fact occurred. Labeling is not the same as understanding. Labeling will never lead to prevention; understanding may.

Notwithstanding these criticisms, however, if there is a need to assign accidents to categories, perhaps for some actuarial or political reason, then HFACS is probably the method of choice. However, there are alternatives, and the interested reader is directed to the excellent review by Beaubien and Baker (2002) of current taxonomic methods applied to aviation accidents for a comprehensive overview and comparative analyses of this topic.

11.5   SPECIAL PROBLEMS IN DOING RESEARCH ON ACCIDENTS

There are several problems that arise when one is conducting research on the causes of accidents. Arguably, the dominant problem is the scarcity of accidents. Before the reader tears this book to shreds, and writes an angry letter to the editor of their local newspaper condemning bloodthirsty aviation researchers, let us assure you that we are not wishing for more accidents. Rather, we are pointing out that the prediction of rare events presents some special difficulties from a statistical standpoint, the details of which are beyond the scope of this book. Some of the difficulties can be illustrated with a simple example, however.

Let us assume that we are interested in predicting the occurrence of fatal accidents among general aviation pilots in the United States. There are roughly 300,000 general aviation pilots in the United States and every year there are about 300 fatal accidents. (For the sake of convenience, let us use rounded numbers that are approximately accurate.) So, if accidents are purely random, the chance of any particular pilot being in a fatal accident is 0.001 (300 divided by 300,000) or one out of a thousand. Imagine then, if we are trying to evaluate whether pilots with beards have more fatal accidents than pilots without beards. We might begin our study in January by identifying a group of 100 pilots, half with beards and half without. Then in December, we would see how many are still alive. Fortunately for the pilots, but unfortunately for our research project, all the pilots will almost certainly still be alive at the end of the year—thus telling us nothing about the accident-causing properties of beards. The difficulty is that if only one pilot out of a thousand has an accident during a year, then we would expect something less than one pilot out of the hundred in our study group to have an accident. Unless the effect upon safety of having (or not having) a beard is tremendous, we are unlikely to obtain any results of interest.

Technically, what we are lacking here is variance (or variability) in the criterion (accident involvement). If there is no variance, then there is no information contained in the observation. This is equivalent to trying to find the smartest person in the class by giving all the students a test. If the test is too easy, then all the students get perfect scores, and we cannot tell from the scores who is smartest. (For additional information, consult Nunnally 1978 and his description of the effects of extreme splits in dichotomous criteria on the point biserial correlation.)

This limitation leads to the use of nonparametric statistics (e.g., chi-square), statistics that do not require normal distributions (e.g., Poisson and negative-binomial regression) and, on occasion, very large samples. It also leads to the use of measures other than accident involvement as the criteria for studies.

Arguably, accidents can be thought of as the tip of an iceberg. There are relatively few accidents, but there are many more incidents and hazardous events that did not result in an accident. Sometimes, the difference between an incident and an accident is very slim—perhaps only a matter of a few feet in clearing a tree on takeoff. Thus, these incidents may represent instances in which had the circumstances been only slightly different (perhaps a slightly hotter day, just a little more fuel on board, only a few less pounds of air in the tires) the incident would have become an accident.

It has been suggested (Hunter 1995) that incidents and hazardous events could be considered surrogates for the actual measure of interest—accident involvement. Finding a significant relationship between some measure of interest (e.g., some personality trait) and the surrogate measure of number of hazardous events experienced during the previous year would therefore be an indication that the measure may be related to accident involvement. This approach has been taken in several of the studies described later in this chapter.

The prevalence of incidents and hazardous events have been examined both in the United States (Hunter 1995) and in New Zealand (O'Hare and Chalmers 1999).

Hunter conducted a nationwide survey of pilots in the United States using a set of questions he termed the Hazardous Events Scale (HES). The HES consisted of questions that asked respondents to indicate the number of times they were involved in potentially hazardous events. The questions and the responses for private and commercial pilots are given in Table 11.6. For this same group of respondents, approximately 9% of the private pilots and 17% of the commercial pilots reported having been in an aircraft accident at some point in their careers. Clearly (since they were alive to respond to the survey), these were nonfatal accidents, which are about 5–6 times more prevalent than fatal accidents (i.e., there were about 300 fatal accidents in 2005 out of about 2000 total accidents).

In a survey of New Zealand pilots, O'Hare and Chalmers (1999) found that encounters with potentially hazardous events were fairly common. Furthermore, the experiences reported by the New Zealand pilots were remarkably similar to those of the U.S. pilots. For example, the proportions of pilots who had entered IMC (slightly under 25%) or inadvertently stalled an airplane (about 10%) were almost identical in both samples. It is interesting that even given the geographic disparity between the United States and New Zealand the experiences of pilots in the two countries were so similar. This is a finding to which we will return later in this chapter.

Findings such as these have encouraged researchers to consider the utility of such measures in accident research. Since there are many more incidents than fatal accidents (perhaps as many as two or three orders of magnitude), then using them, in lieu of accidents in research, alleviates to some degree the problems associated with the prediction of rare events. However, since these are only surrogates for the true criterion of interest, it must be remembered that these results are only suggestive of possible relationships.

11.6   OUT OF THE AIR AND INTO THE LABORATORY

Because of the difficulties associated with conducting naturalistic research—that is, research involving actual pilots engaged in flights—some researchers have chosen to conduct laboratory-based research. Typically, this research utilizes flight simulators of varying degrees of fidelity and flight profiles designed to expose the pilots to the conditions of interest. Laboratory research has the advantage of tight control over the stimuli (e.g., the aircraft capabilities, the weather experienced). However, since the risk of physical injury and death is never present in these situations, it is always a challenge to defend the generalizability of results from the laboratory to actual flight. Both naturalistic and laboratory research have their advantages and disadvantages, and it is incumbent upon the research to utilize their capabilities appropriately and to note the limitations of their research in their reports.

11.6.1   Aviation Weather Encounters

Over the years, encounters with adverse weather have remained one of the largest single causes of fatal general aviation accidents. Particularly interesting are those instances in which the pilot continued a flight from visual to instrument conditions,

TABLE 11.6
Reports of Hazardous Events among U.S. Pilots

	Private Pilot Certificate		Commercial Pilot Certificate	
	Number of Events[a]	Percent Reporting	Number of Events	Percent Reporting
Low fuel incidents	0	80	0	66
	1	16	1	24
	2	3	2	7
	3	1	3	2
	4 or more	0	4 or more	2
On-airport precautionary	0	54	0	41
or forced landing	1	23	1	21
	2	11	2	15
	3	4	3	7
	4 or more	8	4 or more	17
Off-airport precautionary	0	93	0	82
or forced landing	1	5	1	10
	2	1	2	3
	3	0	3	2
	4 or more	0	4 or more	3
Inadvertent stalls	0	94	0	90
	1	5	1	6
	2	1	2	2
	3	0	3	0
	4 or more	0	4 or more	1
Become disoriented (lost)	0	83	0	83
	1	14	1	13
	2	2	2	3
	3	0	3	1
	4 or more	0	4 or more	0
Mechanical failures	0	55	0	33
	1	27	1	26
	2	10	2	17
	3	4	3	9
	4 or more	4	4 or more	16
Engine quit due to fuel	0	93	0	84
starvation	1	6	1	12
	2	1	2	3
	3	0	3	1
	4 or more	0	4 or more	1
Flow VFR into IMC	0	77	0	78
	1	15	1	14
	2	6	2	5
	3	1	3	2
	4 or more	2	4 or more	2

(*Continued*)

TABLE 11.6 (*Continued*)
Reports of Hazardous Events among U.S. Pilots

	Private Pilot Certificate		Commercial Pilot Certificate	
	Number of Events[a]	Percent Reporting	Number of Events	Percent Reporting
Become disoriented	0	95	0%	91
(vertigo) while in IMC	1	4	1	7
	2	1	2	2
	3	0	3	0
	4 or more	0	4 or more	0
Turned back due to	0	29	0	23
weather	1	21	1	16
	2	19	2	18
	3	13	3	11
	4 or more	22	4 or more	32

Source: From Hunter, D.R. 1995. *Airman Research Questionnaire: Methodology and Overall Results.* DOT/FAA/AM-95/27. Washington, DC: Federal Aviation Administration. Table 32.

[a] Number of times this event has been experienced during flying career.

and subsequently either lost control of the aircraft or struck the ground while trying to exit the weather. Several researchers have examined these accidents from a variety of perspectives. One such perspective is to focus on these events as a plan continuation error (Orasanu et al. 2001). This perspective suggests that pilots fail to alter their plans when unforeseen conditions are encountered that make the original plan untenable. This failure can be attributed to the risk perception and risk tolerance constructs suggested by Hunter (2006), and it can also be interpreted in terms of sunk costs (O'Hare and Smitheram 1995). The sunk-cost concept attempts to explain plan continuation error as arising from the inherent desire of the pilot not to waste their previous effort. That is, once a trip has been initiated, each minute of the trip represents the expenditure of resources (time and money) that will be lost if the pilot is forced to return to the origination point without completing the flight. Early in a flight, this potential loss is relatively small, but as the duration of the flight grows, so does the potential loss. This potential loss (the sunk cost in accounting terms) then represents a motivation to continue the flight, even into marginal conditions. O'Hare and Owen (1999) tested this concept by having pilots fly a simulated cross-country flight in which they encountered adverse weather either early or late in the flight. The sunk-cost concept would predict that the pilots who encountered the weather later in the flight would be more likely to press on in an attempt to reach their destination. However, in this experiment, the results failed to support that hypothesis, since a majority of pilots in both conditions diverted their flights. Thus, the validity of this concept, as an explanation for pilot behavior in the face of adverse weather, is questionable.

Overconfidence by pilots was investigated by Goh and Wiegmann (2001), who found that pilots who continued into weather conditions in a simulated flight reported greater confidence in their piloting abilities, even though there were no actual differences in training or experience when compared to pilots who chose to divert. These same pilots also judged weather and pilot error as likely threats to flight safety less than the pilots who diverted, and believed themselves less vulnerable to pilot error.

Recall also the study of American, Norwegian, and Australian pilots described in the previous chapter (Hunter et al. 2003). That study showed that the some pilots may use methods to assess weather information (compensatory models vs. multiple-hurdle models) that could place them at increased risk of a weather accident.

11.7   OTHER PROGRAMS TO IMPROVE SAFETY

Under the sponsorship of the FAA, researchers at the Ohio State University began a program of research in the early 1990s aimed at developing better understandings of the causes of accidents among general aviation pilots, with the explicit goal of developing interventions to improve safety. The approach of this research was more on the development of expertise among relatively inexperienced pilots than on assessing hazardous thoughts or providing heuristics for decision-making (Kochan et al. 1997). This work led to the development of three training products aimed at improving decision-making by pilots (1) during the preflight planning process, (2) when making decisions in-flight, and (3) when making weather-related decisions.

11.7.1   Setting Personal Minimums

The first of these three products trained pilots to recognize the hazards present in flights and to establish a set of minimum operating standards (usually termed personal minimums) that would create a buffer against those hazards (Kirkbride et al. 1996). For example, although it is legal to fly (in the United States) at night with 4 miles visibility and a ceiling of 2000 feet, a prudent pilot lacking an instrument rating might elect to only fly at night when the visibility is greater than 8 miles, and the ceiling is over 5000 feet. These more stringent standards become that pilot's personal minimums, and are recorded in a personal checklist that pilots are encouraged to review before each flight. Evaluations of pilot acceptance of this new training were positive (Jensen et al. 1998), although no evaluation of the impact of the training on external criteria such as involvement in hazardous events or accidents was conducted.

11.7.2   Weather-Related Decision-Making

In contrast to the attempt at procedural standardization incorporated in the personal minimums training, and the hazardous thoughts training contained in the several FAA publications, a skills-based approach has been proposed that would focus on helping pilots improve their skill at recognizing and dealing with hazardous situations. O'Hare et al. (1998) utilized the techniques of cognitive task analysis (CTA) and the critical decision method (CDM) form of CTA described by Klein et al. (1989) to evaluate the decision processes of highly experienced general aviation pilots in adverse weather situations. Use of this technique allowed them to identify the information cues and processes used by these expert pilots in making weather-related decisions. Using these data, Wiggins and O'Hare (1993, 2003a), under contract to the FAA, constructed a training program they called WeatherWise.

WeatherWise is a computer-based training program "designed to provide visual pilots with the skills necessary to recognize and respond to the cues associated with deteriorating weather conditions during flight" (Wiggins and O'Hare 2003b, p. 337). The program consists of four stages:

- *Stage 1*: An assessment of in-flight weather conditions from still images, to demonstrate the difficulty in making determinations of visual flight conditions.
- *Stage 2*: An introduction to the salient weather cues that were identified in previous research as being used by experts to make weather decisions. These cues were
  - Cloudbase
  - Visibility
  - Cloud coloring
  - Cloud density
  - Terrain clearance
  - Rain
  - Horizon
  - Cloud type
  - Wind direction
  - Wind speed
- *Stage 3*: Presentation of a number of images of in-flight weather conditions to identify the point at which a significant deterioration had taken place. During this stage, a rule of thumb was advocated to the effect that, should a significant deterioration occur in three or more of the cues, then a weather-related decision (possibly a diversion) should be made.
- *Stage 4*: Further practice in attending to the salient weather cues. In this stage, participants viewed a sequence of in-flight video recordings and identified the point at which conditions deteriorated below visual flight requirements.

This training program was evaluated using a group of 66 Australian private pilots, none of whom had more than 150 total flight hours. In comparison to the control group, who did not receive the training, the pilots who completed the WeatherWise training were significantly more likely to make a diversion decision at or before the optimal point. In contrast, the pilot who did not receive the training tended to continue on into the adverse weather conditions (Wiggins and O'Hare 2003b).

In addition to the FAA, other civil aviation authorities have recognized the need to improve general aviation safety and have incorporated the previously mentioned training programs as part of their national safety efforts. The civil aviation authorities of both Australia and New Zealand have adopted the personal minimums and WeatherWise training programs and have distributed the training to their general aviation pilots.

11.7.3 COOPERATIVE EFFORTS TO IMPROVE SAFETY

In recognition of the importance of decision-making to accident involvement, the FAA, in cooperation with a coalition of aviation industry organizations, formed a Joint Safety Analysis Team (JSAT) to examine general aviation aeronautical decision-making (ADM), and to develop a program to improve ADM so as to reduce the number of accidents attributable to poor decision-making. The JSAT, in turn, chartered an international panel of human factors experts to address the technical issues of how poor decision-making contributed to accidents, and what might be done to improve aviation safety. That panel's recommendations, listing over 100 specific items, were adopted without change by the JSAT and provided to the FAA as part of its final report (JSAT 2002). Reflecting a pragmatic approach to applying the current knowledge of accident causality among general aviation pilots, the panel's recommendations covered a wide range of possible interventions. Some examples include:

- Create and disseminate to pilots a weather hazard index which incorporates the weather risks into a single graphic or number.
- Reorganize weather briefings so as to present information related to potentially hazardous conditions as the first and last items given to the pilot.
- Increase the use of scenario-based questions in the written examination.
- Include training for Certified Flight Instructors (CFIs) on risk assessment and management in instructional operations.
- Produce a Personal Minimums Checklist training program expressly for use by CFIs in setting their instructional practices.
- Establish a separate weather briefing and counseling line for low-time pilots.
- Require pitot heat to be applied automatically, whenever the aircraft is in flight.
- Develop displays that depict critical operational variables in lieu of raw, unprocessed data (e.g., have fuel indicators that show remaining range or endurance, as well as remaining gallons of fuel).
- Develop and disseminate training which explicitly addresses the issues involved in crash survivability; including crash technique, minimizing vertical loads, and planning for crashes (water, cell phone, matches, etc.) even on flights over hospitable terrain.
- Develop role-playing simulations in which pilots can observe modeled methods of resisting social pressures and can then practice those methods.

Regrettably, these interventions have not yet been implemented, even though they were accepted by both industry and government regulators. This is a reflection, perhaps, of the difficulty of making even well-regarded changes in an established bureaucracy and cost-conscious industry. Clearly, it is not enough for researchers to find better ways to keep pilots safe. They must also find ways to get their discoveries implemented—arguably, the more difficult of the two tasks.

Nevertheless, some progress is being made in training pilots to be more safety-conscious. In 2006, the AOPA Air Safety Foundation (ASF) began sending a free DVD on decision-making to all newly rated private and instrument pilots. The scenarios contained on the DVD focus on VFR into instrument conditions and IFR decision-making—two areas that the ASF has found to be particularly troublesome (AOPA 2006).

There is also evidence that membership in flying clubs promotes safety. Edwards (2015) compared the safety records of members of three aircraft type clubs to non-members. He found that for 2013, members of the American Bonanza Society were 2.5 times less likely to have a serious accident and 11 times less likely than nonmembers to be involved in a fatal accident. For the Cirrus Owners Club, members were 1.8 times less likely to be in accident, and over two times less likely for fatal accident. Similarly, members of the Lancair Owners organization were two times less likely to be involved in an accident, and 11 times less likely to have a fatal accident. It should be noted, of course, that these data do not necessarily indicate that membership itself promotes safety. It could also be the case that pilots who have a greater interest and commitment to safety tend to join clubs. That is simply a limitation with naturalistic research. However, since there is no evidence to suggest that belonging to a club makes you less safe, joining seems like a fairly safe bet.

11.8 SUMMARY

In this chapter, we have examined the issue of safety from the perspective of aviation psychology. We have seen that although flying in large commercial air carriers is quite safe, the situation is not so comforting in general aviation, where the risks of involvement in a fatal aviation accident are somewhat higher than being involved in a fatal motor vehicle accident. Curiously, anecdotal evidence (from the responses of many general aviation pilots when this topic is raised at flight safety seminars) suggests that general aviation pilots are largely unaware of this differential risk and generally believe that they are safer when flying than when driving their cars. Hence, programs to improve safety often receive little more than lip service, since the pilots involved do not really feel that they are at risk.

Scientific research has identified several factors that place pilots at greater risk of accident involvement. Certainly, fatigue, drugs, and the various visual illusions noted in Chapter 3 can degrade performance and increase accident risk. A lack of aptitude or abilities such as those listed in Chapter 5 can play a role, as can organizational and interpersonal issues, such as those discussed in Chapter 9. Among those factors discussed earlier in Chapter 10 were feelings of invulnerability (hazardous attitudes) and feelings of being a victim of outside forces (locus of control), along with issues relating to recognition of the risks inherent to flight.

The advanced technology formerly found only in air carriers and executive jets is now working its way into the general aviation fleet. This technology will make some tasks easier (e.g., navigation), but it will present its own set of unique problems, and will still require pilots to make reasoned judgments about when, where, how, and if they should undertake a flight. The influence of pilots' personality and their skill at acquiring and using information will still be great, even in the aircraft of tomorrow. Safety requires a proactive approach to assessing and managing all the elements that influence the outcome of a flight, including the most important element, the human at the controls.

11.9   OUTSIDE ACTIVITIES

Perhaps, one of the best ways to understand what can happen when multiple factors converge is to review the detailed accounts of actual aviation accidents contained in the reports produced by the NTSB. These reports are available from their Web site: http://www.ntsb.gov/investigations/AccidentReports/Pages/aviation.aspx.

Look at the final (not the interim) reports for a number of accidents, and see how the accidents developed, and all the factors that contributed to the adverse outcome. As you do so, think about some of the topics covered in this book. Were physiological factors, such as hypoxia, fatigue, or drugs involved? If the accident involved a commercial flight, was there evidence that the pilot(s) was ill-suited to the tasks? Would a more stringent selection system or better training possibly have avoided that situation? Were there indications of poor human factors design in the aircraft controls and displays? Were there communications errors among the crew and between the crew and ATC? Would better CRM training have helped? Finally, where pilot error was a contributing or major cause, ask yourself why that error occurred, and what could have been done to prevent the error, or to mitigate its effects. Keep track of these factors as you read the reports, and see if you can find any common themes. If you read a dozen or so of these reports and really think about what happened, you will be a much better and safer pilot.

RECOMMENDED READINGS

Dekker, S. (2002) The Re-Invention of Human Error. (technical report 2002-01). Ljungbyhed, Sweden: Lund University School of Aviation.
Dekker, S. (2006). *The Field Guide to Understanding Human Error.* Aldershot: Ashgate.
Perrow, C. (1984). *Normal Accidents: Living With High-Risk Technologies.* New York: Basic Books.
Reason, J. (1990). *Human Error.* Cambridge: Cambridge University Press.
Reason, J. (1997). *Managing the Risks of Organizational Accidents.* Aldershot: Ashgate.

REFERENCES

AOPA (Aircraft Owners and Pilots Association). 2006. *The Nall Report.* Frederick, MD: Author.
AOPA (Aircraft Owners and Pilots Association). 2015. *The Nall Report.* Frederick, MD: Author.
ATSB. 2007. *Australian Transport Safety Bureau—Data and Statistics.* Retrieved on June 7, 2007 from: http://www.atsb.gov.au/aviation/statistics.aspx
Beaubien, J.M. and Baker, D.P. 2002. A review of selected aviation human factors taxonomies, accident/incident reporting systems, and data reporting tools. *International Journal of Applied Aviation Studies* 2: 11–36.

Dekker, S.W.A. 2001. The disembodiment of data in the analysis of human factors accidents. *Human Factors and Aerospace Safety* 1: 39–57.

Dekker, S.W.A. 2002. *The Re-invention of Human Error*. Technical Report 2002-01. Ljungbyhed, Sweden: Lund University School of Aviation.

Diehl, A.E. 1989. Human performance aspects of aircraft accidents. In Jensen, R.S. (Ed.), *Aviation Psychology* (pp. 378–403). Brookfield, VT: Gower Technical.

Diehl, A.E. 1991. Does cockpit management training reduce aircrew error? *The 22nd International Seminar of the International Society of Air Safety Investigators*, Canberra, Australia, November 1991.

Dismukes, K., Berman, B., and Loukopoulos, L. 2006. Rethinking pilot error and the causes of airline accidents. *The CRM/HF Conference*, Denver, CO, April 16–17, 2006.

Edwards, W.J. 2015. The efficacy of aircraft type club safety. *Journal of Aviation Technology and Engineering* 5: 7–16.

Federal Aviation Administration (FAA). 2012. Administrator's fact book. Retrieved from March 1, 2016 from: http://www.faa.gov/about/office_org/headquarters_offices/aba/admin_factbook/

Gaur, D. 2005. Human factors analysis and classification system applied to civil aircraft accidents in India. *Aviation, Space and Environmental Medicine* 76: 501–505.

Goh, J. and Wiegmann, D.A. 2001. Visual flight rules flight into instrument meteorological conditions: An empirical investigation of the possible causes. *International Journal of Aviation Psychology* 11: 359–379.

Hunter, D.R. 1995. *Airman Research Questionnaire: Methodology and Overall Results*. DOT/FAA/AM-95/27. Washington, DC: Federal Aviation Administration.

Hunter, D.R. 2006. Risk perception among general aviation pilots. *The International Journal of Aviation Psychology* 16: 135–144.

Hunter, D.R., Martinussen, M., and Wiggins, M. 2003. Understanding how pilots make weather-related decisions. *International Journal of Aviation Psychology* 13: 73–87.

Inglis, M., Sutton, J., and McRandle, B. 2007. *Human Factors Analysis of Australian Aviation Accidents and Comparison with the United States*. Aviation Research and Analysis Report—B2004/0321. Canberra, Australia: Australia Transport Safety Bureau.

Jensen, R.S. and Benel, R.A. 1977. *Judgment Evaluation and Instruction in Civil Pilot Training*. FAA-RD-78-24. Washington, DC: Federal Aviation Administration.

Jensen, R.S., Guilkey, J.E., and Hunter, D.R. 1998. *An Evaluation of Pilot Acceptance of the Personal Minimums Training Program for Risk Management*. DOT/FAA/AM-98/7. Washington, DC: Federal Aviation Administration.

Joint Safety Analysis Team. 2002. *General Aviation Aeronautical Decision-making*. Unpublished Report. Washington, DC: General Aviation Coalition.

Kirkbride, L.A., Jensen, R.S., Chubb, G.P., and Hunter, D.R. 1996. *Developing the Personal Minimums Tool for Managing Risk During Preflight Go/No-Go Decisions*. DOT/FAA/AM-96/19. Washington, DC: Federal Aviation Administration.

Klein, G., Calderwood, R., and McGregor, D. 1989. Critical decision method for eliciting knowledge. *IEEE Transactions on Systems, Man, and Cybernetics* 19: 462–472.

Kochan, J.A., Jensen, R.S., Chubb, G.P., and Hunter, D.R. 1997. *A New Approach to Aeronautical Decision-making: The Expertise Method*. DOT/FAA/AM-97/6. Washington, DC: Federal Aviation Administration.

Leveson, N. 2004. A new accident model for engineering safer systems. *Safety Science* 42: 237–270.

Li, W.-C. and Harris, D. 2005. HFACS analysis of ROC air force aviation accidents: Reliability analysis and cross-cultural comparison. *International Journal of Applied Aviation Studies* 5: 65–81.

Markou, I., Papadopoulos, I., Pouliezos, N., and Poulimenakos, S. 2006. Air accidents-incidents human factors analysis: The Greek experience 1983–2003. *The 18th Annual European Aviation Safety Seminar*, Athens, Greece.

Nunnally, J.C. 1978. *Psychometric Theory*. New York, NY: McGraw-Hill.

O'Hare, D. and Chalmers, D. 1999. The incidence of incidents: A nationwide study of flight experience and exposure to accidents and incidents. *International Journal of Aviation Psychology* 9: 1–18.

O'Hare, D. and Owen, D. 1999. *Continued VFR into IMC: An Empirical Investigation of the Possible Causes*. Final Report on Preliminary Study. Unpublished manuscript. Dunedin, New Zealand: University of Otago.

O'Hare, D. and Smitheram, T. 1995. "Pressing on" into deteriorating conditions: An application of behavioral decision theory to pilot decision making. *International Journal of Aviation Psychology* 5: 351–370.

O'Hare, D., Wiggins, M., Williams, A., and Wong, W. 1998. Cognitive task analyses for decision centered design and training. *Ergonomics* 41: 1698–1718.

Orasanu, J., Martin, L., and Davison, J. 2001. Cognitive and contextual factors in aviation accidents. In Salas, E. and Klein, G. (Eds.), *Linking Expertise and Naturalistic Decision Making* (pp. 209–226). Mahwah, NJ: Erlbaum.

Perrow, C. 1984. *Normal Accidents: Living with High-risk Technologies*. New York, NY: Basic Books.

Rasmussen, J. 1997. Risk management in a dynamic society: A modelling problem. *Safety Science* 27: 183–213.

Reason, J. 1990. *Human Error*. New York, NY: Cambridge University Press.

Reason, J. 1997. *Managing the Risks of Organizational Accidents*. Aldershot, UK: Ashgate.

Shappell, S.A., Detwiler, C.A., Holcomb, K.A., Hackworth, C.A., Boquet, A.J., and Wiegmann, D.A. 2006. *Human Error and Commercial Aviation Accidents: A Comprehensive Fine-grained Analysis Using HFACS*. DOT/FAA/AM-06/18. Washington, DC: Federal Aviation Administration.

Shappell, S.A. and Wiegmann, D.A. 2000. *The Human Factors Analysis and Classification System-HFACS*. Technical Report DOT/FAA/AM-00/7. Washington, DC: Federal Aviation Administration.

Shappell, S.A. and Wiegmann, D.A. 2002. HFACS analysis of general aviation data 1990–98: Implications for training and safety. *Aviation, Space, and Environmental Medicine* 73: 297.

Shappell, S.A. and Wiegmann, D.A. 2003. *A Human Error Analysis of General Aviation Controlled Flight into Terrain CFIT) Accidents Occurring Between 1990–1998*. DOT/FAA/AM-03/4. Washington, DC: Federal Aviation Administration.

Wiegmann, D.A. and Shappell, S.A. 1997. Human factors analysis of postaccident data. *International Journal of Aviation Psychology* 7: 67–82.

Wiegmann, D.A. and Shappell, S.A. 2001. *A Human Error Analysis of Commercial Aviation Accidents Using the Human Factors Analysis and Classification System (HFACS)*. DOT/FAA/AM-01/3. Washington, DC: Federal Aviation Administration.

Wiegmann, D.A and Shappell, S.A. 2003. *A Human Error Approach to Aviation Accident Analysis: The Human Factors Analysis and Classification System*. Burlington, VT: Ashgate.

Wiggins, M.W. and O'Hare, D. 1993. A skills-based approach to training aeronautical decision-making. In Telfer, R.A. (Ed.), *Aviation Instruction and Training*. Brookfield, VT: Ashgate.

Wiggins, M.W. and O'Hare, D. 2003a. Expert and novice pilot perceptions of static in-flight images of weather. *International Journal of Aviation Psychology* 13: 173–187.

Wiggins, M.W. and O'Hare, D. 2003b. Weatherwise: Evaluation of a cue-based training approach for the recognition of deteriorating weather conditions during flight. *Human Factors* 45: 337–345.

12 Concluding Remarks

> Everyone thinks of changing the world, but no one thinks of changing himself.
>
> **Tolstoy**

Notwithstanding Tolstoy's comment, humans are not easy to change. However, after reading this book, it is hoped that the reader will recognize that, of all the parts of the aviation system, the human is the part that is most often called upon to change. Fortunately, one of the most characteristic traits of humans is their adaptability—their ability to change their behavior to fit the demands of the situation and to recover from difficulties. There is no more dramatic demonstration of this adaptability than pushing forward on the controls when the aircraft has stalled and the nose is pointing downward, when all one's instincts call for yanking the controls backward.

Nevertheless, humans are not infinitely adaptable. The research on the selection of pilots demonstrates that some individuals are better suited than others. The research on accident involvement also suggests that some individuals are more likely to be in an accident than others—perhaps because they failed to adapt their behavior to the demands of a novel situation. Hopefully, the reader of this book is now better aware of how the human interacts with the aviation system, and has also developed some awareness of the limits of their personal capabilities and adaptability.

Human behavior is not only determined by individual differences, but it is also influenced by organizational factors such as safety culture, leadership, and job demands. The aviation industry is currently undergoing many changes, which may result in more demands and fewer resources available to pilots and other professionals. It is thus important to know how stress may influence both behavior and the mental health and well-being of people working in aviation.

By its nature, this book could only scratch the surface of aviation psychology. The topics covered by each of the chapters in this book are themselves the subject of multiple books and journal articles. However, the references and recommended readings provided in each of the chapters can lead the interested reader to more in-depth information on the topics. This book, we hope, will have prepared you for those readings by providing you with a basic knowledge of the terminology, concepts, tools, and methods of inquiry of psychology. Building upon that foundation, the reader should now be better able to assess reports that purport to show the impact of some new training intervention or to appreciate the impact that fairly subtle changes in instrumentation design and layout can have on aircrew performance. Hopefully, after reading the book, you will be a better consumer of new research findings and be able to use the knowledge to improve practice.

Although we have focused on aviation operations, much of what we have covered is equally applicable to other situations. For example, the task of the pilot has much in common with drivers, operators of nuclear power stations, and surgeons. Poorly designed work stations and controls can contribute to driving accidents and reactor meltdowns as easily as they contribute to aircraft crashes. The principles of designing to meet the capability and characteristics of the operator and the tasks they are required to perform remain the same. Only the specifics of the setting are changed.

Along that same line, our focus in this book has been on the pilot; however, we recognize that they are only one part of an extensive team. The discussions regarding the pilot also apply to the people outside the flight deck, including the maintainers, air traffic control, dispatchers, and managers of aviation organizations. Therefore, what you have learned from this book may also prove useful to you in other settings.

Psychology is concerned with how individuals are alike and also with how individuals differ. Knowing your strengths and weaknesses, knowing where your tendencies can take you, and knowing the limits of your personal performance envelope can help you avoid situations where the demands of the situation exceed your capacity to respond.

We encourage you to broaden your knowledge and acquire new skills, and we sincerely hope that you will use the information from this book to become more competent, more self-aware, and to apply what you have learned to be a better, safer pilot.

Index

Milton Keynes UK
Ingram Content Group UK Ltd.
UKHW031142141024
449569UK00024B/1143

9 781032 569833